# Economics, Business, and Islamic Finance in ASEAN Economics Community

Patricia Ordoñez de Pablos
*The University of Oviedo, Spain*

Mohammad Nabil Almunawar
*Universiti Brunei Darussalam, Brunei*

Muhamad Abduh
*Universiti Brunei Darussalam, Brunei*

A volume in the Advances in Finance, Accounting, and Economics (AFAE) Book Series

IGI Global
DISSEMINATOR OF KNOWLEDGE

Published in the United States of America by
IGI Global
Business Science Reference (an imprint of IGI Global)
701 E. Chocolate Avenue
Hershey PA, USA 17033
Tel: 717-533-8845
Fax: 717-533-8661
E-mail: cust@igi-global.com
Web site: http://www.igi-global.com



Library of Congress Cataloging-in-Publication Data

Names: Ordóñez de Pablos, Patricia, 1975- editor. | Almunawar, Mohammad Nabil, 1960- editor. | Abduh, Muhamad, 1981- editor.
Title: Economics, business, and Islamic finance in ASEAN economics community / Patricia Ordonez de Pablos, Mohammad Nabil Almunawar, and Muhamad Abduh, editors.
Description: Hershey, PA : Business Science Reference, [2020] | Includes bibliographical references and index. | Summary: “”This book examines emerging topics, challenges, and success factors in economics, business and, Islamic finance in the ASEAN region”--Provided by publisher”-- Provided by publisher.
Identifiers: LCCN 2019037714 (print) | LCCN 2019037715 (ebook) | ISBN 9781799822578 (hardcover) | ISBN 9781799822585 (paperback) | ISBN 9781799822592 (ebook)
Subjects: LCSH: Economic development--Southeast Asia. | Finance--Religious aspects--Islam. | Finance--Southeast Asia.
Classification: LCC HC441 .E295 2020 (print) | LCC HC441 (ebook) | DDC 330.959--dc23
LC record available at https://lccn.loc.gov/2019037714
LC ebook record available at https://lccn.loc.gov/2019037715

This book is published in the IGI Global book series Advances in Finance, Accounting, and Economics (AFAE) (ISSN: 2327-5677; eISSN: 2327-5685)

British Cataloguing in Publication Data
A Cataloguing in Publication record for this book is available from the British Library.

# Advances in Finance, Accounting, and Economics (AFAE) Book Series

ISSN:2327-5677
EISSN:2327-5685

Editor-in-Chief: Ahmed Driouchi, Al Akhawayn University, Morocco

**MISSION**

In our changing economic and business environment, it is important to consider the financial changes occurring internationally as well as within individual organizations and business environments. Understanding these changes as well as the factors that influence them is crucial in preparing for our financial future and ensuring economic sustainability and growth.

The **Advances in Finance, Accounting, and Economics (AFAE)** book series aims to publish comprehensive and informative titles in all areas of economics and economic theory, finance, and accounting to assist in advancing the available knowledge and providing for further research development in these dynamic fields.

**COVERAGE**

- Managerial Accounting
- Economics of Natural and Environmental Resources
- Economics of Agriculture and Biotechnology
- Finance and Accounting in SMEs
- Theoretical Issues in Economics, Finance, and Accounting
- Microfinance
- Public Finance
- Economics of Migration and Spatial Mobility
- Applied Accounting
- Taxes

IGI Global is currently accepting manuscripts for publication within this series. To submit a proposal for a volume in this series, please contact our Acquisition Editors at Acquisitions@igi-global.com or visit: http://www.igi-global.com/publish/.

The Advances in Finance, Accounting, and Economics (AFAE) Book Series (ISSN 2327-5677) is published by IGI Global, 701 E. Chocolate Avenue, Hershey, PA 17033-1240, USA, www.igi-global.com. This series is composed of titles available for purchase individually; each title is edited to be contextually exclusive from any other title within the series. For pricing and ordering information please visit http://www.igi-global.com/book-series/advances-finance-accounting-economics/73685. Postmaster: Send all address changes to above address. 

## Titles in this Series

*For a list of additional titles in this series, please visit:*
*http://www.igi-global.com/book-series/advances-finance-accounting-economics/73685*

***Mapping, Managing, and Crafting Sustainable Business Strategies for the Circular Economy***
Susana Serrano Rodrigues (Polytechnic Institute of Leiria, Portugal) Paulo Jorge Almeida (Polytechnic Institute of Leiria, Portugal) and Nuno Miguel Castaheira Almeida (Polytechnic Institute of Leiria, Portugal)
Business Science Reference • ©2020 • 280pp • H/C (ISBN: 9781522598855) • US $195.00

***Growth and Emerging Prospects of International Islamic Banking***
Abdul Rafay (University of Management and Technology, Pakistan)
Business Science Reference • ©2020 • 500pp • H/C (ISBN: 9781799816119) • US $215.00

***Handbook of Research on Theory and Practice of Global Islamic Finance***
Abdul Rafay (University of Management and Technology, Pakistan)
Business Science Reference • ©2020 • 500pp • H/C (ISBN: 9781799802181) • US $445.00

***Challenges and Impacts of Religious Endowments on Global Economics and Finance***
Buerhan Saiti (Istanbul Sabahattin Zaim University, Turkey) and Adel Sarea (Ahlia University, Bahrain)
Business Science Reference • ©2020 • 350pp • H/C (ISBN: 9781799812456) • US $225.00

***Regional Trade and Development Strategies in the Era of Globalization***
Akhilesh Chandra Prabhakar (Lovely Professional University, India) Gurpreet Kaur (Lovely Professional University, India) and Vasilii Erokhin (Harbin Engineering University, China)
Business Science Reference • ©2020 • 325pp • H/C (ISBN: 9781799817307) • US $225.00

***Algorithms for Solving Financial Portfolio Design Problems Emerging Research and Opportunities***
Fatima Zohra Lebbah (Ecole Préparatoire en Sciences et Techniques d'Oran (EPSTO), Algeria)
Business Science Reference • ©2020 • 130pp • H/C (ISBN: 9781799818823) • US $155.00

*For an entire list of titles in this series, please visit:*
*http://www.igi-global.com/book-series/advances-finance-accounting-economics/73685*

IGI Global
DISSEMINATOR OF KNOWLEDGE

701 East Chocolate Avenue, Hershey, PA 17033, USA
Tel: 717-533-8845 x100 • Fax: 717-533-8661
E-Mail: cust@igi-global.com • www.igi-global.com

## Editorial Advisory Board



## List of Reviewers

Wardah Azimah Haji Sumardi, *Universiti Brunei Darussalam, Brunei*
Rizal Abd Hamid Mohd Syaiful, *Universiti Teknikal Malaysia Melaka, Malaysia*
Hassanudin Mohd Thas Thaker, *Sunway University, Malaysia*
Mohd Zaidi Md Zabri, *Universiti Sains Malaysia, Malaysia*
Ali Yusob Md Zain, *Universiti Utara Malaysia, Malaysia*

# Table of Contents

# Detailed Table of Contents

Community economic development is a relatively new strategy employed to increase employment, income, and entrepreneurship activities in small town and communities. The Centre for Islamic Economics, International Islamic University Malaysia (IIUM) has initiated a smart partnership with CIMB Islamic Bank to offer entrepreneurship training and Islamic microfinance facility to the poor in Malaysia. This project adopts several modes of Islamic microfinance financing instruments which include equity-based and debt-based financing. The program aims to educate the communities surrounding the IIUM campus with entrepreneurship knowledge and skill in addition to giving Shariah-compliant micro-financing facility for them to implement their business ideas. CIMB Islamic, which is the main partner for this project, provides funds for Islamic microfinance facilities and IIUM contributes expertise in providing entrepreneurship trainings to the communities located near IIUM campus. It is hoped that this smart partnership would empower the surrounding communities and create more successful entrepreneurs.



Amongst three Muslim majority countries (Indonesia, Malaysia, and Brunei) of ASEAN, Malaysia leads the halal industry globally and considered to be the global halal hub. Simultaneously, the market is growing tremendously in other member countries as well. It has been realized that a number of driving forces are responsible for boosting the expansion of Halal industry globally as well as in ASEAN. While there are a number of factors accelerating the growth of the Halal industry, there are many limitations and challenges that are hindering the market expansion. Therefore, this chapter introduces the overview of Halal industry globally as well as in ASEAN counties. The chapter explores the opportunities of the Halal industry for ASEAN counties followed by identifying the issues and challenges confronted by industry players. Finally, it concludes by providing some recommendations in the ASEAN context based on the current global situation and findings of the Halal industry. The chapter adopts methodology of analyzing secondary data.

This chapter evaluates food security policies and extension policies to the achievement of targets and the results of a development programme such as Food Self Sufficiency village (DMP) used Participatory Poverty Assessments (PPA). The output obtained is information that is an evaluation of how the policy was planned, initiated, and implemented. Participatory Poverty Assessments (PPA) monitoring and evaluation analyse the outcome and impact of the DMP Programme. The output of the PPA process from this chaper is the agricultural policy formulated in terms of practical ways of approaching poverty problems from a local perspective. The success of alternative policy options applied by local government such us Physical, Human Resources, Institution development at the grassroots level should be adopted at the national level. It should represent the best example of a case of successful programme implementation at the grassroots level which can then be used in formulating national policies and strategies.



A two-sided market or two-sided network is made up of two distinct user groups that provide each other with network benefits in which they interact through an intermediary or platform. A digital marketplace makes use of a two-sided market where the two distinct groups are the buyers and sellers. A digital marketplace is a type of e-commerce site where the sellers offer products or services to the buyers, and transactions are controlled and processed by marketplace operators. With the rapid development and adoption of the Internet and digital marketplace globally and also regionally, businesses in Brunei Darussalam are slowly incorporating digital marketplace. This chapter provides an overview of the current state of the digital marketplace in Brunei, and thus, case studies of local digital marketplaces are discussed. A qualitative approach, which consists of interviews with companies, is made for the study. The strengths and problems of employing digital marketplace for businesses and analysis using Michael Porter's five models is also covered in this chapter.

Brunei Darussalam (AMBD). AMBD envisions a vibrant economy powered by ICT through ICT-Smart Citizens as well as being a connected and efficient nation. This chapter discusses the application of Fintech specifically in Islamic finance sector based on the descriptive method of research by concentrating on its regulations. At the end, the research found that though Fintech in Islamic finance sector has been done since it's emerging through Guidelines Fintech Regulatory Sandbox Guidelines Islamic financial Fintech will be strengthened and developed and more diversified.



The Islamic banks in Indonesia have a serious issue of a low market share of 5%. This emerged due to the limited/unvaried product range, low literacy and inclusion level of Islamic finance, unfavorable perception for Islamic banking, and limited distribution networks and outreach. All of these causes could be resolved by using social media, which will bring several opportunities such as transparency and openness, effective marketing channels, stakeholders' relationship, social media content, brand image and reputation, shariah compliance activity, learning and knowledge, and greater personalization. Meanwhile, in using social media, the Islamic banks face few challenges such as network infrastructure, negative comments, information risk management, privacy, and deception. This chapter can be a reference to any institutions, particularly the Islamic banks which associated with digital interfaces and interactions in their daily businesses. Thus expectedly, the Islamic banks could enhance the public trust and establish a good Islamic identity.



Loan shark is a humanitarian problem faced by many countries in the world, including in Asia, even in the Association of Southeast Asian Nations (ASEAN)'s countries. Loan shark activities are found not only in Myanmar and Cambodia, which has the lowest per capita income in ASEAN but also in Indonesia, Thailand, Malaysia, Brunei, and even Singapore, which are the five countries with the highest gross domestic product (GDP) per capita in ASEAN. How are loan shark practices in ASEAN countries? Can nanofinance overcome the microfinance gap to fight the loan shark? How the practice of Bank Wakaf Mikro (BWM) in Indonesia to nanofinance with qardhul hassan contract? Find the answers in this chapter.

# Preface

## INTRODUCTION

Association of Southeast Asian Nations (ASEAN) is the seventh-largest economy in the world. In 2015, members of ASEAN agreed to establish the ASEAN Economic Community (AEC), a regional economic integration. This economic integration opens vast opportunities as the market size is huge with a combined GDP reaches US$2.6 trillion. Collectively, AEC is the third-largest economy in Asia and the seventh-largest in the world.

ASEAN has a young population as half of its 640 million people are less than 30 years old. The growing number of the middle-class segment, which will reach 400 million in 2020, couple with its more than 339 million active Internet users (more than 300 million access the Internet from mobile devices) has made ASEAN an attractive digital consumers.

## CONTENTS OF THE BOOK

The book presents a collection of 15 chapters that addresses key topics to understand business, economics and Islamic finance in ASEAN region and also explored trends and challenges in the region.

It aims to serve as an international platform to bring together academics, researchers, lecturers, decision makers, policy makers, and practitioners to share new theories, research findings, and case studies and have a better knowledge and understanding of problems and opportunities in the region.

Chapter 1, titled "Organizational Factors and the Success of Technology Transfer" (authors: Md Zahidul Islam and Safayet Rahman) explores the relationship between organizational culture, structure, complexity of technology and the success of technology transfer. Technology is one of the key competitive advantages of any organization and plays an important role in the success of both international and domestic firms. Technology can be transferred within the boundaries of an organization, outside of organizational boundaries with strategic partners and also across national boundaries. As it transcends national borders, difficulties in transferring technology are likely to increase. To overcome the difficulties, certain organizational culture could play an important role in the efficient transfer of technology in an organization. Besides culture, organizational structure could also play a major role to achieve technology transfer success. Furthermore, the complexity of technology is also can affect the success of technology transfer.

Chapter 2, titled "Spatial Dynamic Modeling for Increasing the Competitiveness of Small Medium Enterprises: Case Study Bogor City, West Java, Indonesia" (authors: Hartrisari Hanggoro, Harry Imantho and Anissa Damayanti) states that the Role of Small and Medium Enterprises (SMEs) in supporting Indonesian economic activity are significant. SMEs face many obstacles in their business development. Empowerment of SMEs in Bogor by local governments carried out in conjunction with the Department of Cooperatives and SMEs. This study aimed to establish the spatial model design of SMEs in Bogor area in order to improve the competitiveness of products in Bogor city. The analysis has shown that SMEs in Bogor city is still in the phase of development, market penetration and also product development. The model shows the average performance index of SMEs in Bogor is only 62.29, 19 among 41 have index values about 50. From the competitiveness analysis, we could see that among 41 SMEs can be categorized in 4 quadrants. Strategic program could be developed based on the position in the quadrant. It can be concluded that in general SMEs in Bogor city have not been ready for internationally competition. Government should develop specific strategy for each SMEs based on the quadrant position defined by the model.

Chapter 3, titled "Exploring the Entrepreneurial Motivations and Barriers of Agripreneurs in Brunei Darussalam" (authors: Siti Fatimahwati Pehin Dato Musa, Pg Siti Rozaidah Pg Hj Idris and Muhammad Khairul Hidayatullah Haji Basir) studies the motivations and institutional barriers of local agripreneurs who are involved in different branches of agriculture in Brunei. Descriptive analysis and thematic analysis were performed to analyse the data. The agripreneurs in the study consider their venture into agriculture as an act of symbolic nationalistic support whereby they envision Brunei to be a nation less reliant on food imports, in line with the country's vision or better known as Wawasan 2035. In addition, their motivation is also based on Islamic values with the intention of seeking lawful earning and a path to a blessed monetary and hereafter rewards. The main problems faced by the agripreneurs are lack of access to finance, lack of infrastructure and technology and lack of exposure. The research on local agripreneurs in the context of Brunei is scarce, thus this study aims to provide a better understanding of their motivations and constraints in order for Brunei to realize the potential of the agriculture sector as an important driver of the economy and thus develop the sector further.

Chapter 4, titled "Empowering Community Through Entrepreneurship Training and Islamic Microfinancing: Sharing the Experience of IIUM-CIMB Partnership" (authors: Norma Md Saad, Mustafa Omar Mohammad and Mohammed Aslam Haneef) states that community economic development is a relatively new strategy employed to increase employment, income, and entrepreneurship activities in small town and communities. The Centre for Islamic Economics, International Islamic University Malaysia (IIUM) has initiated a smart partnership with CIMB Islamic Bank to offer entrepreneurship training and Islamic microfinance facility to the poor in Malaysia. This project adopts several modes of Islamic microfinance financing instruments which include equity-based and debt-based financing. The program aims to educate the communities surrounding the IIUM campus with entrepreneurship knowledge and skill in addition to giving Shariah-compliant micro-financing facility for them to implement their business ideas. CIMB Islamic which is the main partner for this project provides funds for Islamic microfinance facilities and IIUM contributes expertise in providing entrepreneurship trainings to the communities located near IIUM campus. It is hoped that this smart partnership would empower the surrounding communities and create more successful entrepreneurs.

Chapter 5, titled "Halal Industry in ASEAN: Issues and Challenges" (authors: Moha Asri Abdullah and Md Siddique E Azam) affirms that amongst three Muslim majority countries (Indonesia, Malaysia, and Brunei) of ASEAN, Malaysia leads the halal industry globally and considered to be the global halal hub. Simultaneously, the market is growing tremendously in other member countries as well. It has been realized that a number of driving forces are responsible for boosting the expansion of Halal industry globally as well as in ASEAN. While there are a number of factors accelerating the growth of the Halal industry, there are many limitations and challenges that are hindering the market expansion. Therefore, the first objective of this chapter is to introduce the overview of Halal industry globally as well as in ASEAN counties. Later section of the chapter will be exploring the opportunities of the Halal industry for ASEAN counties followed by identifying the issues and challenges confronted by industry players. Finally, it concludes by providing some recommendations in the ASEAN context based on the current global situation and findings of the Halal industry. The chapter adopts methodology of analyzing secondary data.

Chapter 6, titled "Analysis of Food Security Policy by Participatory Poverty Assessment (PPA) Effort: Case In Indonesia" (authors: Muhamad Rusliyadi, Azaharaini Hj. Mohd and Muhammad Anshari) aims to evaluate food securit policies and extension policies to the achievement of targets and the results of a development programme such as Food Self Sufficiency village (DMP) used Participatory Poverty Assessments (PPA). The output obtained is information that is an evaluation of how the policy was planned, initiated and implemented. Participatory Poverty Assessments

(PPA) monitoring and evaluation analyse the outcome and impact of the DMP Programme. The output of the PPA process from this study is the agricultural policy formulated in terms of practical ways of approaching poverty problems from a local perspective. The success of alternative policy options applied by local government such us Physical, Human Resources, Institution development at the grassroots level should be adopted at the national level. It should represent the best example of a case of successful programme implementation at the grassroots level which can then be used in formulating national policies and strategies.

Chapter 7, titled "The Study of Digital Marketplace in Brunei Darussalam" (authors: Alif Azizi Abdullah, Mohammad Nabil Almunawar and Muhammad Anshari) state that a two-sided market or two-sided network is made up of two distinct user groups that provide each other with network benefits in which they interact through an intermediary or platform. A digital marketplace makes use of a two-sided market where the two distinct groups are the buyers and sellers. A digital marketplace is a type of e-commerce site where the sellers offer products or services to the buyers, and transactions are controlled and processed by marketplace operators. With the rapid development and adoption of the Internet and digital marketplace globally and also regionally, businesses in Brunei Darussalam are slowly incorporating digital marketplace. This chapter aims to provide an overview of the current state of the digital marketplace in Brunei, and thus, case studies of local digital marketplaces will be discussed. A qualitative approach, which consists of interviews with companies, will be made for the study. The strengths and problems of employing digital marketplace for businesses and analysis using Michael Porter's five models will also be covered in this chapter.

Chapter 8, titled "A Study of Quality Tools and Techniques for Smart Manufacturing in Industry 4.0 in Malaysia: The Case of Northern Corridor Economic Region" (authors: Mohd Syaiful Rizal Abd Hamid, Saifuddin Isa and Chew Boon Cheong) analyses the key factors for selecting quality tools and techniques in industrial revolution 4.0, particularly in the smart manufacturing context. This study asked, "What are the factors determining which quality tools and techniques are more applicable in specific circumstances related to quality performance in Industrial Revolution 4.0?" To answer this question, a multiple case study and an in-depth literature review were employed as the research design approach. Two key data collection methods (qualitative methods) were used: (1) Primary data from face-to-face interviews with Toyo Memory Technology and Intel Malaysia (2) Secondary data from previous studies. This review, coupled with the case study analysis, led to the identification of the real implementation of quality tools and techniques in the industries. Finally, this book can enhance the reader understanding of Industrial Revolution 4.0 and quality management practices as well as highlight opportunities for further research.

Chapter 9, titled "Ethnicity and Household Savings in Indonesia" (authors: Shochrul Rohmatul Ajija, Muhamad Abduh, Wasiaturrahma Wasiaturrahma and Ahmad Hudaifah) states that household saving is very important, not only for securing the future spending of the family but also for the country's economy. Using the logit analysis on data of The Indonesia Family Life Survey (IFLS) wave three, four, and five, this study attempts to analyze factors influencing, especially the role of ethnicity, upon the household savings in Indonesia. The result indicates that gender, location, and level of education are the consistent variables affecting the household saving behaviour in Indonesia across the three wave surveys. Meanwhile, as for the ethnic group variable, there are only Sunda, Batak, and Bima-Dompu that can significantly influencing the people's saving behavior across the three wave surveys.

Chapter 10, titled "Strengthening Islamic Finance in South East Asia Through Innovation of Islamic Fintech in Brunei" (author: Abdurrahman Raden Aji Haqqi) observes that fintech solutions can revolutionize Islamic financial services and leverage on the so-called 'Fourth Industrial Revolution' which is the movement towards combining everyday aspects of our lives, such as finance, into the digital realm that will help increase speed, efficiency, and convenience. The most significant challenge for all countries pursuing Fintech is regulating the industry. Following the issuance of the Financial Sector Blueprint, the Fintech Unit was established under Autoriti Monitori Brunei Darussalam (AMBD). AMBD envisions a vibrant economy powered by ICT through ICT-Smart Citizens as well as being a connected and efficient nation. This article discusses the application of Fintech specifically in Islamic finance sector based on the descriptive method of research by concentrating on its regulations. At the end, the research found that though Fintech in Islamic finance sector has been done since it's emerge but through Guidelines Fintech Regulatory Sandbox Guidelines Islamic financial Fintech will be strengthened and developed and more diversified.

Chapter 11, titled "Opportunities and Challenges of Social Media to the Islamic Banks in Indonesia" (author: Ahmad Rafiki) affirms that the Islamic banks in Indonesia have a serious issue of a low market share of 5%. This emerged due to the limited/unvaried product range, low literacy and inclusion level of Islamic finance, unfavorable perception for Islamic banking, and limited distribution networks and outreach. All of these causes could be resolved by using social media which will bring several opportunities such as transparency and openness, effective marketing channels, stakeholders' relationship, social media content, brand image and reputation, shariah compliance activity, learning and knowledge, and greater personalization. Meanwhile, in using social media, the Islamic banks face few challenges such as network infrastructure, negative comments, information risk management, privacy, and deception. All the information in this chapter can be used as a reference to any institutions particularly the Islamic banks which associated with digital interfaces and interactions in its daily businesses. Thus expectedly, the Islamic banks could enhance the public trust and establish a good Islamic identity.

Chapter 12, titled "The Loan Shark in ASEAN Can Nanofinance With Qardhul Hassan Deal With It? Lesson Learned From Bank Wakaf Mikro in Indonesia" (author: Khairunnisa Musari) states that loan shark is a humanitarian problem faced by many countries in the world, including in Asia, even in the Association of Southeast Asian Nations (ASEAN)'s countries. Loan shark activities are found not only in Myanmar and Cambodia, which has the lowest per capita income in ASEAN but also in Indonesia, Thailand, Malaysia, Brunei, and even Singapore, which are the five countries with the highest gross domestic product (GDP) per capita in ASEAN. How are loan shark practices in ASEAN countries? Can nanofinance overcome the microfinance gap to fight the loan shark? How the practice of Bank Wakaf Mikro (BWM) in Indonesia to nanofinance with qardhul hassan contract? Find the answers in this chapter.

Chapter 13, titled "Factors Influence Retail Equity Investors to Patronize Islamic Stockbroking in Malaysia: An AHP Approach" (authors: Muhamad Abduh and Faizal Asfan Mohamad) analyses factors influence retail equity investors to patronize Islamic stockbroking in Malaysia and rank their level of importance using Analytical Hierarchy Process. Data are collected using questionnaire via online and offline survey among clients, individuals who work in the stockbroking industry and stockbroking related industry such as fund managers, unit trust managers and mutual funds. The results show that religiosity and product awareness significantly influence the patronizing behavior of Malaysian retail equity investors. On the other hand, economic motives, convenience, social influence and attractiveness of stock investment ranked below religiosity and product awareness. In view of the findings, stockbroking industry players such as investment bank, stockbroking firm or participating organization should take advantage of the religiosity and product awareness factors as a main focus to develop Islamic stockbroking service in Malaysia. Sales, marketing and business development strategies can be designed according to the said criteria.

Chapter 14, titled "Post-Crisis Interdependence Between Islamic Unit Trust Funds and Islamic Stock Market in Malaysia" (author: Muhamad Abduh) explores the short-run and long-run relationship between 34 Islamic unit trusts and the Islamic stock market after the global financial crisis. The study collects the data from Bloomberg's database from 2009 until 2012 and employs J-J cointegration to identify the long-run relationship while Granger causality test is used to investigate how the changes in Islamic stock market can influence the changes in Islamic unit trusts in the short-run. The finding indicates that 61.76 percent out of the 34 Islamic unit trusts tested do not have long-run equilibrium with the Islamic stock market. Furthermore, only a few Islamic trusts responded to the changes in the Islamic stock market. This study is important at least in two folds. Firstly is its role in fulfilling the gap in the literature of unit trust—stock markets nexus in Islamic finance. Secondly, the findings provide some relevant information to the investors and fund managers so they may take benefit from the situation.

The last chapter of the collection, Chapter 15, titled "Financial Accessibility and Small Medium Enterprise (SMEs) in Malaysia: The Role of Crowdfunding and Islamic Finance" (authors: Mohamed Asmy Bin Mohd Thas Thaker, Hassanudin Bin Mohd Thas Thaker and Choong Pai Wei) affirms that one of the common problems facing by worldwide SMEs including Malaysia is accessing external financial services. Given this fact, this paper attempts to offer a sustainable model of source of financing for Malaysian SMEs in meeting their financial need, which is known as Islamic Crowdfunding-Small and Medium Enterprises (ICSMEs) model. We review comprehensive literature by focusing on the issues of financial accessibility faced by Malaysian SMEs, and the existing studies relating to SMEs, crowdfunding and Islamic finance in support to construct ICSME model. We discussed the modus operandi of the proposed ICSME model and offers several significances of the model.

Before closing this preface, it is important to thank authors for their interest in participation in this book as well as the members of the Editorial Advisory Board of the book and reviewers for the time and efforts they invested in choosing the best collection of chapters for this book. Thank you very much to all of you.

*Mohammad Nabil Almunawar*
*Universiti Brunei Darussalam, Brunei*

*Muhammad Abduh*
*Universiti Brunei Darussalam, Brunei*

*Patricia Ordóñez de Pablos*
*The University of Oviedo, Spain*
*November 2019*

# Chapter 1
# Organizational Factors and the Success of Technology Transfer

**Md Zahidul Islam**
*Universiti Brunei Darussalam, Brunei*

**Safayet Rahman**
*Southeast University, Bangladesh*

## ABSTRACT

*This chapter discusses the relationship between organizational culture, structure, complexity of technology, and the success of technology transfer. Technology is one of the key competitive advantages of any organization and plays an important role in the success of both international and domestic firms. Technology can be transferred within the boundaries of an organization, outside of organizational boundaries with strategic partners and also across national boundaries. As it transcends national borders, difficulties in transferring technology are likely to increase. To overcome the difficulties, certain organizational culture could play an important role in the efficient transfer of technology in an organization. Besides culture, organizational structure could also play a major role to achieve technology transfer success. Furthermore, the complexity of technology can also affect the success of technology transfer.*

## INTRODUCTION

Technology is one of the most important factors determining the outcome of the industrialization process of developing countries. Technology is the application of

DOI: 10.4018/978-1-7998-2257-8.ch001

scientific discoveries to the production of a better quality of goods and services. Eridilek (1986) defined technology as the expertise or know-how required to manufacture a final product or for processing intermediate inputs. Technology helps to create new products or industrial processes; therefore, it is one of the key competitive' advantages of any organization. Technology plays an important role in the success not only of international firms but also that of domestic ones. In other words, technology can play an important role in economic growth and development. As technology has evolved rapidly, the technology gap between developed and developing countries is said to be widening. The developing countries have weak technological bases and, on top of that, their capacities for research and development activities are limited. Such a situation allows these countries no choice but to rely on foreign investment as a major mechanism for technological acquisition.

The transfer of technology from one organization to another can also be explained by the transaction cost theory. Transaction cost economics is concerned with the underlying theory of organizational arrangement that most efficiently economize on transaction costs (Williamson, 1985). A firm has the option to either internalize a function or to contract it out (make or buy). There are costs and risks associated with either choice. Internalizing a function represents some commitment to it. The firm must create permanent internal components devoted to the activity. Contracting out is essentially establishing an agency relationship, and the firm faces the risk associated with an imperfect agency. Normally, technology transfer occurs when transaction costs related to the transfer is less than developing one's own. Every organization needs to consider cost before involved in the transfer. When an organization is able to transfer technology at a reasonable cost, it means it will provide higher profit and satisfaction. Transfer of technology from one organization to another can also be viewed in terms of the resource dependency theory. Resource dependency theory suggests that one organization is dependent on another for essential resources. This dependency can affect the relationship with other organizations (Kotter, 1979). Dependence exists when the decision-makers perceive that the behavior of particular external organizations imposes contingencies and constraints on organizational behavior and its effectiveness (Lynskey, 1999). An appropriate understanding and application of this theory will enable an organization to choose the right transfer, in turn, will increase the possibilities of successful technology transfer.

In simple form, technology transfer means the process that allows the transfer of technology from one organization to another organization (Bozeman, 2000). Technology transfer can be a source of hardware or specialized technical skills, which are transferred to a target group of receivers, those who do not possess those specialized skills. Technology transfer can also be termed as the transmission of knowledge, which enables the recipient firm to manufacture a certain product or provide a particular service (Tsang, 1997). Typically, technology transfer is a continuous process, and it can occur within the boundaries of an organization (e.g., from HQ to its branches or subsidiaries) or across organizational boundaries, as can be seen in strategic alliances. Similarly, the transfer can be transnational, crossing national boundaries. It should be noted that specific difficulties are encountered when a technology is transferred across international borders. Some of the problems are caused by, for example, the differences in technological infrastructure, language, the level of economic development, culture and attitude between home and host countries, as well as high communication costs (Teece, 1977). Failures of technology transfer are all quite common, especially when both sides face communication problems. Furthermore, failures occur when the developers of technical systems or their users are unwilling or unable to adapt (Leonard-Barton & Sinha, 1993). Despite various origins of failure, one thing is certain that failure in technology transfer poses a threat to organizational success in any country and Malaysia is not an exception. Technology is one of the most important features of modern organizations, and it is playing an important role in the development of this nation as well.

Over the years, Malaysia has formulated many policies to facilitate industrialization and technology development to make the country developed by 2020 (Hamdan et al., 2018). Though Malaysia has no specific policy on technology transfer, nevertheless, the use of technology transfer, as a development mechanism, is reflected in the progress of the automotive industry in Malaysia. The country's focus is comprehensible by looking at its third Industrial Master Plan (covering 2006-2020), which was formulated to create a sustainable competitive manufacturing and service sector (Hamdan et al., 2018). The action plan formulated for this master plan is considered the main driver for local Small and Medium Enterprises to use technology transfer to become competitive in the market (Hamdan et al., 2018). As a matter of fact, currently, the business environment in Malaysia is exhibiting increased competition. Hence, failure in technology transfer can result in losing competitive advantage in the market, which in turn, can result in losing the investment in the technology transfer process. Thus, it becomes imperative to ensure successful technology transfer. Though many Malaysian organizations are involved in technology transfer, however, the success of the technology transfers of these organizations is still debatable. With the expansion of the Malaysian economy, it is anticipated that the success of technology transfer will play a very important role in the success of Malaysian organizations in the global market. Therefore, it is important for managers to identify the ideal organizational factors to achieve success in technology transfer.

## THE SUCCESS OF TECHNOLOGY TRANSFER

The success of technology transfer can be discussed into four stages, such as awareness, association, assimilation and application (Lynskey, 1999). The first stage is the awareness of one's own product weakness, and the type of technology competitors possess. The relationship with credible boundary-spanning agents is the second stage. Next stage is the assimilation related to the ability to new inputs of technology, and the final stage is to building sustainable technological capability. The success of technology transfer becomes a reality when the set of goals and objectives combined with the adaptation strategy (Udo & Ehie, 1996). A successful technology transfer brings financial and economic benefits to the organization in the form of increased profitability, more competitiveness and saves costs (Preece, 1989). It also provides technical and production benefits in the form of increased flexibility in organization, improved control and consistency, and improvement in the product (Preece, 1989).

In order to ensure the success of the technology transfer, the recipient needs to think about some important aspects. According to Ratnam (1985), for technology transfer to be successful, a society must first nurture a proper scientific orientation at all levels. This is important not only to create a conducive environment for the introduction of technology but also to promote an entrepreneurial and managerial outlook that is technologically alert and is enthusiastic about investing in research and development. The resource requirement of technology transfer refers to its demand upon the transferor or transferee input of resources. The first factor is the technical absorptive capacity of the transferee. A successful technology transfer needs active participation not only of the transferor but also of the transferee (Tsang, 1997). For a successful technology transfer, recipients would be obligated to devote substantial resources to assimilate, adapt and integrate the technology into the production system. According to Cohen & Levinthal (1989), a firm's ability to evaluate and utilize outside knowledge is largely a function of the level of its prior related knowledge. The other factors like manufacturing experience, the size of the organization and the intensity of the research and development can also play important roles in the technology transfer. The selection of technology also contributes to the success of technology transfer, like in the case of SABIC project in Saudi Arabia. This project was successful because of the right choice of technology. The selection process involves close coordination with R&D and marketing personnel. They made an assessment in its international patent implications and its techno-economic benefits. Recruitment and training of local personnel are some of the aspects behind the success of technology transfer. This becomes very important because local staffs need to perform at a high level of skill acquired from technology suppliers (Germidis, 1977). The training policy varies depending on the job characteristics and industry.

According to Olayan (1999), the difficulties arise in recruiting and training from the level of a technician and it becomes greater at the higher skill level of the technical, and administrative hierarchy.

To measure the success of technology transfer, we need to look at three levels, such as process, output, and outcome. Process relates to the operations that control products or services produced and delivered. Output is the features, values and characteristics desired by the customer and delivered by the process. Outcome is the highest level of measurement and represents the ultimate desired results of technology transfer (Tenner & DeToro, 1992). In technology transfer, process performance parameters measure each step or activity in the process and the characteristics of inputs delivered by the transferor that controls the desired outcome. Outcome determines the ultimate success or failure of the technology transfer. If an organization is able to get the desired outcome, that means the technology transfer is successful. The overall success of a technology transfer depends on the final outcome of any transfer that helps an organization to produce a unique product or gaining more market share (Zoller, 1999). According to Udo & Ehie (1996), the success of technology transfer can be measured with the outcomes such as a reduction in throughput time and production cost, improvement in the quality of products, quick response time, improved working conditions, and relationship.

Technology transfer can be successful when the actual outcome of the transfer process meets the transfer plans. This includes the timeline of the transfer, meeting the budgeted cost, manufacturing starts without any major quality issues. A realistic timeline is very important towards the desired result, and there should be enough time given in meeting the task (Zoller, 1999). The timeline also depends on the location of the transfer, the nature of the technology that is to be transferred, the readiness of the transferee (recipient), and the type of the operations involved. The cost involved in technology transfer is a potential indicator of the success of the transfer process. If the actual spending does not exceed the planned budget, then the technology transfer is considered successful. However, it is really difficult to define the project budget because many unforeseen circumstances that can arise during the transfer (Zoller, 1999) and this can be one of the causes for the technology transfer failure. The satisfaction level also indicates the success of technology transfer. If the satisfaction level is high, then we can consider the transfer to be successful. The satisfaction level also indicates how well the technology transfer process meets all the plans. If the plans are not fulfilled, then the satisfaction level is expected to be low.

With the passage of time, technology became complex, new technology becoming obsolete faster than before. The fourth industrial revolution will make technology more dynamic. Continuous innovation will be the key for organizations to survive. Organizations will be required to absorb technology faster and also innovate and apply technology faster (Hamdan et al., 2018). This situation can be better explained by the "Role Shifting Model" of technology transfer process that emphasizes the creation of innovation instead of just technology transfer (Choi, 2009). In addition, a well-designed structure would facilitate better technology management in the organization (Hamdan et al., 2018). Furthermore, Malaysia's quest towards being a knowledge-based economy will demand its organizations to adopt the knowledge-based view, which requires favorable organizational culture with an effective structure. As it is also mentioned before that, difficulties in transferring technology are likely to increase as it transcends national borders. Therefore, to foster innovation and alleviate difficulties, appropriate organizational culture and structure could play an effective role in the successful transfer of technology.

## ORGANIZATIONAL CULTURE

Organizational cultural difference is crucially important to the efficient technology transfer and poses a major challenge for managers involved in transfer projects. Organizational culture is generally seen as a set of key values, assumptions, understandings and norms that are shared by employees of an organization and also taught to new employees (Daft & Armstrong, 2012). Organizational culture may play both a positive and negative role in technology transfer. Cultural differences between the technology provider and receiver are considered the main issue in the conduct of cross-cultural technology transfer projects (Ganesan & Kesley, 2006; Lin & Berg, 2001). The adverse impact of culture might play an important role to cause failure in the way of successful technology transfer. However, cultural problems can be overcome by nurturing appropriate culture in the organization.

An organization having supportive and innovative culture could easily deal with such problems. Organizations might successfully achieve effective long-term technology transfer performance through the support from their top management, as reflected through policies, commitment mechanisms, and the process of continuous management and evaluation (Gibson & Smilor, 1992). In addition, top management could play an important role by providing the needed resources for achieving a successful technology transfer. Furthermore, establishing a teamwork culture is a critical factor in organizational learning processes, because it creates opportunities to interact with others through the collaborative arrangements, where team members try to achieve mutual objectives (Nguyen & Aoyama, 2015). Team-based activities increase both verbal and non-verbal communication and enhance the integration of specialized and generalized knowledge, which could be useful for successful technology transfer (Achrol & Kotler, 1999). Moreover, teamwork increases interpersonal interactions leading to increased mutual trust and mutual trust, in turn, enriches the exchange of crucial resources and information. These interactions also increase empathy, helpfulness, opinion sharing, a sense of togetherness and social ties. High levels of sharing and understanding reduce the possibility of meeting obstacles to technology transfer during the establishment of cross-cultural alliances (Ding et al., 2009).

The innovative culture is the environment where employees are inspired to be risk-taking, result-oriented, creative, challenging, enterprising, and driving (Wallach, 1983). An innovative culture involves the introduction and application of new and improved ways of doing things (Islam et al., 2017). An innovative organization focuses on developing innovative ideas, continuous improvement and quality management. Innovative organizations thrive to achieve efficiency at every level; therefore, it enhances the success of technology transfer. Furthermore, successful technology transfer is influenced by the knowledge level of the workers, transfer mechanisms and types of technology. Therefore, to ensure the proper use of technology, technology transfer processes should transfer not only technical knowledge but also the supplementary managerial and social knowledge (Attewell, 1992). Therefore, in order to ensure that technology is used successfully, appropriate training approaches are necessary. Innovative organizations are concerned about their employee's development; hence, to make employees more efficient innovative organizations arrange training programs on a regular basis.

## ORGANIZATIONAL STRUCTURE

Organization structure is defined as ways in which job tasks are formally segregated, classed and coordinated (Robbins, 1996). It also governs communication patterns and interactions, which are based on the social networking theory (Islam et al., 2015). According to Gold, Malhotra, & Segars (2001), organizational structure refers to the formal rules, tasks, functions and authorities that exist within an organization, including hierarchic relationships, reward systems, policies, processes and sector boundaries. Organization structure may be classified using various taxonomies such as simple, team structure, bureaucratic, mechanistic, organic and matrix structure. The mechanistic organization is seen as an organizational hierarchy of authority where an organization is operated under specific rules and regulations, with predefined functional roles and decentralization and complexity are relatively low (Burns & Stalker, 1961). The organic structure, on the other hand, is defined as an organizational design in which exists a high level of decision-making, a low degree of authority, and a high degree of complexity (Burns & Stalker, 1961). Examples of organic designs include project and matrix forms of structures (Burns & Stalker, 1961). However, for general discussion, three major types of organizational structures are decentralization, formalization, and size.

Decentralization is an extension of delegation (Sharma, 1989). It is the delegation of authority throughout the organization. It is not necessary that authority flows at the same rate from level to level; however, what is important is that wherever decision-making takes place, that level is provided with the commensurate authority. According to Sharma (1989), decentralization helps an organization by developing and motivating managers and also focuses on business performance. A decentralized organization allows lower-level personnel to participate in the key decisions in the organization and facilitates problem-solving and quicker actions and promotes similar interests between them and the key decision-makers (Robbins, 1996). A decentralized, participatory structure opens up channels of communication and increases cooperation (Chen et al., 2010). Open communication helps an organization to maintain better communication with the transferee and facilitates the sharing of expertise. Decentralization creates an environment that increases communication and commitment of the members of the transfer team. Although decentralization may enhance the initiation of innovative ideas, nonetheless, stricter channels of authority may be needed to reduce conflict and ambiguity that can impair the adoption of technology (Pierce & Delbecq, 1977).

Formalization relates to communication process within the organizations. Formalization measures the degree to which an organization uses its rules and procedures to prescribe behavior (Liao et al., 2011). Formalized structures have explicit rules and procedures, which stress on how organization members should act and behave. The use of explicit rules of relationship has been identified as an impediment to the spontaneity and flexibility needed for internal transfer (Bidault & Cummings, 1994). Between firms, less formality enhances effectiveness and cooperation (Dahlstrom et al., 1995). According to Bums and Stalker (1961), organic organizations with less formalization provide higher capacity in innovation. Less formal structure in an organizational boundary exposes fewer formal rules and regulations, which creates greater flexibility and creativity (Islam et al., 2015). Though success in implementing innovations requires a greater degree of formal structure, however, less formalization creates greater flexibility that reduces rigidity and constraint in problem-solving during the technology transfer process.

Size and the success of technology transfer can be viewed from two perspectives: the availability of resources and complexity of structure. Size of organizations is usually determined by a variety of measures such as total assets, number of employees, and sales value generated. How the size of the organization influences the success of technology transfer, is still in controversy. Research has shown that a large organization does not necessarily result in greater success (Hage, 1980). Small organizations can be more successful because they are highly flexible, a greater ability to adapt and improve, and less difficulty in accepting and implementing change. On the other hand, large organizations have more complex and diverse facilities that aid the adoption of a large number of innovations (Nord & Tucker, 1987). Greater resources give large organizations the leeway to tolerate the potential loss due to unsuccessful transfer. Moreover, large organizations employ more professional and skilled workers; hence, these organizations have high technical knowledge and technical potential. The size of the input and output volumes allows large organizations to accumulate resources that bring them to the forefront of technical development. Availability of resources in any organization ensures greater absorptive capacity to assimilate the technology transfer.

## THE COMPLEXITY OF THE TECHNOLOGY

The complexity of technology could hinder the success of technology transfer. Technology complexity can be categorized along three dimensions, namely radical vs incremental, technological vs administrative, and product vs process (Cooper, 1998). Incremental innovation is the degree of strategic and structural change that the firm must undergo to accommodate innovation. Incremental changes enhance and extend the underlying technology and thus reinforce the established technical order (Tushman & Anderson, 1986). Radical innovations represent advances so significant that brings revolutionary alteration of the organisation, and its support networks must occur to accommodate and implement the change. As innovation is radical, it can be riskier for any organization (Cooper, 1998). Radical product innovations require a greater outlay of resources and are riskier than incremental advances (Kotler, 1997). Radical innovations are inherently more unpredictable and uncertain (Rice et al., 1998). Radical innovations require participants to engage in more learning and unlearning and to develop new capabilities. Consequently, there is a greater need for reorientation of existing structure and process (Nord & Tucker, 1987). The higher stakes involved, demands, unfamiliarity, and unpredictability of radical products make projects prone to communication breakdowns and make the task of coordinating the projects more difficult. Radical innovation projects tend to be star projects and consequently, participants tend to be more committed to them (Schmidt & Calantone, 1998). Administrative innovation refers to the changes that affect the policies, allocation of resources and other factors associated with the firm's social structure of the organization (Daft, 1978). Technological innovation refers to the adoption of an idea that directly influences the basic output. This technological aspect is similar to the classification by Gopalakrishnan, Kessler, & Bierly (1999). They have classified the complexity of innovation into three characteristics, i.e., the degree to which the innovation is divisible, the degree of intellectual sophistication and its originality. Product innovation reflects the end product or service offered by the organization, while the process innovation represents changes in the way firms produce end products or services (Utterback, 1994). Sciulli (1998) showed that large, complex and participative firms adopt product innovation. Process innovation seemed to favor large and bureaucratic firms (Porter, 1980).

The complexity of technology plays a role in the success of technology transfer. The success of technology transfer is affected by the nature of the technology being transferred. The complexity of technology might demand some changes in organizational culture, which could be difficult to implement in a short span of time. The organizational structure could be also get affected by the complexity of technology. For example, decision-making is very important in the technology transfer process. Generally, a decentralized structure is suitable for incremental transfer. On the other hand, radical transfer needs a centralized structure. Furthermore, a larger organization might be favorable for incremental transfer. However, the small organization creates a favorable environment for radical transfer.

## CONCLUSION

Technology is the driving force of modern business and also an important indicator of development progress. Successful technology transfer could transform an organization into an efficient contributing entity to a country's economy. To achieve success in technology transfer, organizational factors such as organizational culture and structure might play an important role. An organization's supportive and innovative culture, which ensures management's support, establishes teamwork, creates room for innovation and provides training might create an appropriate environment conducive to successful technology transfer. Furthermore, choosing the appropriate structure by evaluating the required autonomy, formalization and size might also smoothen the overall process of technology transfer. Though the complexity of technology could moderate the relationship between organizational culture, structure and success of technology transfer, nonetheless, identifying and understanding these factors could enable the managers in Malaysian business organizations to make effective decisions regarding the transfer of technology.

## REFERENCES

Achrol, R. S., & Kotler, P. (1999). Marketing in the network economy. *Journal of Marketing*, *63*(Special Issue), 146–163. doi:10.1177/00222429990634s114

Attewell, P. (1992). Technology diffusion and organizational learning: The case of business computing. *Organization Science*, *3*(1), 1–19. doi:10.1287/orsc.3.1.1

Bidault, M., & Cummings, T. (1994). *Advanced Manufacturing Technology and Work Design*. Chichester: Wiley.

Bozeman, B. (2000). Technology transfer and public policy: A review of research and theory. *Research Policy*, *29*(4/5), 627–655. doi:10.1016/S0048-7333(99)00093-1

Burns, T., & Stalker, G. M. (1961). *The Management of Innovation* (3rd ed.). London, UK: Tavistock Publications.

Chen, C.-J., Huang, J.-W., & Hsiao, Y.-C. (2010). Knowledge management and innovativeness: The role of organizational climate and structure. *International Journal of Manpower*, *31*(8), 848–870. doi:10.1108/01437721011088548

Choi, H. J. (2009). Technology transfer issues and a new technology transfer model. *The Journal of Technology Studies*, *35*(1), 49–57. doi:10.21061/jots.v35i1.a.7

Cohen, W., & Levinthal, D. (1989). Innovation and Learning: The two Faces of R & D. *Economic Journal (London)*, *99*(397), 569–596. doi:10.2307/2233763

Cooper, J. R. (1998). A Multidimensional Approach the Adoption of Innovation. *Management Decision*, *36*(8), 493–501. doi:10.1108/00251749810232565

Daft, R. L. (1978). A Dual Core Model of Orgaizational innovation. *Academy of Management Journal*, *20*, 193–211.

Daft, R. L., & Armstrong, A. (2012). *Organization Theory and Design* (2nd ed.). Toronto, Canada: Nelson Education.

Dahlstrom, R. F., Dwyer, R., & Chandrashekaran, M. (1995). Environment, Structure and Performance in Interfirm Exchange. *Journal of Business-To-Business Marketing*, *2*(2), 37–58. doi:10.1300/J033v02n02_04

Ding, Q., Akoorie, M., & Pavlovich, K. (2009). Understanding the specificity and complexity of inter-firm knowledge flows in alliance networks. *Interdisciplinary Journal of Contemporary Research in Business*, *1*(7), 8–33.

Eridilek, A. (1986). Issues in international technology transfer. *Economic Impact*, *4*(56).

Ganesan, S., & Kesley, J. (2006). Technology transfer: International collaboration in Sri Lanka. *Construction Management and Economics*, *24*(7), 743–753. doi:10.1080/01446190600704703

Germidis, D. (1977). *Transfer of Technology by Multinational Corporationns*. Paris, France: Development Centre of the Organisation for Economic Co-operation and Development.

Gibson, D. V., & Smilor, R. W. (1992). *Technology Transfer in Consortia and Strategic Alliances*. Maryland: Rowman and Littlerfield Publisher.

Gold, A. H., Malhotra, A., & Segars, A. H. (2001). Knowledge management: An organizational capabilities perspective. *Journal of Management Information Systems, 18*(1), 185–214. doi:10.1080/07421222.2001.11045669

Gopalakrishnan, S., Kessler, E. H., & Bierly, R. S. (1999). Innovation Speed: A Conceptual Model of Context, Antecedents and Outcomes. *Academy of Management Review, 21*(4), 1143–1191.

Hage, J. (1980). *Theories of Organizations*. New York: John Wiley & Sons.

Hamdan, A. R., Fathi, M. S., & Mohamed, Z. (2018). Evolution of Malaysia's technology transfer model facilitated by national policies. *IACSIT International Journal of Engineering and Technology, 7*(2), 196–202. doi:10.14419/ijet.v7i2.29.13317

Islam, M. Z., Jasimuddin, S. M., & Hasan, I. (2015). Organizational culture, structure, technology infrastructure and knowledge sharing: Empirical evidence from MNCs based in Malaysia. *Vine, 45*(1), 67–88. doi:10.1108/VINE-05-2014-0037

Islam, M. Z., Jasimuddin, S. M., & Hasan, I. (2017). The role of technology and socialization in linking organizational context and knowledge conversion: The case of Malaysian service organizations. *International Journal of Information Management, 37*(5), 497–503. doi:10.1016/j.ijinfomgt.2017.06.001

Kotler, P. R. (1997). *Marketing Management: Analysis, Planning, Implementation and Control*. Englewood Cliffs, NJ: Prentice Hall.

Kotter, J. P. (1979). *The General Managers*. New York: Free Press.

Leonard-Barton, D., & Sinha, D. (1993). Developer-User Interaction and User Satisfaction in Internal Technology Transfer. *Academy of Management Journal, 36*(5), 1125–1139.

Liao, C., Chuang, S. H., & To, P. L. (2011). How knowledge management mediates the relationship between environment and organizational structure. *Journal of Business Research, 64*(7), 728–736. doi:10.1016/j.jbusres.2010.08.001

Lin, B. W., & Berg, D. (2001). Effects of cultural difference on technology transfer projects: An empirical study of Taiwanese manufacturing companies. *International Journal of Project Management, 19*(5), 287–293. doi:10.1016/S0263-7863(99)00081-2

Lynskey, M. J. (1999). The transfer of Resources and Competencies for developing Technological Capabilities-The case of Fusitsu-ICL. *Technology Analysis and Strategic Management*, *11*(3), 317–335. doi:10.1080/095373299107384

Nguyen, N. T. D., & Aoyama, A. (2015). The impact of cultural differences on technology transfer Management practice moderation. *Journal of Manufacturing Technology Management*, *26*(7), 926–954. doi:10.1108/JMTM-09-2013-0130

Nord, W. R., & Tucker, S. (1987). *Implementing Routine and Radical innovation*. Lexington, KY: Lexington Books.

Olayan, H. B. (1999). Technology Transfer in Developing Nations. *Research Technology Management*, *42*(3), 43–48. doi:10.1080/08956308.1999.11671283

Pierce, J. L., & Delbecq, A. L. (1977). Organization Structure, Individual Attitudes, and Innovation. *Academy of Management Review*, *2*(1), 27–37. doi:10.5465/amr.1977.4409154

Porter, M. E. (1980). *Competitive Strategy: Techniques for Analyzing Industries and Competitors*. New York: Free Press.

Preece, D. A. (1989). *Managing the Adoption of New Technology*. London, UK: Routledge.

Ratnam, K. J. (1985). *Technology and society*. Pulau Pinang: Universiti Sains Malaysia.

Rice, M. P., O'Connor, G. C., Peters, L. S., & Morone, J. G. (1998). Managing Discontinuous Innovations. *Research Technology Management*, *41*(3), 52–58. doi:10.1080/08956308.1998.11671210

Robbins, S. P. (1996). *Organizational Behavior: Concepts Controversies Applications* (7th ed.). Englewood Cliffs, NJ: Prentice Hall International.

Schmidt, J. B., & Calantone, R. J. (1998). Are Really New Product Development Projects Harder to Shut Down? *Journal of Product Innovation Management*, *15*(2), 111–123. doi:10.1111/1540-5885.1520111

Sciulli, L. M. (1998). How Organization Structure Influences Success in Various Types of Innovation? *Journal of Retail Banking Services*, *20*, 13–18.

Sharma, R. A. (1989). *Organizational Theory and Behavior. New Delhi* , India: McGraw-Hill.

Teece, D. J. (1977). Technology Transfer by Multinational Firms: The Resource Cost of Transferring Technological Know-How. *Economic Journal (London)*, *87*(346), 242–261. doi:10.2307/2232084

Tenner, A. R., & DeToro, I. J. (1992). *Total Quality Management*. New York: Addison-Wesley.

Tsang, E. W. K. (1997). Choice of International Technology Transfer Mode: A Resource-based View. *Management International Review*, *37*, 151–165.

Tushman, M. J., & Anderson, P. (1986). Technological Discontinuities and Organizational Environments. *Administrative Science Quarterly*, *31*(3), 439–465. doi:10.2307/2392832

Udo, G. J., & Ehie, I. C. (1996). Advanced Manufacturing Technologies: Determinants of Implementation Success. *International Journal of Operations & Production Management*, *16*(12), 6–26. doi:10.1108/01443579610151733

Utterback, J. M. (1994). *Mastering the Dynamics of Innovation*. Boston, MA: Harvard Business School Press.

Wallach, E. J. (1983). Individuals and organizations: The cultural match. *Training and Development Journal*, *37*(2), 28–36.

Williamson, O. E. (1985). *The Economic Institutions of Capitalism: Firms, Markets, Relational Contracting*. New York: Free Press.

Zoller, A. S. (1999). Are you Satisfied with your Technology Alliance? *Research Technology Management*, *64*(3), 10–12. doi:10.1080/08956308.1999.11671266

## ADDITIONAL READING

Battistella, C., De Toni, A. F., & Pillon, R. (2016). Inter-organisational technology/knowledge transfer: A framework from critical literature review. *The Journal of Technology Transfer*, *41*(5), 1195–1234. doi:10.100710961-015-9418-7

Inkpen, A. C., & Tsang, E. W. K. (2016). Reflections on the 2015 Decade Award—Social Capital, Networks, and Knowledge Transfer: An Emergent Stream of Research. *Academy of Management Review*, *41*(4), 573–588. doi:10.5465/amr.2016.0140

Ismail, M., Hamzah, S. R. & Bebenroth, R. (2018). Dfferentiating Knowledge Transfer and Technology Transfer: What Should an Organization Managers Need to Know? *European Journal of Training and Development*, doi:10.1108/EJTD-04-2018-0042

Khan, Z., Shenkar, O., & Lew, Y. K. (2015). Knowledge transfer from international joint ventures to local suppliers in a developing economy. *Journal of International Business Studies*, *46*(6), 656–675. doi:10.1057/jibs.2015.7

Latilla, V. M., Frattini, F., Petruzzelli, A. M., & Berner, M. (2018). Knowledge management, knowledge transfer and organizational performance in the arts and crafts industry: A literature review. *Journal of Knowledge Management*. doi:10.1108/JKM-08-2017-0367

## KEY TERMS AND DEFINITIONS

**Organizational Culture:** A set of key values, assumptions, understandings and norms that are shared by employees of an organization and also taught to new employees (Daft & Armstrong, 2012).

**Organization Structure:** The ways in which job tasks are formally segregated, classed and coordinated (Robbins, 1996).

**Technology:** The expertise or know-how required to manufacture a final product or for processing intermediate inputs. (Eridilek, 1986).

**Technology Transfer:** The process that allows the transfer of technology from one organization to another organization (Bozeman, 2000).

# Chapter 2
# Spatial Dynamic Modeling for Increasing the Competitiveness of Small Medium Enterprises:
## Case Study of Bogor City, West Java, Indonesia

**Hartrisari Hanggoro Hardjomidjojo**
*IPB University, Indonesia*

**Harry Imantho**
*SEAMEO BIOTROP, Indonesia*

**Anissa Damayanti**
*IPB University, Indonesia*

## ABSTRACT

*The Role of Small and Medium Enterprises (SMEs) in supporting Indonesian economic activity are significant. SMEs face many obstacles in their business development. Empowerment of SMEs in Bogor by local governments carried out in conjunction with the Department of Cooperatives and SMEs. This study establishes the spatial model design of SMEs in Bogor area to improve the competitiveness of products in Bogor city. The analysis shows that SMEs in Bogor city is still in the phase of development, market penetration, and also product development. The model shows the average performance index of SMEs in Bogor is only 62.29, 19 among 41 have index values about 50. From the competitiveness analysis, authors could see that among 41 SMEs can be categorized in 4 quadrants. Strategic program could*

DOI: 10.4018/978-1-7998-2257-8.ch002

*be developed based on the position in the quadrant. It can be concluded that in general SMEs in Bogor city have not been ready for internationally competition. Government should develop specific strategy for each SMEs based on the quadrant position defined by the model*

# INTRODUCTION

## Background

The role of Small and Medium Enterprises (SMEs) in supporting economic activities in Indonesia's national real sector is very important. Within the framework of the national economy, SMEs have contributed to the recruitment of workers, increasing the Gross Domestic Product (GDP) as well as increasing the value of exports and national investment. SMEs has shown their performance at the economic crisis situation became the locomotive of the national economic movement since the raw materials used came from within the country. At present there are 56 534 591 SMEs units throughout Indonesia representing 99.9% of the total number of industries / businesses in Indonesia (Ministry of Cooperatives and SMEs, 2013 and 2015).

The ASEAN Free Trade Area (AFTA) implemented since 2015 should be used optimally to provide the equitable economic benefits for industry especially SMEs in the country. Indonesia as one of the ASEAN members has prepared facing AFTA by developing the important infrastructure, such as airports and ports in various places in Indonesia. Reform of procedures and bureaucracy has been done also to provide better social and economic services. This is a step to build a basis for the country's economic resilience facing the free market. A large number of Indonesian SMEs should be able to take advantage of the AFTA market opportunities so as to increase the country's foreign exchange and public welfare by producing products that have competitive and comparative advantages.

The facts show that although the number of SMEs is dominant, in general they face various obstacles in developing their businesses. Some of the obstacles include: capital, marketing, raw materials, technology, management, bureaucracy, infrastructure and partnerships. In this government and related agencies should take the role to solve the problems. Ministry of Cooperatives and SMEs has made policies and programs that can help the development and maintenance of SMEs. The policies of the Ministry of Cooperatives and MSMEs in 2015-2019 are aimed to: increasing productivity, feasibility and added value of Cooperatives and SMEs so that they are able to grow to a larger scale ("grade up") and be competitive. The policy direction implemented through five strategies as outlined in the 2015-2019 National Medium-Term Development Plan (RPJMN), namely: improving the quality of human resources, increasing access to finance and expanding financing schemes, increasing product value added and marketing reach, strengthening business institutions and ease, certainty and business protection. Meanwhile the challenges that need to be addressed in the development of SMEs are particularly related to the improvement of SME conditions, including: (1) Improvement of business formalization with better business governance; (2) Increasing productivity supported by skilled workforce and applying technology; (3) Capacity building to build partnerships and join global production and marketing networks; (4) Utilizing increasingly open opportunities from the application of the ASEAN Economic Community (AEC) and bilateral economic cooperation agreements and other regions and (5) Improving policies and regulations that are responsive to improving the performance and competitiveness of MSMEs. The various problems and challenges, especially for micro and small business actors mentioned above, direct efforts to empower MSMEs in the future need to be focused on handling two strategic issues, namely business growth and competitiveness.

The use of information technology in this era could be integrated in the modeling stage in order to present more clearly the simulation result of different scenarios. Spatial form can be used to present location about SMEs included basic information needed by other parties in order to know better about the SMEs or to take opportunities to collaborate with the SMEs.

A dynamic spatial model for enhancing MSME competitiveness needs to be developed in order to help decision makers make policies related to increasing product competitiveness both nationally and internationally for the improvement of people's welfare.

## Objectives

The purpose of this study is to develop a prototype of the SME spatial mapping model as a tool for policy analysis, to develop appropriate strategy for developing SMEs on improving the competitiveness of SMEs' products both nationally and internationally for the improvement of people's welfare. The prototype model will be equipped with analytical tools for mapping SMEs categories in readiness to compete on a local, national or international scale so that the specified strategy will be right on target and effective. The model is validated with SMEs data at Bogor City.

The steps taken for this research are as follows: (1) identification of selected SMEs at Bogor city and mapping in spatial information systems based on index value, (2) mapping of SMEs positions individually based on the readiness to increase competitiveness, (3) development of competitive strategies based on mapping positions, (4) validation of dynamic spatial models for increasing SMEs competitiveness in the city of Bogor.

## LITERATURE REVIEW

### Definition of SMEs

Pursuant to Law Number 20 of 2008 concerning SMEs, small business is a productive economic business that stands alone, which is carried out by individuals or business entities that are not subsidiaries or branch companies that are owned, controlled, or become a part either directly or indirectly of medium or large businesses with a net worth of more than fifty million rupiahs to a maximum of five hundred million rupiahs excluding land and buildings for businesses or has annual sales of more than three hundred million rupiahs up to a maximum of two billion five hundred million rupiahs. Medium business is a productive economic business that stands alone, which is carried out by individuals or business entities that are not subsidiaries or branch companies that are owned, controlled or become a part either directly or indirectly with small businesses or net businesses with a net worth of more than five hundred million rupiahs up to a maximum of ten billion rupiahs excluding land and buildings for business premises or annual sales results greater than two billion five hundred million rupiahs up to a maximum of fifty billion rupiahs. The World Bank defines small businesses with the criteria of the number of employees less than 30 people, annual income does not exceed $ 3 million and total assets do not exceed $ 3 million. For medium-sized businesses the number of employees is a maximum of 300 people, a yearly income of up to $ 15 million and assets of up to $ 15 million

### Mapping, Geographic Information Systems and Dynamic Spatial Models

Mapping is a grouping of territories related to several geographical locations of the region which include the highlands, mountains, resources and population potential that have socio-cultural influences that have special characteristics in the use of appropriate scales. According to Prahasta (2002) a map is a representation or picture of abstract elements or features selected from the surface of the earth or celestial bodies and is generally depicted on a flat plane and reduced or scaled. Map classification can be grouped into three, namely: (1) classification of maps according to content in the form of a map of the earth (topographic map) that describes the landscape in general on the surface of the earth, using certain scales, thematic maps that contain special themes for specific interests, which are useful in research, science, planning, tourism, etc. and navigation maps are maps that are made specifically or for practical purposes to help sea, aviation and travel navigation; (2) map classification based on scale that is very large scale map, with scale> 1: 10,000, large scale map, <1: 100,000-1: 10,000, medium scale map, 1: 100,000-1: 1,000,000 and small scale map, > 1: 1,000,000 and

(3) classification of maps based on uses which include educational maps, maps of science, general information, tourists, navigation, engineering applications and planning.

Prahasta (2002) states that a Geographic Information System (GIS) is a computer-based system that is used to store and manipulate geographical information. GIS is a computer-system used to collect, examine, integrate and analyze information related to the surface of the earth. Meanwhile according to Burrough and Mc. Donnel (2000), GIS is an organized collection of computer hardware, software, geographic data and personnel that are efficiently designed to obtain, store, update, manipulate, analyze and display all forms of geographic reference information.

Dynamic systems are computer-based approaches that are used for designing and analyzing policies by taking into account the complexity of the problems encountered such as in social, managerial, economic and ecological systems. In general, a dynamic system approach is characterized by dependence and interaction between elements and information feedback. Dynamic spatial models use mathematical models by combining textual and geo-spatial data to be represented in spatial form or mapping (Hartrisari et al, 2013).

## SMEs Competitive Strategy

Every company, both engaged in services and non-services, in conducting business activities requires a strategy that is able to put the company in the best position, able to compete and continue to develop by optimizing all the potential of its resources (Sitepu, 2005). The final goal of a competitive strategy according to Porter (1998) is to tackle environmental forces in the interests of the company which consists of 5 competitive forces namely the entry of new competitors, the threat of substitute products (substitutes), the power of supply (bargaining) of buyers, strength of supplier supply, and competition among existing competitors.

Aaker (1998) states there are at least five strategic forces namely differentiation, low-cost, focus, preemption, and synergy. The five factors forming the strategic strength, namely differentiation, that is the uniqueness of the products produced by the company, which is felt valuable to customers; low cost, is the ability of companies to work and invest in order to support the creation of products at low prices but produce relatively high profits; focus, the company's concentration on one market segment or part of a certain product line; preemption or pioneering work so that company is able to create a "barrier" for competitors to enter its market segment; and synergy, the cooperation within the same type of industry.

In reality, increasing the competitiveness of SMEs can be done through growth strategies by changing the conditions of factors affecting SMEs or by collaborating strategies with other industries to enter a wider market (Centenaro and Laimer, 2017; Laforet (2008)

# METHODOLOGY

## Time and Place

The research was conducted from April to November 2015 located in Bogor city. Survey has been done to all existing SMEs at Bogor city. Analysis at the System and Computing Laboratory at SEAMEO BIOTROP Campus, Jalan Raya Tajur, Km 6, Bogor and Laboratory of Industrial System Engineering, Department of Agroindustrial Technology, IPB University at Dramaga Campus.

## Equipment Needed

Selection of the right hardware and software in maintaining compatibility needs to be considered so as not to cause problems in the analysis process. A computer supported with a high-speed-internet connection is needed for the purpose of downloading data. The software used is Net-logo, Arc View, Arc GIS and Microsoft Office software. The city map of Bogor is also used as a basic map in a dynamic spatial model.

## Data Sources and Data Collection

The data needed for this research is detailed data about SMEs, including location coordinates, company name, address, owner's name, products produced, production capacity of marketing detail and marketing network of SMEs' products. The primary data survey was conducted on MSME data obtained from the Bogor City Industry Office.

## Methods

The systems approach is used for this research (Hartrisari, 2007). The system approach is a holistic perspective, which focuses on integration and linkages between components. This approach can change the way of thinking in dealing with problems using a model that is a simplification of a system (Hartrisari, 2007). The stages in the system approach are as follows: (1) Requirement Analysis, (2) Problem Formulation, (3) System Identification, (4) Modeling, (5) Verification and validation and (6) Implementation. Requirement analysis is the initial stage of assessing a system. At this stage, the needs of each system player are identified. Based on the results of the needs analysis, synergistic or contradictory needs can be identified. Understanding the system mechanism is carried out at the system identification stage, usually stated in the input-output diagram. The model is developed after understanding the mechanism of the system. Model verification and validation is done to ensure that the model built can be used to solve problems encountered in the actual system. If the model has been proven to be valid, then it could be proposed to implement in the real situation (Tobing et al., 2018). The dynamic spatial model of increasing SME competitiveness is designed at the system modeling stage. Data about SMEs such as production capacity, capital, raw materials, the number of workers and others are in the form of statistical data (non-spatial) so it needs to be prepared so that it can be integrated in the spatial model. This non-spatial data input will use Microsoft Excel. Net logo, Arc View and Arc-GIS will be used for spatial modeling.

The method used to determine strategies on improving the competitiveness of SMEs' products is the SMEs index value. Calculation of the index value is adopted from the calculation of the village development index value (IPD) used in determining the classification of village typologies by Indonesian Ministry of National Development and the Central Statistics Agency (2014). The stages of calculating the index are: determining the indicators, the indicators weight and scores. Index values then are obtained from a total sum of each indicator scores.

The SMEs index is calculated based on a composite of 14 indicators, grouped in external and internal dimensions according to Potter (1998) and Brouthers et al. (2009). Indicators taken into account in the calculation of the SMEs are derived from primary data collected during the survey. They consist of: the number of workers, production capacity, operating costs per month, management, technology used, continuity of raw materials, suppliers, adequacy of raw materials, marketing, market coverage area, export experience to foreign countries, waste management, monthly turnover and total capital. Experts are needed to give the value of indicators weights and scores. The index value then is calculated by the total of the weight multiply by the score for each indicator.

The index values ranging from 0 to 100 are categorized into 4 groups as follows: index values 0-25 indicate that SMEs are still classified as primary SMEs which usually only market in the surrounding area; index values 26-50 are categorized at developing SMEs, index values 51- 75 indicates the status of developed SMEs while the index value above 76 indicates an independent status of SMEs.

Based on the SMEs index values mapping, we can further analyze the SMEs condition by determining the SMEs readiness zones in increasing competitiveness using IFA (Internal Factor Evaluation) and EFA (External Factor Evaluation). Based on the results of IFA and EFA analysis, SMEs at Bogor city will be mapped into 4 categories, based on readiness of competition versus added values of their products. The competitive readiness is represented by internal factors and the value added of SMEs products represented by external factors according to Aaker (1998).

Descriptively, quadrant I showed that SMEs do not yet have high competitiveness and there is no potential to compete internationally (primary SMEs). Quadrant II showed SMEs that have the potential to compete internationally but need to be encouraged for export market opportunities (SMEs are developing). Quadrant III presented SMEs that have the potential to enter the export market, but are not yet aware of the opportunity to enter the export market (SMEs are progressing), while SMEs in quadrant IV indicated that SMEs have products that meet the standards and have entered the international market (SMEs independent). The operational strategy developed is based on the four MSME categories that are produced from the IFA and EFA analysis

## RESULT AND DISCUSSION

### Identification of SMEs at Bogor City

Identification of SMEs in Bogor city was carried out based on field surveys of SMEs locations from the list of SMEs provided by the City of Bogor Industrial Service. We found that the government should update the data of SMEs existence in Bogor city. Many SMEs that are registered are no longer operational or they are not found in the location. In designing the spatial dynamic model, updated data is very important. If the data used is inaccurate or not up-to-date, the resulting decision may be inappropriate. The results of the SMEs identification survey in Bogor city informed that only 41 SMEs were still identified as operating SMEs in the city of Bogor, categorized in 21 non-food businesses / industries and 20 food businesses / industries.

### Spatial Dynamic Design of SMEs in Bogor City

Spatial mapping of 41 SMEs was designed in the form of a spatial information system. Each SMEs coordinate is plotted on the city map of Bogor. Each point indicating the position of SMEs is complemented with data about SMEs such as the name, owner, product produced, capacity, marketing area, level of technology used and capital allocation. The appearance of the SMEs information system can be seen in Figure 1. In the picture 21 SMEs are mapped according to the coordinates of the location obtained during the survey. This information system is designed on a web-based basis so that it can be accessed via cell phones to facilitate users in obtaining SMEs information in an area in this case the city of Bogor.

The SMEs spatial information system is continued with the SMEs index mapping display as presented in figure 2. Like the previous SME existence information system, the index mapping display can also be accessed via cell phone, but given relatively small display screen, the possibility of display results is less clear.

*Figure 1. Performance example of spatial information system of SMEs at Bogor city*

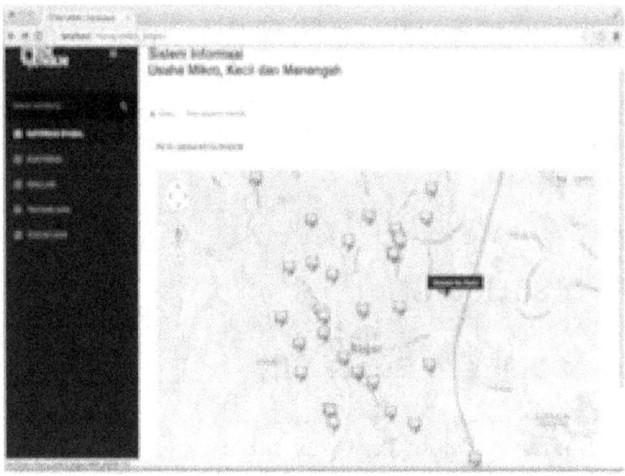

Figure 2 shows the status of SMEs in the city of Bogor based on the index values. In the picture it can be seen that difference color at the point representing the status of SMEs (red, yellow and blue). The circle size and color represents the SMEs status: developing, advancing and independent. Bigger size of the circle indicates higher index values.

## Zonation Mapping Analysis

Based on the SMEs index value, an analysis is conducted to map the zoning of SMEs' readiness in increasing competitiveness, especially in global markets. Analysis of the mapping of SMEs zone based on index values is presented in Figure 3. The average SMEs index of Bogor city is about 62.29 (above 50). In the figure it is seen that 19 of 41 MSMEs (46%) have an index above 50 so that they are included in the advanced and even independent MSME categories. This shows that some SMEs that are generally said to have many weaknesses in terms of capital, marketing, raw materials, technology, management, bureaucracy, infrastructure and partnerships have become developed and independent businesses and are ready to penetrate international markets. The government should be able to give priority to these SMEs in order to accelerate competitiveness in the international market so that the existence of SMEs can be a potential resource in the context of regional development.

The government of Bogor city needs to consider the existence of SMEs as regional economic drivers considering that the SMEs are considered as developed and even independent SMEs' status. Priority strategies for developing SMEs need

*Figure 2. Performance of SMEs status at Bogor city*

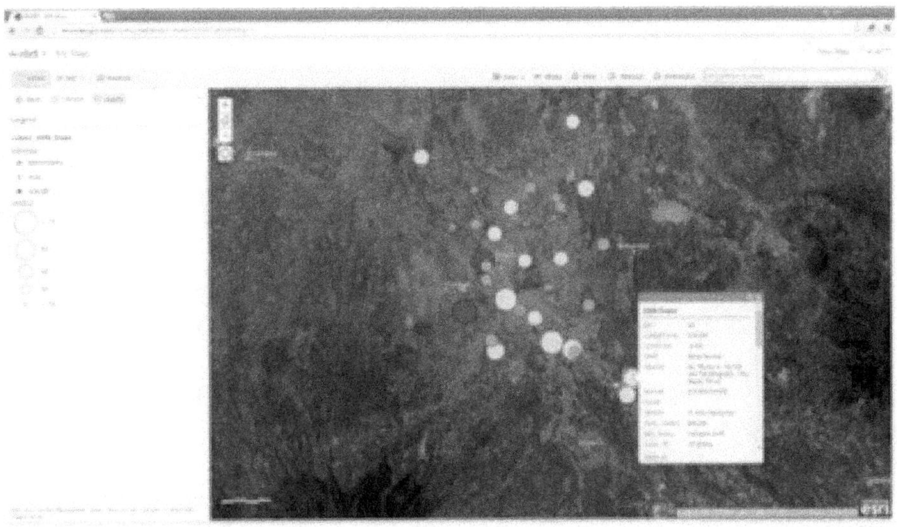

to be carried out to prepare internationally competition. The development of the SMEs in the city of Bogor could become an indicator of community welfare, and a sustainable development program that can be used as an example for other regions.

## Competitive Strategy Development

The determination of the SMEs competitive strategy has been done through IFA and EFA analysis. Basically this analysis is similar to the SWOT analysis which consists of Strength, Weaknesses, Opportunity and Threats analyzes by stating that the strength and weakness factors are internal factors, whereas the threat and opportunity factors are categorized as factors external. For this research, the SMEs zone is determined based on the mapping of internal and external values as shown in Figure 6. Based on the picture it appears that from 41 sample SMEs found 8 SMEs included in quadrant 4, namely SMEs that have high competitiveness and are ready to enter the global market, 12 SMEs categorized at SMEs that have high competitiveness but are not ready to enter the international market. As many as 5 SMEs are included in the category that has potential to compete in the international market, but SMEs are not ready internally, while 16 SMEs are still in quadrant I, namely SMEs that have not been able to increase the added value of products for the international market.

Based on the mapping of SMEs zoning, it can be seen that strategies to improve SME competitiveness could not be generalized. Strategies need to be built based on

*Figure 3. SMEs status based on index values analysis*

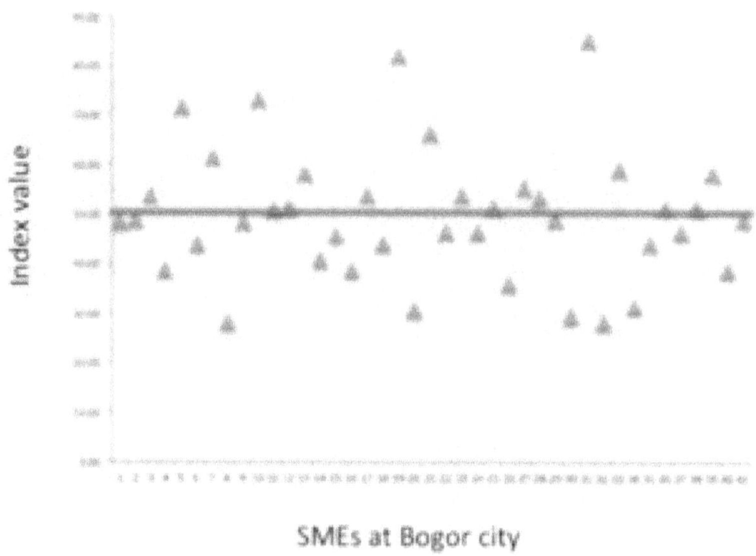


the needs of SMEs. From the results of SMEs zone, at least 4 strategies can be made to improve SMEs competitiveness. The strategy development for SMEs that have potential products but are not ready to compete globally (quadrant III) is assistance in the framework of product development in accordance with global market demand that wants a competitive advantage. For SMEs that are ready to compete but need assistance in entering the global market (quadrant II) the strategy that must be done is assistance in the context of market development so that SMEs can enter the global market. For SMEs that are in the first quarter, it is expected to be able to develop and dominate the local and national markets first, whereas for SMEs that are ready to compete globally and have entered the global market (quadrant IV), the government must maintain this condition so that SMEs can develop more fine again. Simulation with specific strategy implementation could increase 11.30% of index values.

The dynamic spatial model of increasing SMEs competitiveness has been able to demonstrate the performance as a tool for the decision-making in prioritizing programs and targets for SMEs according to the needs based on the readiness of SMEs in increasing their competitiveness.

*Figure 4. SMEs analysis based on index value analysis*

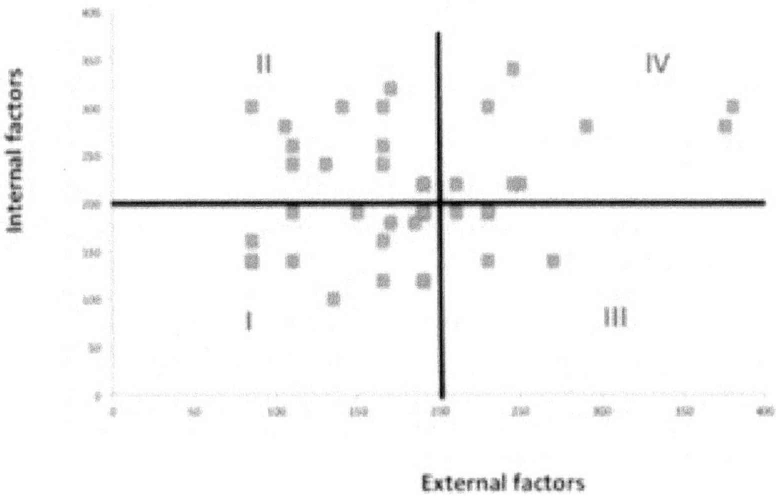


## CONCLUSION AND RECOMMENDATION

### Conclusion

The dynamic spatial model for enhancing SME competitiveness with the Bogor MSME case study has been able to demonstrate its performance as a tool to assist decision makers in order to determine the strategies that need to be carried out for SMEs. The status of SMEs in different quadrants will result in different MSME coaching strategies. This dynamic spatial model is expected to be an example to be implemented in other regions

### Recommendation

The first prototype of dynamic spatial model for increasing SME competitiveness is able to map SMEs locations, present SMEs specific data, calculate and display index values and determine the strategies that need to be done in order to improve competitiveness. The model prototype needs to be validated in other regions in order to assure the performance of the model. Development of the prototype could be done with the sensitive analysis in order to get the dominant factors affecting the competitiveness of SMEs.

## ACKNOWLEDGMENT

We present our gratitude to SEAME BIOTROP that has given us research funding for conducting this research.

## REFERENCES

Aaker, D. A., & Adler, D. A. (2001). *Developing business strategies*. Sons New York, NY: John Wiley.

Anonim. (2013). Undang-Undang no 20, tahun 2008 tentang Usaha Mikro Kecil dan Menengah. Kementerian Koperasi dan Usaha Mikro, Kecil dan Menengah.

Anonim. (2015). Indikator Industri Kecil dan Menengah Indonesia. Badan Pusat Statistik, Jakarta.

Brewer, C. (2014). *Designing better maps. A guide for GIS users*. Esri Press.

Brouthers, L. E., Nakos, G., Hadjimarcou, J., & Brouthers, K. D. (2009). Key factors for successful export performance for small firms. *Journal of International Marketing, 17*(3), 21-38.

Burrough, P. A., McDonnell, R., McDonnell, R. A., & Lloyd, C. D. (2015). *Principles of Geographical Information Systems*. OUP Oxford.

Burrough, P. A., McDonnell, R., & McDonnell, R. A. (2000). Principles of Geographical Information System, New York: Oxford University Press.

Centenaro, A., & Laimer, C. G. (2017). Cooperative Relationship and Competitiveness in Supermarket Sector. *Review of Business Management., 19*(63), 65–81. doi:10.7819/rbgn.v0i0.3070

Hartrisari. (2007). Sistem Dinamik. Konsep Sistem dan Pemodelan untuk Industri dan Lingkungan. SEAMEO BIOTROP. Bogor.

Hartrisari, H., Imanto, H., & Suyamto, D. (2013). Decision Support Planning for Food Security (case study at Jawa barat province). SEAMEO BIOTROP. Bogor.

Laforet, S. (2008). Size, strategic, and market orientation affects on innovation. *Journal of Business Research, 61*(7), 753–764. doi:10.1016/j.jbusres.2007.08.002

Nohong, M., Sanusi, A., & Nurqamar, I. F. (2018, May). Suriadi Harun Strategic Model in Increasing the SMEs Competitive Advantage in South Sulawesi. *International Journal of Administrative Science & Organization, 25*(2), 57–65.

Penyusun, T. (2015) Indeks Pembangunan Desa 2014: Tantangan pemenuhan standar pelayanan minimum desa. Kenenteian PPN/Bappenas dan Badan Pusat Statistik, Jakarta.

Porter, M. (1998). *Competitive Advantage*. USA: Waterstone. doi:10.1007/978-1-349-14865-3

Prahasta, E. (2002). Sistem Informasi Geografis. Konsep dasar Informasi Geografis. I nformatika. Bandung.

Sage, A. P. (1991). *Decision Support Systems Engineering*. New York: John Wiley.

Sitepu, J. (2005). *Manajemen Strategik*. Jakarta: Gramedia Group.

Sulianti, K. T. D., Fathorazz, M., & Ayu Wulandari, G. (2018). Mapping the Competitive Advantage of SMEs in East Java, Indonesia. *Jurnal Dinamika Manajemen*, *9*, 1.

Turban, E., Sharda, R., & Delen, D. (2014). Business intelligence and analytics: Systems for decision support. Pearson Higher Ed.

## ADDITIONAL READING

Adam, I. O., & Musah, A. (2015). Small and Medium Enterprises (SMEs) in the Cloud in Developing Countries: A Synthesis of the Literature and Future Research Directions. *Journal of Management and Sustainability*, *5*, 115.

Attempt to extend knowledge of Decision Support Systems for small and medium-sized enterprises—IEEE Conference Publication. (n.d.). Retrieved November 1, 2019, from https://ieeexplore.ieee.org/abstract/document/7733409

Chalal, M., Boucher, X., & Marques, G. (2015). Decision support system for servitization of industrial SMEs: A modelling and simulation approach. *Journal of Decision Systems*, *24*(4), 355–382. doi:10.1080/12460125.2015.1074836

Eiriz, V. (2019). Spatial proximity and SME strategy in local networks. Journal of Business & Industrial Marketing, (ahead-of-print). doi:10.1108/JBIM-10-2018-0283

Neuwirth, C., Hofer, B., & Schaumberger, A. (2016). Object view in spatial system dynamics: A grassland farming example. *Journal of Spatial Science*, *61*(2), 367–388. doi:10.1080/14498596.2015.1132641 PubMed

## KEY TERMS AND DEFINITIONS

**Asean Economic Community (AEC):** is a regional economic integration with the goal of establishing ASEAN as a single market, with the free flow of trade and investment among the 10 member states.

**(GDP):** is the total monetary or market value of all the finished goods and services produced within a country's borders in a specific time period.

**Small Business:** a business with a number of employees less than 30 people, annual income does not exceed $ 3 million and total assets do not exceed $ 3 million. for medium-sized businesses the number of employees is a maximum of 300 people, a yearly income of up to $ 15 million and assets of up to $ 15 million Gross Domestic Product

**The Asean Free Trade Area (AFTA):** is a trade bloc agreement by the Association of Southeast Asian Nations (ASEAN) supporting local trade and manufacturing in all ASEAN countries, and facilitating economic integration with regional and international allies.

# Chapter 3
# Exploring the Entrepreneurial Motivations and Barriers of Agripreneurs in Brunei Darussalam

**Siti Fatimahwati Pehin Dato Musa**
https://orcid.org/0000-0003-1987-4595
*Universiti Brunei Darussalam, Brunei*

**Pg Siti Rozaidah Pg Hj Idris**
*Universiti Brunei Darussalam, Brunei*

**Khairul Hidayatullah Basir**
*Universiti Islam Sultan Sharif Ali, Brunei*

## ABSTRACT

*This study explores the motivations and institutional barriers of local agripreneurs who are involved in different branches of agriculture in Brunei. Descriptive analysis and thematic analysis were performed to analyse the data. The agripreneurs in the study consider their venture into agriculture as an act of symbolic nationalistic support whereby they envision Brunei to be a nation less reliant on food imports, in line with the country's vision or better known as Wawasan 2035. In addition, their motivation is also based on Islamic values with the intention of seeking lawful earning and a path to a blessed monetary and hereafter rewards. The main problems faced by the agripreneurs are lack of access to finance, lack of infrastructure and technology, and lack of exposure. The research on local agripreneurs in the context of Brunei is scarce, thus this chapter provides a better understanding of their motivations and constraints for Brunei to realize the potential of the agriculture sector as an important driver of the economy and thus develop the sector further.*

DOI: 10.4018/978-1-7998-2257-8.ch003

## INTRODUCTION

Agriculture was once an important economic activity in Brunei but has declined in importance since the discovery of oil in 1929. In 1947, more than 50% of the population was employed in agriculture but by 1971 this had decreased to 10% (Franz, 1990). In the early 1960s, there was concern about the economic effects of over-dependency on oil and the Second National Development Plan of 1962-1968 focused on agriculture. Increasing rice production was one of the strategies adopted to achieve self-sufficiency and to diversify the economy (Yakub, 2012). In 1970, rice production reached 35% of the self-sufficiency level (Yakub, 2012) and by 1975, it peaked at 38% but has since declined and in 1978 was 14% (DAA, 1990). In the 1970s, farming was characterized by small, family farms: the average farm size was 2.6 hectares and the main crops were paddy, rubber, sago, coconut and pepper (Groome, 1978). Production was mainly for self-consumption and any surpluses were exchanged for other food commodities. Groome (1978) argues that agricultural productivity in the 1970s was low whether measured by output, area, or *per capita* because production was not market-orientated but was more on meeting the needs of individual households. The agricultural sector combined with forestry and fisheries only contributed 11% to GDP in 1974 and it continued to decline to 8% in 1975 and 5% in 1980. In 2014, the agricultural sector contributed 1% to the GDP (DAA, 2009).

Agriculture still lags behind other sectors. In 2011, it constituted only 3% of the labour force and less than 1% of GDP. This compares with 63% and 72% in the industrial sector and 33% and 27% in the services sector (World Bank, 2012). Nevertheless between 1999-2008, agricultural production nearly doubled in value terms from US$80m to US$160m (DAA, 2009), and in 2011, agriculture, forestry and fisheries recorded the highest annual growth of 5%, followed by construction and manufacturing which grew 2% each.

To assist farmers, the government provides free insecticides and fungicides, technical support, training in modern cultivation techniques and funding incentives. For example, the government under the Paddy Guarantee Price Purchasing Scheme subsidizes rice consumption by buying it from producers at a price more than the market price with the aims of incentivizing more farmers to grown paddy and to ensure that the price of the local rice is competitive. Under this subsidy scheme, the DAA bought rice from local producers at US$12 per 10kg while the retail price for consumers was US$9 per 10kg (DAA, 2009).

However, there is still a problem of labour scarcity in the agricultural sector in Brunei where there exists a poorly skilled, ageing workforce and a high dependency on migrant labour. In 2014, the number of people working in agriculture was 5,218 of which 704 were involved in livestock production, 4,382 in crops and 132 in agri-

*Figure 1. Conceptual framework for agripreneurial motivation*

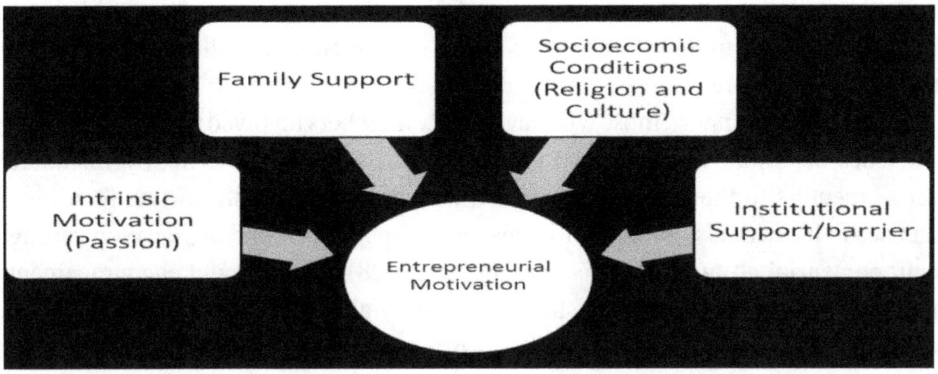


food processing (Brunei Government, 2015). Statistics has also shown a decrease in the percentage of labour force in agriculture from 0.69% in 1998 to 0.54% in 2008 and the percentage decrease in the rural population which can be partly attributed to the declining agricultural labour force. Under the DAA's mid-term action plan (2008-13), increased efforts to upgrade technology and human resource capacity are highlighted.

This study examines the entrepreneurial motivations of fifteen agripreneurs in Brunei with the aim of learning from their experiences so that further improvements can be made in the agriculture sector in order for Brunei to successfully achieve its vision of food security and self-sufficiency.

## Conceptual Framework and Literature Review

Entrepreneurial motivation is a state of mind that leads to an individual to start up a business or entrepreneurial activity (Shiri et al. 2012). The diagram above represents the conceptual framework for the factors influencing entrepreneurial motivation studied in this chapter. Some of the factors widely studied that have shown to have an impact on entrepreneurial motivation are (i) intrinsic motivation of the individual like a strong passion for entrepreneurial venture; (ii) family support (iii) socioeconomic conditions (culture and religion) and (iv)institutional support or barrier.

Passion is defined as a strong desire toward an activity that we love, in which we invest a substantial amount of time and energy in to (Vallerand and Houlfort, 2003). Harmonious passion for work, on the other hand develops when an individual highly value and enjoys engaging in the work activities consistently resulting in the integration of work into their overall identity. Entrepreneurship is one of the emerging fields that uses the concept of passion to study entrepreneurial motivation. Research finds that there is a positive correlation between passionate entrepreneurs and venture effectiveness and performance (Cardon et al., 2009; Chen et al., 2009). It is also observed that individuals that follow their passion are more likely to persevere and put more effort in spite of the low profit and challenges faced from the business venture.

As for family support, those who have family members involved in entrepreneurial activities are more likely to start their own businesses. These family members act as mentors to the younger generation who are interested in starting their own business. Individuals with family business experience tend to develop strong entrepreneurial attitudes (Harris and Gibson, 2008). Support and encouragement from family members have been shown to have a high correlation with development of entrepreneurs (Baughn et al., 2006). It is also shown to be important in shaping the perceived attractiveness of a particular business venture as well as providing financial assistance.

Socioeconomic conditions also play a role in influencing entrepreneurial motivation. For example the religion in Brunei, Islam, has its own entrepreneurship characteristic and guiding principles based on al-Qur'an and al-Hadis to guide entrepreneurship operation (Oukil, 2013). From the Islamic point of view, spirituality is an important aspect of entrepreneurship (Mohd Zain Mubarak, Asyraf Abd. Rahman, Mohd Rafi Yaacob, 2014). In Brunei, Malay Muslims entrepreneurs' achievement are associated with internal religious values based on their attitudes in running their businesses. As for the culture component, a study by Hofstede (2001) shows that Malays lack of entrepreneurial culture. This can be related to one of the cultural values put forward by Hofstede (2001) whereby Malays have high uncertainty avoidance. This refers to the extent to which the members of a culture feel threatened by ambiguous or unknown situations (Hofstede, 2001). This view is further reinforced by Hayton *et al.* (2002) who argues that cultures that encourage entrepreneurship are those that have a low uncertainty avoidance, high individualism, low power distance and high in masculinity. Based on these cultural values, Brunei has a culture that has a weak entrepreneurship culture.

Institutional support is crucial in the development of entrepreneurship in a country. Institutional theory assumes that institutions constitute the "rules of the game" that shape the course of individuals' behavior and beliefs (Kazumi and Kawai, 2017, p.347). Bruton, Ahlstrom and Li (2010) further explain that institutional theory plays a major role in explaining the forces that result in entrepreneurial success, apart from organisational (or entrepreneurial) resources. Watson, Hogarth-Scott and Wilson (1998) emphasise the importance of institutional support where these institutions are extremely important elements of entrepreneurs' external environment, on which both the survival and further development of enterprises are based. Thus, Institutional theory can be used to explain the factors of institutions which enable and constraint entrepreneurs.

Institutional support is in the form of a supportive environment which includes government policies and procedures. This is highlighted by Bruton, Ahlstrom and Li (2010) that governments can ensure markets function efficiently by removing conditions that create entry barriers, market imperfections, and unnecessarily stifling regulation. Individuals are more motivated to engage in entrepreneurship activities if they perceive that the business environment and business opportunities are encouraging and vice versa. This is because, entrepreneurial mind-sets and behaviors are shaped by the regulatory, normative and cognitive institutional systems that control access to a wide range of critical resources (Kazumi and Kawai, 2017). In addition, according to Lim *et al.* (2010) government policy shapes the institutional environment in which entrepreneurial decisions are made and hence, can influence the allocation of entrepreneurial activities.

Institutional barrier, on the other hand, includes difficulties in securing loans for business start-ups, availability of land and infrastructure and up to date technology. The strength of entrepreneurial efforts may be shaped by the extent to which socially supportive institutional norms reward or discourage entrepreneurial thinking and innovative behaviors (Baumol, 1990). The presence of an unconducive business environment such as restrictive loan requirement will result in individuals becoming less likely to venture into entrepreneurial activities regardless of their interest towards entrepreneurship.

## RESEARCH METHODOLOGY

This study uses a qualitative research method by conducting in-depth interviews with fifteen agripreneurs. The list of agripreneurs were obtained from the Department of Agriculture and Agrifood Brunei and letters were sent out to set up interviews appointments. There have been many more selected but these agipreneurs were the ones who promptly replied and shared their experiences willingly. The fifteen companies are involved in various parts of the agriculture sector which can be categorized into ‘crops and vegetables’ and ‘poultry and aquaculture’. They also varied in terms of agripreneurship levels from micro to established companies.

This research uses thematic analysis to analyse and organise the data. Braun and Clark (2006) define thematic analysis “as a method for identifying, analysing and reporting patterns (themes) within data. It minimally organises and describes data sets in detail and most of the time it goes further than this, and interprets various aspects of the research topic.” The first step of familiarizing with the data involves listening to the audio of the recordings, transcribing and reading repetitively all the transcripts from the interviews. In the second stage of the data analysis, ‘coding’ is undertaken whereby data is organised into meaningful groups. Codes identify a feature of the data that appears interesting to the researcher, and refers to "the most basic segment, or element, of the raw data or information that can be assessed in a meaningful way regarding the phenomenon" (Braun and Clarke, 2006).

In phase three, the researcher's task is to "re-focus the analysis at the broader level of themes, rather than codes, involves sorting the different codes into potential themes, and collating all the relevant coded data extracts within the identified themes" (Braun and Clark, 2006). This is done by extracting the most significant themes in the text segments of each code to identify the underlying patterns and structures. Phase four involves the refinement of themes. According to Braun and Clarke (2006), "data within themes should cohere together meaningfully with identifiable distinctions between themes". Phase five begins when there is a satisfactory thematic map of the data. The themes should be more "defined and refined" meaning that it should cover the "essence" of what each theme is about and what aspect of data each theme consist of.

Below are the brief profiles of the agribusinesses that were interviewed

**Agrotechnology**

1. MADGrow Tech Brunei was established and registered in February 2017. Leading the team of MADGrow Tech is Managing Director, Wan Muhammad Syazwan Bin Haji Hijazi @Wanzzy Hijazi and Mohd Hijazi Bin Haji Juli@Temengong A.M.H Shibli as the Corporate Advisor. MADGrow Tech aims to provide methods and technologies that sought to improve farming in everyday use.

**Aquaculture**

2. Usaha Asilati Sendirian Berhad is a private limited company and one of the very few in Brunei to specialize in shrimp farming. It joined the local aquaculture scene in 1994 and officially began operations in March the following year. The company is currently being managed by Ampuan Ammilee Farahiyah who inherited the business from her father, and founder, the late Ampuan Haji Mohamad bin Ampuan Haji Yusof. The company's mission is to supply quality organic rostris blue shrimps that are completely devoid of pesticide and antibiotics as well as guaranteed disease-free.
3. Nur Az-Zahra Aquaculture, located in Sungai Bunga, was established in 2016 and managed by Mohammad Azhar who bought the farm — using a $40,000 loan his parents gave — from his uncle in 2014. The company was first worked on by Mohammad Azhar alone, but now it has employed two other people on Mohammad Azhar's other farm in Pelumpong. The company act as suppliers, selling fish to restaurants; although that is contingent upon demand.

## Crops and Vegetables

4. Syarikat Pertanian Tropikal Utama operates on 19 hectares of land, producing various crops at the Rampayoh Agricultural Development Site in Mukim Labi, Belait District. Awang Yong Khian Fook, owner and manager of the Tropikal Utama Agriculture farm started operations in 1995 with 14 hectares and added another 5 hectares, 5 years later. The farm's most popular product is its coffee crop. Syarikat Pertanian Tropikal Utama has penetrated markets in China, Jordan, Kuwait, Singapore, and Korea for Arabica and Robusta coffee products.
5. Marsya Farm, situated atop a 2.8-hectare plantation, is a company that has been at the forefront of agricultural innovation having experimented with more conventional methods as well as new technologies such as drip irrigation, fertigation, hydroponics, and rain shelter. Located in *Kawasan Kemajuan Pertanian* (KKP), Kampung Sungai Liang, Daerah Belait, Marsya Farm is currently cultivating a variety of crops including fruits like menas and mulberry, and vegetables like mustard leaf, cucumber, cherry tomato, and corn, among many others.
6. Eco Nadi Agrobiz is operated by Haji Mohd Ayub bin Haji Suhaili and Khairuddin bin Mohammad. It is a successful local chilli plantation located in Kampong Sinaut, Tutong District. The company, which has been operating a four-hectare farm since November 2016, uses fertigation system and focuses on chilli production for domestic market. After acquiring the necessary experience and knowledge in farm management from running their two farms in Kampong Bukit Udal and Kampong Bangungos, the company was awarded with the Brunei Good Agricultural Practice (Brunei GAP) certification by the Agriculture and Agrifood Department under the Ministry of Primary Resources and Tourism (MPRT).
7. AgroMetro Company is a partnership founded by four inspiring youths namely Dayang Norisa 'Azuma binti Mohd Norazmi (Director), 29; Dayang Siti Badariah binti Darius (Resident Seedling Expert), 29; Dayang Nursalwana binti Kamidi (Marketing Manager), 20; and Awang Norwardi bin Griffin (Head Manager), 22. AgroMetro specialises in the hydroponic system which is a modern method of cultivating vegetables. The mission of the company is to revamp and transform farming technology so as to make advancements suitable to Brunei.
8. S & R Aquafarm was founded back in 2011 which utilizes modern farming method known as Aquaponics. Aquaponics is the integration of both aquaculture and hydroponics in a closed loop system. S & R Aquafarm is currently managed and operated by Syazwan bin Haji Suni. Syazwan became interested in agriculture while he was studying for his bachelor

degree in Perth, Australia, when he observed his housemates growing Kankong using hydroponics.

9. Ayesha's Farm is a home-based business based in Perumahan Lugu selling hydroponics sets to households for personal or home. It is owned by a husband and wife and they do most of the farming themselves, starting from seeding all the way through to harvesting. They started at the end of 2017. The business is done on a part-time basis. Through this business, they hope to educate people on how to maximize the benefits of utilizing hydroponics so as to make farming more efficient. Ayesha's Farm also offers farming lessons for children to expose them early to and get them interested in agriculture.
10. Haji Zainal is the main benefactor of Katimahar Agri Park, a nature park that was created to answer the Government's call to boost village economies and eco-tourism through the One Village One Product campaign. Alongside promoting employment opportunities for village youths and providing a place of entertainment and family fun for local and foreign visitors, the park's main vision is also to preserve wildlife and fruits of Brunei and prevent them from extinction.
11. Hyren Agrotex Global Success Enterprise is a company owned by Hairinshah Haji Tahirudin. It was officially registered on the 4th of October 2016, though the company has begun operations since 2015 following Hairinshah's completion of the Belia Berpadi course in January that year. Hairinshah sells his farm output to the Department of Agriculture and Agrifood, who are his main clients, as well as other private customers.
12. Syarikat Al Rasyid is owned and managed by Muhammad Abdul Rasyid Bin Kamarudjaman. It was registered on the 4th of October 2016. Syarikat Al Rasyid is an agriculture company that focuses on paddy cultivation. It has begun operations since 2015 following Rasyid's completion of the Belia Berpadi course in January 2015. The farm is managed on 1 hectare of land located in MPK Kampung Bebuloh.
13. U-Nos K Enterprise is a private limited company specializing in paddy farming. It is owned by 31-year-old Mohamad Yunos bin Kepli. U-Nos K Enterprise is a fairly new business; having only been established and officially starting operations in January 2019 with the help of start-up capital received from LiveWIRE. The company's mission is to provide consistent and top-quality service to their customers, including the Department of Agriculture who are its main client and helps distribute the company's output to shops throughout the country.

**Eggs and Poultry**

14. Ideal Multifeed Farm Company was founded by the late Pehin Orang Kaya Di-Gadong Seri Diraja Dato Laila Utama Haji Awang Abdul Rahman, father of current managing director, Haji Awang Ahmad Morshidi. Ideal Multifeed Farm produces and supplies Halal poultry meat and graded eggs. It was established on 16th July 1969. As of now, the company is rearing enough chickens to not only distribute to their restaurants but also supply to supermarkets. The company butchers 200 chickens a day as well as produces about 40,000 eggs every month.
15. Hazeeyah Agro Farm is a duck farm producing salted eggs based in Temburong. It is managed by a couple, Nur Haziyah Abdul Rahman and her husband Muhd Hazim Abdul Rahim Mangkiling. They began in 2015 and started out with just 12 ducks. At that time, they were still unsure about the market and how to rear ducks. Currently, the farm is about 0.7 acres and just enough to fit all the ducks. They bought a batch of 450 ducks which is the standard ration for what their farm can currently accommodate. This is to ensure the ducks to be free-range and able to produce high quality eggs.

## FINDINGS AND DISCUSSION

Based on the thematic analysis conducted, the most common motivation that can be observed among the agripreneurs are passion, family support, religious motivation and cultural motivation whereas institutional barriers consists of the following factors: lack of access to financial support, lack of infrastructure and technology and lack of exposure.

### Intrinsic Motivation: Passion and Family Support

Most of the agripreneurs mentioned that having a strong passion is important. Among the reasons for their perseverance is the passion for farming and this comes from the strong support system from their families who have been their source of motivation. The passion can also come from the exposure towards agriculture from a young age whereby some of their parents are farmers. Having a family member working in agriculture sector is a significant factor in influencing young people expectations of that sector. For example, Hj Ayub stated that farming is in his blood. He used to plant durians in his village when he was small. Similar to Hj Muliadi, his passion for farming developed since he was a child when he would help out his parents with subsistence farming. This is also true for most of the agripreneurs interviewed.

Having a family member working in agricultural sector is a significant factor in influencing young people expectations of that sector. Families are "the key, and often the single most important source of guidance, information and influence" (Taylor, 1992, pp. 19). This is further supported by Wildman and Torres (2001) where he found that youths that have experience in agriculture, have been living or working on the farm, and have exposure to information about the agricultural sector, are also more likely to have a positive perception of agriculture.

## Socioeconomic Condition: Religious Motivation

The agripreneurs main motivations are mostly driven by spiritual values and not solely on profit. According to Faizal et.al. (2013), there is no separation between entrepreneurial activities and religion in Islam. The spiritual aspects that have been identified in the interviews which have had a significant impact on their motivations are as follows:

*Believing in Greatness of Allah in Terms of Ikhlas (Sincere) and Tawakkal (Reliance on Allah)*

For instance, Haji Ayub's strongest motivation is Allah and whatever he does is sincere for Allah. SWT. He endeavours to be as giving to HIS creatures as HE is to them, remarking that, "Every time I need anything, when I am faced with hardship, when I want guidance, I seek HIS help and I talk to HIM directly. As a Muslim, I fear nobody else but Allah the Almighty". After he puts all his efforts, he leaves everything to Allah. He humbles himself to learn more to worship and praise Allah the Almighty. With dua, he is putting his trust in Allah and depending on Him to succeed.

*Earning Barakah (Blessing) by Practicing Amanah (Trust) and Honesty in Business*

Seeking a lawful earning is our duty as Muslims. This is in accordance to Prophet Muhammad (PBUH), "God loves those who work and strive for their livelihood" and "to search lawful earning is obligatory after the compulsory things (like prayer, fasting, and belief in God) (Abdul Ghafar Ismail et.al. 2011, p.249).

Practicing ***amanah*** and honesty are very important towards the survival and development of their business and how these will lead to ***barakah*** in their earnings when they are doing their business. This will also give positive impacts on the reputation of their business. In a study by Tlaiss (2015), Muslim women entrepreneurs perceived Islamic work-related values of good and hard work (amal salih), honesty and truthfulness (sidik and amanah), fairness and justice (haqq and adl), and benevolence (ihsaan) as instrumental to the survival and success of their enterprises.

According to Hj Awg Ahmad Morshidi, in running his business, he emphasized on the seriousness and responsibility of providing halal poultry in order to maintain trust among Muslim customers. He mentioned that *What He (Allah) gives, He (Allah) can also take away.* He always ensure that success has to be earned earnestly and honestly.

**Barakah** *can also be earned by fulfilling our responsibilities towards the society. Islam requires all commercial activities to be undertaken in accordance with principles laid down in shari'ah in order to obtain barakah for the sake of achieving Al-falah (everlasting success) which is the ultimate goal of a Muslim's life (Rusnah Muhamad et.al. 2008, p.47).*

Hj Ayub sees farming as an opportunity to seek Allah's blessings. He highlighted his favourite Hadith:

*Tidaklah seorang muslim menanam pohon atau menanam tetumbuhan kemudian burung, manusia, dan haiwan ternak memakan buah-buahan dari pohon yang dia tanam kecuali hal tersebut terhitung sedekah baginya. What it means is that whatever you do, you owe back to your community.*

*Parents' Blessing*

Islam commands us to honour, obey and respect our parents. This is mentioned in the Quran:

*Your Lord has commanded that you worship none but Him, and that you be kind to your parents. If one or both of them reach old age with you, do not say to them a word of disrespect, or scold them, but say a generous word to them. And act humbly to them in mercy, and say, My Lord, have mercy on them, since they cared for me when I was small (17: 23-24).*

Businesses shall yield bountifully when blessing from the parents is earned. This is highlighted by Rasyid where parents' blessings and encouragement represent the main source of motivation for Rasyid. He has received unconditional morale and financial support from both his parents. Rasyid's father reassured him to see this through and not to lose hope. Overall, his parents' blessings and encouragement represent the main source of motivation for Rasyid.

This shows that the aspect of spirituality, particularly Islamic motivations, plays an important role in the motivation of Malay Muslim entrepreneurs. A strong sense of spirituality based on faith towards Allah SWT creates a positive attitude among the agripreneurs and has an impact on their practice of entrepreneurship.

## Socioeconomic Condition: Cultural Motivation

All of the agripreneurs in this study stated that one of their motivation towards farming and setting up an agribusiness is considered as an act of symbolic support towards His Majesty the Sultan and Yang Di-Pertuan of Brunei Darussalam's *Titah*. They envision Brunei to be a nation less reliant on food imports, in line with Wawasan 2035.

The agripreneurs commented that people are anxious about change. Change is uncomfortable and implies a high chance of failure. It is natural that people will prefer to stay within their comfort zones rather than risk costly failures. These agripreneurs asserts that one should spend time with people that encourages them to undertake risks and reassuring them that those risks are necessary and worth taking. Fear of failure often inhibits people from pushing themselves to new limits. This fear of failure is often misconstrued or misconceived as laziness and even lack of intelligence or otherwise often explained as the "Malay problem". One of the agripreneur; Hj Ayub highlighted that we need to debunk this myth of lazy Malays. He believes Malays are capable to achieve success like any other race and was ashamed that Malays had been left behind by the forward-thinking Chinese entrepreneurs. However, it is inherently flawed to use the cultural deficit misconception to explain the lack of entrepreneurial spirit of the Malays. These misconceptions assume homogeneity of the Malays, which is far from the reality. Agripreneurs like Hj Ayub and Hj Morshidi believe Malays are responsible to encourage and support other Malays to succeed. More importantly, they take full ownership and responsibility of their actions in achieving success. They do not believe in shortcuts and being lazy.

These agripreneurs challenge the negative stigma by boldly taking risks and pushing boundaries towards success. They made no excuses but remind others that for those who is undertaking a risky initiative, one needs freedom and also mentoring and guidance. Communication is the key. Informed people do not fear change. A mindset change is required. The population can start by being more empathetic towards the entrepreneurial under-attainment of the Malays, and cast aside the cultural prejudices people have of the Malay community. By viewing the issue of entrepreneurial attainment as a 'socioeconomic' issue instead of an 'ethnic' issue, hopefully the population will relate to the issue as a responsibility of the entire Bruneian community instead of solely the Malay community.

The agripreneurs basis of motivation was human needs for achievement, power and affiliation. Notably, it was their filial piety towards the Sultan, personal satisfaction, monetary benefits and independence that had motivated them to become agripreneurs and sustain their agripreneurship (see Bolton & Thompson, 2004). The agripreneurs exhibited perseverance and determination, and the ability to take calculated risks, initiatives and responsibility. The agripreneurs were goal- and opportunity- orientated. This is an important observation that challenges the stereotype that Malays had been associated with a blatant lack of competitive and enterprising spirit because of which it was thought that they would never belong to the world of modern business (see for example, Winstedt, 1947; Mahathir, 1970). Specifically in the case of Brunei their sense of loyalty and filial piety towards the Sultan motivated them to strive and change such misconception. In several studies on Brunei's ILT or Implicit Leadership Theory, where the studies focused on a follower-centric study on leadership in Brunei. Followers or the ruler's subjects rely on their cognitive schema to assess whether to accept a leader's influence attempt. This cognitive schema is known as "the implicit leadership theory" (ILT) which individuals have on the qualities of a leader. When a leader is perceived as conforming to this ILT, followers tend accept their influence attempt (see Lim et al., (2012); Md Zain et al., (2014); Md Zain et al., (2015)).

The call for Bruneians to be entrepreneurial and risk-takers in the field of agriculture could be seen as an attempt by Bruneian youths to heed their leader, His Majesty's request. And His Majesty's role as a nurturing and supportive leader has helped paved several opportunities for agripreneurs to excel.

## Institutional Barriers (Lack of Access to Financial Support, Lack of Infrastructure and Technology and Lack of Exposure)

According to our studies, the role of support institutions in encouraging entrepreneurial activity and economic growth is extremely important. Early institutional theory reviews confirm the explanatory limitations face by the agripreneurs. The success of the agripreneurs is possible by identifying the barriers in that process, that is, removal thereof. From the findings below, we can suggest the supports needed by our agripreneurs for the support institutions to consider which can result in their success.

### Lack of Access to Financial Support

The major challenge posed by the agripreneurs is access to financial support. The most common way of accessing credit is through loans from financial institutions. However, banks often place stringent rules when lending money to agripreneurs and usually require collateral such as land or savings (Herbel *et al.*, 2010). Banks refused to lend out money for their start-up capital due to the risky nature of agricultural production which are associated with unpredicted weather conditions, floods and droughts, pests and some harvest which may take time. Furthermore, young agripreneurs are perceived as risky and their business plans are often not considered substantial (FAO, 2010). This results in youths gaining access to finance through informal sources such as family and friends (IFAD, 2009).

The agripreneurs in this study recalled the difficulty they faced when applying for bank loans from financial institutions. However these agripreneurs refused to let this challenge to restrict their involvement in agriculture. Most of them looked for other avenues to develop their agribusiness. Some resort to borrowing funds from family and friends. As Hj Muliadi recalled: "The bank would not approve our request for a loan; we had to take out a collateral, be able to meet their repayment deadlines and the minimum amount payable, etc. We were not financially stable when I first wanted to start the farm business; there was no way we could meet any of the demands of the bank. So we ended up depending on people and convincing them to place their faith in our business plans, that we were worth investing on."

On the other hand, the youths in the Belia Berpadi Programme participated in the BSP LiveWire Business Awards Startup Funding Scheme (BASfS) in January 2019. LiveWire Brunei is an enterprise development programme created by BSP in 2001 which runs training workshops to support local entrepreneurship and stimulate sustainable economic development. To help young people in their pursuit of starting their own companies, LiveWIRE provides seed capital to fledgling establishments.

Accessing finance for starting up businesses is a difficulty in Brunei due to the absence of a capital market and a stock exchange. In addition, Brunei has no central bank and the banks are highly regulated by the Ministry of Finance (Oxford Business Group, 2014). Polsaram *et al.* (2011) observes that 76% of SMEs had no access to financing and had to resort to personal and family funds for start-up, 18% received financing from local banks while 5.4% received loans from foreign banks. It is difficult to obtain financial funding from the banks for business start-ups because Brunei does not have access to credit scoring to identify high risk consumers and there is no information on business finances. Banks therefore resort to traditional methods of lending inspection like property or land title as collateral as well as personal or business credit record. Therefore, improving the opportunity space of agriculture, agribusiness and the ease of doing business may result in more young people participating in agriculture.

## Lack of Infrastructure and Technology

The agripreneurs also stressed their concern over the insufficient infrastructure. For example, the youths involved in paddy plantation had problems with respect to irrigation system and drainage. Several rice fields are without proper irrigation systems, the water supply is not always sufficient to meet the requirements of irrigation systems of paddy fields in Wasan. Further, there is a problem of lack of up-to-date technology in Brunei. The farmers pointed out that they need suitable machinery that operates well for the soil. The use of machinery and new technology in farming in Brunei still lags behind other countries. Further, there is a problem of lack of up-to-date technology in Brunei. Heavy tractors always sink down into the soil and slow down ploughing and harvesting processes. The farmers pointed out that they need suitable machinery that operates well for the soil. To achieve food security in the circumstances of low land availability, the Minister of Industry and Primary Resources stated that Brunei will focus more on the "technology and know-how" which use higher variety of crops and more productive farming techniques, rather than the practice of clearing forests for agriculture (Maierbrugger, 2014). However, the use of machinery and new technology in farming in Brunei still lags behind other countries.

As stated by the founder of MADGrow Tech; Wan Muhammad Syazwan bin Haji Hijazi: "there is a mentality in Brunei where the standard of job is very low, we just expect to call foreign labour to come and do manual labour for us since it is cheaper". This is mostly due to the crowding-out effect of cheap foreign labours that can easily be obtained and results in outdated farming methods, which coupled with ageing farmers, is creating a sector that looks traditional and unattractive to the youths. In Brunei, the use of technology is still in its infancy and technology substitution is slow. In theory, technology-substitution happens when the cost of labour rises in relation to the cost of capital as wages are increased in a growing economy creating a shift from labour-intensive to capital-intensive production techniques (Webster, 1993). In Brunei, this shift has not taken place because the rise in local wages has led to the use of low wage foreign labour, and this is a common feature of oil exporting country (Heeks, 1998). Therefore, the use of foreign labour which is easily available is more economical than using machinery.

## Lack of Exposure

It can be observed that there is lack of exposure of agripreneurs and their agribusinesses in Brunei. Not many are aware of their existence and this creates the typical stereotypes that farming is unprofitable and unpopular. One of the ways that the agripreneurs can change this is by utilizing the social media.

In this age of technological advancement, social media such as Instagram and Facebook proves to have a significant impact on marketing businesses. It has the ability to reach out to target audience on a daily basis. It has been reported that Brunei is among the thirteen countries with the highest social media penetration.

According to We Are Social and Hootsuite's Digital 2019 report, Brunei is among countries with highest social media penetration (Xuxin, 2019) while Brunei continues to have the highest Instagram penetration in the world (BizBrunei, 2019). Thus, social media can be a game changer for the agripreneurs especially start-ups that should not be overlooked. Some of the benefits can be seen as follows:

- Social media can be used for international market penetration

Mohammad Yousef Abuhashesh (2014) identified the integration of the social media identified as one of the most important factors in the current business environment and companies have to ensure that they are able to highlight the demands of the global business environment and adequately react to the trends. For example, Khian Fook asserts that marketing and advertising are the most important things for expansion and he hopes that the government will be able to support him in terms of expanding his agribusiness outside of the local market. Thus, social media can be used to reach and market their products in international market. However, it needs to be studied which social media is best to be used.

- As a platform to gain support and publicise more training opportunities

According to Haji Ayub of Eco Nadi, there are students who showed interest in farming but due to lack of institutional support, the programmes he initiated had to be put in to a halt. Social media can be used as a medium to expose to the public and the institutions on their activities in order to convince them on the benefits of joining the programmes. This will help to gain support from targeted or interested party. This is explained by Hanna, Rohm & Crittenden (2011) that the core business functions such as marketing, advertising, customer service and public relations development; are dependent on the social media integration of the organization.

Some of the agripreneurs offers firsthand experience. For example, Khian Fook welcomes dedicated and committed local interns to work with him on his plantation, Haji Muliadi offers life skills classes and Ayesha's Farm also offers farming lessons for children to expose them early to and get them interested in agriculture. With the use of social media, it will reach out to greater audience especially youth who are interested to gain firsthand experience in agriculture.

## POLICY IMPLICATIONS

### Exposure to Agriculture: Education and Mentoring

Passion of farming can be nurtured from knowledge in agriculture gained from education. However, in Brunei there is a lack of agriculture exposure in schools. Agriculture is slowly losing its importance even as an optional subject due to its low status and lack of emphasis in the school curriculum. As a result of the lack of agricultural component in the education curriculum, students tend to progress through education with little appreciation of the source of food they consume and the food supply chain. It is therefore important that there is some form of agricultural component from an early start.

The agripreneurs in this study highlighted the importance of practical and experiential based knowledge and their eagerness to continuously update themselves with the technical know-how and developmental trends of paddy farming. They asserted that education plays a significant role in changing mind-sets. They further added that raising awareness through formal and informal education is key to sparking the passion amongst youth in Brunei. Specifically looking at strategies to make the Bruneian youth of today be more informed about the current situation of agriculture in the country.

In 2018, Minister at the Prime Minister's Office called for the integration of agriculture and agricultural entrepreneurship education within national school curricula for early exposure and to promote interest in the agri-sector (Idris, 2018). One problem with the basic education system is that for decades it has focused on preparing students for higher and/or tertiary education. This emphasis is now to encourage students to take the agripreneurship route to improve their employability because unfortunately not all graduates are able to obtain employment in their field of study.

In addition to that, last year the DAA has started an initiative to encourage more youth participation in agriculture in order supply domestic market demand and replace Brunei's ageing farmers with the introduction of free agricultural courses to teach interested or potential young farmers to build their own vertical gardens at home. A specialized program, *Kursus Pendedahan Teknologi Mudah dan Murah*, to educate youth on inexpensive methods to start an agricultural business. Participants are taught the importance of market analysis to prepare them for the struggles upon entering the open, and unpredictable market (Wasli, 2018).

According to Santiago and Roxas (2015), there are various ways of marrying agriculture and entrepreneurship as drawn from small pockets of non-government intervention in the Philippines. For agripreneurship to work, the two tracks of hard technical know-how needs to be combined with innovative and entrepreneurial skills.

To have more students engaged in agripreneurship, alternative learning systems must be introduced at the basic education level such as the Family Farm School (FFS) model for young children in the Philippines. High school graduates who were unable to pursue higher education can generate income from selling the crops they harvest at school whilst studying. Upon graduating, students are well-equipped with the necessary skills to run both a farm and a company. There is also the Social Enterprise Model, targeted at young graduates who can finance entrepreneurial businesses in the farm village university, a positive initiatives that local institutions like Universiti Brunei Darussalam (UBD) could establish in the near future.

## Access to Finance

A good example of a favourable financial aid for agripreneurs to gain credit for start-up is the Agro Bank of Malaysia. With 40 years of experience in agricultural banking, Agro Bank can be considered as a leading bank with focus on the agricultural sector. It plays an important role as a development financial institution in enhancing the agricultural sector in Malaysia. As a statutory body, the Bank is in charge of arranging, providing, supervising and coordinating credit for agricultural purposes in Malaysia.

The Paddy-i Financing or formerly known as the Paddy Credit Scheme is an award winning innovative financing by Agrobank with the aim to cater the seasonal needs of paddy farmers and suitable for the plantation and replantation of paddy (Agrobank, 2016). The scheme was first introduced in 1970 after the Bank's establishment and has been instrumental in the development of commercialised and progressive paddy plantation industry in Malaysia. It was the first financing customised to meet the needs of paddy farmers since then and remains the first of its kind in Malaysia.

One of the key success factors for the scheme was the ability of the Bank to structure a working capital financing for them. Under normal commercial financing practices, the paddy farmers will not be able to have easy access to financing due to the nature of paddy planting where the cash flows for repayment is seasonal and the plantation is susceptible to paddy price risks, adverse weather and excess supply. With this scheme, farmers are able to obtain financing of up to RM2,500 per hectare or maximum financing of RM50,000 to meet the requirement for the purchase of paddy, seeds, fertilisers, land preparation and other production costs associated with the paddy farming. The scheme also provides low profit rate subject to 3.25% profit rate per harvest season and no collaterals and guarantors required for the financing. The features and benefits of the schemes significantly helped the paddy farmers especially to increase the production output and income.

## Entrepreneurial Opportunity and Exposure through Social Media

As there is a lack of exposure of agripreneurs and their agribusinesses in Brunei and not many are aware of their existence, this is the time where the use of social media to promote agriculture should be maximised. The lack of exposure has created the typical stereotypes that farming is unprofitable and unpopular.

As mentioned in the earlier sections, Brunei is one of the highest users of social media, particularly instagram. According to BizBrunei (2019) Brunei continues to have the highest Instagram penetration in the world, with 63% of the population above 13-years-old using the photo and video sharing platform. Awareness and exposures through social media which will reach most of the population, especially youth, will give indirect impact to the youth of changing the negative mindset about agriculture. Brunei should make use of this opportunity to further promote agriculture through social media and help to change the mindset among youth.

In 2016, Dr Amin Mugera, an agribusiness specialist at the University of Western Australia's (UWA) School of Agriculture and Resource Economics, said the sultanate, like many other countries in the world, is struggling to attract and convince its youth to take up agriculture and Brunei's must look at agriculture as a business opportunity (Rasidah Hj Abu Bakar, 2016). Thus, with exposures through social media, to understand what agriculture is, and learn from the inspiring or successful agrirpeneurs, this will slowly help to convince youth and make them understand about agriculture and later consider it as a business opportunity.

It was also reported that, among the achievements of mobile penetration to a higher level, the number of smartphone user or smart devices are estimated at about 90 per cent in the country from the overall number of mobile users (BruDirect, 2019). Broadband penetration and Mobile Broadband penetration are at 115 per cent, 4G Long Term Evolution, LTE devices are at 90 per cent of the country's residents and Fixed broadband penetration is about 50 per cent of the number of households and business premises (BruDirect, 2019). Furthermore, it was also reported that the government is looking to improve telecommunications infrastructure and make it more conducive for e-commerce (Rasidah Hj Abu Bakar, 2019). Thus, the future prospect of social media in e-commerce should not be overlooked.

## CONCLUSION

Agriculture has always been an important driver of the world's economy and was once the main source of income for the Brunei economy. It is important for Brunei to achieve food self-sufficiency and food security to safeguard against any food crisis like the ones in 2008 and 2010. This study provides an overview of the motivations and challenges of agripreneurs in Brunei. The agripreneurs noted on areas of improvement particularly the need for more opportunities in securing financial support like or similar to the one offered by LIVEWIRE as well as the key importance of having updated and accessible knowledge be it formal or informal education and even current updates as well as technological developments on farming. This paper also alluded to successful initiatives in countries like Philippines and Malaysia to adopt and customise to further assist agripreneurs in Brunei.

This study contributes empirically based on the findings on religious and cultural motivation of entrepreneurship. It can be seen in the case of Brunei that religious and cultural values plays a significant role in influencing the motivation for entrepreneurial activity more specifically in the venture of agribusiness. The theory of uncertainty avoidance put forward by Hofstede (2001) which observes the nature of Malays to be less of a risk taker is flawed based on the findings in this study. It can be seen that the nationalistic or patriotism value of the agripreneurs studied in this research outweighs the theory of uncertainty avoidance. The religious value of entrepreneurship is also an area which is rarely explored and in this study, it is observed that religious values plays a significant role in entrepreneurial motivation. However, this study has its own limitations. It is a qualitative study based on the responses of fifteen agripreneurs in Brunei and it may be too ambitious to be generalized for the whole population. Nevertheless, the study provides a solid foundation for further exploration and confirmation of these entrepreneurial motivation factors through different forms of analysis.

The way forward for Brunei is to benefit and learn from these agripreneurs and hopefully in the next few decades ideally by 2035, the future innovators and entrepreneurs will be able to improve the agriculture sector in Brunei and ultimately achieve our vision of food self-sufficiency and food security.

## REFERENCES

Al Quran[1].

Zain, M., Yusob, A., Othman, R., Lim, S., & Idris, P., & Siti Rozaidah, D. (2015). Attributes of effective leadership from the perspectives of implicit leadership theory (ILT): A study in Brunei. *International Journal of Science Commerce and Humanities*, *3*, 58–64.

Baughn, C. C., Chua, B. L., & Neupert, K. E. (2006). The normative context for women's participation in entrepreneurship: A multicountry study. *Entrepreneurship Theory and Practice*, *30*(5), 687–708. doi:10.1111/j.1540-6520.2006.00142.x

Baumol, W. J. (1990). Entrepreneurship: Productive, unproductive, and destructive. *Journal of Political Economy*, *98*(5), 893–921. doi:10.1086/261712

BizBrunei. (2019). Brunei's Instagram penetration highest in the world. Bizbrunei (Online) Retrieved from https://www.bizbrunei.com/2019/04/bruneis-instagram-penetration-highest-in-the-world/

Bolton, B., & Thompson, J. (2004). *Entrepreneurs: Talent, temperament, techniques* (2nd ed.). Oxford, UK: Elsevier Butterworth-Henemann.

Braun, V., & Clarke, V. (2006). Using thematic analysis in psychology. *Qualitative Research in Psychology*, *3*(2), 77–101. doi:10.1191/1478088706qp063oa

BruDirect. (2019). Development of 4th Industrial Revolution. BruDirect (Online). Retrieved from http://brudirect.com/news.php?id=65263

Brunei Government. (2015). *Brunei Darussalam Key Indicators 2014*. Brunei Darussalam: Department of Statistics, Department of Economic Planning and Development, Prime Minister's Office.

Bruton, G. D., Ahlstrom, D., & Li, H.-L. (2010). Institutional theory and entrepreneurship: Where are we now and where to we need to move in the future. *Entrepreneurship Theory and Practice*, *34*(3), 421–440. doi:10.1111/j.1540-6520.2010.00390.x

Cardon, M. S., Wincent, J., Singh, J., & Drnovsek, M. (2009). The nature and experience of entrepreneurial passion. *Academy of Management Review*, *34*(3), 511–532. doi:10.5465/amr.2009.40633190

Chen, X. P., Yao, X., & Kotha, S. (2009). Entrepreneur passion and preparedness in business plan presentations: A persuasion analysis of venture capitalists' funding decisions. *Academy of Management Journal*, *52*(1), 199–214. doi:10.5465/amj.2009.36462018

Department of Agriculture and Agri-food. (2009). *Mid-term Plan 2008-2011*. Retrieved from http://www.agriculture.gov.bn/DOA2009/pdf%20Publication/Pelan%20Strategik%202008-2013.pdf

Faizal, P. R. M., Ridhwan, A. A. M., & Kalsom, A. W. (2013). The Entrepreneurs Characteristics from al-Quran and al-Hadis. *International Journal of Trade. Economics and Finance*, *4*(4), 191–196.

Franz, J. C. (1990). The Sultanate of Brunei: Oil Wealth and problems of Development. (M. Schmitz, & A. Sharp, Trans.) In Universitat Nuremberg, Nuremberg.

Groome, J. (1978). *Farming in Brunei: current systems and prospects for beef production.* (Master's thesis). Durham University (Online). Retrieved from http://etheses.dur.ac.uk/9736/1/9736_6529.PDF?UkUDh:CyT

Hanna, R., Rohm, A., & Crittenden, V. L. (2011). We're all connected: The power of the social media ecosystem. *Business Horizons*, *54*(3), 265–273. doi:10.1016/j.bushor.2011.01.007

Harris, M. L., & Gibson, S. G. (2008). Examining the entrepreneurial attitudes of US business students. *Education + Training*, *50*(7), 568–581. doi:10.1108/00400910810909036

Hayton, J. C., George, G., & Zahra, S. A. (2002). National culture and entrepreneurship: A review of behavioural research. *Entrepreneurship Theory and Practice*, *26*(4), 33–52. doi:10.1177/104225870202600403

Heeks, R. (1998). Small Enterprise Development and the 'Dutch Disease' in a Small Economy: The Case of Brunei, *IDPM Discussion Paper Series Paper*, No. 56, Development Policy and Management, University of Manchester.

Herbel, D., Croweley, E., & Lee, M. (2010). *Good practices in building innovative rural institutions to increase food security*. FAO Issue.

Hj Abu Bakar, R. (2016). Youth must see agriculture as a business opportunity. The BT Archive (Online). Retrieved from https://btarchive.org/news/national/2016/04/24/youth-must-see-agriculture-business-opportunity

Hj Abu Bakar, R. (2019). Flexing digital economy muscle key to enabling growth in other sectors. The Scoop (Online). Retrieved from https://thescoop.co/2019/01/31/flexing-digital-economy-muscle-key-to-enable-growth-in-other-sectors/

Hofstede, G. (2001). *Culture's Consequences: Comparing Values, Behaviours, Institutions, and Organizations across Nations*. Thousand Oaks, CA: Sage.

Idris, A. (2018). Incorporate agriculture in school curriculum, says minister at PMO. Borneo Bulletin (Online). Retrieved from https://borneobulletin.com.bn/incorporate-agriculture-in-school-curriculum-says-minister-at-pmo/

International Fund for Agricultural Development (IFAD). (2009). *Gender in Agriculture Source book.*

Ismail, A. G., Shamim, S., & Possumah, B. T. (2011). Bringing work back in Islamic perspectives. *Prosiding PERKEM*, *5*(2), 247–262.

Kazumi, T., & Kawai, N. (2017). Institutional support and women's entrepreneurial self-efficacy. *Asia Pacific Journal of Innovation and Entrepreneurship, 11*(3), 345–365. doi:10.1108/APJIE-12-2017-041

Lim, D., Morse, E., Mitchell, R., & Seawright, K. (2010). Institutional environment and entrepreneurial cognitions: A comparative business system perspective. *Entrepreneurship Theory and Practice, 34*(3), 491–516. doi:10.1111/j.1540-6520.2010.00384.x

Lim, S., Othman, R., Zain, M., Yusob, A., & Pengiran, S. R. (2012). Implicit leadership theories of Bruneians. *Journal of Asia-Pacific Business, 13*(4), 302–319. doi:10.1080/10599231.2012.718674

Maierbrugger, A. (2014) Brunei limits agricultural land use to 1% to protect tropical forests. Retrieved from http://investvine.com/brunei-limits-agricultural-land-use-to-1-to-protect-tropical-forests/

Mohamad, M. (1970). *The Malay dilemma*. Singapore: Asia Pacific Press.

Mohammad Yousef, A. (2014). Integration of social media in business. *International Journal of Business and Social Science, 5*(8), 202–209.

Mohd Zain, M., Asyraf, A. R., & Mohd Rafi, Y. (2014). Spirituality in Islamic Entrepreneurship: Motivation and Achievements of Successful Entrepreneurs in Kelantan. *Journal of Techno Social, 6*(2), 27–36.

Oukil, M. S. (2013). Entrepreneurship and entrepreneurs in an Islamic context. *Journal of Islamic and Human Advanced Research, 3*(3), 111–131.

Oxford Business Group. (2014). *The Report: Brunei Darussalam 2013*. London, UK: Oxford Business Group.

Polsaram, P., Kulsiri, P., Techasermsukkul, L., Dar Htwe, T., & Kwanchainond, K. (2011). Small and medium enterprises development policies of 4 ASEAN countries: Brunei Darussalam, Cambodia, Lao PDR, and Myanmar. *Japan Overseas Development Corporation (JODC)*. Retrieved from http://www.asean.org/storage/images/documents/SME%20Policies%20in%204%20ASEAN%20Countries%20-%20Brunei%20Darussalam.pdf

Rusnah, M., Edil, A. S., & Mohd Rizal, M. (2008). Corporate social responsibility: An Islamic perspective. *Journal of Accounting Perspectives, 1*, 43–56.

Santiago, A., & Roxas, F. (2015). Reviving farming interest in the Philippines through agricultural entrepreneurship education. *Journal of Agriculture, Food Systems, and Community Development, 5*(4), 15–27.

Shiri, N., Mohammadi, D., & Hosseini, S. M. (2012). Entrepreneurial intention of agricultural students: Effects of role model, social support, social norms and perceived desirability. *Archives of Applied Science Research*, *4*(2), 892–897.

Taylor, M. J. (1992). Post-16 options: Young people's awareness, attitudes, intentions and influences on their choice. *Research Papers in Education*, *7*(3), 301–335. doi:10.1080/0267152920070305

Tlaiss, H. A. (2015). How Islamic business ethics impact women entrepreneurs: Insights from four Arab middle eastern countries. *Journal of Islamic Business Ethics*, *129*(4), 859–877. doi:10.100710551-014-2138-3

Vallerand, R. J., & Houlfort, N. (2003). Passion at work: toward a new conceptualization. In S. W. Gilliland, D. D. Steiner, & D. P. Skarlicki (Eds.), *in Emerging Perspectives on Values in Organizations*. Greenwich, CT: Information Age Publishing.

Wasli, W. (2018). Jobseekers, youths encouraged to start vertical farming. The Scoop (Online). Retrieved from https://thescoop.co/2018/09/15/jobseekers-youths-encouraged-to-start-vertical-farming/

Watson, K., Hogarth-Scott, S., & Wilson, N. (1998). Small business start-ups: Success factors and support implications. *International Journal of Entrepreneurial Behaviour & Research*, *4*(3), 217–238. doi:10.1108/13552559810235510

Webster, A. (1993). Comparative advantages and long run Dutch disease effects: The international trade of Trinidad and Tobago. *Development Policy Review*, *11*(2), 153–155. doi:10.1111/j.1467-7679.1993.tb00034.x

Wildman, M., & Torres, R. M. (2001). Factors identified when selecting a major in agriculture. *Journal of Agricultural Education*, *42*(2), 46–55. doi:10.5032/jae.2001.02046

Winsteadt, R. O. (1947). *The Malays: A cultural history*. Singapore: Kelly & Walsh.

World Bank. *(2012) The World Bank Data Bank.* Retrieved from http://databank.worldbank.org/data/views/reports/tableview.aspx

Xuxin. (2019). Brunei among countries with highest social media penetration, Xinhua. Feb. 1, 2019. Available at http://www.xinhuanet.com/english/2019-02/01/c_137792631.htm (Accessed: 27 June 2019).

Yakub, K. (2012) *An Ethnographic Study of Wasan Rice Farm in Brunei Darussalam*. (Master's Thesis). Ritsumeikan Asia Pacific University. Retrieved from http://r-cube.ritsumei.ac.jp/bitstream/10367/3915/1/51110003.pdf

Zain, M., Yusob, A., Othman, R., Lim, S., & Idris, P. (2014). Brunei implicit leadership theories: Impacts of expectation gap. *Review of Strategic and International Studies*, *6*, 12–21.

## ADDITIONAL READING

Dhindsa, H. S., & Md-Hamdilah, A.-Z.-A. (2014). Societal Perceptions of Agriculture: A Brunei Case Study. *Journal of Agricultural Education and Extension*, *21*(5), 441–465. doi:10.1080/1389224X.2014.971828

Fox, S. (2016). Reframing the influence of national culture with theory-based multi-resolution simulation models. *Management Research Review*, *39*(5), 521–545. doi:10.1108/MRR-09-2014-0211

Ibrahim, A. L. (1996). *Cultural and counter-cultural forces in contemporary Brunei Darussalam in Thumboo E Cultures in ASEAN and the 21st Century*. Singapore: University of Singapore Press.

Johnston, B. F., & Mellor, J. W. (1961). The role of agriculture in economic development. *The American Economic Review*, *51*(4), 566–593.

Lassa, J. A. (2015). *Brunei's Vision 2035: Can It Achieve Food Self-Sufficiency? RSIS Commentary, no.34*. Singapore: Nanyang Technological University.

Shams, S., Shafiuddin, K. H., Sultan, A. M. S. B. H. M., & Juani, R. B. H. M. (2015). Agriculture Adaptation to Climate Change in Brunei Darussalam. *Environment & Urbanization Asia*, *6*(1), 59–70. doi:10.1177/0975425315585193

Touburg, G. (2016). National habitus: An antidote to the resilience of Hofstede's "national culture"? *Journal of Organizational Change Management*, *29*(1), 81–92. doi:10.1108/JOCM-11-2015-0219

## KEY TERMS AND DEFINITIONS

**Agripreneur:** An entrepreneur involved in agricultural activities.

**Cultural Motivation:** An individual's actions, desires, and needs to learn about and engage with culture based incentives which plays an important role in the generation of agripreneurs decision to venture into agripreneurship for e.g. a sense of loyalty to support the family, a sense of nationalistic pride.

**Entrepreneurial Motivation:** The process of transforming an individual in to an entrepreneur.

**Institutional Barriers:** Barriers such as lack of government assistance, lack of funds, infrastructure issues, lack of training, poor contract and property laws and corruption that discourages entrepreneurial activities.

**Institutional Support:** Policies and practices aimed at creating a conducive business environment characterized by attractive opportunities for new entrepreneurs.

**Intrinsic Motivation:** Behaviour that is driven by personal satisfaction and reward.

**Religious Motivation:** Behaviour that is driven by ethical principles founded in religious beliefs.

## ENDNOTE

1 https://www.soundvision.com/article/the-quran-and-sunnah-on-the-elderly

# Chapter 4
# Empowering Community Through Entrepreneurship Training and Islamic Micro-Financing:
## Sharing the Experience of IIUM-CIMB Islamic Smart Partnership (i-Taajir)

**Norma Md Saad**
*International Islamic University Malaysia, Malaysia*

**Mustafa Omar Mohammad**
*International Islamic University Malaysia, Malaysia*

**Mohammed Aslam Haneef**
*International Islamic University Malaysia, Malaysia*

## ABSTRACT

*Community economic development is a relatively new strategy employed to increase employment, income, and entrepreneurship activities in small town and communities. The Centre for Islamic Economics, International Islamic University Malaysia (IIUM) has initiated a smart partnership with CIMB Islamic Bank to offer entrepreneurship training and Islamic microfinance facility to the poor in Malaysia. This project adopts several modes of Islamic microfinance financing instruments which include equity-based and debt-based financing. The program aims to educate the communities surrounding the IIUM campus with entrepreneurship knowledge and skill in addition to giving Shariah-compliant micro-financing facility for them to implement their business ideas. CIMB Islamic, which is the main partner for this*

DOI: 10.4018/978-1-7998-2257-8.ch004

*project, provides funds for Islamic microfinance facilities and IIUM contributes expertise in providing entrepreneurship trainings to the communities located near IIUM campus. It is hoped that this smart partnership would empower the surrounding communities and create more successful entrepreneurs.*

## INTRODUCTION

Entrepreneurship has long been recognized to have an influential role in the economic development of a country. One of the most important contributions of entrepreneurship is in community development (Van de Ven, 1993; Bryant, 1989; Gartner, 1985). Research indicates that if the community members are able to motivate themselves, self-development strategies are great tools to empower the community to enhance their economic condition (Korsching & Allen, 2004). Despite the heavy preference and emphasis on centralized approach of economic development, researchers such as Loveragde (1996) and Flora and Flora (2004) state that professionals and government agencies who are involved in community economic development programs continuously assert that attracting industry and entrepreneurship is an effective strategy to create jobs and empower a community.

A survey conducted by the US Chamber of Commerce reveals that the biggest business challenge faced by entrepreneurs is getting access to business financing (CO, US Chamber of Commerce). The findings of the survey are consistent numerous studies which indicate one of the major difficulties faced by micro, small, and medium-size enterprises (MSMEs) is getting access to financing (Teo & Cheong, 1994: Mensah et al., 2015; Peprah, C. 2016). The ability to access financing is a crucial factor for MSMEs to start, grow, sustain, and improve themselves.

Microfinance service has been developed in order to provide financing needed by micro and small enterprises. Microfinance has been acknowledged as one of the easiest ways for micro and small entrepreneurs to obtain financing as well as an effective tool to alleviate poverty. The microfinance movement started because many people believed that thousands of creditworthy poor and minority borrowers were sometimes excluded from the formal credit market. Many people argue that excluding such individuals will permanently affect their chances to help themselves to come out of poverty (Aghion & Boltin, 1997; Banerjee & Newman, 1993 (cited in Aghion & Boltin, 1997)). Traditionally, the poor in developing countries resort to borrowing from informal sectors that impose exorbitantly high-interest rates (Sen, 1981; De Aghion & Morduch, 2005).

Offering relatively cheap credit to the poor and providing basic business skills to micro-entrepreneurs are believed to be an appropriate development strategy, therefore, many governments and non- governmental agencies (NGOs) have provided aids, subsidies and technical assistance to many firms and agencies that are involved in micro-lending activities. Grameen Bank from Bangladesh is considered to be a pioneer microfinance institution assisting the poor by giving them small loans to be involved in business and generate income to sustain themselves and their families.

Islamic microfinance is a combination of two rapidly growing industries that are microfinance and Islamic finance. It has the potential to not only respond to unmet demand but also to combine the Islamic social principle of caring for the less fortunate with microfinance's power to provide financial access to the poor (Karim et al., 2008). Base on Islamic doctrines of social and economic justice, Islamic microfinance will be a key to provide financial access to millions of Muslim poor who currently reject microfinance products which are not *Shariah* compliant. Despite the expansion of Islamic microfinance (IMF), the institution continues to face three primary challenges: lack of access to affordable finance, overreliance on debt-based financing and the poor quality of human resources, both as providers and recipients of microfinance services. These have hampered efforts towards developing entrepreneurial and investment societies particularly among the Muslim communities.

Studies have shown that there has been a complete shift in Islamic banking and finance from supposedly PLS banking to a sales-based and debt-based system (Saeed, 2004; Dusuki & Abozaid, 2007; Asutay, 2007). The activities of Islamic banks depend largely on contracts that are regarded as "mark-up" based, rather than on PLS contracts such as a *Mudharabah* and *Musharakah.* The latter, argued as being preferable by academics, has thus far been minimally used in practice.

The current practice in Islamic microfinance is very much similar to that of Islamic banking. According to Obaidullah (2008), Islamic microfinance institutions (IMFs) across the globe utilize a variety of *Shariah*-compliant mechanisms, such as *Murabahah,* Bai-*Bithaman-Ajil, Ijarah, Bai-Salam,* etc. All these modes of financing create debt. In Indonesia, even though Obaidullah & Khan (2008) report that IMFs there uses reasonably balanced with an array of products - based on *Mudharabah, Musharakah, Murabahah, Ijarah* and *Al-Qard al-hasan,* this is a new trend because Seibel (2005) reports that in BPRS (one of IMFIs operating in Indonesia), the main financing product is *Murabahah,* i.e., a sales contract between bank and customer with a fixed profit margin for the bank. Flexible profit- sharing, which is cumbersome to calculate, is of minor importance. In the Middle East, the *Hodeida* Microfinance Program in Yemen followed the model practiced by Grameen Bank in Bangladesh. However, it uses *Murabahah* mode of financing instead of PLS mode of financing. Obaidullah & Khan (2008) report that in Bangladesh, the Islamic microfinance institutions there have been depending on deferred-payment sales (*Bai mu'ajjal*) mode of financing.

## IIUM-CIMB ISLAMIC MICROFINANCE AND ENTREPRENEURSHIP DEVELOPMENT PROGRAM (*I-TAAJIR*)

The Centre for Islamic Economics (CIE), International Islamic University Malaysia (IIUM), henceforth will be known as CIE, IIUM, has initiated a smart partnership with CIMB Islamic Bank to offer entrepreneurship training and Islamic microfinance facility to the poor in Malaysia. This project adopts several modes of Islamic microfinance financing which include equity-based and debt-based financing. The program aims to educate the communities surrounding the IIUM campus with entrepreneurship knowledge and skill in addition to giving *Shariah*-compliant micro-financing facility for them to implement their business ideas. CIMB Islamic which is the main partner for this project provides funds for Islamic microfinance facilities and IIUM contributes expertise in providing entrepreneurship trainings to the communities located near IIUM campus.

The collaboration between CIE, IIUM and CIMB Islamic Bank is based on the premise that microfinance as a method to provide capital to empower the working poor can be replicated but requires tailored adjustments to the local socio-economic and cultural characteristics (Segrado 2005; Saad 2012). This research also focuses on the application of *Mudharabah* and *Musharakah,* the equity-based modes of financing in Islamic microfinance scheme. Dusuki & Abozaid (2007) argue that the provision of equity based financing by Islamic financial institutions will facilitate toward achieving the Islamic socio-economic objectives which include social justice, economic growth, efficiency and stability.

The CIE-CIMBi Entrepreneurs Program (*i-Taajir*) is a program implemented by the Centre of Islamic Economics, KENMS, IIUM to offer Islamic micro-financing scheme to micro entrepreneurs in Gombak area, where the University is located. The program is a pioneer study to test the possibility of several Islamic microfinance models developed by researchers from Centre of Islamic Economics. This program aims to guide people around Gombak and Selangor with entrepreneurial knowledge and skills besides providing Islamic micro-financing facilities for entrepreneurs to implement their business ideas.

This program is implemented to achieve the following objectives:

1. Enhancing community life through entrepreneurship.
2. Providing microfinance facility to communities around Gombak and IIUM.
3. Empowering and providing capital to the selected working local poor with financing using *Al-Qard al-Hasan* (zero-interest financing), sale based *Murabahah* and the PLS modes.
4. Implementing the concept of inclusive finance by providing access of credit/ financing to the poor.

5. Enhancing the level of *amana* (trust) and sense of *syukur* (appreciation) among the selected working local poor so that they are able to donate a portion of their profit to a pool of *Tabarru'* Fund.
6. Conducting an impact study on the success of the project in general and on the effectiveness of using the PLS and sale based modes for Islamic microfinance.

## Theoretical Foundation

*I-Taajir* is a community-based program. It is quite similar to the Nebraska EDGE program administered by the Center for Applied Rural Innovation at the University of Nebraska-Lincoln, USA, where both programs are built upon community interaction field theory and community development theory. Wilkinson (1991) states that the community is an interaction field between individuals, groups, and organizations. The bond among the different entities in the community is the shared interest in the locality that they share with each other. Community economic development through entrepreneurship increases peoples' willingness to come together and take action to empower the community. The approach of empowering the community through entrepreneurship and providing access of financing has been proven successful by the Nebraska EDGE program which started in 1993, where more than 1,600 new and existing entrepreneurs have been assisted in either starting of expanding their businesses. Emery, Wall, and Macke (2004) undertake a study to examine the result of another community-based entrepreneurship program called Energizing Entrepreneurship (E2). Based on the initial results, they report that E2 approach in engaging and providing entrepreneurship trainings are producing positive result in empowering small communities and expanding local businesses.

## Benefits of Joining *i-Taajir*

There are a number of microfinance institutions operating in Malaysia providing financing to the poor in the country. As a new microfinance player in the country, *i-Taajir* needs to have some unique features to attract participation from the poor. Among the unique features of the program, besides the opportunity to get Islamic financing facilities up to RM10,000 (USD2500) are as follows:

- Participants get free trainings from experts coming from IIUM or outside of IIUM
- Participants receive personal business guidance/coaching
- Participants are educated on the ethical and spiritual aspect of doing business

## *I-Taajir* Organizational Structure

The organizational structure of *i-Taajir* involves three Advisors, a project manager, four research assistants and over 70 student volunteers. Figure 1 below shows the organizational structure of *i-Taajir.*

The advantages of the *i-Taajir* organizational structure shown in Figure 1 above are the following, among others. Firstly, it is simple to allow easy flow of information and easy accessibility of members. Secondly, since all the members are staff and students of IIUM, they can hold meetings at any time at their conveniences. This also allows them to keep abreast with the activities of the project.

The Advisors who are also the pioneers of *i-Taajir* are: Professor Dr. Norma Md Saad, Professor Dr. Mohamed Aslam Mohamed Haneef, and Associate Professor Dr. Mustafa Omar Mohammed. The three advisors have the experience in conducting several research on entrepreneurship and microfinance, and have developed financing instruments to be used in *i-Taajir.* They provide leadership role for *i-Taajir* and assist in developing *i-Taajir*'s long and short term plans, strategies and activities, and oversee their implementations. They also ensure that finances of the project are managed within the authorized budget, and there is an effective internal control to ensure the activities are conducted lawfully and ethically and with integrity.

The project manager is a person who is equipped with the necessary knowledge and skills related to planning, organizing and controlling of the project to ensure proper supervision, process Improvement and efficient performance management.

*Figure 1. Organizational structure of i-Taajir*

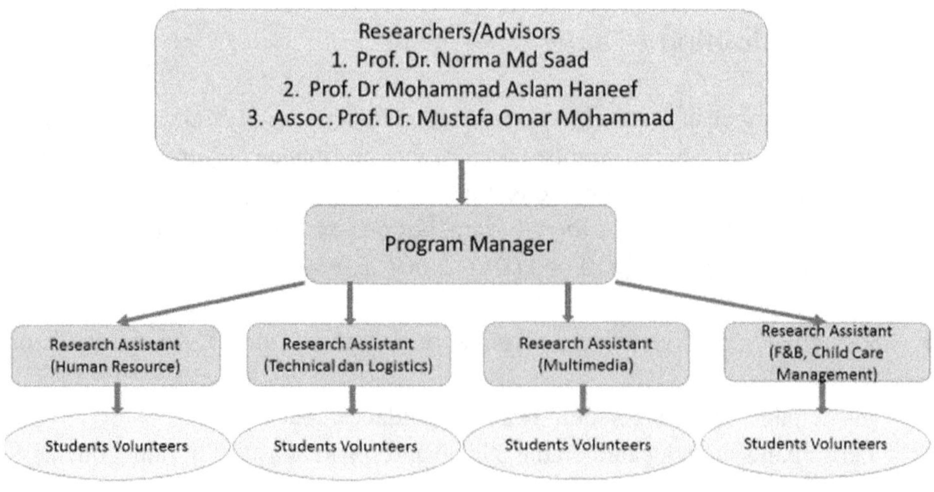

The following are the duties of the Project Manager:

**Planning**

1. Create a detailed work plan which identifies and sequences the activities needed to successfully complete the project
2. Develop a schedule for project completion that effectively allocates the resources to the activities
3. Determine the objectives and measures upon which the project will be evaluated at its completion

**Organizing**

1. Execute the project according to the project plan
2. Develop forms and records to document project activities
3. Set up files to ensure that all project information is appropriately documented and secured
4. Write reports on the project for the Advisors and for funders
5. Manage project funds according to established accounting policies and procedures

**Controlling**

1. Review the project schedule with the Advisors and revise it if required
2. Ensure that the participants' files are properly maintained and kept confidential
3. Ensure that the project deliverables are on time, within budget and at the required level of quality
4. Ensure that all financial records for the project are up to date
5. Monitor cash flow projections and report actual cash flow to the Advisors on a regular basis (bi- weekly/monthly)

Project manager is assisted by four Research Assistants (RAs) who are given responsibility to handle different portfolios, namely: Human Resource; Technical and Logistics; Multimedia; Food and Beverages, as well as Child Care Management. The four RAs are assisted by a number of student volunteers divided according to the different portfolios.

## Different Phases of *i-Taajir* Program

### Motivation

The first phase is the motivation, or program kick-off. IIUM students who are involved in the program will identify the target group and area for the *i-Taajir* program to be held. The residents of the targeted area would be informed that date

*Figure 2. Different phases of i-Taajir*

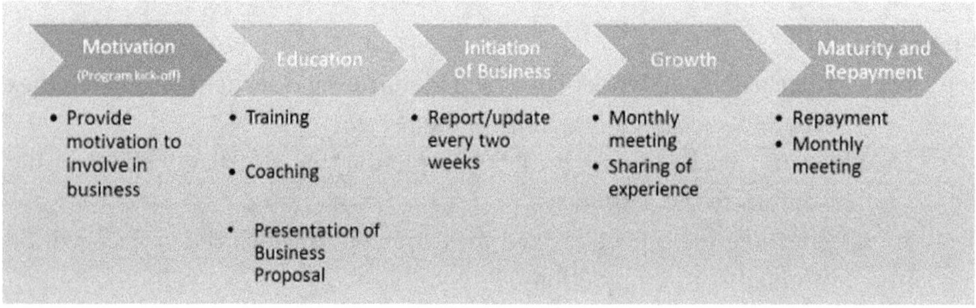


and venue of the motivation program. In order to encourage the potential participants to attend the event, they were invited to come together with their family members, which include spouses and children. Special facilities were arranged to entertain the children while their parents attended the program. The children were managed by the student volunteers who had developed modules to manage and entertain the children during the motivation sessions.

During the official launch, motivation sessions were held by inviting successful entrepreneurs to deliver talks to encourage and inspire the participants and instill in them the spirit of entrepreneurship. They were also reminded about integrity in business and upholding moral principles and ethical values. Lucky draws were conducted from time to time. At the end of the motivation sessions, the student volunteers conducted interview with the participants for ice breaking, establishing rapport and to know more about their business skills, financial and social status. This additional information would later be triangulated with the information the participants provided earlier in the household survey.

## Education Phase

Second part of the program is the Education Phase which consists of training, coaching, and presentation of business proposal. *I-Taajir* offers to the participants four modules of training programs:

1. Introduction to Business
   Under this module, participants would be asked to identify specific businesses that they want to venture/expand. The will be exposed on the legal and other requirements to set up business entities.
2. Basic Accounting Skills
   Participants are taught to prepare business proposal which would include among other things cash flow, revenue, expenditure, and profit.

*Figure 3. Training modules*

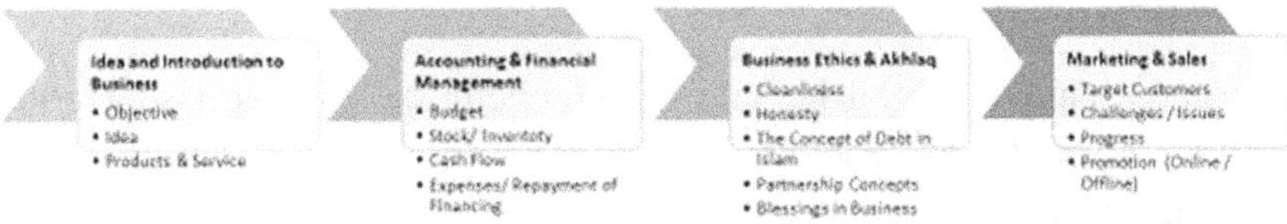


3. Marketing Skills
   Marketing experts from IIUM or outside of IIUM are invited to teach the participants on the various ways to market their products.
4. Business Ethics and *Akhlaq*
   Under this module, participants are taught to adhere Islamic ethic and *akhlaq* in doing business. They are reminded that profit should not be the only reason in venturing into business. Other reasons such as providing solutions to others, giving the best and efficient service, and observing the cleanliness and good manners are equally important reasons to ensure success in any business venture.

Participants who have successfully undergone the four-module trainings would be paired with a student who has been trained to provide personal coaching to the participant in order to prepare a business proposal. Student Coach, SC visits participants at their residences, associations and business premises to arrange for coaching whose duration ranges between 1 to 5 hours. The coaching time is flexible in order to accommodate the study schedule of SC and the working hours of the participants. The coaching sessions are also part of due diligence process as the SCs are required to write their observations on the participants' commitment and efforts in preparing the business proposal. The business proposal must include the type of business, risks involved, rate of success, amount of financing required, tools to be purchased duration of financing, and estimated monthly repayment amount.

Upon the completion of the business plan draft, the student volunteers arrange for the participants to have preliminary presentations before selected members of staff from IIUM. The main objectives of the preliminary presentations are to solicit feedback for improving the proposal before the final presentation. The final presentations are conducted in parallel sessions with a panel comprising at least two expert judges in each session. The expert judges are selected staff from IIUM, CIMB Islamic and professionals from the industry. The presentations are done in power point slides in a duration of 20 to 25 minutes followed by the question and answer session from the experts. The results of all the presentations are then forwarded to *i-Taajir* management for the final selection for award of contracts.

The committee which consists of Advisors of *i-Taajir,* and CIMB officers adopts the following benchmarks for the award of contracts:

1. The participant fulfills all the criteria set for being called poor: visual indicators of poor, level of income and asset size.
2. The participant has attended all the required sessions: motivation, training, couching and presentations.
3. The participant has obtained a pass for his/her proposal and presentation from the
   expert judges.
4. Other additional information on the participant obtained from the household survey and through informal interviews and interactions with student couches and volunteers.
5. The extent to which the business proposal is sound and viable.

## Initiation of Business, Growth, and Maturity

The selection committee decides and matches the kind of financing mode suitable for each type of business and the amount of financing applied for. As a rule of Thumb, *Al-Qard al-Hasan* mode is offered to participants who apply for a financing amount of Malaysian Ringgit RM5000 or less, and the other modes: *Murabahah, Musharakah Mutanaqisah* and *Mudarabah* are offered to those who have applied for RM10, 000 financing facility. There are also cases where the committee has offered a hybrid contract of *Murabahah* and *Al-Qard al-Hasan*.

Funds are disbursed to successful participants in three different stages to ensure that the money is properly used and not diverted to personal or other usage. SC will be monitoring the usage of the fund and making progress report on the development of the participant attached to him/her. If the report from the SC about the business progress of the participant is satisfactory, then only the second and third disbursement would be released. The SC will continue to monitor the progress to ensure that the participant's business is growing and able to make monthly repayment of the financing given to him/her.

In order to ensure that the businesses undertaken by the participants are running well, a unique program called Sharing Session is organized for the entrepreneurs to come together and share their business experience. In this session, each entrepreneur is given an opportunity to briefly talk about his or her business, whether it is operating well or not. A business consultant is invited to handle the Sharing Session. He starts the program by giving a short motivation talk and then he would invite the entrepreneurs to share the problems that they are facing in running their businesses.

The session would end by the business consultant addressing and giving solutions to common as well as specific problems faced by the entrepreneurs. All *i-Taajir* participants who attended the program indicate that they benefit tremendously from the Sharing Session as they are given practical solutions by the consultant on how to solve their business problems.

## Types of Business

*I-Taajir* has completed the Education phase and Awarding ceremony for Cycle 1 where 12 participants have been awarded financing with a total of RM47,000 (USD11,500). In Cycle 2, the number of participants who are awarded with financing is more than doubled. A total of 27 participants receive a total of RM174,000 (USD42,500) worth of financing.

Table 1 displays the types of business, number of participants involved in each business, amount of financing as well as contract awarded to each business category. Majority of the participants are involved in food and beverage sector with the highest amount of financing (RM124,000). Repair service comes at a distance second whereby only four participants are involved in this activity with a total financing of only RM29,500.00. Very few participants are venturing into other types of businesses.

*Table 1. Types of business, amount of financing and contracts*

| No | Number of Participants | Type of Business | Amount of Fund (RM) | Contract |
|---|---|---|---|---|
| 1 | 22 | Food and Beverage | 124,080.00 | *Al-Qard al-Hasan, Murabahah,* Hybrid |
| 2 | 2 | Tailoring, textile and clothing | 8,000.00 | *Murabahah* |
| 3 | 1 | Hardware store | 10,000.00 | *Murabahah* |
| 4 | 3 | Massage, Traditional Medicine, Facial, and Cosmetics | 11,650.00 | *Al-Qard al-Hasan, Murabahah* |
| 5 | 4 | Repair Services (phone, motorcycle, car) | 29,500.00 | *Al-Qard al-Hasan, Mudarabah,* |
| 6 | 2 | Trading | 12,105.00 | *Murabahah and Al-Qard al-Hasan* |
| 7 | 1 | Multi-service | 3,500.00 | *Al-Qard al-Hasan* |
| 8 | 2 | Agriculture | 18,190.00 | *Mudharabah* Hybrid |
| 9 | 2 | Printing Service | 18,520.00 | *Al-Qard al-Hasan* |

## Modes of Financing

*I-Taajir* is designed specifically to offer different mode of financing to its clients. The modes of financing developed and offered under *i-Taajir* program are namely, *Al-Qard al-Hasan, Murabahah, Musharakah Mutanaqisah* and *Mudarabah*. In special cases, it also offers hybrid contracts. These contracts and their steps are discussed below:

### Al-Qard al-Hasan

Figure 4 shows the first mode of financing offered by *i-Taajir* which is *Al-Qard al-Hasan*. Steps involved in *Al-Qard al-Hasan* contract are as follows:

1. The participant applies for *Al-Qard al-Hasan* facility from *i-Taajir.*
2. *I-Taajir* provides the *Al-Qard al-Hasan* (zero-interest) financing in cash to the participant.
3. The participant accompanied by Student Coach (SC) uses the money to buy equipments and raw materials for business activity.
4. The participant submits monthly reports to *i-Taajir.*
5. The participant repays the *Qard* to a Trust fund.
6. The participant is encouraged to contribute/donate at least 10% of his/her profit to the *Tabarru'* Fund.

*Figure 4. Mode of financing 1: Al-Qard al-Hasan*

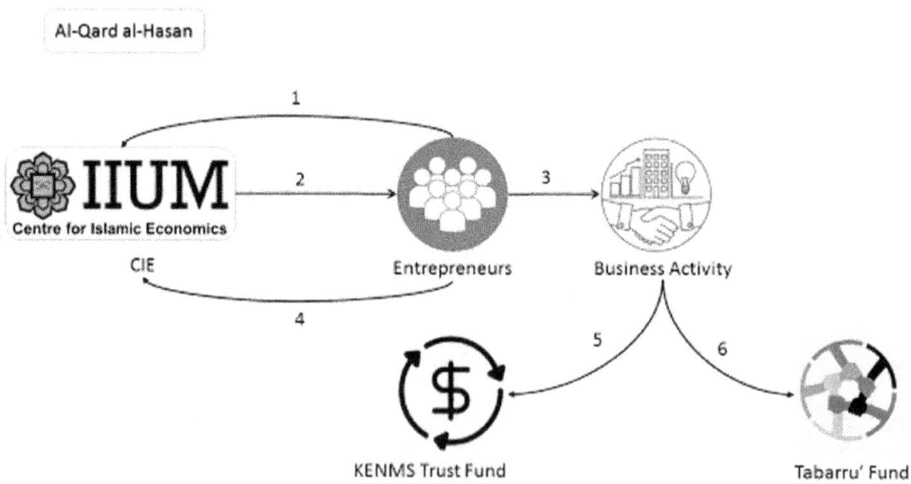

*Figure 5. Mode of financing 2: Murabahah*

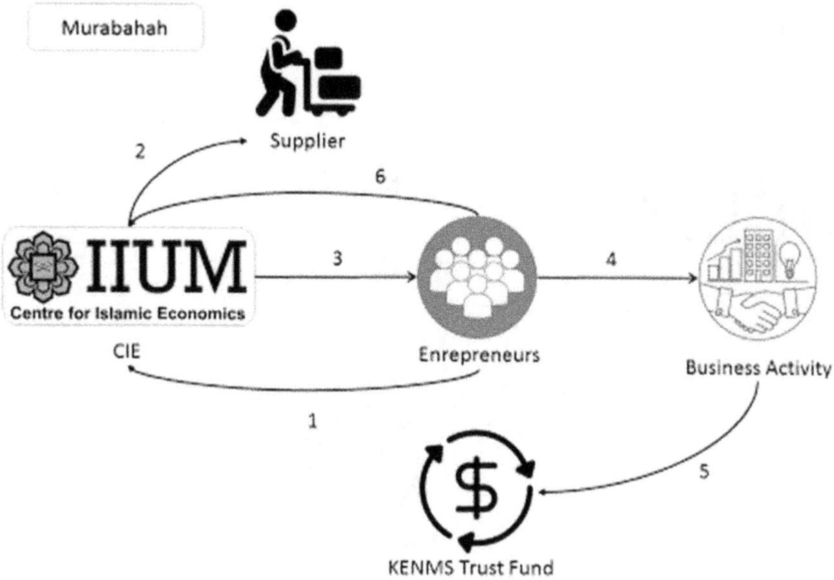


## Murabahah

Figure 5 displays the flow under the second mode of financing which is *Murabahah*. Steps involved in *Murabahah* contract are as follows:

1. The participant identifies the tool or materials needed to run the business and obtains invoice from the seller.
2. *I-Taajir* appoints participant as an agent to buy the tools or materials from the supplier.
3. *I-Taajir* sells the tools or materials at cost-plus to the participant.
4. The participant uses the tools or materials for the business activity.
5. The participant pays the selling price by instalments to KENMS Trustee Fund.
6. The participant submits monthly reports to *i-Taajir*.

## Mudharabah

Figure 6 exhibits the third mode of financing which is *Mudharabah*. Steps involved in *Mudharabah* contract are as follows:

*Figure 6. Mode of financing 3: Mudharabah*

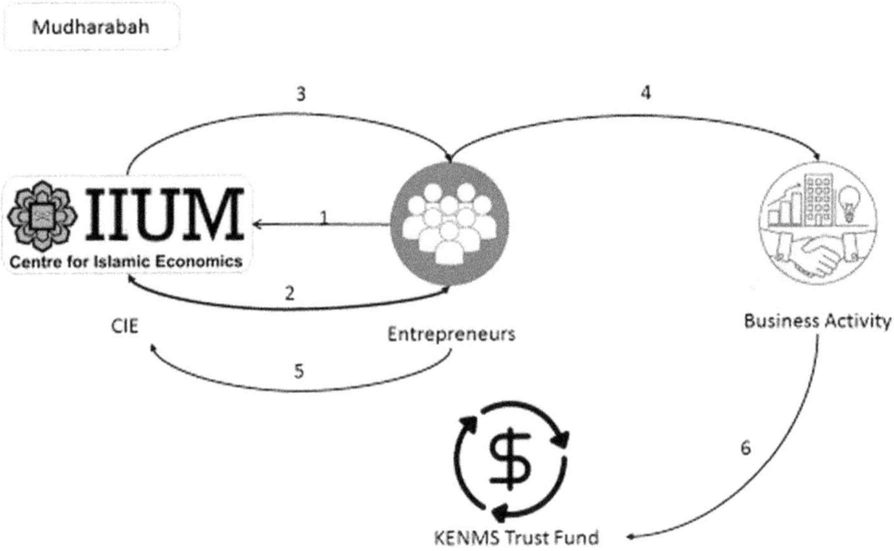


1. The participant presents business project to *i-Taajir* and provides detail of the amount of financing required.
2. *I-Taajir* and the participant agree on a profit-sharing ratio, usually 95:5. Participant is allowed to keep 95% of his or her profit, and share only 5% of the profit with *i-Taajir.*
3. *I-Taajir* provides financing to participant to run the business project.
4. The participant invests the fund in the business activity.
5. The participant redeems *i-Taajir*'s capital plus share of the profit and submits monthly reports to *i-Taajir*.
6. *I-Taajir*'s capital plus share of the profit is redeemed from the business activity periodically to KENMS Trustee fund.

## Musharakah Mutanaqisah

Figure 7 demonstrates the fourth mode of financing which is *Musharakah Mutanaqisah*. Steps involved in *Musharakah Mutanaqisah* are as follows:

1. The participant identifies the tools or materials needed for the business and obtains invoice from the supplier.
2. The participant provides 10% of the cost of the tools or materials and *i-Taajir* provides 90% of the cost.

*Figure 7. Mode of financing 4: Musharakah Mutanaqisah*

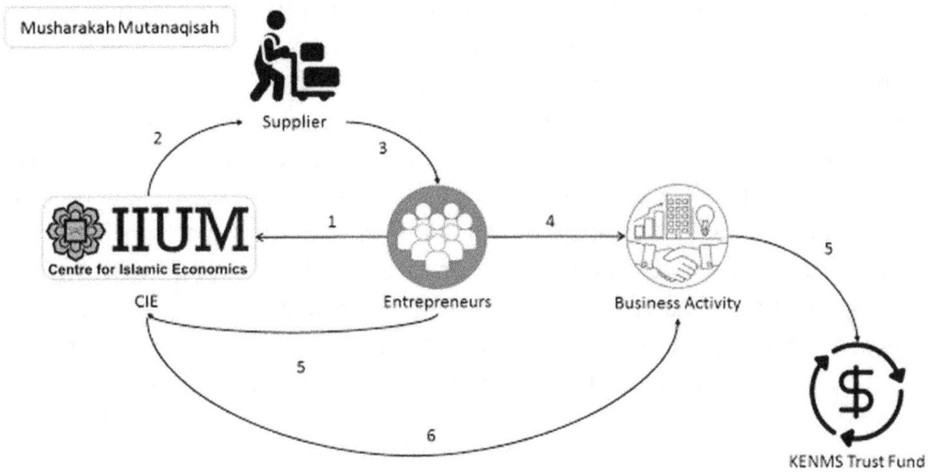


3. *I-Taajir* appoints the participant as an agent to buy the tools or materials from the supplier and they both jointly own the asset.
4. The supplier delivers the tools or materials to the participant.
5. The participant uses the tools or materials for the business activity.
6. The participant is pays periodic rent and purchase of equity in separate contracts to KENMS Trustee Fund and submits monthly reports to *i-Taajir*.
7. The participant takes full ownership of the asset after a symbolic sale.

The duration of financing for all the four modes is approximately 12 months. The student coaches, SCs, are assigned to monitor the business progress of each participant. SC would be visiting the participant on a bi-weekly basis.

## CONCLUSION

*I-Taajir* is a young and new player in the entrepreneurship and microfinance industry. The program is developed to fill in the gap or shortcomings of existing microfinance institutions in Malaysia in offering diverse types of Islamic micro-financing instruments to their clients. In addition, the novelty of *i-Taajir* is in its approach of combining microfinance and entrepreneurship trainings in building as well as empowering local communities. It is hoped that through this program, entrepreneurs who are given training and financing are able to improve their businesses and progress from initially being the zakat recipients to become zakat payer. That would be the ultimate success of *i-Taajir* program.

At present, *i-Taajir*'s target groups include people at the bottom 40% in terms of income (B40) and residential areas around Gombak and IIUM. Future plan would be to expand this program to a wider area to cover for other areas in the State of Selangor. There is also potential to expand *i-Taajir* model to develop entrepreneurship in poor communities in neighboring countries. Due to its unique feature in combining entrepreneurship development and Islamic microfinance, *i-Taajir* advisors has received request to expand *i-Taajir* program in Cambodia, Indonesia, and Tunisia.

In addition, in order to scale up the program and involve more participants, plans are under way to collaborate with relevant government and non-governmental agencies for program enhancement. Collaboration with other agencies are also important to provide additional trainings to participants and exposed them to other types of profitable businesses rather than concentrating only in the food and beverages sector.

## REFERENCES

Aghion, P., & Bolton, P. (1997). A theory of trickle-down growth and development. *The Review of Economic Studies*, *64*(2), 151–172. doi:10.2307/2971707

Asutay, M. (2007). Conceptualization of the second best solution in overcoming the social failure of Islamic banking and finance: Examining the overpowering of Homoislamicus by Homoeconomicus. *IIUM Journal of Economics and Management*, *15*(2), 167–196.

Banerje, E. A., & Newman, A. (1993). Occupational choice and process of development. *Journal of Political Economy*, 101, 274-298.

Bryant, C. (1989). Entrepreneurs in the rural environment. *Journal of Rural Studies*, *5*(4), 337–348. doi:10.1016/0743-0167(89)90060-0

CO. US Chamber of Commerce. (2019). Retrieved October 3, 2019 from https://www.uschamber.com/co/run/business-financing/business-financing-challenges

De Aghion, B. A., & Morduch, J. (2005). *The economics of microfinance*. Cambridge, MA: The MIT Press.

Dusuki, A. W., & Abozaid, A. (2007). A critical appraisal on the challenges of realizing Maqasid al-Shariah in Islamic banking and finance. *IIUM Journal of Economics and Management*, *15*(2), 143–166.

Emery, M., Wall, M., & Macke, D. (2004). From theory to action: Energizing entrepreneurship (E2), strategies to aid distressed communities grow their own. *Journal of the Community Development Society*, *35*(1), 82–96. doi:10.1080/15575330409490123

Flora, C. B., & Flora, J. L. (2004). *Rural communities: Legacy and change* (2nd ed.). Boulder, CO: Westview Press.

Gartner, W. B. (1985). A conceptual framework for describing the phenomenon of new venture creation. *Academy of Management Review*, *10*(4), 696–706. doi:10.5465/amr.1985.4279094

Karim, N., Tarazi, M., & Reille, X. (2008). Islamic microfinance: An emerging market niche. *CGAP Focus Note*, No. 49.

Korsching, P. F., & Allen, J. C. (2004). Local entrepreneurship: A development model based on community interaction field theory. *Journal of the Community Development Society*, *35*(1), 25–43. doi:10.1080/15575330409490120

Loverigde, S. (1996). On the continuing popularity of industrial recruitment. *Economic Development Quarterly*, *10*(2), 151–158. doi:10.1177/089124249601000202

Mensah, H. K., Azinga, S. A., & Sodji, J. A. M. (2015). Challenges faced by small and medium-size enterprises in accessing credit facilities from financial institutions: An empirical assessment incorporating the perceptions of both borrowers and financiers. Retrieved October 1, 2019 from https://www.researchgate.net/publication/286238910

Obaidullah, M., & Khan, T. (2008). Islamic microfinance development, challenges and initiatives. *Policy Dialogue Paper No. 2*, Islamic Research and Training Institute, Islamic Development Bank. Retrieved July 6, 2011 from http://www.imad.in/mf-obaidullah1.pdf

Peprah, C. (2016). *Challenges SMEs face in acquiring loans from banks: A comparative study between Finland and Ghana*. (Unpublished doctoral dissertation). Centria University of Applied Sciences.

Saad, N. (2012). Microfinance and prospect for Islamic microfinance products: The case of Amanah Ikhtiar Malaysia. *Advances in Asian Social Science*, 1(1).

Saeed, A. (2004). Islamic banking and finance: In search of a pragmatic model. In V. Hooker, & A. Saikal (Eds.), *Islamic perspectives on the new millenium*. Singapore: ISEAS. doi:10.1355/9789812305367-009

Segrado, C. (2005). Case study: Islamic microfinance and socially responsible investment. *MEDA Project*, University of Torino MED. Retrieved July 2, 2012 from http://www.gdrc.org/icm/islamic- microfinance.pdf

Seibel, H. D. (2005). Islamic microfinance in Indonesia. Division Economic Development and Employment Sector Project Financial Systems Development. Retrieved July 6, 2011 from http://www.gtz.de/de/dokumente/en- islamic-mf-indonesia.pdf.pdf

Sen, A. (1981). *Poverty and famines: An essay on entitlement and deprivation.* Oxford, UK: Clarendon Press.

Teo, S., & Cheong, S. (1994). Difficulties faced by SMEs in obtaining financing from financial institutions. *Journal of Enterprising Culture*, *2*(4), 955–968. doi:10.1142/S0218495894000355

Van de Ven, A. H. (1993). The development of an infrastructure for entrepreneurship. *Journal of Business Venturing*, *8*(3), 211–230. doi:10.1016/0883-9026(93)90028-4

Wilkinson, K. P. (1991). *The rural community in America.* New York: Greenwood Press.

## ADDITIONAL READING

Flora, C. B., Flora, G. P., Green, G. P., & Schmidt, F. E. (1991). Rural economic development through local self-development strategies. *Agriculture and Human Values*, *8*(3), 19–24. doi:10.1007/BF01591839

Lyons, T. S. (2015). Entrepreneurship and community development: What matters and why? *Community Development (Columbus, Ohio)*, *46*(5), 456–460. doi:10.1080/15575330.2015.1085194

Saad, N., & Abdul Razak, D. (2013). Towards an application of musharakah mutanaqisah principle in Islamic microfinance. *International Journal of Business and Society*, *14*(2), 221–234.

Schell, D. W., & Davig, W. (1981). The community infrastructure of entrepreneurship: A socio-political analysis. In K. H. Vesper (Ed.), *Frontiers of entrepreneurship research.* Wellesley, MA: Babson College.

Summers, G. F. (1986). Rural community development. *Annual Review of Sociology*, *12*(1), 347–371. doi:10.1146/annurev.so.12.080186.002023

Wall, M., & Luther, V. (2003). Nurturing entrepreneurship in rural communities. Lincoln, NE: Heartland Center for Leadership development.

Walzer, N. (2004). Introduction: Entrepreneurship in community development. *Journal of the Community Development*, *35*(1), 1–4. doi:10.1080/15575330409490118

## KEY TERMS AND DEFINITIONS

**Al-Qard al-Hasan:** A loan contract between a debtor and creditor. Debtor only pays back the principal amount which is borrowed. The debtor can pay more than the amount borrowed so long that it is not stated in the contract.

**Centre for Islamic Economics:** A network collaborator which links research, training and consultancy activities of the Kulliyyah of Economics and Management Sciences (KENMS), IIUM to the wider community in the areas of Islamic economics, management, accounting and finance. The CIE conducts training and consultancy programmes for both academics and industry players in Malaysia and regionally/ globally.

**CIMB Islamic Bank:** A global Islamic banking and finance services franchise of CIMB Group. The Bank offers innovative and comprehensive *Shariah*-compliant financial products in investment banking, consumer banking, asset management, private banking, and wealth management. Headquartererd in Kuala Lumpur, Malaysia and is the fifth largest banking group in ASEAN with over 39,000 staff.

**Gombak:** Administrative district located in the state of Selangor, Malaysia. It was created on February 1, 1974. The International Islamic University Malaysia (IIUM) is located in Gombak district.

**Kulliyyah of Economics and Management Sciences:** One of the first two faculties established when the International Islamic University Malaysia was established in 1983. There are four academic departments within the Kulliyyah: Department of Economics, Department of Business Administration, Department of Accounting, and Department of Finance. The Kulliyyah's vision is to be a leading faculty of international excellence in teaching, research and consulting services integrating conventional economics, accounting, business and finance with values and morality based on revealed sources of knowledge.

**Mudharabah:** A widely known profit sharing contract in Islam in which one party (the Rab al Maal) provides funds and the other (the managing trustee, the Mudarib) party provides management expertise. Profits are shared between the Rab al Maal and the Mudarib in a proportion agreed in advance. Losses, if any, are the liability of the former, and the latter loses his share in the expected profits. If, however, the loss is due to the negligence, fraud, or a breach of trust on the part of the Mudarib in handling the funds, he/she is totally responsible for the losses. Funds are to be used for *Shariah*-compliant activities.

**Murabahah: A**n Islamic financing structure in which the seller provides the cost and profit margin for the purchase of an asset. Murabaha is not an interest-bearing loan but is an acceptable form of either cash or credit sale under Islamic law. In the case of credit sale, the buyer does not become the owner of the asset until the loan is fully paid.

**Musharakah Munataniqah:** Musharakah Mutanaqisah is a contract of partnership between two parties, where initially the two parties jointly purchase an asset, then, one partner gradually buys over the whole shares of the property. The buying and selling agreement must be independent of the partnership contract. It is not permitted that one contract is combined with another contract as a condition for concluding the other.

**Nebraska:** A midwestern state in the United States. Lincoln is the capital city and a lively university town.

*Shariah*-**Compliant:** An act or activity that conforms with the requirements of the *Shariah*, or Islamic law. The term is frequently used in the Islamic banking and finance industry as a synonym for "Islamic"—for example, *Shariah*-compliant financing or *Shariah*-compliant product.

# Chapter 5
# Halal Industry in ASEAN:
## Issues and Challenges

**Moha Asri Abdullah**
https://orcid.org/0000-0002-5178-2300
*International Islamic University Malaysia, Malaysia*

**Md Siddique E Azam**
*International Islamic University Malaysia, Malaysia*

## ABSTRACT

*Amongst three Muslim majority countries (Indonesia, Malaysia, and Brunei) of ASEAN, Malaysia leads the halal industry globally and considered to be the global halal hub. Simultaneously, the market is growing tremendously in other member countries as well. It has been realized that a number of driving forces are responsible for boosting the expansion of Halal industry globally as well as in ASEAN. While there are a number of factors accelerating the growth of the Halal industry, there are many limitations and challenges that are hindering the market expansion. Therefore, this chapter introduces the overview of Halal industry globally as well as in ASEAN counties. The chapter explores the opportunities of the Halal industry for ASEAN counties followed by identifying the issues and challenges confronted by industry players. Finally, it concludes by providing some recommendations in the ASEAN context based on the current global situation and findings of the Halal industry. The chapter adopts methodology of analyzing secondary data.*

DOI: 10.4018/978-1-7998-2257-8.ch005

## INTRODUCTION

ASEAN is an association of free trade agreement amongst ten South-East Asian countries where the Halal industry has potential opportunities because of the integration of non-tariff protection in international trade. The halal market is no more limited to the boundary of the food sector. While spreading its territory to other sectors it is being encountered by a number of issues and challenges also. Researchers have already addressed some of these issues and challenges in their studies and drawn the attention of industry players and policymakers. The global halal industry as a whole is estimated to worth around USD2.3 trillion (excluding Islamic finance) a year (Global halal market - Statistics & Facts, (Shahbandeh, 2019)). The integration of ethical values along with religious values opens up the boundary of the halal industry from 2.8 billion Muslim consumers to non-Muslim consumer as well around the world. For example, Brazil, Australia, and Singapore are in the list of top ten countries with highest GIEI (Global Islamic Economy Indicator) score in the halal food market in 2017-2018, although they are non-Muslim countries (Thomson Reuters and Dinar Standard, 2017). In the halal food industry, the largest market is meat and poultry which is, surprisingly, led by non-Muslim countries. New Zealand and Australia are leading worldwide in exporting halal meat. Brazil and Argentina, at the same time, are the biggest poultry producer (Nor Ai'han Mujar, 2015). The current Muslim population is 2.18 billion which is 28.26% of the total population is increasing at 1.84% a year ("Muslim Population in the World," n.d.). As the consumer size is increasing, the market size of the halal industry is also increasing at an annual rate of 20% with a value of US$560 billion a year (Pacific, 2010). Such growth is also noticeable in ASEAN counties like Malaysia, Indonesia, Thailand, Brunei and so on. Moreover, the GDP in terms of purchasing power of ASEAN has also increased significantly since 1990. All these driving forces like the Muslim population seize, GDP (PPT), emerging industry players and market, and free trade agreement are the indicators of Halal industry growth globally as well as in ASEAN. However, to utilize all the driving forces effectively and efficiently, issues and challenges faced by the halal industry should also be identified and addressed by policymakers, researchers, academics, governments, and respective authorities in ASEAN.

Thus, this chapter starts with an overview of the current situation and prospects of the global halal industry followed by the Halal market in some counties of ASEAN. It continues by identifying the driving forces that determine the rapid growth of the global halal market in ASEAN. As the main objective of this chapter, it investigates issues and challenges in ASEAN halal market regarding the identified driving forces. Finally, the chapter draws the conclusion by providing recommendations based on the findings.

Government and policymakers can use the results to develop policies and programs improving halal markets in respective countries. The methodology applied was reviewing the literature and secondary data from available resources through library search that comprised of online and offline materials like articles in journals, newspaper, books and thesis and data from different statistical websites and research papers. Selection of the literature was made by looking into the relevancy of the objectives of this chapter. Statistical websites and literature were cited based on the availability of the most recent data.

## GLOBAL HALAL INDUSTRY

The term 'halal' comes from the Arabic word namely *halla, yahillu, hillan, wahalalan* which means allowed or permissible by the Shariah law. According to Sharia'h law, every Muslim must ensure whatever they consume comes from a halal source. This confirmation shouldn't be limited to only ingredients but also the whole process of production and services (Zakaria, 2008). The study by Malboobi and Malboobi 2012 defines halal as lawful, beneficial, and not a serious threat or harm to human. The definition given by Jabatan Kemajuan Islam Malaysia (JAKIM), in Trade Description Order 2011, covers products and services encompassing all the business operations like packaging, marketing, manufacturing, logistic, supply, maintain premises, slaughtering and so on (JAKIM, 2015).

*Figure 1. Muslim population globally in 2018 (in million)*
*Source: www.muslimpopulation.com*

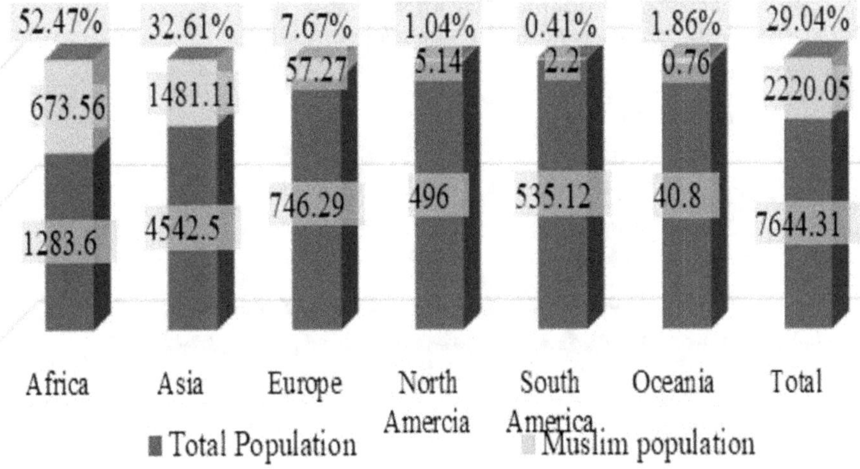

Realizing the significance of halal and its impact on the global economy, FAO (Food and Agriculture Organization) of United Nations has also prepared guidelines for using the term 'halal' to be adopted by its member countries (Ager, 2015).

The global Muslim population was 1.8 billion in 2015 comprising 24% of the total population (LIPKA, 2017). Stating Islam as the fastest-growing religion the report also projected the Muslim population of India to surplus the largest Muslim population of Indonesia by 2050. Surprisingly, according to www.muslimpopulation.com, it has already surpassed in 2018. As of 2018 global Muslim population is 2.2 billion which is 29.04% of the total world population (Figure 1). As the consumers around the world are growing and becoming aware of the concept 'halal' which is not anymore confined to food only, halal industry has been identified as the fastest-growing market in the global economy. The industry is growing at 20 percent per year estimating a value of US$560 billion (Elasrag, 2016). As of 2017, the total estimated value of the global halal market was US$4.54 trillion and expected to reach US$9.71 trillion by 2025 (Thomson Reuters and DinarStandard, 2018). This growth and spread of the industry is no more limited to only 2.18 billion Muslims, rather it is also the market for non-Muslims. Besides Malaysia, other countries like China, Thailand, Indonesia, Singapore, Korea, Philippine, and Australia have already tapped on the market. Many non-Muslim majority countries have also realized the potential of the halal industry. In fact, some countries like Brazil, Australia, New Zealand, Italy, India, Germany are occupying the top ten positions in GIE (Global Islamic Economy) score in different halal sectors.

According to the study by Elasrag (2016), the Halal Industry has extended not only its product sectors like pharmaceuticals, health products, toiletries, and cosmetics, but also in-service sectors like marketing, supply chain, logistic, packaging,

*Figure 2. Market share of Halal industry worldwide*
*(**Source:** https://www.statista.com/topics/4428/global-halal-market/)*

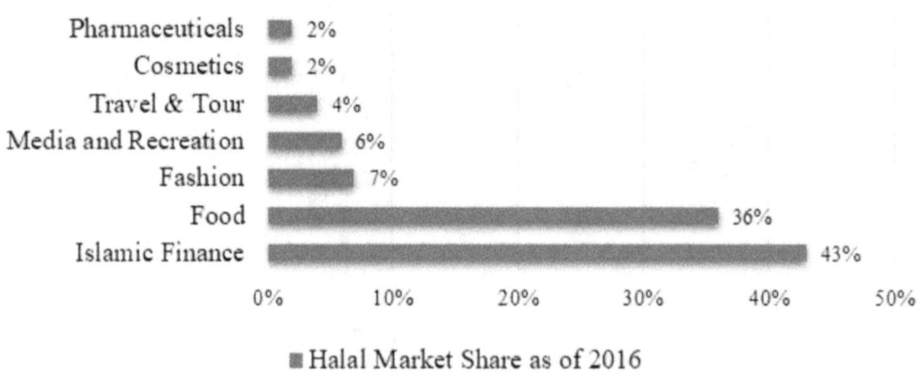

*Table 1. Potential growth sector in Halal industry*

| Clusters | Potential Value for the Halal Market (USD) (Based on 5% of Global Halal Trade) |
|---|---|
| **Cosmetic / Personal Care** | 177 Billion |
| **Agriculture** | 41.5 Billion |
| **Pharmaceutical** | 30.3 Billion |
| **Logistic** | 25.0 Billion |
| **Islamic Finance** | 0.17 Billion |
| **Travel Industry** | 0.13 Billion |
| **Total Value for Halal New Growth Clusters** | **274.1 Billion** |

Source: Halal Industry Development Corporation

manufacturing, branding, and financing. the study also implies that lifestyle offerings like travel & tourism, hospitality management, and the fashion industry are now also a major sector of extended halal industry.

A study by Dar et. al. (2013) shows that the Muslim population has a growth rate of 3 percent per annum and constitute 23 percent of the world's population. Although some of the Muslim countries have higher purchasing power and a growing economy, the rest of the countries, on the other hand, have low per-capita income. The Third Industrial Master Plan; 2016-2020 of Malaysia indicates the aim of Malaysia to become the world's leading halal hub. In this regard, the halal industry is projected to contribute about 5.8% to the GDP of Malaysia as well as a significant contribution to the ASEAN economy. The global market is now following Malaysia and competing to be a global hub in the halal industry.

## HALAL INDUSTRY IN ASEAN

China, Malaysia, Indonesia, South Korea, Taiwan, Japan, Hong Kong and 10-member countries of ASEAN comprise the East Asia and ASEAN halal market. ASEAN nations are one of the world's driving providers and furthermore merchants of halal confirmed items globally. In spite of the fact that these nations compete in the global front, there has been significant exchanging halal items among them. Indonesia in excess of 200 million Muslims (Table 9.5); Malaysia – *Halal* Hub market in the world; Brunei – higher purchasing power; Singapore – the strong purchasing power of Muslim consumers and staging of events on halal market and industry. China is a huge and an untapped market, but speedily growing market; recently developing *halal* park and *halal* supply chain. ASEAN counties have greater prospects to tap the potential halal markets in other East Asian countries like China, South Korea, Taiwan. The general overview of the Halal industry in some of the ASEAN counties are as follows-

## Malaysia

Malaysia has been leading the Global Islamic Economy Indicator score for the last five years in a row and 38 points ahead of UAE in the year 2018-2019. Malaysia ranks number one in Islamic finance and number two in halal food, halal travel, and halal pharmaceutical & cosmetics market which indicates a strong Islamic economy in Malaysia (Figure 3). Malaysia emphasizes creating awareness on halal lifestyles which made Malaysia resume its position from sixth to number one and leading in other sectors as well. Government of Malaysia has taken several approaches to make Malaysia as the global halal hub by 2020 with a contribution of 5.8% to the GDP (Mustapa Mohamed, 2018).

In addition, the following eleven strategic thrusts have been set by the Halal Research Council for the progress and advertisement of Malaysia as the global *halal* hub (MiTi, 2012):

1. increasing the awareness of Malaysia as the center for *halal* products and services;
2. dealing with the rising rivalry from other economies in the region;
3. subsidizing external investments to access crude materials and improve intensity;
4. enhancing R&D in item and process improvements and utilizing upon most recent innovative advancements to grow the product range;
5. developing halal-compliant services;
6. utilizing and leveraging upon Malaysian Halal Standard to distinguish Malaysia's *halal* items;
7. guaranteeing item quality and sustenance wellbeing;
8. undertaking foundational advancement of *halal* parks;
9. harmonizing the *halal* accreditation process;
10. enhancing the coordination among agencies engaged with the improvement and advancement of the business; and
11. strengthening the institutional limit of organizations engaged in the advancement and promotion of *halal* products and services.

The halal industry master plan 2008-2020 identified four key halal industry sectors focusing on foods, ingredients, cosmetics, and personal care, and animal husbandry. Figure 4 illustrates the four key sectors and their goals specified in the plan. The agencies and institutes other than JAKIM (Jabatan Kemajuan Islam

*Figure 3. Top 15 countries in GIE*
*Source: Thomson Reuters and DinarStandard, 2018*

| TOP 15 COUNTRIES | GIE Indicator Score | Halal Food | Islamic Finance | Halal Travel | Modest Fashion | Halal Media and Recreation | Halal Pharmaceuticals and Cosmetics |
|---|---|---|---|---|---|---|---|
| **Malaysia** | 127 | 81 | 173 | 92 | 33 | 51 | 96 |
| **UAE** | 89 | 91 | 83 | 97 | 106 | 109 | 104 |
| **Bahrain** | 65 | 45 | 86 | 20 | 19 | 44 | 45 |
| **Saudi Arabia** | 54 | 48 | 64 | 34 | 16 | 33 | 47 |
| **Oman** | 51 | 62 | 52 | 28 | 25 | 28 | 43 |
| **Jordan** | 49 | 60 | 49 | 35 | 23 | 25 | 58 |
| **Qatar** | 49 | 49 | 55 | 27 | 12 | 63 | 36 |
| **Pakistan** | 49 | 58 | 53 | 15 | 22 | 9 | 58 |
| **Kuwait** | 46 | 42 | 57 | 12 | 12 | 30 | 34 |
| **Indonesia** | 45 | 48 | 46 | 65 | 34 | 16 | 44 |
| **Brunei** | 45 | 58 | 43 | 26 | 12 | 37 | 57 |
| **Sudan** | 37 | 55 | 34 | 29 | 8 | 11 | 21 |
| **Iran** | 34 | 36 | 37 | 19 | 11 | 22 | 37 |
| **Bangladesh** | 32 | 35 | 33 | 19 | 28 | 7 | 34 |
| **Turkey** | 31 | 44 | 21 | 71 | 32 | 25 | 41 |

*Figure 4. The 4 key Halal industry sectors and their goals in the Halal industry master plan*
*Source: Adapted from Halal Industry Development Corporation Malaysia (2015)*

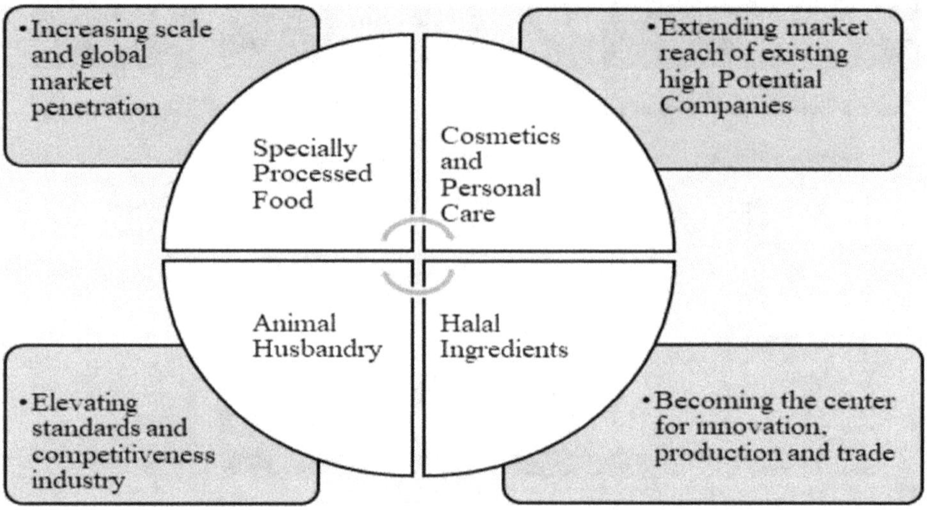


Malaysia), that are engaged in the development and promotion of halal industries in Malaysia are listed here-

1. Ministry of Domestic Trade, Cooperatives & Consumerism (MTDCC)
2. Ministry of Trade and Industry (MITI)
3. Malaysian Industrial Development Authority (MIDA)
4. Malaysia Productivity Corporation
5. Standards Malaysia
6. SME Corporation Malaysia
7. International Institute for Halal Research and Training (INHART)

Another indicator for Malaysia to be the global hub in halal industries is the hosting of 'Malaysia Halal Week' which is an annual event combining three major events namely- International Halal Showcase (MIHAS), World Halal Research (WHR) summit and World Halal Forum (WHF). The government of Malaysia has introduced several incentive plans besides other programs to motivate and promote the halal industry in Malaysia. Some of the Incentive plans are shown in figure 4.

*Figure 5. Incentives for the promotion of the Halal industry in Malaysia*
*Source: Adapted from Halal Industry Development Corporation (2015)*

| | |
|---|---|
| **Halal Park Operators** | - Income Tax Exemption (100% tax exemption for 10 years) OR; Investment Tax Allowance (100% for 5 years)<br>- Exemption on import duty & sales tax for cold room equipment |
| **Halal Industry Players** | - Income Tax Exemption on export revenue (100% for 5 years) OR; Investment Tax Allowance (100% for 10 years); Exemption from import duty on raw materials; |
| **Halal Logistic Operators** | - Income Tax Exemption (100% tax exemption for 5 years) OR; Investment Tax Allowance (100% for 5 years)<br>- Exemption on import duty & sales tax for cold room equipment |

## Indonesia

Indonesia has the potential of becoming one of the major markets and producer in the halal industry with its' largest Muslim population in the world. Based on GIE score by Thompson Reuters' report 2017, Indonesia is in 11th position globally with securing the 4th and 8th position in Halal travel and Halal Pharmaceuticals & Cosmetics respectively (Figure 3). The production of halal products in Indonesia is mainly for domestic consumption. The highest authority of Islamic affairs in Indonesia which is the Indonesian Ulama Council (MUI) issues the halal certificate. According to the governmental regulations of Indonesia, it is required by all manufacturer or importer to declare their consumable products as halal while labeling and advertising.

As of 2017 report, 127,286 products have been certified by the MUI which proves the booming halal market in Indonesia (Riza Roidila Mufti, 2018). Indonesia is also the largest importer of halal F&B products globally. Indonesia's Halal tourism contributes significantly in ASEAN economy through a number of strategies and initiatives. The recent launch of global halal travel alliance by Indonesia amongst ASEAN counties is a great initiative in developing the flow of intra-ASEAN tourism. Issues and challenges for Indonesia to overcome include- lack of comprehensive halal regulation, lack of efficient and skillful monitoring authority to monitor halal practices, and lack of awareness among producers about the need of halal certification (Pacific, 2010).

*Figure 6. Indonesia Halal F&B market ($Billion)*
*Source: https://www.grandviewresearch.com/industry-analysis/halal-food-market*

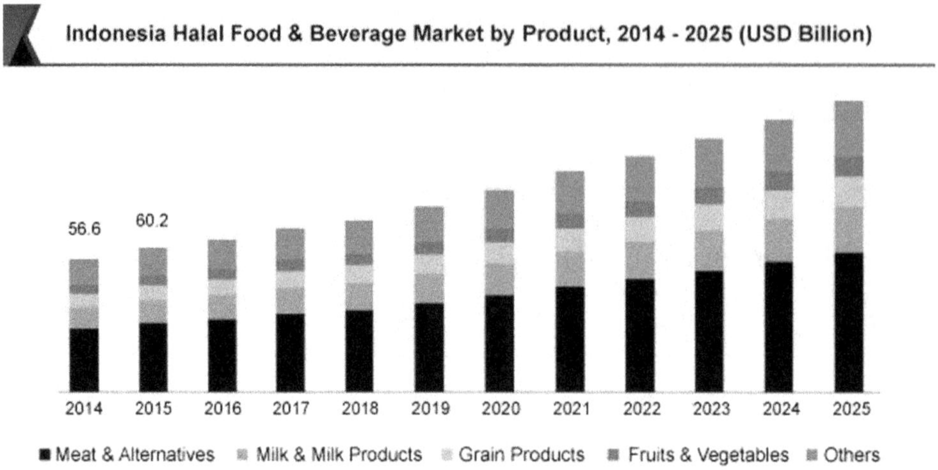


## Thailand

To achieve the export strategy "Kitchen of the world" undertaken by the government of Thailand, the halal market has got significant importance in Thailand. In fact, it is the fifth largest exporter in halal food with a significant share in the global halal food market. The Halal Standard Institute was established in 2003. The central Islamic committee of Thailand developed standard THS24000:2552 which covers guidelines for Halal products (Johan, 2018). Thailand also established Halal Science center. Such initiatives by the government of Thailand, yet after being a non-Muslim major country, shows its' commitment to recognizing Thailand as a global halal hub. Some other strategies that have been taken by Thailand are- strengthening the country's halal industry particularly in meeting world standards, promoting the competitiveness of entrepreneurs, increasing capability in halal certification and formulating standards, and upgrading research and development (Pacific, 2010).

The halal industry in Thailand is focused on Halal F&B market which is mainly based on the tourists. Therefore, Muslim friendly tourism (tourism services that serve halal restaurants, Muslim friendly accommodations, tour guide, halal F&B and other needs by Muslim tourists) is another potential area for Thailand to tap into. According to Crescentrating, 2018 Thailand was ranked 2$^{nd}$ as the most Muslim friendly destination after Singapore. However, the rank went down from 5$^{th}$ in 2017 to 6$^{th}$ position in 2018 in Halal travel sector in terms of GIE score (Thomson Reuters and DinarStandard, 2018). Additionally, as of 2015, there were 581 halal restaurants in Thailand reported by The Tourism Authority of Thailand (Wannasupchue, Othman, Abidin, Ishak, & Mohamad, 2019).

## Brunei

Brunei is one of the important economies amongst ASEAN counties as it is the 5th largest oil producer in South East Asia, 9th largest exporter of liquified natural gas globally, and 2nd highest GDP (PPP) amongst ASEAN counties (Khalid, Haji Masr, Muhammad, & Pang, 2018). Simultaneously, in the halal industry, figure 2 shows that Brunei has been ranked 11th globally based on GIE score in 2018 securing its 7th and 10th position in Halal food and Halal media & recreation sector (Thomson Reuters and DinarStandard, 2018). It has the potential to achieve the economic diversification in Brunei which is the main objective of its national development plan (Oh, bin Pg Hamir, & Mohd Shah, 2018). Realizing such significance Brunei became the first East Asian country to adopt *Shariah Law* in April 2014. Moreover, through ASEAN Brunei has concluded Free Trade Agreement (FTA) with Australia, New Zealand, Japan, China, India, and South Korea. Consequently, Indonesia has launched an Islamic educational game app for children in Brunei; Japan's Mitsubishi company is trying to get halal certification in Brunei for manufacturing and selling its MC Biotech products; Halal Science and Metrology Centre in Brunei with Osaka University Japan was established; A joint venture, Simpor Pharma, has been developed between Canadian pharmaceutical company and investors in Brunei; Golden Corporation, a Taiwan Foreign Direct Investment (FDI), was established in 2010 for seafood processing, fishing, and aquafarming (Thomson Reuters and DinarStandard, 2018).

The halal certification law in Brunei is based on Halal Certificate and Halal Label Order, 2005 and Brunei Darussalam Standard for Halal food PBD 24:2007. The responsible bodies for halal certification are Ministry of Religious Affairs, Department of Syariah Affairs, and Halal Food Control Division which are also supported by the Ministry of Energy and Industry. Additionally, Brunei also has its official guidelines for halal certification which explains about halal certification, auditing, and application procedure for the applicants (Smart Shield International Sdn Bhd, 2016).

## Singapore

Singapore is a non-Muslim majority nation and at the same time the only developed country in ASEAN. Halal industry has gained no less importance in Singapore than other Muslim countries. Singapore has been recognized as one of the global halal hubs and halal food has been significantly important for a few facts. Firstly, tourism and business location in Singapore. Secondly, the food safety law by the government which is maintained strictly, and finally the well-recognized halal standard. Yet, Singapore is not in the list of top 15 GIE scored countries in the report by Thomson

*Figure 7. Brunei Halal*
*Source: Smart Shield International Sdn Bhd, 2016*

Tablets and toiletries of Simpor Pharma

*Figure 8. Halal certification by MUIS 2010-2017*
*Source: Ira Sugita, 2017 and MUIS, 2018*

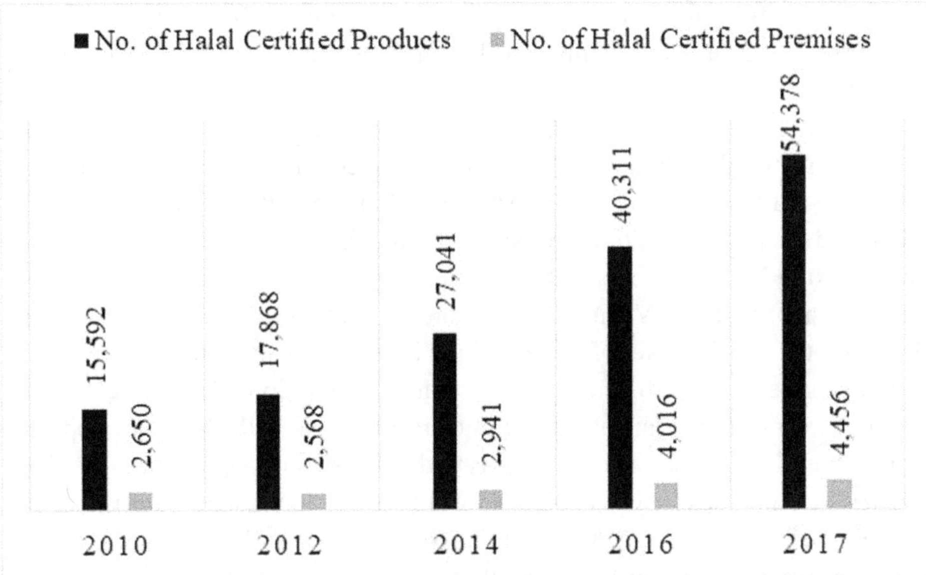


Reuters and DinarStandard, 2018. However, it has secured 3rd position in the field of Modest fashion, and halal pharmaceuticals and cosmetics, and 2nd ranking in Halal media and recreation sector of Halal industry (Figure-3). Simultaneously, in 2015 it has exported $79 million meat and livestock to OIC member countries.

The Islamic Religious Council of Singapore (MUIS) is the responsible organization of halal certification and also have the authority of Muslim affairs in Singapore. MUIS also have the ISO accreditation which has made its halal certification logo more assured and recognized in middle east countries. The introduction of Muis e-halal system 3.0 (MeS 3.0) enabled the halal certification faster and user-friendly in Singapore. With an annual growth of 10 percent in halal certification, MUIS has certified more than 4,400 premises and 54,378 types of products made in Singapore which is five times more than past decades (MUIS, 2018). The enforcement team in monitoring and taking actions on the use of the halal mark is very strong in Singapore. The annual report 2017 states that MUIS has detected 103 halal related violations from 2015 to 2017 and took actions that included warning, suspension of certificate, revoking certificate permanently or for 3 to 6 months. Additionally, the report also states to have an operating income of $6.5 million in 2017 which was only from Halal certification.

## Other ASEAN Counties

The halal industry is influentially spreading in other ASEAN counties also. **Philippine**, for example, is aiming to become the leaders of halal products for which it is developing a 100-hectare processing facility named, Asia Halal Centre. Additionally, to gain a significant share of the halal export opportunity, Halal development board of Philippine has accepted the conditions of Halal Export Act 2016. Similarly, the bilateral trade between **Vietnam** and UAE is valued at $9 billion and the recent visit of Al-Maya group, that imports jasmine rice and dairy products from Vietnam companies, to Vietnam, shows a greater prospect of halal industry opportunity in Vietnam (Thomson Reuters and DinarStandard, 2018). Moreover, the Halal market of **Cambodia** is based on its Halal tourism sector. In 2016 it experienced a 24.5 percent increase in tourists from middle east countries. The same year the government entered into an agreement with Halal Development Corporation (HDC) Malaysia to investigate the investment opportunities of Halal industry in Cambodia. It has been observed that Muslim friendly tourism is the common business sector amongst ASEAN that has opened the halal market niche in these counties. According to CrescentRating, 2018 while Malaysia and Indonesia were ranked number one tourist's destination country, **Laos** was also ranked (126th) as one of the total 130 Muslim friendly tourist destination countries.

## OPPORTUNITIES AND DRIVING FORCES OF HALAL MARKET IN ASEAN

There are certain factors that drive the rapid growth of the halal industry globally as well as in ASEAN. These factors may include the rapid growth of Muslim population size, increase in purchasing power and GDP growth, emerging halal industry players, and Muslim lifestyle offerings. These driving forces, however, also indicate the underlying opportunities of the halal industry. The following section identifies the mentioned factors as driving forces and shows the opportunities of the global halal industry.

## Growing Muslim Population

The rapid growth of the Muslim population around the world is the factor that driving the expansion of the global halal market most. About 43.5% of the ASEAN population is Muslim which also represents 12.7% of the global Muslim population (Table 2).

Millennials, also known as Generation Y, a driving factor in the growth of the economy as well as the global halal industry. It is they who address the needs of

*Table 2. Muslim population in ASEAN countries and world population, 2018.*

| No. | Country | Total Population (in million) | Muslim Percentage (%) | Muslim Population in 2018 (in million) |
|---|---|---|---|---|
| 1. | Indonesia | 265.2 | 88 | 233.38 |
| 2. | Malaysia | 32.5 | 61.3 | 19.92 |
| 3. | Philippine | 107 | 10 | 10.70 |
| 4. | Myanmar | 53.9 | 15 | 8.09 |
| 5. | Thailand | 66.2 | 10 | 6.62 |
| 6. | Cambodia | 16 | 7 | 1.11 |
| 7. | Vietnam | 94.7 | 1 | 0.95 |
| 8. | Singapore | 5.7 | 16 | 0.91 |
| 9. | Brunei | 0.4 | 67 | 0.27 |
| 10. | Laos | 7 | 1 | 0.07 |
| Total | | 648.60 | 43.48% | 282.02 |
| **Global Statistics** | | | | |
| Globally Total | | 7644.31 | 29.04%<br>ASEAN= 12.7% | 2220.05 |

Source: www.muslimpopulation.com

Muslim millennials and set the brands by bringing changes across the retail economy. They are the driving force in terms of entrepreneurship, innovation, technology-savvy, and potential strength. By 2027, Millennials are set to 2.8 billion of the world's population as core consumer force. At the same time, Generation Y amongst the OIC countries will be reaching to 0.7 billion with an increasing average age 28.2 which is less than the age of the global young population (Thomson Reuters and DinarStandard, 2017). As the fastest growing religion in terms of population, Islam is projected to be the most popular religion by 2070, which is another significant sign of halal industry growth (LIPKA, 2017).

## GDP Growth in ASEAN

Gross Domestic Product by purchasing power parity or GDP (PPP) is another driving force of global halal industry growth and it is one of the economic tools to measure the potential strength of an economy. The definition of GDP (PPP) given by world bank is *"the number of units of a country's currency required to buy the same amount of goods and services in the domestic market"* compared to the United States market; based on the US dollar.

*Figure 9. GDP of the ASEAN countries from 2008 to 2018 (in billion US$)*
*Source: https://www.statista.com/statistics/796245/gdp-of-the-asean-countries/*

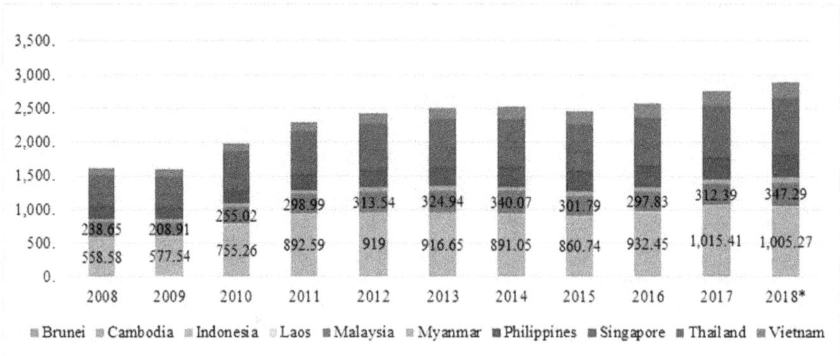


*Table 3. ASEAN GDP per-capita PPP (USD)*

| ASEAN Counties | GDP PPP (in US$) from 1990 to 2017 | | | |
|---|---|---|---|---|
| | 1990 | 2000 | 2010 | 2017 |
| Cambodia | - | 1384 | 2522 | 3652 |
| Myanmar | 743 | 1306 | 3721 | 5612 |
| Vietnam | 1453 | 2562 | 4408 | 6172 |
| Laos | 1708 | 2485 | 4218 | 6397 |
| Philippine | 4010 | 4224 | 5596 | 7599 |
| Indonesia | 4625 | 5805 | 8433 | 11189 |
| Thailand | 6650 | 9189 | 13486 | 16279 |
| Malaysia | 10,552 | 16310 | 21107 | 26824 |
| Brunei | 84672 | 82049 | 80552 | 71809 |
| Singapore | 34345 | 51706 | 72115 | 85535 |

*Source*: https://data.worldbank.org

*Figure 10. ASEAN average GDP per-capita (PPP) growth from 1990 to 2017*
*Source: https://data.worldbank.org*

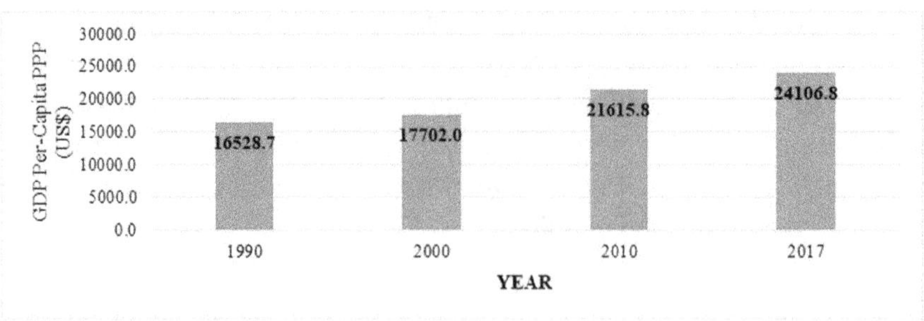

Figure 9, 10 and Table 3 shows an increasing trend in both GDP and GDP (PPP) amongst ASEAN economy during the last decade. It also shows that ASEAN average GDP (PPP) growth increased by 45.5% from 1990 to 2017. Global GDP, in PPP terms, is set to reach $168 trillion with a growth rate of 5.8 percent between 2016 and 2022. The 57 Muslim majorities of OIC countries are set to grow by 6.2 percent between 2016 and 2022 (Thomson Reuters Global Islamic Economy Report 2017/2018). The report also indicates China as the game-changing player in the Islamic economy trade. The "One Belt One Trade" initiative of China involves 28 OIC countries and stands to benefit from $3 trillion in infrastructure-related investments. This will have a positive impact on ASEAN economy as well.

## The Emergence of Halal Markets and Industry Players

In many countries around the world, the industry players have a lot of campaign that creates indirect awareness about halal products and services that results in Halal market force. Consumers around the world are becoming aware of the importance of Halal, not only in terms of food consumption, but also the ethical values integrated to it, e.g. Muslim friendly tourism (MFT), modest fashion, logistic, pharmaceuticals, and many others. The trillion-dollar business in the halal industry is the result of this emerging consumer need.

It is evident that Muslim majority countries like Malaysia, Indonesia, Saudi Arabia, and Pakistan and other non-Muslim countries are also leading in the GIE

*Table 4. Key Halal Industry Players in ASEAN*

| ASEAN Counties | Key Industry Players |
|---|---|
| Malaysia | Rex Industry food processor, QSR Malaysia, Aidijuma Colors Group in retail sector, Duck Group in Cosmetics, Dagang Halal and Marrybrown distribution channel and retailer, Waqf Airlines, KPJ Healthcare Berhad in halal travel; Naelofer, Nashata, and Alya Sarah in Modest Fashion sector; Islamic Tunes in Halal Media and recreation sector; CCM Chemicals Sdn. Bhd., Halalgel, and AJ Pharma (Vaccines) in Halal Pharmaceuticals, PrettySuci, and Aisa in Halal Cosmetics. |
| Indonesia | Unilever Indonesia in halal cosmetics, Kalbe Farma in Halal Pharmaceuticals; Moshaict, Hijup, Saqina, Itang Yunasz, Dian Pelangi, Elzatta, and Dian Pelangi in Modest Fashion; Sofyan Hotels and indonesiahalal.com in Halal travel industry; |
| Singapore | Halal Supermarket MyOutlets, HealthFX with blockchain technology focused on pharmaceuticals, Finterra ledger technology of Singapore has enhanced the Islamic charitable activity creating a smart contract in specific waqf projects. |
| Thailand | In Halal Tourism Al Meroz Hotel, Macia Condor, Anantara Group's and five-star resort at Oman's mountain |
| Brunei | Ghanim International Corporation, Western Foods & Packaging Sdn. Bhd., and Sahtain Sdn. Bhd. in Halal Food sector. |

Source: Thomson Reuters and DinarStandard, 2017, Thomson Reuters and DinarStandard, 2018

*Figure 11. Merchandise trade by ASEAN economies 2007-2017 ($Billion)*
*Source: World Trade Statistical Review 2018*

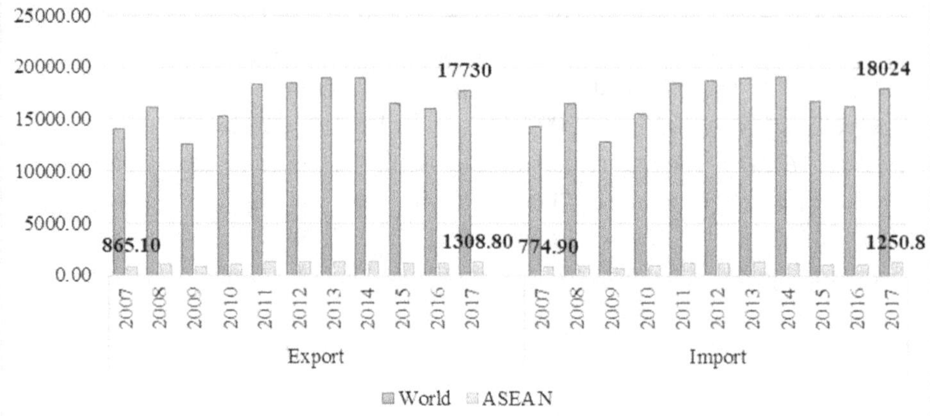


indicator score. However, the emerging markets in other countries like Thailand, Philippine, China, and Singapore show the potential growth in the halal industry. The emerging markets of all these countries view halal as a means to stimulate the economy through exports, tourism, value-add, trade, research, certification expertise, training programs, a halal science symposium, raw material supplier and some other aspects (imarat Consultants, n.d.). Table 4 shows some examples of emerging market and halal industry players in ASEAN.

Countries around the world are emerging as market players competing each other in the halal industry which mad the ASEAN counties to maintain their merchandise trade consistent in terms of both export and import (Figure 11).

## Muslim Lifestyle Offerings and Halal Ecosystem

As the Muslim population is increasingly growing worldwide, halal industry has extended its offerings into lifestyle fields that include halal dining (ensuring halal food), Muslim friendly tourism and hospitality services, halal pharmaceuticals and cosmetics as well as the fashion industry and entertainment. Figure 12 shows the Muslim spending in different lifestyle sectors in 2016 and also the projection in 2022. There are significant opportunities for investment and creation of global halal foods as the sector is growing at nearly double that of global growth. The demand of food is expected to increase by more than 70% by 2050 which indicates a strong demand of halal food in future (Personal, Archive, Puah, Voon, & Entebang, 2009). In Halal travel industry, Malaysia is leading globally amongst ASEAN counties including Indonesia and Thailand in fourth and fifth place respectively. Additionally,

*Figure 12. Global Muslim spend on Halal life-style sectors ($ Billion)*
*Source: Thomson Reuters Global Islamic Economy Report 2017/2018*

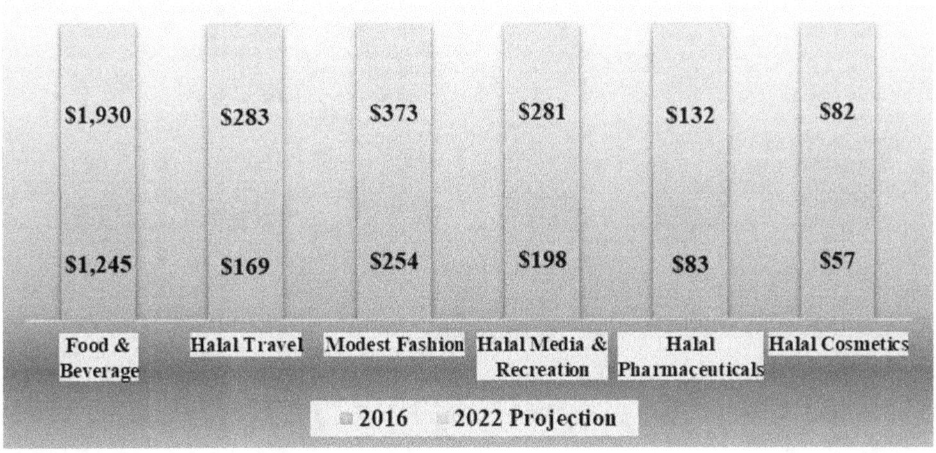


the Global Halal Travel Alliance among ASEAN launched by Indonesia, and the Indonesia-Malaysia-Thailand Growth Triangle (IMT-GT) project are initiatives to increase the intra-ASEAN tourism flow and accelerate the growth of this industry.

There are a huge demand and supply gap in Halal cosmetics and personal care sector globally, which is a great opportunity for the halal industry to tap into. Currently, the supply of Halal cosmetics and personal care is only 18% of the total USD56 billion demand worldwide. Exporters globally are supplying only USD10 billion leaving a huge demand-supply gap estimated to be USD46 billion (HDC, Bio Malaysia & ASEAN Bioeconomy Conference, 2015).

## Halal Ecosystem

The halal industry ecosystem is the core of global as well as ASEAN halal industry growth which is comprised of various clusters and industries. The clusters and industries co-exist and supported by proper policy, legislation, halal integrity management, and industry development. As the industry is huge, each component creates potential opportunities in different aspects for ASEAN countries globally. For example, Halal hubs and parks, Halal certification, standards development, logistic and supply chain management, online B2B and many more (Figure 13).

**Halal parks** in different countries can play an important role in the ecosystem of the halal industry creating opportunities in different ways. For example, in Malaysia, there are 21 halal parks serving 18 multinational companies with the employment of 5,274. Moreover, these halal parks involve more than 110 SMEs (Small and Medium Enterprises) and the investment is RM8.07 billion (Nor Ai'han Mujar, 2015).

*Figure 13. Halal eco-system as the new source of economic growth*
*Source: Economic Planning Unit, Prime Minister's Department, Malaysia*

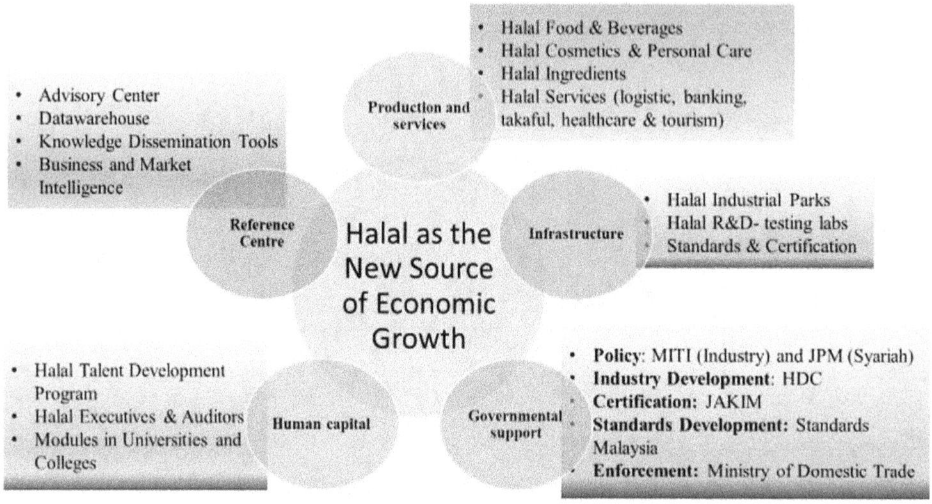


The integrity of the entire **Halal supply chain** is a very important component for the halal industry to take care of the effective control of the halal supply chain is more complex than traditional logistic operations. In Thailand Kosol Surinandha (head of Halal Logistics and Tourism at Chulaongkorn University) is leading a logistic program, Business Incubation for Halal Products (Bihap), that includes R&D into new manufacturing techniques and logistic procedures to meet Halal export requirement (Catto-Smith, n.d.).

## LIMITATIONS AND CHALLENGES IN ASEAN

While in one side, the Muslim consumers around the world represent a great opportunity for the halal industry, on the other side, it is also a great challenge to deal with the diversity of the same population. Although the religious belief of Muslims is the same around the world, they have their own culture, regional or local shades, preferences, and practices. Such diversity is also observable in ASEAN counties (Personal et al., 2009).

The growing Muslim population and the growth of the halal industry could be under threat by the non-Muslim population as well. The non-Muslim manufacturers, especially in the food and beverage industry. The unfriendly and malign act of introducing non-halal elements into foods, clothing, and other services claimed to be halal by the non-Muslim industry players poses a big challenge to the growth of the halal industry globally. It may turn into a destructive threat as this intention of an evil act by non-Muslims will decrease the halal integrity of the products and services and erode the confidence of the consumers (Personal et al., 2009).

One of the biggest challenges for the Halal industry is establishing an internationally recognized halal standard and accreditation, especially in the food sector. In ASEAN every country has different Halal logo as well as Halal standard which is not only creating confusion amongst consumers but also hindering the growth of the industry (Thomson Reuters and Dinar Standard, 2016). This challenge was also addressed by Johan, 2018 in his study and many other scholars as well.

The challenge of establishing Halal standards and accreditation is also pivotal to remove the confusion surrounding halal standards both in consumer and producer level. There's no international scheme to accredit Halal Certification Bodies (HCBs) in respective countries. Too many standards developing bodies create confusion to decide on which one will provide market access, and in many cases, multiple certificates are necessary for exporters (Personal et al., 2009). Similar challenges were mentioned at Bio Malaysia & ASEAN Bioeconomy Conference, 2015 stating a capacity and capability gap among the certification bodies and preserving halal integrity throughout the supply chain and logistics management from farm to fork.

To be specific, the challenge lies in every sector of the Halal industry like food and beverage as mentioned earlier. For example, the Halal travel market faces challenges in terms of accommodation of both Muslims and non-Muslims in same hotel, lack of investment and shariah-compliant funds, lack of common halal travel standards, dilemma in marketing, and no agreed definition of different terms used in the market e.g. Halal holiday, Muslim-friendly, and Family oriented hospitality (Personal et al. 2009, Thomson Reuters Report 2017/18).

The modest fashion, an emerging market segment in the halal industry, with plenty of opportunities is also facing challenges. The regulations imposed by certain governmental agencies against religious attires put a big challenge for the industry to reach non-Muslim countries. other challenges in this sector include lack of marketing sophistication, lack of product innovation, and the reluctance of investors to finance due to limited global success stories.

Halal media and recreation, another emerging market segment in the industry, that can experience substantial growth through multi-channel expansion, also holding risk and challenges at the same time to overcome. Unlike other sectors, getting financed and governmental support is a more promising challenge for this sector. The growth can also be hindered because of poor intellectual property (IP) rights that limit innovation as well as the sector to religious shows only. Diversification in cultural and religious-themed shows and addressing the demand of young generations also add to the challenges in this sector (Thomson Reuters Report 2017/18).

*Table 5. Global Halal industry: summary of opportunities and limitations*

| Opportunities | Limitations |
|---|---|
| **Halal Food Sector** | |
| - **Products and Market**: Halal organic and healthy, emerging exporters, halal ingredients, halal baby foods, online restaurant booking, halal food B2B and retail commerce | Lack of global OIC brands |
| - **Consumer Need Ecosystem:** influence/ social media, non-Muslim consumers, increasing retail availability, sponsorship | Fraudulent in Halal labeling, Negative media Backlash |
| - **Financing:** Halal company IPOs (Initial Public Offerings), Halal food Sukuk/debt, crowdfunding, start-up accelerators, shariah-compliant trade finance, Halal food equity investment. | Lack of OIC Brands, lack of available finance |
| - **Policies, Regulation, and Investment:** Emerging Halal accreditation, Halal food incubators, Halal parks | High-cost operations, anti-stunning legislation, limited standardization, lack of harmonized regulation |
| **Halal Travel** | |
| - **Products and services:** Iran as a travel destination, adventure travel packages for millennials, Halal foods, ecotourism, Halal beach resorts, the entrance of mainstream players in the market. | Limited private equity interest in MFT, fragmented market. |
| - **Consumer needs ecosystem:** Global Cooperation Council (GCC) countries are diversifying into tourism due to fall in oil price, positioning GCC destinations as family-friendly, increase in halal conferences | Limited awareness among OIC countries, accommodation of both Muslims and non-Muslims together, underdeveloped branding, niche market |
| - **Policies, Regulation, and Investment:** Halal certification of the hospitality business, opportunities for destination agencies | Lack of unified halal travel standards, US travel restriction |
| **Modest Fashion** | |
| - **Products and Services:** Luxury modest wear, modest sportswear, fashionwear for teens and tween | Limitation of product lines, western brands as competitor creating modest fashion lines |
| - **Consumer needs ecosystem:** Co-branding with cosmetics, hijab-wearing role model, untapped Muslim minority markets, co-marketing with halal travel, peripheral services (media, modeling agency), collaboration with mainstream retailers. | Limited modest fashion incubators or accelerators, lack of sharia'h compliant investment. |
| - **Policies, Regulations, and Investment:** Vertical integration, sports federations relaxing regulations on hijabs | Islamophobia, banning of hijabs in different countries, talent scarcity, patent/copyright issue |
| **Halal Media and Recreation** | |
| - **Products and services:** young millennials are as key growth drivers, Islamic media content like films, drama, documentaries, and talk shows based on history, Islamic culture, Islamic knowledge and so on. | Lack of well-established brands, bad press getting worse, rising Islamophobia restricts the growth beyond the Muslim world. |
| - **Operations:** Rising demand for value-based content across all media platforms, Generation Z creating new demand subsets. | Lack of financial support as most of the investors have poor understanding and confidence in the media business |
| - **Policies, Regulations, and Investment:** Halal media and recreation can act as a conduit for halal media advertising, robust convergence opportunities with Islamic education. | Inadequate IP right protection in OIC countries, creativity is hindered by political/cultural policies, content creation and skills are harmed by sectarianism |
| **Halal Pharmaceutical and Cosmetics** | |
| - Halal medical tourism, prescriptive halal medicines, vaccines, ingredients, GCC, East-Asia key development market, halal medical equipment.<br>- Certification and Standards. Dedicated free zones may result in the emergence of major trading hubs in OIC markets | Lack of awareness, lack of universal standards, lack of availability of ingredients, still seen as a market niche, possibility to be limited to Muslim consumers only. |

Source: Extracted from Thomson Reuters Global Islamic Economy Report 2017/2018

As Muslims are becoming concerned more and more about what they consume, a number of companies are offering pharmaceutical and cosmetic products that are free from animal-sourced ingredients. However, the segment is not free from challenges either. Lack of halal ingredients availability, potential investors, limited standardization, and the fear of being limited to Muslim consumers only are some of the challenges the market is to face to ensure its growth globally. (Thomson Reuters Report 2017/18).

A summary of the opportunities and limitations in the Halal industry in ASEAN has been presented in Table 5.

## CONCLUSION AND RECOMMENDATION

As the concept *Halal* is associated to '*toyyib*', meaning good, and is applicable to all activities of human life, it has been observed from the literature and data from different sources that the Halal industry is spreading in every aspect of business and has become a potential growth sector globally. According to 6$^{th}$ Halal Expo 2018, recently held in Turkey, global Halal market has a current volume of $4 trillion (including Islamic finance) and is expected to reach $7 trillion in three years. The growth of the Halal industry is driven by certain forces which are the growing Muslim population size, GDP growth of Muslim countries, emerging halal markets and players, Muslim lifestyle offerings, and Halal ecosystem. While boosting the expansion of halal industry globally, these factors also are creating opportunities in every market segments of the economy.

The halal food sector has shown a significant achievement and Muslim spend continues to increase with a 6 percent growth from 2015. The potential opportunity in halal food and beverage sector is addressed by even non OIC countries. Halal food companies could be a multi-billion dollar, publicly listed enterprises through trade finance, working capital, and capital expansion. Halal food companies can also become halal lifestyle conglomerates through developing product categories and lines, and emerging dedicated halal free zones. Notable investment by different firms worldwide like Nestle, Janan Halal Meat, Kingsley, etc. implies that Halal is becoming an area of focus for private equity firms.

In general, the industry is facing challenges in terms of standards recognized and adopted globally, research and development, innovations, alternative ingredients, and preserving Halal integrity throughout the supply chain management from farm to fork. This is supported by the report published by Bio Malaysia & ASEAN Bioeconomy Conference, 2015. The problem is being faced by the Halal industry from the very beginning is the absence of any viable international schemes to accredit Halal certification bodies (HCBs). It is the non-Muslim countries that produce a major part of the halal foods globally. To strengthen the accreditation of the independent HCBs in these countries, initiatives are being taken by SMIIC (Standards and Metrology Institute for the Islamic Countries), GSO (G.C.C. Standardization Organization), and ESMA (Emirates Standards and Metrology Authority).

The core challenge is the lack of harmonized standards which is holding back the industry causing confusion. Having a common standard in ASEAN will also reduce the production costs for export companies (Johan, 2018). Halal travel and tourism are one of the potential sectors of the halal industry that can grow globally faster by identifying the relevant sectors and developing products accordingly. Products of both travel and other relevant sectors can be promoted to airlines. An effective system of standards like HOTREC Hotel stars Union and The Green Key Global are two successful examples of Halal travel industry to look into and realize the essence of unified global standards. Modest fashion companies need to appeal to both Muslims and non-Muslims by embracing a broader consumer base. Besides focusing on quality, strong DNA, and workmanship, the industry should strategize policies of creating a brand. The brand that speaks the demand of modest fashion style of all demographics especially the Muslim community. One more emerging market is Halal media and recreation where companies can grow through multi-channel expansion. The scope can be extended by shifting the focus beyond religious sectors. Diversification in cultural and religious-themed media proposition can excel for a significant minority population. However, government and investor involvement to facilitate the growth is necessary which is a challenge for the industry. Other challenges for the industry include marketing to non-Muslim audiences and meeting the needs of millennials. All halal products produced in ASEAN and certified by different HCBs need more regulatory oversight. More coordination between the accreditation bodies is needed to avoid unnecessary duplication or competition. Finally, the establishment of the "ASEAN General Guidelines on the Preparation and Handling of Halal Food" in 2001 by ASEAN could be improved and expanded further to come up with a unified halal standard and logo in ASEAN.

## REFERENCES

Ager, S. N. S., Abdullah, M., Shahwahid, F. M., Wahab, N. A., & Saidpudin, W. (2015). An analysis of the definition of halal: shari'ah vs statutes. In World Academic and Research Congress. 2015 (World-AR 2015) Ar-Rahim Hall, YARSI University, Jakarta, Indonesia, Dec. 9-10, 2015.

BioMalaysia & ASEAN Bioeconomy Conference. (2015). *Halal economy : Opportunity and Challenges*. Retrieved from http://biomalaysia.bioeconomycorporation.my/speakerssliders/day1/session2perlis/BioMalaysia 2015-v4(17.08.2015).pdf

Catto-Smith, C. (n.d.). *The weekly link Halal logistics a fast-growing market*. Retrieved from http://www.halalrc.org/images/Research Material/Literature/Halal logistics a fast-growing market.pdf

CrescentRating. (2018). Global Muslim Travel Index 2018. (April). Retrieved from https://www.crescentrating.com/download/thankyou.html?file=X7UrOM8Y_GMITI-Report-2018-web-version%281%29.pdf

Crescentrating, M. (2018). *Mastercard-Crescentrating GMTI 2018 Global Muslim Travel Index 2018*. Retrieved from https://www.halalmedia.jp/wp-content/uploads/2018/04/GMITI-Report-2018.pdf

Economy of the Organisation of Islamic Cooperation. (n.d.). *Arabian Business*. Retrieved from http://www.arabianbusiness.com/muslim-tourism-sector-said-be-worth-over-138bn--growing-656633.html

Fleishman Hillard Majlis. (2011). The Market Opportunity of the Muslim World. Bio Malaysia & ASEAN Bioeconomy Conference. (2015). *Halal economy : Opportunity and Challenges*. Retrieved from http://biomalaysia.bioeconomycorporation.my/speakerssliders/day1/session2perlis/BioMalaysia 2015-v4(17.08.2015).pdf

Imarat Consultants. (n.d.). *An Overview of the Global Halal Market South East Asia Driving the Halal. Media*. Retrieved from http://www.halalrc.org/images/Research Material/Presentations/overview of global halal market.pdf

Ira Sugita. (2017). *Halal in Singapore*. Singapore. Retrieved from https://gain.fas.usda.gov/Recent GAIN Publications/Halal in Singapore_Singapore_Singapore_3-28-2017.pdf

JAKIM. (2015). Manual Procedure for Malaysia Halal Certification (Third Revision) 2014. [Third Revision]. *Manual Procedure for Malaysia Halal Certification, 2014*, 67. doi:10.1017/CBO9781107415324.004

Johan, E. (2018). New Challenges in ASEAN Regional Market: International Trade Framework on Halal Standard. *Jurnal Dinamika Hukum, 18*(1), 93. doi:10.20884/1.jdh.2018.18.1.809

Khalid, A. M., Haji Masr, M., Muhammad, N., & Pang, W. L. (2018). *Halal Meat and Meat Products Processing*. Brunei Darussalam: ERIA; Retrieved from http://www.eria.org/uploads/media/RURB_2018_Chapter_4_Halal_meat_Brunei.pdf

LIPKA. M. (2017). Muslims and Islam: Key findings in the U.S. and around the world. Retrieved November 5, 2018, from http://www.pewresearch.org/fact-tank/2017/08/09/muslims-and-islam-key-findings-in-the-u-s-and-around-the-world/

MiTi. (2012). *Development of the halal industry*. Retrieved from http://www.miti.gov.my/miti/resources/fileupload/Chap 21.pdf

MUIS. (2018). *MUIS Annual Report 2017*. Retrieved from https://www.muis.gov.sg/-/media/Files/Corporate-Site/Annual-Reports/MUIS_AR_Full_2017.pdf

Muslim Population in the World. (n.d.). Retrieved October 31, 2018, from http://www.muslimpopulation.com/

Mustapa Mohamed. (2018). World Halal Week 2016 Speech. Retrieved from http://www.miti.gov.my/index.php/pages/view/3195

Nor Ai'han Mujar, N. H. (2015). The economics of halal industry. *Journal of Experimental Psychology. General*, *136*(1), 23–42.

Oh, Y., bin Pg Hamir, A. M. H., & Mohd Shah, M. A. S. bin. (2018). The viability of halal food industry for Brunei economic diversification: SWOT analysis. *People: International Journal of Social Sciences, 3*(3), 1220–1233. doi:10.20319/pijss.2018.33.12201233

Pacific, A. (2010). Global Halal Industry : An Overview. *Global Islamic Finance Report 2013*, 140–159. Retrieved from http://www.gifr.net/gifr2013/ch_13.PDF

Personal, M., Archive, R., Puah, C., Voon, S., & Entebang, H. (2009). Halal Industry : key challenges dan Opportunities, (10679).

Shahbandeh, M. (2019). Global halal market - Statistics & Facts. Retrieved March 17, 2019, from https://www.statista.com/topics/4428/global-halal-market/

Smart Shield International Sdn Bhd. (2016). *Study on Halal Industry Investment in Brunei Darussalam*. Retrieved from http://www.eria.org/old/events/Brunei_Halal_EN.pdf

Thomson Reuters and DinarStandard. (2017). Outpacing The Mainstream. *State of the Global Islamic Economy Report, 2017*(18). doi:10.100700348-013-1600-9

Thomson Reuters and DinarStandard. (2018). *State of Global Islamic Economy Report 2018/19. Dubai International Financial Centre*. Retrieved from https://haladinar.io/hdn/doc/report2018.pdf

Wannasupchue, W., Othman, M., Abidin, U. F. U. Z., Ishak, F. A. C., & Mohamad, S. F. (2019). Current Trends and Opportunities for Halal Restaurants in Thailand: A Conceptual Framework. *International Journal of Academic Research in Business and Social Sciences*, *9*(1), 235–247. doi:10.6007/IJARBSS/v9-i1/5392

WTO. (2018). *World trade statistical review 2018*. Retrieved from www.wto.org/statistics

Zakaria, Z. (2008). Tapping into the world halal market: Some discussions on Malaysian laws and standards. *Shariah Journal*, *16*(3), 603–616.

## ADDITIONAL READING

Ab Talib, M. S., Md. Sawari, S. S., Abdul Hamid, A. B., & Ai Chin, T. (2016). Emerging Halal food market: An Institutional Theory of Halal certificate implementation. *Management Research Review*, *39*(9), 987–997. doi:10.1108/MRR-06-2015-0147

Anggara, F. S. A. (2017). Development of Indonesia Halal Agroindustry Global Market in ASEAN: Strategic Assesment. *Al Tijarah*, *3*(1), 65–78. doi:10.21111/tijarah.v3i1.940

Dubé, F. N. HaiJuan, Y., & Lijun, H. (2016). Halal certification system as a key determinant of firm internationalisation in the Philippines and Malaysia. Asian Academy of Management Journal, 21(1), 73.

Hashimi, D., Saifuddeen, S. M., & Salleh, S. M. (2010, December). A background on Halal industry and principles. In *International workshop for Islamic scholars on agribiotechnology: Shariah compliance* (p. 12).

Othman, B., Shaarani, S. M., & Bahron, A. (2016). The potential of ASEAN in halal certification implementation: A review. *Pertanika Journal of Social Science & Humanities*, *24*(1), 1–24.

Othman, P., Sungkar, I., & Hussin, W. S. W. (2009). Malaysia as an international halal food hub: Competitiveness and potential of meat-based industries. *ASEAN Economic Bulletin*, *26*(3), 306–320. doi:10.1355/AE26-3F

Roberts, C., & Onn, L. P. (2009). Brunei Darussalam: Cautious on political reform, comfortable in ASEAN, pushing for economic diversification. *Southeast Asian Affairs*, 61-82.

Thambipillai, P. (2012). ASEAN Economic Integration: Challenges to Brunei Businesses. *Achieving the ASEAN Economic Community 2015. Challenges for Member Countries & Business*, *216*, 181.

## KEY TERMS AND DEFINITIONS

**ASEAN:** An acronym stands for 'Association of South-East Asian Nations. It is an association of free trade agreement amongst ten South-East Asian countries.

**Driving Forces:** Factors that drive or enhances the growth of the Halal industry globally.

**GDP (PPP):** Gross Domestic Product (GDP) by Purchasing Power Parity (PPP) is one of the economic tools to measure the potential strength of an economy.

**GIEI Score:** The Global Islamic Economy Indicator (GIEI) score is a composite weighted file contained six area level pointers crosswise over 73 center nations to demonstrate the present territory of Islamic Economy markers over every one of the Islamic Economy pillars.

**Global Halal Industry:** An industry in the global economy that is comprised of Halal food, Halal cosmetics, Halal pharmaceuticals, Muslim friendly tourism, Halal logistics and supply chain, Modest fashion, Halal media and recreation, and other markets targeting to fulfill the needs of Muslim consumers globally.

**Halal Ecosystem:** The entire atmosphere of Halal industry that comprises of production (food, pharmaceuticals, cosmetics, ingredients etc.), services (logistics and supply chain, tourism, banking and takaful etc.), governmental support, and human capital (halal auditors & executives, academicians, halal knowledge workers, syllabus in universities and colleges).

**Halal Park:** HALAL PARK is a community or network of manufacturing and service industries located on a common territory with the objective of preserving the integrity of halal products and services and improving the economic performance of the participating companies.

**Halal Supply Chain:** The type of supply chain in the production and manufacturing industry that preserves the halal integrity from farm to table.

**Key-Industry Players:** Brands or countries that are leading globally for different halal products and services.

**Millennials:** It is a phrase also know as Generation-Y which is used to indicate the people who reached their adulthood in the early 21st century. This term, according to the U.S. Census Bureau, involves the generation of people born in between 1980-2000.

# Chapter 6
# Analysis of Food Security Policy by Participatory Poverty Assessment (PPA) Effort:
## Case in Indonesia

**Muhamad Rusliyadi**
https://orcid.org/0000-0003-4632-5671
*Polytechnic of Agricultural Development Yogyakarta Magelang, Indonesia*

**Azaharaini Hj. Mohd. Jamil**
*College IGS Brunei Darussalam, Brunei*

**Muhammad Anshari**
https://orcid.org/0000-0002-8160-6682
*Universiti Brunei Darussalam, Brunei*

## ABSTRACT

*This chapter evaluates food security policies and extension policies to the achievement of targets and the results of a development programme such as Food Self Sufficiency village (DMP) used Participatory Poverty Assessments (PPA). The output obtained is information that is an evaluation of how the policy was planned, initiated, and implemented. Participatory Poverty Assessments (PPA) monitoring and evaluation analyse the outcome and impact of the DMP Programme. The output of the PPA process from this chaper is the agricultural policy formulated in terms of practical ways of approaching poverty problems from a local perspective. The success of alternative policy options applied by local government such us Physical, Human Resources, Institution development at the grassroots level should be adopted at the national level. It should represent the best example of a case of successful programme implementation at the grassroots level which can then be used in formulating national policies and strategies.*

DOI: 10.4018/978-1-7998-2257-8.ch006

## INTRODUCTION

Poverty reduction is the key to the success of a country's development. Encouraging economic development is an effective policy for poverty reduction. One of the policy measures to effectively address the issue of poverty is the adoption of participatory approaches in the planning, monitoring and evaluation of poverty reduction policies. A participatory approach is used to address weaknesses which could not be effectively addressed previously. Variations regarding the evaluation of poverty reduction policies are dominated by top-down approaches. A less top-down approach to evaluating policies will accommodate the needs and aspirations of the poor.

Participatory Poverty Assessment (PPA) is a method of analysis of data aggregation. It seeks to recognise deficiency scope within the public, cultural, financial and political atmosphere in a particular region. It focuses on the local peoples' perceptions. Different research methods can be contextualised to different degrees. These categorisations with participatory methods aim to standardise the data collection and analysis with the sample in a large household study. The course of classification approaches offers the advantage of inferring qualitative information from quantitative evaluations, which characterises the comparison of survey and participatory data. Nevertheless, it does not include the perspective of acquiring quantitative data from the PPA.

Participatory Poverty Assessment (PPA) was introduced by the World Bank to assess the poverty in a region from top level down to village level. People facing poverty would be were identified and so were the causes of poverty, and recommendations for poverty reduction effort at household level were proposed. The variation or diversity of indicators that exists in the country and villages are taken to be representative of poverty at household level. However, this implies a methodology that is diverse, and is capable and flexible enough to respond to the needs of the subject of policies (ADB, 2001).

PPA generally uses several tools to analyse the characteristics of poor families with poverty reduction in mind. PPA is a method of evaluating the characteristics of the poor through observation and analysis of policy implementation. The requirement of this method is the participation of the community and stakeholders to discover alternative solutions to poverty problems at the grassroots level. It is a practical tool of solving poverty problems, such as increasing farmer income and reducing poverty.

## BACKGROUND

PPA initiates a participatory method that thrives in the viewpoint of Participatory Rural Appraisal (PRA). They become key to mechanisms for advance policy agency by embodiment of the community's participation. PRA has been seen as a family of approaches and methods to enable local people to share and analyse their knowledge of life and conditions, and to plan and to act (Chambers, 1994). It emerged in the early 1990s, building on insights and methodological innovations from various study methods. Agro-ecosystem analysis provided the series of diagramming, mapping, scoring and grading methods of the different natural processes; insight provided by the work of practical and development anthropologists and those of field research in farming systems emphasised villagers' capability in conducting their own personal analysis; and most notably there was the development of Rapid Rural Appraisal (RRA) (Laderchi, 2001).

Conservative poverty estimates, together with equally conservative financial and qualification estimates, have been criticised for leading to external enforcement, and for not taking into account the views of poor people themselves. The participatory approach's purpose is to change this and to enable the people themselves to take part in decisions about what it entails to be poor and the level of poverty (Chambers, 1994; 1997). The implementation of PPA, evolved from PRA, is described as "a rising family unit of approaches and methods to enable local people to distribute, develop and analyse their understanding of living and circumstances, to plan and to effort" (Chambers, 1994). Originally, it was intended for small projects, then the World Bank, to complement to its poverty assessments, scaled up PPA. By 1998, the World Bank's poverty assessments included a participatory aspect. A widespread multi-country workout (of 23 countries) was similarly incorporated as conditions for the World Development Report, available as Voices of the Poor (Narayan-Parker & Patel, 2000). According to Cornwall (2000), there are three types of PA: (1) those connected with self-determination and empowerment; (2) those linked with raising the effectiveness of programmes; and (3) individuals' emphasis on common learning. The role of participatory movements as defined by the World Bank, particularly in their poverty assessments, has tended to be compliant. It adopts PPA so that the poor will join forces with programmes rather than to modify the pattern of the programmes themselves (type 2), and the Voices of the Poor emphasises the third type.

Study and policy points of reference on poverty issues have undergone a shift in conceptualisation of the poor from passive recipients of development efforts to those who can contribute to their own livelihood improvements (Chambers, 1996). To facilitate this shift, state institutions should provide the conditions for the poor to do so. The terms 'poor' and 'non-poor' can be perceived as externally imposed categories that do not reflect locally perceived differences, as well as possibly being derogatory. Subjective valuation of wellbeing can provide a divergence and more contextually specific perspective on living conditions. Since poverty is embedded in a socioeconomic system, it is always relative to a socially defined threshold. An individual with a given level of income, food, protection, or clothing may be considered inadequate in one context, but not in another. Thus, the distinction between absolute and relative poverty is important (Lok-Dessallien, 1998).

According to Norton et al. (2001), the purpose of PPA is to improve the strength of public activities aimed at poverty reduction. PPAs are generally taken to be

*Table 1. Approaches to PPAs*

| No | | First generation PPAs | Second generation PPAs |
|---|---|---|---|
| 1 | Focus of PPA process | Generating textual representation of realities of the poor, to contribute to policy recommendations | Creating new relationships within the policy process – bridging public policy, civil society, people in poor communities, donor agencies. |
| 2 | Means of influencing policy change | PPA influences donor country assessment documents (country poverty assessment). PPA is a 'product' which seeks to influence another product. Policy influence therefore is largely contingent on the quality of the policy process associated with the overall document. | PPA influences country policy-making processes: budget process (pro-poor allocation of public resources); sector policy; regulatory function (land reform, informal sector); poverty monitoring system; local government policy and budget processes. |
| 3 | Institutional location | Designed/supervised by donor agency staff. Donor 'publishes' PPA. PPA managed and implemented by NGO or research institute, chosen by the donor according to criteria of technical and logistical competence to deliver PPA report. | Chosen to maximise potential contributions to policy process. Institutional partnerships created to introduce logistical and technical capacity |
| 4 | Time-frame | Period necessary to complete one round of national fieldwork and generate report. | Process approach allowing for PPA to work with planning and budget formulation processes at national, sectoral and local levels.<br>PPA may or may not be produced.<br>Follow-up with specific studies possible. |
| 5 | Substantive focus | Focus on: poor people's understanding of poverty and deprivation, constraints in accessing public benefits and services, poor people's priorities for public policy. | As in left column, but with increasing emphasis on: access to information for action for people in poor communities; governance, accountability and transparency. |
| 6 | Key skills | For PPA implementation<br>Social analysis (synthesis of results)<br>Training skills in research field methods<br>Research design logistical support for policy analysis | For PPA implementation social analysis (synthesis of results)<br>Training skills in research field methods<br>Research design<br>Logistical support for policy analysis for policy mainstreaming<br>Understanding macro policy, sector policy and budget formulation processes<br>Advocacy skills institutional change management |

Source: Norton et al. (2001)

policy research exercises, linked to governmental policy processes, directed at understanding poverty from the perspective of poor people, and their priorities in terms of actions to improve their conditions. PPAs can strengthen poverty assessment processes through broadening stakeholder involvement, thereby increasing general support and legitimacy for anti-poverty strategies, enriching the analysis and understanding of poverty by letting in the perspectives of the poor, and providing a diverse scope of valuable information on a cost-effective, rapid and timely basis, creating new relationships between policymakers, service suppliers and people in poor communities. PPAs may originate from a mixture of dissimilar institutions, including NGOs, donors and research establishments. They may address different audiences – including policy-makers, politicians, advocates and activists.

According to Norton et al. (2001), the impact to date of PPAs has been the finding that all stakeholders have had significant changes in knowledge, understanding, and military strengths in one or more of the following areas: the nature and causal factors of poverty; greater solidarity with or sympathy for the poor; increased commitment to consulting the poor; better understanding of and/or increased commitment to participate or 'bottom-up' research, planning, and monitoring; better understanding of local conditions such as recognition of inequities which are important at the household level, particularly gender-based issues; greater willingness to acknowledge sensitive issues such as domestic violence or marginalisation of some social groups; increased need for better social services and programmes; and increases in commitment to or demand for participation and grassroots democracy.

## METHODOLOGY

The four villages in Central Java province in this study are regarded as the main representatives for assessment of the Programme by PPA analysis. This study is a pioneer in the area of PPA in Indonesia, and it links to agricultural policy. The PPA concept is used in synthesising the problem of poverty at village level with the participation approach. Every report shows a naturalistic depiction of poverty commonly found in rural areas. Both qualitative and quantitative data were analysed. Most data generated come from the Participatory Rural Appraisal (PRA), based on poverty analysis. The participatory method is one method that uses PRA as data base analysis with decision making from stakeholders or villagers in order to examine poverty in the village.

Data related to the DMP Programme and extension service were collected using unstructured and semi-structured questionnaire. The survey was conducted in four villages; 100 samples from each, using a purposive and clustered sampling technique based on some particular sample criteria. Criteria of the sample chosen were based on farmer characteristics such as their level of wealth, farmer leader, the village leader, and gender. (Rusliyadi et al, 2019). The purposive sampling technique is a type of non-probability sampling that is most effective when one needs to study a certain cultural domain with knowledgeable experts within. Purposive sampling may also be used with both qualitative and quantitative research techniques. This type of sampling can be very useful in situations when one needs to reach a target sample quickly, and where sampling for proportionality is not the main concern (Rusliyadi & Libin, 2018)

Data collection in the field during research work in four villages took almost two months. PPA was a key element in the survey, where the results reflect the rural poverty level. Fieldwork carried out in the research involved various multidisciplinary teams, derived largely from existing local extension officers. A series of meetings addressed provincial and regency governments, cross-sector institutions and community organisations around the villages researched. Fieldwork in the PPA was carried out by local participants with a participatory approach. The PPA is actually a visual Participatory Rural Appraisal (PRA) tool to retrieve data from focus group discussions with groups of respondents where they scored wellbeing rankings, rated or scored preference data, and mapped and illustrated social resources.

## PPA AND AGRICULTURAL POLICY LINKING

Poverty reduction and fair distribution of economic growth are significantly meaningful to the Indonesian government. Poverty reduction is constantly determined in terms of the social safety nets, as opposed to sharpening and focusing on addressing macro weakness, at the structural and sectoral level. Therefore, this requires an approach that is able to consider all of them in the form of PPA. People rarely get information about government plans and in the policy formulation phase. The government should be transparent in every policy. The role of stakeholders is indispensable in policy implementation. This method is robust, because it involves many stakeholders in finding alternative solutions to address public problems, especially in poverty reduction policies.

The blueprint of a policy initiation plan provides users with direct impacts on policy strategy. It intends to clarify the problems from the grassroots level. Discussion at the household level facilitates the government in allocation of funds and budgets in accordance with the scheme of policy implementation. The government's current top-down policy looks at civil society as an entity that cannot contribute to the development plan. This is the bridge that the participatory approach is expected to address in a strategic plan based on assessment of threats and problems encountered at the grassroots level.

PPA is the basic method, like a baseline study, to assess the poverty level in the country. The focus in this context is rural areas in Indonesia. In this case, rural areas cannot be separated from the agriculture sector. Most rural policies are derived from agricultural policy. The closeness and relationship between agricultural policy and objects in PPA are strongly interrelated. The PPA results from other countries are based on the analytical characterisation of livelihoods in agriculture, forestry and fisheries. The root causes of poverty are expected to be revealed from livelihood analysis. Therefore, the strategic plan becomes more concentrated and comprehensive for the policy focus after the DMP Programme.

Figure 1 shows the link of PPA findings in each village on agricultural and food security analysis with poverty assessment. These PPA results can be synthesised for each village in order to draft a proposal for provincial and national poverty assessment reports. The reports can be circulated at district, regency and province levels for discussion by the local government and agencies to assist them produce a model for development. Hopefully the synthesis of information using the PPA approach will assist the local government in the formulation of policy actions.

A collection of site 'synthesised reports' of each hamlet/village can become a national synthesised report that can be published internationally as a global national voice of the poor. A site report of each village can also be specific in representing a unique case study from each village. This is a contribution to global reporting on the poor: a valuable document, because it contains rich information as a result of the PPA process. Firstly, it highlights specific information in each site report. Second, it provides opportunities to reinforce the finding of sites with varying socioeconomic and geographical environments. Thirdly, it enables synchronisation and merging of local-level findings to be turned into national poverty quantitative data for analysis.

Figure 1 shows the results of the research report covering all village sites in terms of the PPA. The analysis of household surveys is mainly told in terms of food security and agricultural policy analysis. The analysis can become a resource for national poverty assessment resources. PPA findings are a national poverty assessment that can attract the attention of national policy makers and be published internationally. The Indonesian study findings can be employed to represent the voices of the poor in global studies. Government involvement in the synthesis of the results of the PPA is indispensable, especially in making constructive comments and giving feedback to improve implementation policy and practice in the alleviation of poverty. National poverty assessment summaries obtained as the outcomes of the PPA and other data can be used in future strategic planning operations by the government.

The relationship between PPA results and agricultural policy can be considered complementary. The PPA result is an official document, while the outcome is the strategic plan involving participation of the community. A part of the strategic plan is a strategic programme of agricultural policy on poverty reduction and other research reports. The agriculture policy in the PPA is practical; it examines policy implementation at the grassroots level, especially in how to increase farmers' income and reduce poverty.

The agricultural policy formulated using PPA in terms of practical policy analysis is sourced from local understanding/knowledge. Indonesia has many provinces with a progressive and proactive policy in the agriculture sector. The success of alternative policy options by local government should be enlarged to the national stage.

The local government (province level) is required to carry out a specific policy to alleviate hunger and poverty. Specific local policies should strong and have comprehensive analysis at grassroots level and solve the problem for sustainable development. The PPA process of collecting data can be adopted as a tool for monitoring and planning based on local practice in pro-poor policies with real objectives. In attempting to reduce poverty, the local policies should take into consideration the strength of local economic conditions in terms of agricultural and potential resources.

PPA is a tool used in the analysis of household- or community-level framework, with data derived from discussions with participants. The DMP is meant for poor rural villages. More than 30% of the people in each village are poor, which is why these villages are suitable for PPA implementation PPA. Contributions of PPA in the DMP Programme are based on analysis of the sustainability of existing livelihoods of villagers in order to see the strengths and shortcomings in such areas as human imagination, social capital, natural resources, infrastructure and institutions at the community level. The PPA process involves consolidation, observation and intensive discussion of the poor in the rural Programme sites about the causes of impoverishment. The conditions of the local community become the baseline in the analysis so that tool used are adjusted from real conditions

The livelihood analysis shows different results, depending on the availability of local natural resources in the villages. The four villages in the DPM Programme show that the main livelihood of the villagers is based on farming, livestock, fisheries, forests and tourism. These sectors play a significant role in the village in terms of providing primary income for most villagers. The features of livelihood of the villages can be described as follows. Firstly, the most important aspect of the livelihood of rural communities is paddy cultivation. Ownership of paddy land varies from around 0.1 to 3ha. The land area that generates a relatively small income of farmers is very small (0.25ha). Secondly, livestock production in the countryside is a direct savings mechanism for villagers. If they need small amount of cash such as for buying cooking oil, they can sell chickens to solve their financial constraints. This practice occurs in almost all four villages. Thirdly, fishery brings additional income for most rural communities. Alternatively, fish can also be used as a source of protein to meet the dietary needs of families. Fishing also plays an important

*Figure 1. The link of PPA findings on agricultural and food security analysis with poverty assessment*
*Resources: inspired and adapted from Turk (2001)*

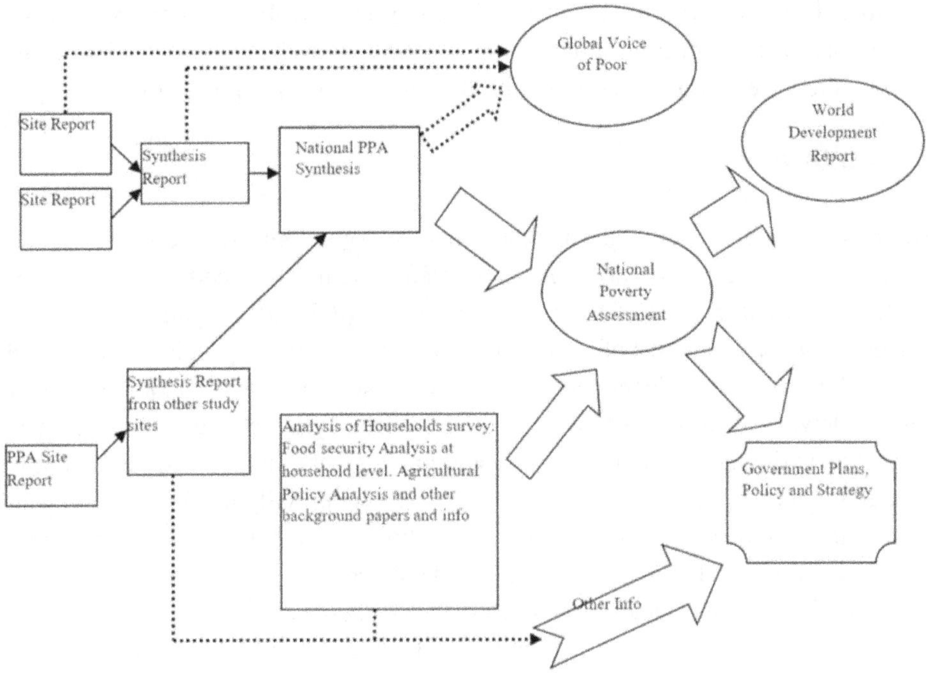


role in the welfare mechanism of the villages by maintaining social security. In Madukoro, fishing is the main source of livelihood for some people. Fourth, NTFPs are major resources for poor communities that currently do not have paddy land; they can collect firewood or wild animals, bamboo and rattan for sale as daily income. Fifth, tourism is the main livelihood for two villages in the researched village sites, because they have many tourist facilities and are frequently visited by foreign and domestic tourists. Tourism has been contributing significantly to the local economy by raising income of the villagers.

The DMP Programme has resulted in the establishment of a microfinancial institution (Lembaga Keuangan Desa - LKD) in the village, participated in by farmer groups. However, the funds allocated for the LKD are limited and they cannot cover the needs of all villagers. There remains a lack of capital necessary to start businesses for some farmers. The villagers proposed establishing a farmer cooperative in the village to support 'off-farm' and 'on-farm' activities and to be managed by farmer groups. The aim of the cooperative is to provide the place for savings and loans with low interest rates and to gain profits for the villagers.

## Livelihood Resources Analysis in the Community

The framework of analysis employed in this work is the sustainability of living resources from time to time. Indexes in the analysis of livelihood focus on how the availability of livelihood resources can cause poverty at the community level. The solutions received from the community discussions are shown in Table 2.

## Agriculture

The most important aspect of the livelihood of rural communities is paddy cultivation. Ownership of paddy land varies from around 0.1 to 3ha. The land area that causes a relatively small income of farmers is very small (0.25ha). Irrigation in the four villages is only a small part of technical irrigation; the other aspect is non-technical irrigated rice, rain–fed, dependent on the rainy season. With cultivation technology handed down it is to be expected that the productivity is not high. Thus, farmers receive a yield which is enough for household consumption. The crop is generally enough to meet needs for three to six months. To cover daily need over a full year farmers usually work in the off-farm sector as labourers, or in livestock or non-timber forest production (NTFS). For example, wild pandan leaves are used as a handcraft in Candirejo, resulting in additional income for villagers.

According to the villagers in Candirejo, "because of land degradation and the limited availability of water, it is very difficult to cultivate paddy and also the lack of fertile land". These conditions are some of the causes of food shortage, which results in poverty being experienced by some villagers. With the increasing population in the village, the land area is reduced and there is a tendency to decrease production, which hinders attainment of food self-sufficiency in the villages. It is necessary for the food supply to come from outside the area for daily consumption and this is the experience of most villages. It can be concluded, then, that land ownership is a key factor in household welfare.

## Livestock

Livestock plays a very important role in the livelihood of the villagers. Most villagers are engaged in keeping livestock (cattle raising). Other community members are engaged in raising chickens. Community members are aware that chickens are nutritious food. People can also readily sell chickens at the local market. The cattle production system implemented in the villages is based on traditional practices and therefore productivity tends to be low. Although some activities of the DMP Programme had already started in villages at the time of study, there remains a need to improve the Programme, especially in rural Madukoro and Candirejo, by introducing,

*Table 2. Changes in livelihood availability and their causes*

| Resources | Year 1990 | Condition | Year 2000 | Condition | Year 2010 | Condition |
|---|---|---|---|---|---|---|
| Fish | 10 | - Fewer people use traditional fishing gear<br>- few market | - 8 | - Many fish from outside and inside village<br>- Use of hand grenades, poison<br>- More markets<br>- Merchants want to buy<br>- Water supply for fishpond decreased | - 6 | - Increased population<br>- High consumption<br>- Use illegal fishing<br>- Competitive fish market |
| Rice | 9 | - Fertile soil<br>- Fewer people<br>- Plenty of farmland and rice available<br>- Fewer people | - 8 | - Increased population<br>- Low crop productivity<br>- No maintenance | - 8 | - More people<br>- Infertility of soil floods<br>- Insufficient food consumption |
| Domestic vegetables and fruits | 9 | - Newly settled<br>- Not many crops | - 7 | - Additional planting<br>- Increasing population<br>- Few market needs<br>- No processing of product | - 6 | - Vegetable gardening<br>- Expansion of crop areas<br>- More markets<br>- Processing product |
| Wild vegetables and fruit | | - Plenty of forest<br>- Not many people extracting<br>- Far from market<br>- Small population<br>- Household Consumption | - | - Extracting by people from outside<br>- Availability of markets<br>- Clearing for farmland, increasing paddy land | - | - Logging concession<br>- Availability of market<br>- Clearing for paddy land and plantation<br>- Bush fires |
| River water | 10 | - Good quality<br>- Deep water<br>- Narrow river<br>- Riverbank not yet broken<br>- Fewer floods | - 8 | - Floods damage crops<br>- River became wider and broke riverbanks<br>- Water got shallow planting crops in riverbank | - 6 | - Quality of water got worse<br>- Floods<br>- Shallow river<br>- Many boats<br>- Cutting forest on the riverbanks |
| Water resources | 9 | - Easy to get water<br>- Plenty of water resources | - 7 | - Degradation of soil<br>- More difficult to get | - 6 | - Population increased<br>- Construction more develop<br>- Difficult to get<br>- Climate change |
| Wild animals | 10 | - Many wild animals in the wild habitat<br>- Household consumptions<br>- Few hunter<br>- No market | - 8 | - Availability of markets<br>- Decreased habitat<br>- More hunters<br>- Markets available<br>- Loss of certain species | - 4 | - Markets increased<br>- Exotic wild animal markets<br>- Illegal hunting |
| Timber | 9 | - Plenty of forest<br>- Not many people logging | - 8 | - Availability of markets<br>- Clearing for plantation, settlement | - 6 | - Bush fires<br>- Illegal logging<br>- Clearing for plantation |
| Total Score | 38 | | 31 | | 22 | |

NB: Scoring is out of 10; the higher the score, the higher the availability of food
Sources: Field Work Primary Data (2013)

for example, a mix of local and etawa goat farming, which can show a fairly high production yield. Livestock technology should be implemented systematically so that diseases can easily be controlled and detected should there be any problem in the livestock. This can be done with the assistance of extension service officers of animal husbandry in the villages.

Livestock production in the countryside is a direct savings mechanism for villagers. If they need small amounts of cash, such as for buying cooking oil, they can sell chickens to mitigate their financial constraints. This practice occurs in almost all four villages. However, for issues like paying high school fees, sending children to university and costs of illness or family, people sell goats or sheep, cattle and timber at their backyards. Livestock health is the major issue for the villagers. It is an even greater concern than people's health from the villagers' perspective.

## Fisheries

Fisheries play an important role in people's lives in the village through the DMP Programme in Madukoro and Kedungdowo, which have developed means of livelihood around fishing, with the availability of lakes and rivers, and people have utilised these available resources to keep fish farms and ponds. Kedungdowo is surrounded by the large river almost like a lake, so most villagers keep fish cages or nets on almost every bank of the Luk Ulo river. The villagers keep catfish, carp, tilapia and pomfret. In Madukoro the river water source is relatively small, but it can be used for small fish farmed in ponds. The villagers in Madukoro usually maintain types of fish such as carp and catfish or fish that are in high demand in the market.

Findings from several group discussions in the four villages indicate that families generated additional income in the range of 20-40% in a year from the contribution of aquaculture. This is a great help economically for villagers to support their livelihood. In small-scale aquaculture, it remains very profitable, but flooding sometimes affects Kedungdowo so that cages installed in the river are washed away by the strong currents due to continuous rain. The concept of small-scale aquaculture is aimed at creating a small pond at the back or side of the house by using a large tarp box shaped like a pool. It is quite efficient, because the capital investment required is reasonable in buying a tarp and fingerlings and fish are fed by using food scraps.

## Forestry

In general, macro-level forest resources are important factors in socio-economic development, especially around the villages in the PPA site. Timber and non-timber forest products (NTPFPs) provide a significant contribution to national GDP, for domestic use and for overseas exports. This is a very high-value contribution to poverty reduction in the rural population, especially for those who live on a forest's edge. The question is: why does the population remain poor in these areas? One needs to examine the case study in the research site. Local villagers usually obtain resources from the forest, particularly for their own consumption. Most villages in the hills are surrounded by tropical forests and therefore they are rich in forest resources, especially timber. However, government regulation prohibits them from selling forest resources. Local villagers normally use these resources for housing and clear them for farming. However, illegal cutting of timber by outsiders still happens.

Villagers reported that tropical forests are found around villages, as well as NTFPs such as bamboo, rattan, mushrooms, wild animals, wild fruits, wild pandan leaves, herbs, wood and fuel. NTFPs are major resources for poor communities that currently do not have paddy land: they collect firewood, wild animals, bamboo and rattan for sale as daily income. One example is Candirejo, where the majority of the poor collect wild pandan leaves, which they dry and sell. If villagers can make crafts from the pandan leaves, the sale value of the product increases and they can sell to the tourist villages nearby. The government's efforts need to be intensified by providing the villagers with extension services and training in making handcrafts from local raw materials. This will help villagers earn higher incomes than before.

### Tourism Resources

Tourism is actually not a natural resource, but it is a social capital resource. However, there is potential for tourism to become a promising industry nowadays. The researcher's opinion is that the main livelihood for two villages in the researched sites is tourism, because the villages have many tourist facilities frequently visited by foreign and domestic tourists. Candirejo has become a tourist destination since the initiation of a Jogjakarta NGO because the location of the village is close to the largest temple in the world, Borobudur Temple. The other village is Kedungdowo in Kebumen Regency, which is adjacent to Jembangan tourist village.

## WEALTH RANKING

The wealth ranking analysis of family groups is divided into three categories: rich, average, poor and hungry. Several indicators are used in the analysis: livestock ownership, possession of a deficit of food stocks, and land ownership of paddy fields, dry land and gardens. There are differences in the ownership of livestock within the category of 'rich'. This is because each village has different characteristics of ownership of animals, which is determined by the estimation of livestock price. In general, the greater proportion of the population do not have enough food to sustain their living because paddy land ownership is relatively low and rice production is not high enough to meet their daily needs. The 'average' ranking shows that the rice shortage period is about 1–4 months, which usually occurs during August to October. This period represents the time of drought or dry season, so plants are not growing very well. Rice cultivation is only possible in areas where water is available for growth. Nevertheless, the key indicator in wellbeing is the availability and adequacy of rice and ownership of livestock, especially cattle and goats. When the quantity of rice and livestock is reduced significantly, the family is said to be poor. This means that poverty remains a very big challenge to communities who have severe food shortages and the lack of livestock ownership.

The primary aspect of the livelihood in every village shows that the key indicator in wellbeing is availability or adequacy of rice and ownership of livestock, especially cattle and goats. Households face poverty when rice and livestock ownership reduce significantly and suddenly. This means that poverty remains a very great challenge to communities that have experienced severe food shortages and lack of livestock ownership. In a focus group discussion, all group members said that the context of poverty for them is ownership of rice for food, and livestock (cattle, goats and chickens) for savings, and these are used for an emergency situation such as daily food needs and children's schooling. Rice and livestock are crucial. Decline in rice and livestock ownership results in imbalance in their livelihoods and daily lives. Therefore, the core of poverty from the villagers' perspective is the inability to meet basic needs through income improvement and development.

An interesting finding that needs to be addressed by the government is seen in the 'poor' and 'hunger' categories. Some of the families could afford to send their children to school, because there are no school fees, but the school is comparatively distant from home. Some villagers were able to send their children to primary school but were unable to send them to middle and high school. On average, every village has a primary school but middle and high schools are quite far from the village. The daily cost for sending a child to school is relatively high for middle and high school. Although public schools are free, the schools location of the school is still relatively distant. In addition, poor family awareness on the need to send their children to school in the village is low and some children are engaged in 'child labour' and some drop out of school. The government needs to address the problem other than by adding more school buildings and to emphasise the policy focus on increasing understanding of the importance of schooling for poor families.

A diagram of cause and effect is very useful in characterising the root problems of poverty at village level. This helps to coordinate the development of action plans and sets priorities in the completion of policy plans. The goal in using causal diagrams is to determine the top priority issues in the research and bottlenecks in analysing problems. This is done by PPA ranking, looking at any obstacles and problems faced

*Table 3. Wealth and wellbeing ranking in DMP programme villages*

| | Kebumen Regency | | Magelang Regency | |
|---|---|---|---|---|
| **Categories** | **Kedungdowo Village** | **Selogiri Village** | **Candirejo Village** | **Madukoro Villaage** |
| Rich | - Several cows / Ownership of cattle (3-5)<br>- Large permanent house<br>- Large paddy field (2-5ha)<br>- Some pond fish (1-3)<br>- Large forestry (2-3ha)<br>- Have ownership of rice milling units and own barns<br>- Have ownership of car transportation<br>- Enough food for the entire year<br>- Large garden and other small livestock<br>- Inheritance from parents | - Several cows/cattle (2-3)<br>- Several goats (8-10)<br>- Large and permanent house<br>- Large yard (2-3ha)<br>- Large garden/ forestry (3-5ha)<br>- Have their own business<br>- Enough food for the whole year<br>- Inheritance from parents<br>- Good health and enough labour | - Several cows (1-3)<br>- Several goats (10-25)<br>- Permanent large house<br>- Large yard (3-5ha)<br>- Large paddy field (2-3ha)<br>- Large garden/Forestry (2-3ha)<br>- Have their own business<br>- Enough food for the whole year<br>- Inheritance from parents | - Several cows (1-3)<br>- Several goats (10-25)<br>- Permanent house<br>- Large yard (3-5ha)<br>- Several fish ponds (2-5)<br>- Large paddy field (2-3 ha)<br>- Large garden/Forestry (2-3ha)<br>- Have their own business<br>- Have their own car transportation<br>- Enough food for the whole year<br>- Good health and enough labour |
| Average | - Some cattle (1-2)<br>- Permanent house<br>- Paddy field (1- 2ha)<br>- Food shortage for 1-3 months a year<br>- Small garden Small livestock (chickens) Enough labour forces | - Some goats (10-25)<br>- Paddy field (0.5- 1.0ha)<br>- Some cattle<br>- Permanent house<br>- Enough labour<br>- Little food for 1-4 months a year<br>- Selling some goods in and outside the village<br>- Daily labour | - some goat (10-25)<br>- Paddy field (0.5-1.0ha)<br>- Children attend school<br>- Some cattle<br>- Permanent house<br>- enough labour<br>- Little food for 1-4 months a year<br>- Selling some goods in and outside the village<br>- Daily labour | - Several goat (10-25)<br>- Paddy field (0.5-1.0ha)<br>- Children attend school<br>- Some buffaloes<br>- Permanent house<br>- Enough labour<br>- Little food for 1-4 months a year<br>- Selling some goods in and outside the village<br>- Daily labour |
| Poor | - Not good house<br>- No cattle<br>- Small house<br>- Paddy field less than 0.1-0.2ha<br>- Stock food for 2-5 months a year<br>- With or without a boat<br>- Poor health | - With or without cows/ cattle<br>- With or without paddy field<br>- Stock food for 2-6 months a year<br>- Not enough clothes<br>- Not all children attend school<br>- No money for medicine when ill | - With or without a buffalo<br>- With or without paddy field<br>- Stock food for 2-6 months a year<br>- Not enough clothes<br>- Not all children attend school<br>- No money for medicine when ill | - With or without a buffalo<br>- With or without paddy field<br>- Stock food for 2-6 months a year<br>- Not enough clothes<br>- Not all children attend school<br>- No money for medicine when ill |
| Hungry | - No cow<br>- No paddy field<br>- Wood house<br>- Food more than 6 months per year<br>- Elderly or young couples<br>- Really poor health | - No cow<br>- With or lacking paddy field<br>- Wood house<br>- Food more than 6-7 months per year<br>- Not enough clothes<br>- No money for children to attend school<br>- No money for drugs when ill<br>- Disabled- and women-headed | - No cow<br>- No paddy field<br>- Wood house<br>- Food more than 6 months per year<br>- Elderly<br>- Really poor health | - No cow<br>- No paddy field<br>- Wood house<br>- Food more than 6 months per year<br>- Elderly or<br>- Really poor health |

Sources: Field work primary data (2013)

by a representative sample of key informants. The respondents were interviewed to learn the various obstacles and problems in poverty alleviation efforts. This helped to determine the level of priorities in a single diagram.

The main cause of poverty, in general, from several focus group discussions in the villages is lack of access to income resources. Revenue, in general, is obtained by earnings of permanent employees from resources such as land, crops, and livestock or fisheries and forestry. *Figure 2* is a general causal diagram of the four study villages. The first cause of poverty is the lack of physical capital due to the effect of rural isolation. Secondly, there is lack of natural capital caused by marginal or low productivity, the environment's decreased stability, climate change and environment shock, and underutilised options. Thirdly, there is lack of financial capital, which is due to lack of saved financial assets, few credit facilities, and few employment options. Fourthly, there is lack of human capital, caused by effects of increasing population, decreases in health quality, low entrepreneurial skills, lack of public sector leadership and lack of social capital due to overly rapid decentralisation, socially inadequate institutions, increasing mortality, violence and corruption, and inadequately focused policies.

Lack of access to financial capital is a major factor in causing poverty. The results show that according to the villagers most poor people were unable to get financial capital for their businesses. There are some opportunities for opening up businesses in rural areas. However, the access of villagers to credit facilities from financial institutions is limited. Financial capital with low interest is preferred by villagers. The easy way to get financial capital is by selling livestock. It is a rare case for livestock or saving to be used for starting a business, as such saving is normally used for urgent matters such as paying when a family member is sick or for school fees of children. Therefore there is a need for alternative capital resources that could be used for opening a business. One solution for this is borrowing from private financial institutions in the village. There is little availability of credit and credit institutions that secure low interest loans for villagers: unfortunately many financial institutions have high interest rates, using, for example, middleman. The DMP Programme has established a micro-financial institution (*Lembaga Keuangan Desa* - LKD) in the village participated in by farmer groups. However, the funds allocated for the LKD are limited and they cannot cover the needs of all the villagers. There remains a lack of capital necessary to start businesses for some farmers. The villagers proposed the establishment of a farmer cooperative in the village in the off-farm sector and on-farm activity, to be managed by farmer groups. The aim of cooperative would be to generate savings and provide loans at low interest rates to facilitate profit-making for villagers.

Lack of human capital in the village is an important factor that causes poverty. Villagers revealed that they need training to develop the skills necessary to secure capital. The level of motivation to work in the village is so low that concerted efforts should be made to increase the motivation of village heads and their staff members to start enterprises and provide jobs. The solution to some of these problems has been incorporated in the DMP Programme, which has proven itself to be helpful to villagers. Health is also one of the important contributing factors in terms of its impact on poverty. Health services in the village are still very basic. For example, one village is served by only one midwife. The Community Health Centre is only provided at the district level. For remote villages like Kedungdowo, it is even more difficult to access health services in case of emergencies.

In regard to social capital, decentralisation policies give local governments the authority to manage their own regions effectively. This means the local government needs to create effective policies to be implemented at district and regency level. One example is the policy of the local government that allowed conversion of agricultural land to settlement. In addition, the focus of implementation of pro-poor policy should be geared towards addressing specific problems at the village level. There was a policy designed to integrate the needs of different sectors in terms of

*Figure 2. Diagram of the causes and effects of poverty in DMP programme villages*

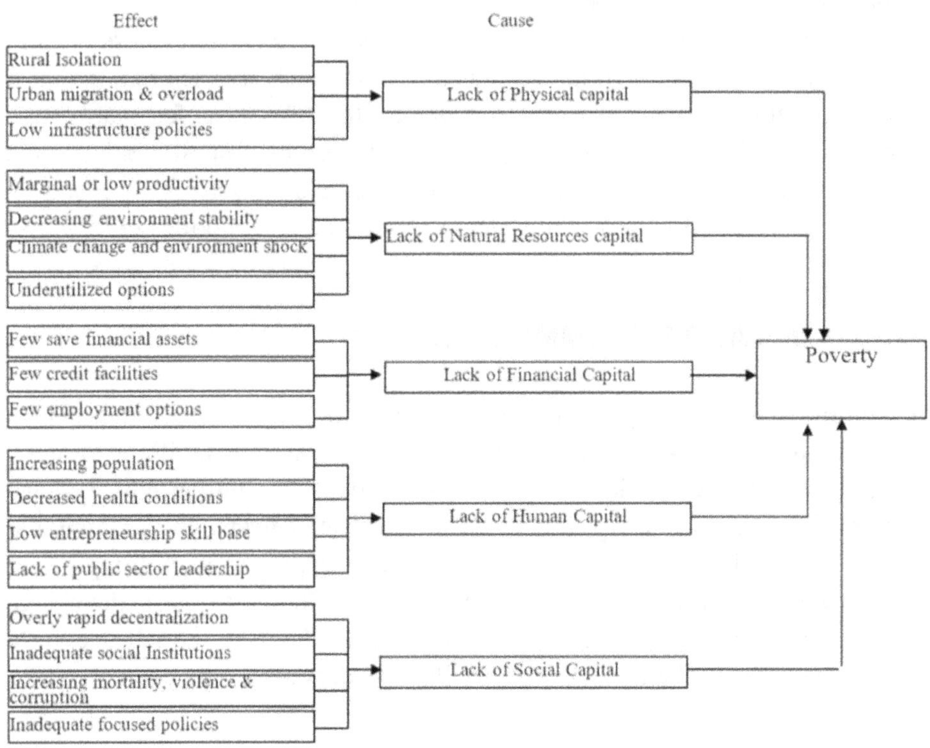

*Figure 3. Root causes/causal analysis of poverty in the village*

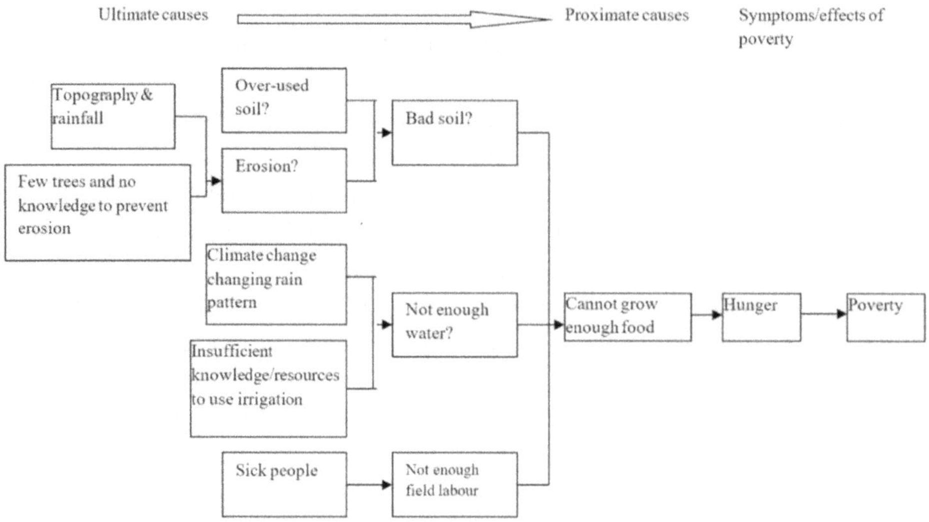


implementation. However, the initiated pattern of policy integration should start from the province level right to the village level with the creation of institutions responsible for policy execution.

The village community believes that poverty is caused by different reasons in each village and they are multidimensional. This research revealed that the most important factor in poverty is scarcity of water. This is because, for many years, people have had difficulty in accessing sources of clean and safe water due to the location of their villages in hilly areas. The diagram below describes the condition of Candirejo with respect to lack of water as the main cause of poverty.

## SOLUTIONS AND RECOMMENDATIONS

Active institutions play a very important role in supporting the DMP Programme. There were institutions in the village sites before the introduction of the DMP Programme, such as the village leader, village councils, farmer groups, rice milling units, a village health station unit, a school, a mosque, a church, private lenders, village shops and traders. New institutions introduced by the Programme are affinity groups, food village teams, rice barns and microfinance institutions. In Kedungdowo, the village leader is serving his second elected term. This shows the trust that villagers have for the village head. The relationship of village leader and village council should be harmonious in order to ensure good consultation with the village council, which typically advises and monitors every village activity.

The institutions, organisations, groups and individuals provide information on the relationships between these entities in the delivery of programme activities and these help planners in identifying and characterising the different factors (impacts, cooperations, linkages, leadership) involved in different circumtances to bring about successful implementation in rural development. Firstly, in Kedungdowo, the important institution is the RMU. Although it is relatively small, it is useful because it is close by. Its function is like a ricebarn or financial institution. It provides villagers with farming inputs and stores of rice stock. Since the launching of the Programme in Kedungdowo, village rice barns and micro financial institution (LKD) have been established, making the function of the RMU less important and its role has been taken over by farmer groups now managing the rice barn and LKD. Low interest loans are an important factor for poor farmers to be motivated to apply and the loan applications are processed in the regular meeting of farmer groups. The poor families find the rice barn beneficial, especially during periods of food shortages. Secondly, in Selogiri, the Affinity Group (AG) formed as a result of the DMP activities consists of four groups of farmers with different business areas of agriculture, livestock, fisheries and cassava cracker manufacturers. Fifty percent of funds are channelled to agricultural groups, so that many more farmers can become involved. The village food team (FVT), which consists of representatives of each affinity group, holds regular meetings every month attended by the head of the village and the village council. The constraints faced in the implementation of activities and future implementation plans are being worked out together so as to encourage the participation of all levels of the society. Thirdly, in Candirejo, farmer groups are relatively more dynamic than those in other villages. The fundamental difference is absence rice milling units because farmers grind their rice in a neighbouring village. Grants are not allocated to the building of rice barns, but are used to purchase livestock (local and etawa goats). The allocation of funding is for poor families who are involved as farmer groups. Their tourism resources contribute to revenue. Some villagers earn money through sales to local and foreign tourists. Fourth, in Madukoro, an individual or group has self-motivation initiated by the village leader. High responses of the public to the programme makes it easy to introduce and implement. The important success factor is the efforts of the leader driving activities initiated by the DMP Programme. The role of the leader is critical to the village's development. The leader should have the ability to mobilise the community to be active in most programmes. A key person with great influence can have a significant impact on programme success through community participation. Policies targeted at the family level such key people to have a significant impact on rural development.

## FUTURE RESEARCH DIRECTIONS

Analysis on sources of funding shows that villages receive funding mostly from the national budget, implemented through local government. To ensure sustainability in efforts to alleviate poverty central government should continue to consideration the local situation in allocation of funds. The local government is currently striving to boost revenues by looking to local and foreign investors to invest in their villages so that the budget can be increased. The local government should be proactive in generating financial sources through local revenue. In this way the gap between the national and regional budgets can be reduced.

Extension officers play an important role in every activity in the village. Their function is to disseminate knowledge and information on programme implementation. However, that information is mostly obtained from friends, relatives and parents. If extension officers are to play their role they need to frequently visit villages and come to the problems faced. Extension activities should not be only from the district level but also from regency or province level. Information disseminations is more effective if officers are experienced and come from various sectors, such as agriculture, husbandry, fisheries and health. Extension officers need to know villagers' problems through close observation. Information should include up-to-date technology and information in terms of programme implementation.

## CONCLUSION

The output of the PPA process from this study is the agricultural policy formulated in terms of practical ways of approaching poverty problems from a local perspective. Indonesia has many provinces with a progressive and proactive policy in the agriculture sector. The success of alternative policy options applied by local government at the grassroots level should be adopted at the national level. It should represent the best example of a case of successful programme implementation at the grassroots level which can then be used in formulating national policies and strategies. The PPA analysis carried out in this study revealed that the main problem facing most villages is physical development. The government needs to pay more attention to infrastructure development. Infrastructure development such as irrigation and roads should be given high priority in poor villages. The impact of infrastructure development is clear, in that it raises the chances of the poor family fighting against poverty and enhancing food security. The policies on rural development should be comprehensive enough to integrate infrastructure development with community development. The integration between various sectors also plays a crucial role in enhancing infrastructure development. Several programmes have been implemented successfully in one of the villages associated with the Programme, various agencies' cooperation gave rise to high impact contribution to the development of the village. In some villages the Programme was not implemented with other programmes but different times, making them less successful. Programmes should be integrated for more significant impact.

## REFERENCES

Asian Development Bank (ADB). (2001). *ADB Annual Report 2001*. ISSN 306-8370 (print). Retrieved from https://www.adb.org/documents/adb-annual-report-2001. Accessed on 29 September 2014.

Chambers, R. (1994). The Origins and Practice of Participatory Rural Appraisal. *World Development, 22*(7), pp. 953-969, 1994 Copyright 0 1994 Elsevier Science Ltd. 0305750X(94)E0029.

Chambers, R. (1996). *Relaxed and Participatory Appraisal. Notes of Practical Approaches and Methods:* Brighton: Institute of Development Studies.

Chambers, R. (1997). *Responsible Well-being*: A Personal Agenda for Development. *World Development, 25*(11), 1743–1754. doi:10.1016/S0305-750X(97)10001-8

Cornwall, A. (2000). *Making Differences? Gender and Participatory Development.* IDS Discussion Paper 378. Institute Development Studies.

Laderchi, R. C. (2001). *Participatory methods in the analysis of poverty: a critical review.* QEH Working Paper Series No. 62, Oxford. Retrieved from http://www2.qeh.ox.ac.uk/Re- PEc/qeh/qehwps/qehwps62.pdf

Lok-Dessallien, R. (1998). Review of Poverty Concepts and Indicators. SEPED Series on Poverty Reduction. New York, Social Development and Poverty Elimination Division, UNDP.

Narayan-Parker, D., Chambers, R., Shah, M. K., & Petesch, P. (2000). *Voices of the Poor: 32 Crying Out for Change*. New York, N.Y.: Published for the World Bank, Oxford University Press. doi:10.1596/0-1952-1602-4

Norton, A., Bird, B., Brock, K., Kakande, M., & Turk, C. (2001). A rough guide to PPAs Participatory Poverty Assessment: An introduction to theory and practice, Department for International Development's Social Development Department, Overseas Development Institute.

Rusliyadi, M., Jamil, M. A., & Kumalasari, R. T. (2019). *Analysis of household food security policy: Case of food security village programme*, Indonesia. *Asian Journal of Agriculture and Rural Development*, *9*(1), 19–32.

Rusliyadi, M., Jamil, M. A., Maseleno, A., Kumalasari, R. T., & Othman, M. (2019). Agricultural extension policy, agricultural growth and poverty reduction in Indonesia. *IACSIT International Journal of Engineering and Technology*, *7*(4), 5539–5550. doi:10.14419/ijet.v7i4.13337

Rusliyadi, M., & Libin, W. (2018). *Agriculture development programs for poverty reduction evidences from Indonesia and China* - comparative study case. *Asian Journal of Agriculture and Rural Development*, *8*(2), 104–118.

## ADDITIONAL READING

Pair, T. R. (1997). *Wise ranking made easy PLA Notes CD-ROM 1988–2001 Source, PLA Notes, Issue 28* (pp. 25–26). London: IIED.

Pair, T. R. (1997). wise ranking made easy PLA Notes CD-ROM 1988–2001 Source: PLA Notes (1997), Issue 28, pp.25–26, IIED London

Patnaik, U. (2008). Theorizing poverty and food security in the era of economic reforms. In G. Lechini (Ed.), *Globalization and the Washington Consensus: Its influence on democracy and development in the South.* Buenos Aires: CLACSO, Consejo Latinoamericano de Ciencias Sociales; http://bibliotecavirtual.clacso.org.ar/ar/libros/sursur/lech/12patna.pdf

Pearson, S., Gotsch, C., & Bahri, S. (2003). *Applications of the Policy Analysis Matrix in Indonesian Agriculture*. Ithaca, London: Cornell University Press.

Reganit, M. P. (2005). *Analysis of Community's Coping mechanisms in Relation to Floods: A Case Study in Naga City, Philippines.* Thesis, International Institute for Geo-Information Science and Earth Observation Enschede, The Netherlands.

Timmer, C. P. (1989). Food *price policy: The rationale for government intervention. Food Policy*, *14*(1), 17–27. doi:10.1016/0306-9192(89)90023-7

Timmer, P. (2008). *Agriculture and Pro-Poor Growth*: An Asian Perspective. *Asian Journal of Agriculture and Development*, *5*(1), •••.

Turk, C. (2001). *Linking Participatory Poverty Assessments to Policy and Policy Making; Experience from Vietnam.* Policy Research Working Paper 2526. The World Bank East Asia and Pacific Region, Hanoi Country Office, January.

## KEY TERMS AND DEFINITIONS

**AG:** Affinity Group

**DMP Programme:** Desa Mandiri Pangan Program (Food Self Sufficiency Village Programme)

**FVT:** The Village Food Team

**GDP:** Gross Domestic Product

**LKD:** Lembaga Keuangan Desa (Microfinancial Village Institusional)

**NGOs:** Non-Governmental Institution

**NTFS:** Non-Timber Forest Productions

**NTPFPs:** Timber and Non-Timber Forest Products

**PNPM:** Program Nasional Pemberdayaan Masyarakat Mandiri (National Programme Community Empowerments)

**PPA:** Participatory Poverty Assessment

**PRA:** Participatory Rural Appraisal

**RMU:** Rice Milling Unit

# Chapter 7
# The Study of Digital Marketplace in Brunei Darussalam

**Alif Azizi Abdullah**
https://orcid.org/0000-0001-6760-6902
*Universiti Brunei Darussalam, Brunei*

**Mohammad Nabil Almunawar**
https://orcid.org/0000-0001-5296-2576
*Universiti Brunei Darussalam, Brunei*

**Muhammad Anshari**
https://orcid.org/0000-0002-8160-6682
*Universiti Brunei Darussalam, Brunei*

## ABSTRACT

*A two-sided market or two-sided network is made up of two distinct user groups that provide each other with network benefits in which they interact through an intermediary or platform. A digital marketplace makes use of a two-sided market where the two distinct groups are the buyers and sellers. A digital marketplace is a type of e-commerce site where the sellers offer products or services to the buyers, and transactions are controlled and processed by marketplace operators. With the rapid development and adoption of the Internet and digital marketplace globally and also regionally, businesses in Brunei Darussalam are slowly incorporating digital marketplace. This chapter provides an overview of the current state of the digital marketplace in Brunei, and thus, case studies of local digital marketplaces are discussed. A qualitative approach, which consists of interviews with companies, is made for the study. The strengths and problems of employing digital marketplace for businesses and analysis using Michael Porter's five models is also covered in this chapter.*

DOI: 10.4018/978-1-7998-2257-8.ch007

## INTRODUCTION

With the accelerating progress of the Internet, businesses can generate new opportunities that create values through digital technologies of the Internet. Lumpkin and Gregory (2004) state that the Internet has a significant impact on the economy that acts as a technology-driven initiative. The rapid progress of the Internet is genuinely fast that it dictates the expansion patterns of other sectors in which businesses that conduct their operations through the Internet have proposed appropriate recommendations to thrive in the marketplace (Mahadevan, 2000).

The Internet has changed how businesses conduct transactions, along with creating a new form of interaction with consumers, which leads to electronic commerce (e-commerce). Andam (2003) states that e-commerce is associated with a vast range of business activities made online that incorporates products and services. These include any forms of business transactions that involve in the interaction between parties that made electronically rather than by physical purchase or direct physical contact. Business transactions made can be B2B (business to business) e-commerce, a form of e-commerce between companies, that deals with the relationships between and among companies. Another type of e-commerce is B2C (business to consumer) e-commerce, which is e-commerce between companies and consumers. These involve consumers collecting information, buying physical products (furniture and consumer goods), or information goods (e-books or software) which received over an electronic network. While C2C (consumer to consumer) e-commerce refers to commerce between individuals or consumers, which are identified by the advancement of electronic marketplaces and online auctions. (Andam, 2003)

Bakos (1991) states that the presence of a transaction process generally indicates the interactions between buyers and sellers of a market where products and services exchanged between consumers and suppliers. A typical e-commerce is digital marketplace that consists of the sell-side (allowing businesses to sell their products to buyers), buy-side (enabling companies to carry out procurement tasks), and a marketplace (electronic marketplaces lead numerous buyers and sellers together in a single web) that mediate transactions (Durfee & Chen, 2002). E-commerce recent technologies on the internet have modified the range of capability of conducting operations in the marketplace (Chircu & Kauffman, 2013).

The presence of these technologies in the current fast-paced, innovative environment has enabled products and services offered in a new and better way for consumers. Giaglis, Klein, and O'Keefe (2000) state that the function of electronic markets as digital intermediaries brings buyers and sellers together on a digital platform. eBay was one of the earliest digital intermediaries of platforms that mediate transactions in which did not previously exist (Bailey & Bakos, 1997). According to Sarkar, Butler, & Steinfield (2006), almost every digital intermediary supports the interactions between buyers and sellers. Where new regulatory form recognized acts as a digital intermediary, operating as a digital support role that prioritizes the intermediation between buyer and seller. Bakos (1998) mentioned the benefits of digital intermediaries include assuring that the transaction can deliver expertise on products and operations along with informational support and guarantee on successful completion of transactions.

Chircu & Kauffman (2013) state that digital intermediaries generally revolve around the communication enhancing capability that the Internet provides. Digital intermediaries can introduce aggregation, support, expertise, search, and matching agreement potentials into a virtual capacity of the new marketplace. Digital intermediaries are similar to a digital marketplace where they act as platforms as a middle man between users and businesses. A digital marketplace demands a robust and rightly managed, IT-based system to innovate, update and introduce a multitude of digital services for the consumers. There are various types of digital marketplaces available in the world, commonly e-commerce, e-services, digital media, smart home, e-health, FinTech, e-travel, and digital advertising (Islam, 2018). The objective of this article is to determine the current state of the digital marketplace in Brunei Darussalam.

## BACKGROUND

The universal adoption of the Internet throughout the world and the expansion of the Web have undoubtedly transformed the way consumers conduct business electronically. The Internet, wireless communications, and digital technologies represent a technology-driven source that generates a noticeable influence on the economy. These technologies driven initiatives change the way businesses interact with each other and their consumers. The changes created an environment where companies are required to perform at a higher level – smarter, faster, cheaper, and initiating new business opportunities (Lumpkin & Gregory, 2004). The digital world of the Internet has been continuously changing, which produced evolving technologies, the way the world uses them, the way information is retrieved. The Internet is also reconstructing the interaction and communication of the society with one another globally, which also affects the products and services bought and selected by the consumers (Ryan & Jones, 2016).

### E-Commerce

The web is an effective medium to conduct e-commerce, which makes web-based e-commerce more preferred. The growing number of consumers choose to adopt the

Internet to shop for products and services (Wolfe, Hsu, & Kang, 2004). Especially services and products that are information-based where consumers can get immediately after their transactions are accepted and confirmed.

E-commerce defined as both informational and financial transactions that transacted electronically between an organization with any third party. E-commerce operations include management of online sales transactions and non-financial transactions, which are inbound customer service inquiries and outbound email broadcasts. There are two perspectives in e-commerce, sell-side e-commerce, which refers to the transactions between a supplier and its customers and buy-side e-commerce that relates to the transactions between a buying organization and its suppliers.

Electronic business (e-business) is the management of business operations on the Internet and digital technologies. E-business operations include the buying and selling of products, services, supplies, assisting customers, handling payments, supervising production control, working together with business partners, information sharing, handling computerized employees' services, recruiting, and more (Damanpour & Damanpour, 2001). In recent times, e-business has been globally recognized for its vast potential to transform business structures effectively, models, and operations of a company or business (Kirs & Bagchi, 2012; Zhu, Kraemer, & Xu, 2006). A company or industry that adopts e-business into their business structure can influence their relationships with customers, suppliers, and other business partners (Grünhagen et al., 2014).

According to Turban, King, Lee, and Viehland (2004), the combination of business and management practices using the Internet enables e-business to accommodate communication technologies. Murphy and Taylor (2004) argue that businesses adopting e-commerce is a crucial factor. This factor contributes to the rise of economic growth, provided that these businesses have considerable buyers, sellers, employers, and innovators. Greenspan (2002) states that the rapid advancement of network technologies and open standards, including lowered communication rate, businesses are shifting into a digital platform. That is internet-based that guarantees a considerable rise in productivity. Technological innovations generally acknowledged as a primary driver of productivity in industries, but if promising innovations are not taken advantage of, benefits from the changes are decreased (Zhu et al., 2006).

## Digital Marketplace

The digital marketplace refers to a type of e-commerce platform where various third parties provide products and services, and third parties include businesses, vendors, consumers, and firms. As a consequent of the rise in the application and rapid advancement of digital marketplaces globally, adopting the digital marketplace became an essential aspect for businesses. The digital innovation and new technologies aided in the progress of digital marketplaces (Aldrich, 1999), have enabled marketplaces owners to attain more customers globally (Eng, 2004) with acceptable costs (Rask & Kragh, 2004).

Kirchner and Schüßler (2019) defined the digital marketplace as a platform that aids in improving socio-technical infrastructures. The digital marketplace establishes new forms of internet intermediaries between buyers and sellers that are not associated with the platform openly. According to Beckert (2009), digital marketplaces represent an extension of general market models. It is considering that public markets contain at least three participants – one buyer and two rival sellers. Digital marketplaces need an additional fourth participant, the market organizer. Market organizers assist in market transactions by creating and running a market order for external sellers and buyers (Evans, Schmalensee, Noel, Chang, & Garcia-Swartz, 2011).

Digital marketplaces conducted throughout various domains: e-commerce marketplaces (AliBaba.com, Amazon.com) (Guo et al., 2006; Mahadevan, 2000), group buying marketplaces (Groupon.com, LivingSocial.com) (Edelman, Jaffe, & Kominers, 2011), online auctions marketplace (Apple's AppStore, Google Play) (Hyrynsalmi et al., 2012; West & Mace, 2010). Amazon and eBay are the earliest adopters of digital marketplaces, which then grew into well-established e-commerce firms. These e-commerce firms provide a platform for buyers and sellers, enabling them to interact with each other and handle transactions through the related platforms. Platforms produce a system to assist transactions between strangers, which can be remarkable as well as eliminating the time and geographical restrictions of the two parties.

## Two-Sided Markets

The digital marketplace, in terms of two-sided markets, functions as a platform for two specific groups, which are the buyers and sellers. Two-sided networks, which are another term for two-sided markets, refer to the platforms that support the interaction between a distinct but inter-dependent group of users. These groups consist of buyers and suppliers, making the platform of two-sided networks an essential aspect in the current business environment. Presently, new projects created on the model of two-sided networks, and sellers are suggesting platform-type services that can connect buyers with numerous sellers simultaneously (Koh & Fichman, 2010).

Rochet and Tirole (2006) define two-sided markets as the dimension in which transactions between end-users rely on their structure and not merely relying on the level of fees imposed by the platform. Usage of the platform or variable charges affects the two sides' readiness to trade once on the platform. Resulting in net revenue from potential interactions; membership provided by the platform or fixed fees demanded from end-users on the platform. Examples of two-sided markets are videogame platforms, such as Nintendo, Sega, Sony Play Station, and Microsoft X-Box. These videogame platforms are required to attract gamers to convince game developers to develop or dock games to their platform. As well as influencing players to buy and use their videogame consoles.

In two-sided networks, network externalities categorized as either intra-network externalities or internetwork externalities. Inter-network externalities are features of one side of the platform that affect users on the other side of the platform. In the majority of situations, the inter-network externalities on the two-sided networks are positive, where the expected gain of users on one side of the platform rises with growing activity levels on the opposite side of the system (Eisenmann, Parker, & Van Alstyne, 2006).

## Digital Platform

The Digital platform has transformed nearly every business today, and it is the first approach chosen to organize an extensive range of human activities, including economic, political, and social interaction (Tan et al., 2015). A digital platform referred to as a two-sided market that comprises an environment of a supplier and consumer groups that participates in transactions and exchanges (Amit & Zott, 2001). According to (Spagnoletti, Resca, & Lee, 2015), digital platforms are changing the development of the entire IS landscape, the interaction between user and organizations are changing as digital platforms aid in online communities of consumers. The growth of digital platforms has changed well-established industries, for instance, in transportation (Grab, Uber), hospitality (Airbnb, Couchsurfing) and software development (Android, iOS)

Different characteristics of digital platforms can indicate its benefits to businesses. First, it helps with the considerable transaction costs, which include search, distribution, contracting, and monitoring costs (Eisenmann et al., 2006; Pagani, 2013). For example, a group of platforms, namely TripAdvisor and Expedia, gather and incorporate travel information from various sources into a single platform, which can reduce the cost of searching for information as well as acquiring support from intermediary agents. Second, through the assistance of governing bodies and digital modularity, platforms support the integration of technological advancement of products (Boudreau, 2010; Tiwana, Konsynski, & A. Bush, 2010). For instance, Google's Android and Apple's iOS provide individual software developers with technical and regulatory structures, which can encourage and assist their support in developing applications. Apart from these aspects, another feature broadly discussed, such as the cross-side network effect (Hagiu, 2014; S. Evans, Hagiu, & Schmalensee,

2006). Cross-side network effects indicate the significance of a platform for a user on one side increases as the number of users on the other size increases. For example, e-commerce platforms such as Amazon and eBay, the significance of the platform from the seller will increase when there is an increase of buyers on the other side, and vice versa.

## Michael Porter Five Forces

Porter's five forces are the suggestion in which includes the industry organization theory (IO). The theory suggests that the attractiveness of industries, a firm's operation, is determined by the market structure that affects the market participants (Raible, 2013). Porter's model was recommended to aid in the analysis of forces inside an industry that encourages competition, therefore, to understand the attractiveness of entering the sector with regards to the investments as well as the vulnerable points that need reinforcing (Cafferky, 2005). The model includes – the threat of new entrants, threat of substitute products, rivalry among existing competitors, the bargaining power of buyers, and the bargaining power of suppliers.

The threat of new entrants is the new entrants penetrating the industry that carry new scope and ambition to obtain the market share that impacts costs, prices, and rate of investment which are required to compete. The threat of substitute products refers to the substitute products that accomplish the same or in a similar function as an industrial product in a different nature. It leads to the indirect threat of substitute products when it displaces a buyer industry's product, and substitutes often disregarded because of their difference from an industry's product. Prices discounts, new products, advertisements, and proved services are different types of rivalry among existing competitors.

The presence of intense rivalry between competitors tends to limit the profitability of an industry, in the intensity of rivalry that reduces an industry's potential profit relies on the magnitude in which companies compete and the platform on which they compete. Bargaining power of suppliers reveals that influential suppliers get more value for themselves by demanding higher prices, decreasing the quality of products and services, and transferring cost to industry participants. Prominent suppliers and suppliers of labor can acquire profit from an industry that is unable to pass on, increasing the cost of its prices. The bargaining power of buyers is identical to influential suppliers in which convincing buyers can get more value by lowering prices and encouraging better quality or additional services, which can increase costs. Influential buyers possess negotiating advantage comparable to participants of the industry, especially when buyers are price-sensitive, exploiting their power to influence price reductions (Porter, 2008)

## AIM OF ARTICLE

Bruneians become well adapted to the idea of utilizing the digital marketplace into their lives, but local businesses are yet to fully grasp the importance of integrating digital marketplace and e-commerce into their business structures. However, there is a lack of research in finding factors of adopting the digital marketplace amongst businesses in Brunei Darussalam. This article aims to investigate elements of selecting the digital marketplace and challenges faced by the companies to gain access to accurate insights regarding the current state of the digital marketplace in Brunei Darussalam. By organizing interviews with businesses, it will help to identify important factors of adopting digital marketplace as well as determining the challenges faced by local businesses. By analysing the considerations and challenges, it is hoped to provide clarification on the current overview of the state of the digital marketplace in Brunei Darussalam.

### Issues, Controversies, Problems

Digital marketplace adoption in Brunei is still in the initial stages of its development, where a reasonable number of companies or businesses incorporate the digital marketplace into their business as well as to market their products and services. The most prominent usage of the digital marketplace used by the population of Brunei is for shopping (e-commerce) (AITI, 2018), found that approximately 78 percent of the population is utilizing e-commerce to shop, bank, and pay bills. The survey reveals the Malaysian digital marketplace (ZALORA) and Chinese shopping site (Alibaba) have gained a strong position amongst e-commerce users of Brunei, in which 47 percent of respondents of e-commerce users shopped on eBay, 36 percent belongs to ZALORA and 18 percent for Amazon. The survey states that only 5 percent of the respondents use local e-commerce sites that include Royal Brunei Airlines, Telbru, and DST's online payment site (The Scoop, 2018). This statistical information shows that the population of Brunei Darussalam favours using the international digital marketplace rather than local ones.

## METHODOLOGY

### Study Design

A case study approach was selected in this qualitative research to gather information needed regarding the study. Face to face interviews suggested, given its ability to specify and produce follow up questions and issues throughout the period of the discussion, in addition to the exploratory nature of the study. In regards to the positive factors that digital marketplaces offer, this study attempts to determine the elements of adoption as well as challenges businesses faced upon adopting it. For this reason, a questionnaire was developed specifically to retrieve relevant information about those as mentioned earlier. The study examined five local e-commerce digital marketplaces operated by local Bruneians. Respondents of the interview range from 23 to 40 years old. Interviews were carried out from March to May of 2019, depending on the availability of the interviewee and held at the business's premises. The average time to complete the interview was approximately 20 minutes. Conversations were recorded using a voice memo application through a smartphone. Since there is limited availability of suitable digital marketplaces in regards to the study, only two local digital marketplaces were chosen to participate in the interviews. Of each company, a leading person(s) who has in-depth knowledge of the business was contacted to participate in the meeting.

Interviews were carried out to determine the current state of their business with the adoption of the digital marketplace. Strengths and weaknesses derived from the information gathered and then analysed. Furthermore, the strengths and weaknesses identified are then put into categories to give better insights into local businesses. In the form of observation and first-hand experience, local businesses platform is taken into account to gain the understanding and usability of the business platforms. Note that the tool for gathering information from the respondents' can be found in the appendix.

## Data Analysis

Information gathered from the interviews was analysed thoroughly, interpreting the data, understanding, and listening to the conversations repeatedly, which includes necessary observations and transcribing data. Concerning the objective of the study, it is hoped that the information collected can answer the purpose of this study. Analysed data from the local businesses are expected to provide the current state of the digital marketplace in Brunei Darussalam.

# FINDINGS AND DISCUSSION

The case study method chosen in this qualitative research, which includes several digital marketplaces cases. By applying the case study method, similarities and differences of the digital marketplaces can outline and analyzed to devise conclusions among the examples.

*Figure 1. Sequence of case study method*
*(Source: Author's compilation, 2019)*

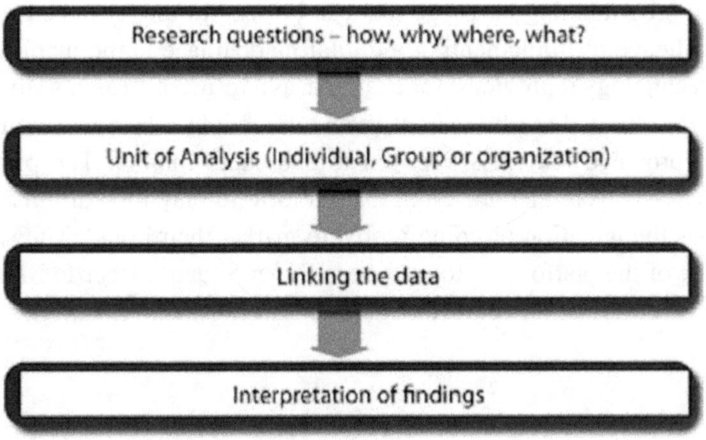


The study unveils the numerous reasons from the businesses, and these reasons contribute to the adoption of the digital marketplace into their business structure. (Yin, 1994) states that case studies are the investigation of a particular event empirically within its surroundings, in which the relationship between the surroundings and the situation is unclear. Hence, a case is investigated to identify an issue or provide input to an existing theory or theoretical concept in which a case study's unit of measure is related to the entity concept.

## Super Squad Soccer

Super Squad Soccer, formerly known as Weekend Warriors, was founded in 2018 and is an online football/futsal platform. In Brunei Darussalam, football/futsal is one of the most popular sports, and therefore, the need to create a platform where players can play as an individual or as a team in different venues is essential, and the company managed to establish this platform. Super Squad Soccer is the first online platform for football/futsal in Brunei Darussalam, which acts as an intermediary to provide venues and bring players together under one platform.

Firstly, by making use of a digital marketplace, Super Squad Soccer eliminates the tedious process of having to gather players, providing the right equipment, and obtaining a facility to play football/futsal. Secondly, by having a digital marketplace, it enables Super Squad Soccer to take full advantage of the smartphone usage in Brunei Darussalam, the ability to attract players across the country to use their platform through the use of social media mainly Instagram as well as verbal communication. A website is provided for players to register their details, purchase credits (credits to play one session), book slots for upcoming sessions, and to attend the football/futsal session.

Some of the challenges they face include the difficulty in recruiting personnel with specific skill sets needed, for example, hiring a programmer whose expertise is in Avalon programming language that can be used to improve their operations. Another challenge of implementing a digital marketplace is the inability to fully utilize the technology it provides, for example, as a result of Brunei's small market. The platform is limited to said market, even though it has the opportunity to grow even more, provided that it is exposed to a broader market. The platform has over 700 active players that are using the platform to play football/futsal, and the company has the intention of going global to market their brand. The subsequent development of the platform is to introduce Super Squad Soccer to Malaysia and the rest of Southeast Asian countries.

## Al-Huffaz

*Al-Huffaz* was founded in 2016 and is an online platform that provides Islamic religious-based services. The main activity of the company is to teach *Al-Quran* recitations by matching *Al-Quran* tutors with a student who wishes to learn *Al-Quran*. It acts as an intermediary that provides expertise in teaching *Al-Quran* recitations to the public. *Al-Huffaz* started from the experiences of an individual from teaching. *Al-Quran* recitations to the public for 13 years, and as it proceeded, there was an increase of demand for *Al-Quran* classes in Brunei Darussalam, which led *Al-Huffaz* to start recruiting tutors to cater to the growing number of students. Brunei Darussalam is well known for its status as an Islamic monarchy that practices Islamic teachings in their everyday lives; the rise of *Al-Huffaz* was well received by the public.

By employing the digital marketplace into their business structure, *Al-Huffaz* can provide a platform where the public can learn *Al-Quran* recitations at their convenience rather than attending fixed schedule classes that can be inconvenient to their schedule. Most of the users using the platform are young parents and the elderly population of Brunei. Some of the challenges faced by *Al-Huffaz* include gaining the trust of the public to use the platform since the audience is familiar with traditional ways of learning *Al-Quran* recitation mainly through classes that are provided by mosques on public holidays.

The platform provides a website where the public can seek tutors according to their current location, review the tutor's schedule, book their preferred slots, and attend the arranged class. A reminder is usually sent via email to both student and tutor a few hours before their respective classes begin. Currently, *Al-Huffaz* has 1500 students, with 150 tutors recruited into their system. The goal of *Al-Huffaz* is to become the world's largest *Al-Quran* teaching platform, targeting to develop in 3 countries in Southeast Asia (Brunei, Singapore, and Indonesia) in the future.

## Naindah

Initially launched by its parent company, an IT company (TechBru Solutions (B) Sdn Bhd), *Naindah* is an online marketplace for both businesses and the public to buy and sell used and new items securely. It launched in 2017 in the hope of revitalizing Brunei's shopping culture. *Naindah* acts as an intermediary that inspects the new and used products in their warehouse before posting it online into the website, fulfilling the issue customers are facing where they are unhappy with the quality of the products in terms of its authenticity and damages to it. Firstly, by making use of an online marketplace, *Naindah* provides a solution to locals and international customers to market their used and new products in Brunei Darussalam. Secondly, by having an online marketplace is the easiest way to reach customers rather than going to physical shops.

*Naindah* aims to help customers to get the products undamaged and in excellent condition when delivered to them. *Naindah* owns a delivery service called *Naindah*Go that delivers its items to customers provided with tracking options to know the location of the package, and it offers same-day delivery even in Kuala Belait. *Naindah* is creating a win-win situation with local vendors with low cost marketing for their products, they focus on local vendors to help them be relevant in the market. *Naindah* has been marketing its brand to international vendors in more varieties of products and vendors into the platform. Some of the challenges they face are the difficulty of attracting local and global vendors to join their online marketplace, and the struggle to maintain the platform in terms of outsourcing or insourcing the maintenance works to minimize cost and the lack of familiarity. *Naindah's* future projects include integrating their business into a mobile application that incorporates grocery shopping, international payments as well as mobile payments for shops in Brunei, which all are accessible through a smartphone.

## Babakimpo

*Babakimpo* is an e-commerce platform that sells household appliances, groceries, cosmetics, and electronics. The company started recruiting employees in 2017, and its parent company Goldmyne funded it. *Babakimpo* owns a logistics company to deliver its merchandise from suppliers to Brunei, which can save costs as well as saving time.

Products are stored in their warehouse, which is in a separate location than their main office. They bought their first server from Malaysia to support the functions and to store the data of their website. Firstly, implementing an online marketplace into their business makes it easier for their customers and for the company gaining the ability to monitor massive amounts of orders through the system as well as storing customer details into the server. Thus, the company will be able to create statistics based on the data collected, which can help the company improve its business structure. Secondly, taken into account the nature in which the population of Brunei Darussalam tends to use smartphones everywhere and anywhere in their daily life, *Babakimpo* took advantage of the matter by creating an online marketplace. *Babakimpo* provides locals with a platform where they can sell their products; some of the local vendors are from 1K1P (1 kampong 1 product), which markets the product of villages in Brunei Darussalam. In the early stages of the company, they started exposing *Babakimpo* to the locals by selling online and offline to build-up the brand name as well as attracting customers to buy from *Babakimpo*.

Some of the challenges they have faced are the challenge to educate the locals on the benefits of making use of an e-commerce marketplace, which can be beneficial for them and local vendors. The difficulty of understanding and catering demands of locals in terms of variety of products they want and need tends to be one of the biggest challenges for *Babakimpo* as well as gaining their trust to conduct transactions through the website. *Babakimpo* is expanding its business by opening a new physical shop to sell their products and a new office to incorporate their growing company. They also improved their shopping experience for customers by introducing cash on delivery (COD) for their customers.

## J3smart

J3smart is an e-commerce platform that caters to everything that consumers need, ranging from electrical appliances, clothing, toys, and types of machinery. J3smart received funding by its parent company Sivli Logistics, which provides logistics solutions to the consumers. The company was established in 2017, aiming to be a one-stop online shop for regular customers or businesses. By creating an online marketplace, J3smart intends on providing consumers a range of products that are absent in Brunei, thus making it easy and convenient for consumers to get what they want. Firstly, by recognizing the growing trend for online shopping in Brunei, it was ideal for J3smart to create an online marketplace to fulfill consumers' spending. Secondly, by having an online marketplace, J3smart can provide consumers with a variety of products with affordable prices that depends on the quantity and the delivery services.

J3smart attracts customers by offering promotions in terms of free delivery and discounts. Some of the challenges faced by J3smart are gaining trust from the locals to use the platform to order products since locals are unconvinced of making transactions on the website, and locals tend to be concerned about the quality of the products. Another challenge is the maintenance of the site since it was outsourced and maintained by a foreigner; it takes time to fix issues regarding the website. The next plan of J3smart includes the introduction of Jpay, which is a form of e-wallet that enables consumers to store points and store digital cash in it.

## STRENGTHS OF ADOPTING DIGITAL MARKETPLACE FOR THE BUSINESSES

### Local Service Center

With the availability of a service center in the country, it enables consumers and users to get assistance promptly. Consumers buying products from the local e-commerce marketplace can change or refund their products faster compared to buying from an international digital marketplace where the process is tedious. Users of services can get in touch with customer service personally for assistance on their matters. Local service center shows consumers and users their existence and credibility of their firms to gain their trust.

### Support for Local SMEs

Entrepreneurship in Brunei Darussalam is still developing an entirely new, where the majority of the digital marketplace in Brunei Darussalam are startups developed by entrepreneurs bringing life into their business ideas. The businesses are established and managed by locals, which provides employment opportunities to fresh graduates as well as the unemployed. Due to the small market of Brunei Darussalam, purchasing products or services from these businesses show support for local products (1K1P – 1 product 1 kampong) and services they provide, by doing so, contributing to the growth of their companies that can enable them to improve their business structure.

### Attraction Power

With Internet penetration more than 90% in Brunei Darussalam, smartphones became a necessity for Bruneians. With access to the Internet, it enables the consumer to access the local digital marketplaces with ease from their smartphones in terms of mobile applications and websites. By utilizing the digital marketplace into their business structure, they can attract more consumers to visit and potentially buy their products and use their services. With access to the Internet, businesses can advertise their products and services through emails, social media, and mobile application notifications through consumer's smartphones.

## Variety and Greater Choices

Local e-commerce marketplaces such as *Babakimpo* and J3smart contains more than 3000 products offered in their platforms. Having a variety and more excellent choices of products provide consumers with an appealing factor to shop in their platforms. The products offered range from clothing, household appliances, cosmetics, electronics, and types of machinery. More significant choices of products mean a better deal for consumers.

## Reviews from Consumers

The digital marketplace enables consumers to give reviews of products and services offered on the platform. Reviews of products and services can help build loyalty and trust of consumers. Reports allow potential consumers to know the product much clearly and the aspects that distinguish the products from others in different marketplaces in which ultimately increase sales. With excellent reviews from consumers, the e-commerce marketplace can easily advertise its potential/prospects via consumer feedback. Reviews are also a great way to interact with consumers directly, knowing the details of the products instantly from their point of view and making development wherever necessary. By making full use of reviews from consumers, it can lead to a positive experience for the consumer, which will help the business in the future.

## Problem Solving Digital Marketplace

SuperSquadSoccer and *Al-Huffaz* management are examples of digital marketplaces that solves problems that the population of Brunei Darussalam has experienced. SuperSquadSoccer provides a platform in which football players can meet and play with minimal requirements in which the company offers everything in terms of fields, jerseys, football necessities (ball, post, referees) and players, which replaces the tedious traditional process of getting a venue, players and essentials for playing football whereas *Al-Huffaz* acts as an intermediary that provides expertise in teaching *Al-Quran* recitations to the public, offering flexible schedules for the public to learn recitation in their convenience and in the comfort of their homes, which replaces the traditional method of learning recitation on fixed programs at mosques and halls.

## PROBLEMS OF ADOPTING DIGITAL MARKETPLACE FOR THE BUSINESSES

### Delivery Times

The average time for products to get delivered to the doorsteps of consumers is in 2-3 weeks. As all the items from the local e-commerce digital marketplace are pre-order, it can be frustrating for consumers due to the longer delivery times. These delivery times are preliminary without taking into account customs problems, courier schedules, and notification cards (authorization items have arrived at local post depot). These factors will potentially delay the arrival of products purchased to the consumers, which will damage the business to consumer relationship.

### Competition with Foreign Digital Marketplace

Locals prefer to shop using a foreign digital marketplace due to their shorter delivery times and better prices. Most foreign digital marketplace provides options of standard or express delivery depending on consumer needs. They also offer better rates compared to the local businesses to attract international consumers, where local businesses focus on domestic spending power. The gap between the foreign digital marketplace and local ones can be shown by their duration of operation, where big companies such as Amazon, eBay, Zalora boasts many years of operating in the vast market and processing high levels of transactions. The credibility of these companies already established, and consumers know what to expect for in their products and services.

### Penetration of International Brands

Local e-commerce marketplace lacks the penetration of international brands, in which unbranded products offered in their platforms compared to products such as Nike, Adidas, LG, Samsung, Uniqlo, H&M, and Bosch in foreign e-commerce marketplaces. Thus, affecting consumer's decision to purchase products due to its credibility compared to branded products in which consumers know what to expect. With the absence of international brands from the local e-commerce marketplace, it is difficult to compete with the foreign marketplace, which provides consumers with branded products.

### Privacy and Security

Privacy and security play a significant role in consumers using e-commerce marketplaces in which incorporate consumers' personal information. It directly influences consumer's decision to shop in e-commerce marketplaces. Local consumers of Brunei Darussalam are wary of the possibility that their personal information may be at risk of being misused by unwanted parties. Consumer's trust in the e-commerce marketplace influences their decision on using them.

### Consumer Understanding

With the rising implementation of the digital marketplace in Brunei Darussalam in which businesses are still entirely new to it, consumer understanding towards the digital marketplace is significant in attracting consumers to shop using the local e-commerce marketplace. Local e-commerce marketplaces expressed their issue on this in which locals have problems using the e-commerce marketplace in terms of ordering and payment of products. On another note, consumers are unable to realize that the digital marketplace can be beneficial to them, and it can improve their shopping experience.

### Quality of Products and Services

Quality is the ability of a product or service to meet a consumer's expectations for that product or service. Quality includes the appearance, durability, usability, and standard of the product or service. Based on a survey made by AITI (2018), one of the problems encountered by 34% of respondents is that products purchased did not meet their expectations. If the quality of the product or services does not meet the expectations of consumers, consumers will potentially choose new places to get products and services.

## PORTER'S FIVE FORCES MODEL

By enforcing the five forces model, it enables an organization to attain a great sense of knowledge on the way profit is divided between the five forces in a particular industry. It is allowing the organization to gain a better insight into participants of the industry that have the power and control over the rules of activities of a particular industry. It permits an organization to analyze the sector of potential changes in the future and at a specific point in time. Using the five forces to analyze an industry, it would help to assess the attractiveness of entering the industry (Bruijl, 2018). Porter's five forces model could be observed in the businesses of Brunei Darussalam.

## Threat of New Entrants (Services)

**Current situation:** High
**Near future:** High

According to (Rajak, 2018), The Bruneian, a trusted e-source in Brunei Darussalam. Brunei Darussalam has placed 4th globally, with 95% of the nation have access to the Internet and are utilizing it through digital media. A survey made by the Authority for Info-communications Technology Industry (AITI) in 2018 (AITI, 2018), found that 83% of the respondents use their smartphones to acquire products and services online. These statistics support that the population of Brunei Darussalam is well-acquainted with technological trends through the Internet and social media such as Instagram and Facebook. Local e-commerce platforms use the Internet and social media for marketing their products and services as well as to attract customers.

There is a considerable number of digital marketplaces that provide products and services in Brunei Darussalam, but their attractiveness depends on the products and services they offer to locals. *Al-Huffaz* and Super Squad Soccer can penetrate and be relevant in the Brunei market because of the demand for their services (football/futsal platform and *Al-Quran* lessons). Therefore, it can be considered that the threat of new entrants to be high. The market for e-commerce platforms is easily accessible to locals, but new entrants will be competing against established e-commerce platforms such as Super Squad Soccer, *Al-Huffaz*, *Naindah*, *Babakimpo*, and J3smart. New entrants may find it difficult to build-up their company due to the market's need for relevant products and services that enable them to compete.

## Bargaining Power of Suppliers (Services)

**Current situation:** Medium
**Near Future:** Low

Considering Super Squad Soccer and *Al-Huffaz* are successful startups, they have developed their company by relying on local personnel and facilities. As a consequent of the limited presence of facilities locally that are needed for Super Squad Soccer to achieve their business model and the limited number of tutors that are *Al-Quran* literate in Brunei Darussalam, the bargaining power of suppliers is considered to be medium. Medium bargaining power of suppliers means that they have slightly more control over companies that use or need the facilities or workforce, which in this case are the football/futsal venues and *Al-Quran* tutors. It also means that there is a limited number of suppliers to choose from. An e-commerce platform needs to recruit a team of specific skill sets for the business to operate, for example, a programmer, an *Al-Quran* tutor. The bargaining power of suppliers may be low in the future when the company grows or venture out into other regions gaining access to more significant facilities and tutors as well as a broader market.

## Bargaining Power of Buyers (Services)

**Current situation:** Low
**Near Future:** Medium

With an internet penetration of over 90%, the population has a limited choice of alternatives to Super Squad Soccer and *Al-Huffaz*. Consumers confined to these choices due to their popularity and dominance in the market. The bargaining power of buyers is considered low due to the options they have. Switching costs can be regarded as high because no other alternatives are present other than traditional methods of the services provided by the Super Squad Soccer and *Al-Huffaz*. Switching cost refers to the effect consumers face in terms of investment and loss by changing service providers (Ting, 2014). At present, consumers are expected to return to a trusted e-commerce platform, in which consumers have built trust with them beforehand.

## Threat of Substitute Products and Service (Services)

**Current situation:** Low
**Near future:** Medium

As a result of high switching costs, options available to consumers are limited. Consumers can opt for the traditional methods of acquiring the same services. However, the process can be tedious and time-consuming. Consumers can get better services with the time-saving process by using these platforms. The threat of substitute services for Super Squad Soccer and *Al-Huffaz* is considered low due to the disadvantageous nature of substitute services. The general need for consumers is to get excellent services, services that solve consumer's need, time-saving, and convenient.

## Rivalry Among Existing Competitors (Services)

**Current situation:** Low
**Near future:** Medium

There is limited availability of e-commerce platforms that provides the same services as Super Squad Soccer and *Al-Huffaz*. Super Squad Soccer provides the venue to play football/futsal, equipment, and the platform in which brings players together in a single website. *Al-Huffaz* matches students with *Al-Quran* tutors at their convenience. The general function of local e-commerce is to sell their services to consumers, although the services provided by Super Squad Soccer and *Al-huffaz* targets specific audiences, making the industry competition to be low. The reason for the little rivalry between industries is the variety of wants and needs of the local market for services marketplaces. Considering football/futsal is the nation's most popular sport, Super Squad Soccer took the initiative to develop the platform to cater to the number of football/futsal players that would use the platform. *Al-Huffaz* operations coincide with Brunei's status as an Islamic nation incorporating Islamic teachings and practices *Al-Quran* as life guidance. *Al-Huffaz* developed a platform to cater to the nation's demand in which was well received by the population and growing ever since.

## Threat of New Entrants (Products)

**Current situation:** High
**Near future:** High

Brunei Darussalam has the highest Instagram penetration in the world includes 63% of the population uses the video and photo-sharing platform. A survey made by the Authority for Info-communications Technology Industry (AITI) in 2018 found that 83% of respondents used their smartphones to purchase products or services online. These statistics verify that the population of Brunei Darussalam is well familiar with technological trends through the use of social media (Facebook, Instagram) and the Internet. Local e-commerce platform utilizes the Internet and social media to attract customers. With Internet penetration well over 90%, online shopping is becoming a nationwide trend in Brunei Darussalam. Online shopping gives customers the ability to gain access to online sources, a wide variety of products and services, secure payment platform, convenience, and faster delivery times. It can be considered the threat of new entrants to be high. The market for an e-commerce platform seems accessible in Brunei Darussalam, but new entrants will be competing against established local ones in Brunei Darussalam. With the likes of *Naindah*, *Babakimpo*, J3smart vying to be the to-go-to e-commerce platform, and the more popular ones amongst Bruneians, which are eBay, ZALORA, and Amazon. New entrants may find it hard to establish themselves by lacking the capital and experience to expose their brand through online/offline marketing, which can be costly and time consuming to gain credibility and trust of the customers.

## Bargaining Power of Suppliers (Products)

**Current situation:** Low
**Near future:** Medium

*Naindah*, J3smart, and *Babakimpo* get their supply from outside of Brunei due to its unavailability locally, gaining access to a range of substitutes abroad. Due to the presence of a wide range of suppliers, companies that cater to a variety of products and services to establish an e-commerce platform, the bargaining power of suppliers is considered to be low. Low bargaining power of suppliers means that they have minimal influence over companies that they sell to, which in this case, an e-commerce platform. It also means that there a lot of suppliers to choose from given the bargaining power of suppliers is low. Different suppliers would offer various quality products, prices of products, uniqueness of products, which can be found in the presence of substitutes. An e-commerce platform needs to order products in bulk, considering the cost, delivery, and human resources incorporated into it. Primary inputs that an e-commerce platform needs are a server for the back-end operations of the platform and its products (e.g., clothing, electronics, and furniture).

## Bargaining Power of Buyers (Products)

**Current situation:** High
**Near future:** High

With an Internet penetration of well over 90%, the population of Brunei Darussalam has a wide range of alternatives available. Consumers can search for the same products at different prices as well as comparing products. Consumers have access to different e-commerce platforms that offer different products. Users can sell their products and services on Instagram, and Facebook provides a platform to buy and sell products and services. The switching cost can be considered low due to the freedom of choice consumers have on where to purchase products and services, which offers alternatives to *Naindah*, J3smart, and *Babakimpo*. Switching cost is defined as the consequence customers face in terms of invest and lost by switching service providers (Ting, 2014). Consumers are likely to return to a trusted e-commerce platform where familiarity and trust between them have already built.

## Threat of Substitute Products and Service (Products)

**Current situation:** High
**Near Future:** High

Due to the low switching cost, consumers can explore other options that are available to them in terms of shopping online. Consumers can get better prices and faster delivery services from ZALORA and Amazon compared to J3smart and *Babakimpo*. In terms of shopping online, the general need for consumers is to get quality products with low costs and getting products swiftly and safely. J3smart and *Babakimpo* can retain their customers or attract new ones by giving them promotions on products and shipping charges, giving them loyalty points for every transaction they make and improving delivery time for customers.

## Rivalry Among Existing Competitors (Products)

**Current situation:** High
**Near future:** High

There is limited availability of e-commerce platforms in Brunei Darussalam; J3smart and *Babakimpo*, whereas *Naindah* sells new and used products from vendors and individuals. The general function of the local e-commerce platforms is to sell products to consumers, making the industry competition to be high. Local e-commerce platform also competes with the foreign e-commerce platforms that are well-known by the locals, which are eBay, Zalora, and Amazon. Online shopping can be competitive because of several reasons that include selling the latest products, selling trendiest products, low-cost shipping, and better delivery time. Taking notice of these reasons and improving them can be the catalyst in growing the business and thrive from other competitors. According to a trusted e-source in Brunei Darussalam, The Scoop (The Scoop, 2018), a survey made by Brunei's Internet regulator, 76% of Bruneians are using e-commerce to shop, pay bills and bank. While 57% of respondents prefer to shop via e-commerce websites, and 72% of respondents used e-commerce platforms to buy clothing and accessories

# CONCLUSION

The digital marketplace can change the interactions of businesses with consumers and the way businesses manage their operations. The presence of a digital marketplace provides an intermediary between buyers and sellers that reduces search costs, acquiring access to a variety of substitute products and services. In this study, some of the e-commerce platforms in Brunei Darussalam investigated, namely Super Squad, *Al-Huffaz, Naindah, Babakimpo,* and J3smart. It can be concluded that local businesses can manage to intercorporate digital marketplace into their business structure and that some of the e-commerce platforms in Brunei Darussalam have successfully secured themselves in the local markets through meeting demands of the market. The challenges faced by these local e-commerce platforms upon implementing the digital marketplace were also studied and determined using a qualitative approach through which a series of interviews were done. In addition to that, the factors of adopting the digital marketplace were identified and analyzed. From this study, it was also found that there is a very high tendency of individual customers who prefer to use foreign e-commerce platforms to buy their products and services. The reasons could be due to a better quality of services and services that provide solutions to problems and shorter delivery times.

This research received no specific grant from any funding agency in the public, commercial, or not-for-profit sectors.

## REFERENCES

AITI. (2018). AITI. Retrieved June 12, 2019, from https://www.aiti.gov.bn/SitePages/Surveys.aspx

Aldrich, D. F. (1999). *Mastering the Digital Marketplace: Practical Strategies for Competitiveness in the New Economy*. John Wiley & Sons.

Amit, R., & Zott, C. (2001). Value creation in E-business. *Strategic Management Journal*, *22*(6–7), 493–520. doi:10.1002mj.187

Andam, Z. R. (2003). E-Commerce and e-Business. *E-ASEAN Task Force UNDP-APDIP*, 47.

Bailey, J. P., & Bakos, Y. (1997). An Exploratory Study of the Emerging Role of Electronic Intermediaries. *International Journal of Electronic Commerce*, *1*(3), 7–20. doi:10.1080/10864415.1997.11518287

Bakos, Y. (1991). A Strategic Analysis of Electronic Marketplaces. *Management Information Systems Quarterly*, *15*(3), 295. doi:10.2307/249641

Bakos, Y. (1998). The emerging role of electronic marketplaces on the Internet. *Communications of the ACM*, *41*(8), 35–42. doi:10.1145/280324.280330

Beckert, J. (2009). The social order of markets. *Theory and Society*, *38*(3), 245–269. doi:10.100711186-008-9082-0

Bruijl, G. (2018). *The Relevance of Porter's Five Forces in Today's Innovative and Changing Business Environment*. SSRN Electronic Journal; doi:10.2139srn.3192207

Cafferky, M. (2005). *The Porter Five-forces Industry Analysis Framework For Religious Nonprofits: A conceptual analysis*.

Chircu, A. N., & Kauffman, R. J. (2013). *E-Commerce and V-Business*. Routledge.

Damanpour, F., & Damanpour, J. A. (2001). E-business e-commerce evolution: Perspective and strategy. *Managerial Finance*, *27*(7), 16–33. doi:10.1108/03074350110767268

Edelman, B., Jaffe, S., & Kominers, S. D. (2011). *To Groupon or Not to Groupon: The Profitability of Deep Discounts*. 24.

Eisenmann, T., Parker, G., & Van Alstyne, M. (2006). Strategies for two-sided markets. *Harvard Business Review, 84*, 92-101, 149.

Eng, T.-Y. (2004). The Role of E-Marketplaces in Supply Chain Management. *Industrial Marketing Management*, *33*(2), 97–105. doi:10.1016/S0019-8501(03)00032-4

Evans, D. S., Hagiu, A., & Schmalensee, R. (2006). *Invisible Engines: How Software Platforms Drive Innovation and Transform Industries*. doi:10.7551/mitpress/3959.001.0001

Evans, D. S., Schmalensee, R., Noel, M. D., Chang, H. H., & Garcia-Swartz, D. D. (2011). *Platform Economics: Essays on Multi-Sided Businesses* (SSRN Scholarly Paper No. ID 1974020). Retrieved from Social Science Research Network website: https://papers.ssrn.com/abstract=1974020

Giaglis, G. M., Klein, S., & O'Keefe, R. M. (2000). *The Role of Intermediaries in Electronic Marketplaces: Assessing Alternative Hypotheses for the Future*.

Greenspan, A. (2002). FRB: Testimony, Greenspan—Monetary policy report to the Congress, U.S. Senate—July 16, 2002. Retrieved May 20, 2019, from https://www.federalreserve.gov/boarddocs/hh/2002/july/testimony.htm

Hagiu, A. (2014). Strategic Decisions for Multisided Platforms. *MIT Sloan Management Review*, *55*, 92–93.

Hyrynsalmi, S., Mäkilä, T., Järvi, A., Suominen, A., Seppänen, M., & Knuutila, T. (2012). App Store, Marketplace, Play! An Analysis of Multi-Homing in Mobile Software Ecosystems. *IWSECO@ICSOB*.

Islam, N. (2018, March 15). *Making Digital Marketplaces Fairer [Keynote Paper presented in the "World Consumers Right Day 2018" on 15 March 2018 at Osmani Sriti Auditorium Organized by Ministry of Commerce, People's Republic of Bangladesh]*.

King, D., Chung, H. M., Lee, J. K., & Turban, E. (1999). Electronic commerce: A managerial perspective. Prentice Hall PTR.

Kirchner, S., & Schüßler, E. (2019). *The Organization of Digital Marketplaces: Unmasking the Role of Internet Platforms in the Sharing Economy*.

Kirs, P., & Bagchi, K. (2012). The impact of trust and changes in trust: A national comparison of individual adoptions of information and communication technologies and related phenomenon. *International Journal of Information Management, 32*(5), 431–441. doi:10.1016/j.ijinfomgt.2012.02.003

Koh, T. K., & Fichman, M. (2010). *Multi-Homing Users' Preferences for Two-Sided Exchange Networks* (SSRN Scholarly Paper No. ID 1635615). Retrieved from Social Science Research Network website: https://papers.ssrn.com/abstract=1635615

Lumpkin, G. T., & Gregory, G. D. (2004). E-Business Strategies and Internet Business Models. *Organizational Dynamics, 33*(2), 161–173. doi:10.1016/j.orgdyn.2004.01.004

Mahadevan, B. (2000). Business models for Internet-based e-commerce: An anatomy. *California Management Review, 42*(4), 55–69. doi:10.2307/41166053

Murphy, A., & Taylor, M. (2004). SMEs and e-business. *Journal of Small Business and Enterprise Development, 11*(3), 280–289. doi:10.1108/14626000410551546

Pagani, M. (2013). Digital Business Strategy and Value Creation: Framing the Dynamic Cycle of Control Points. *Management Information Systems Quarterly, 37*(2), 617–632. doi:10.25300/MISQ/2013/37.2.13

Porter, M. E. (2008). The Five Competitive Forces That Shape Strategy. *Harvard Business Review*, 19. PMID:18271320

Raible, M. (2013). *Industrial Organization theory and its contribution to decision-making in purchasing.*

Rajak, W. (2018). Brunei is world's 4th highest in social media penetration—The Bruneian. Retrieved June 10, 2019, from https://www.thebruneian.news/brunei-is-worlds-4th-highest-in-social-media-penetration

Rask, M., & Kragh, H. (2004). Motives for e-marketplace Participation: Differences and Similarities between Buyers and Suppliers. *Electronic Markets, 14*(4), 270–283. doi:10.1080/10196780412331311720

Rochet, J.-C., & Tirole, J. (2006). Two-sided markets: A progress report. *The Rand Journal of Economics, 37*(3), 645–667. doi:10.1111/j.1756-2171.2006.tb00036.x

Ryan, D., & Jones, C. (2016). *Understanding digital marketing: Marketing strategies for engaging the digital generation.* Kogan Page Publishers.

Spagnoletti, P., Resca, A., & Lee, G. (2015). A Design Theory for Digital Platforms Supporting Online Communities: A Multiple Case Study. *Journal of Information Technology, 30*(4), 364–380. doi:10.1057/jit.2014.37

Tan, B., Pan, S., Lu, X., & Huang, L. (2015). The Role of IS Capabilities in the Development of Multi-Sided Platforms: The Digital Ecosystem Strategy of Alibaba.com. *Journal of the Association for Information Systems*, *16*(4), 248–280. doi:10.17705/1jais.00393

The Scoop. (2018, July 15). Millennials driving e-commerce, says new report from AITI. Retrieved June 11, 2019, from The Scoop website: https://thescoop.co/2018/07/15/millennials-driving-ecommerce-report-aiti/

Ting, S.-C. (2014). *The Relationship between Customers' Switching Cost and Repurchase Intention: The Moderating Role of Satisfaction*. doi:10.4236/jssm.2014.74028

Turban, E., King, D., Lee, J. K., & Viehland, D. W. (2004). *Electronic commerce 2004: A managerial perspective* (International edition). Retrieved from https://trove.nla.gov.au/version/42646354

West, J., & Mace, M. (2010). Browsing as the killer app: Explaining the rapid success of Apple's iPhone. *Telecommunications Policy*, *34*(5–6), 270–286. doi:10.1016/j.telpol.2009.12.002

Wolfe, K., Hsu, C. H. C., & Kang, S. K. (2004). Buyer Characteristics Among Users of Various Travel Intermediaries. *Journal of Travel & Tourism Marketing*, *17*(2–3), 51–62. doi:10.1300/J073v17n02_05

Yin, R. (1994). Case study research: Design and methods (2nd ed.). Beverly Hills, CA.

Zhu, K., Kraemer, K. L., & Xu, S. (2006). The Process of Innovation Assimilation by Firms in Different Countries: A Technology Diffusion Perspective on E-Business. *Management Science*, *52*(10), 1557–1576. doi:10.1287/mnsc.1050.0487

## ADDITIONAL READING

Corbitt, B. J., Thanasankit, T., & Yi, H. (2003). Trust and e-commerce: A study of consumer perceptions. *Electronic Commerce Research and Applications*, *2*(3), 203–215. doi:10.1016/S1567-4223(03)00024-3

Guo, J., Lam, I. H., Lei, I., Guan, X., Iong, P. H., & Ieong, M. C. (2006). Alibaba International: Building a Global Electronic Marketplace. *2006 IEEE International Conference on E-Business Engineering (ICEBE'06)*, 545–548. 10.1109/ICEBE.2006.19

Hernández, J. (2015). Strategies for the Adoption of E-commerce. *Journal of Global Economics, 03*. doi:10.4172/2375-4389.1000157

Järvinen, J., Tollinen, A., Karjaluoto, H., & Jayawardhena, C. (2012). DIGITAL AND SOCIAL MEDIA MARKETING USAGE IN B2B INDUSTRIAL SECTION. *Marketing Management Journal, 22*(2).

Laudon, K. C., & Traver, C. G. (2016). *E-commerce: Business, technology, society*.

Molina-Castillo, F.-J., López-Nicolás, C., & Bouwman, H. (2008). Explaining mobile commerce services adoption by different type of customers. *Journal of Systemics, Cybernetics and Informatics, 6*, 73–79.

Pucihar, A., & Podlogar, M. (2005). E-Marketplace adoption success factors: Challenges and opportunities for a small developing country. *Electronic Business in Developing Countries: Opportunities and Challenges*, 88–117. doi:10.4018/978-1-59140-354-8.ch005

Rysman, M. (2009). The Economics of Two-Sided Markets. *The Journal of Economic Perspectives, 23*(3), 125–143. doi:10.1257/jep.23.3.125

Schafer, J. B., Konstan, J., & Riedl, J. (1999). Recommender systems in e-commerce. *Proceedings of the 1st ACM Conference on Electronic Commerce*, 158–166. ACM. 10.1145/336992.337035

van der Merwe, R., & Bekker, J. (2003). A framework and methodology for evaluating e-commerce Web sites. *Internet Research, 13*(5), 330–341. doi:10.1108/10662240310501612

## KEY TERMS AND DEFINITIONS

**Digital Marketplace:** A type of e-commerce site where product or service information is provided by multiple third parties, whereas transactions are processed by the marketplace operator.

**Digital Platform:** A digital environment of supplier and consumer groups that participates in transactions and exchanges.

**E-Commerce:** The activity of buying or selling of products on online services or over the internet.

**Two-Sided Market:** A firm of having two distinct user groups that provide each other with network benefits.

# Chapter 8
# A Study of Quality Tools and Techniques for Smart Manufacturing in Industry 4.0 in Malaysia:
## The Case of Northern Corridor Economic Region

**Mohd Syaiful Rizal Abd Hamid**
*Universiti Teknikal Malaysia Melaka, Malaysia*

**Saifuddin Isa**
*Universiti Teknikal Malaysia Melaka, Malaysia*

**Chew Boon Cheong**
*Universiti Teknikal Malaysia Melaka, Malaysia*

## ABSTRACT

*This chapter explores the key factors for selecting quality tools and techniques in industrial revolution 4.0, particularly in the smart manufacturing context. What are the factors determining which quality tools and techniques are more applicable in specific circumstances related to quality performance in Industrial Revolution 4.0? To answer this question, authors employ a multiple case study and an in-depth literature review as the research design approach. Two key data collection methods (qualitative methods) are used: (1) Primary data from face-to-face interviews with Toyo Memory Technology and Intel Malaysia (2) Secondary data from previous studies. This review, coupled with the case study analysis, leads to the identification of the real implementation of quality tools and techniques in the industries. The*

DOI: 10.4018/978-1-7998-2257-8.ch008

*chapter can enhance the reader understanding of Industrial Revolution 4.0 and quality management practices as well as highlight opportunities for further research.*

## INTRODUCTION

The world is facing a tremendous 4th industrial revolution with being dominated by the penetration of internet technologies into smart manufacturing environments and a paradigm shift from hierarchic production management to self-organization and self-optimization on the manufacturing floor, also the changes in quality control will be revolutionary (Gluck, M., Wolf, J. 2014). With the involvement of the Industrial Revolution it is important to have a good through quality management where is a source that become the competitive advantage and leadership that carry the values in the organization and successfully not neglecting the technology and the capabilities of the organization have to analyse and operationalize that data towards optimizing and benefiting the organization, (Davenport et al., 2012; McAfee and Brynjolfsson, 2012; Constantiou and Kallinikos, 2015; Henke et al., 2016).

Likewise, the advanced technical features suggest that Industry 4.0 exhibits an attractive and promising production paradigm. It has a significant contribution to the quality improvement system as well as a product that can cope with global challenges. As such, customized products can be produced effectively, efficiently, and profitably (Gluck, M., Wolf, J. 2014).

In turn, the measure of modern quality management aiming for sustainable success means not only to avoid the delivery of defective products to the customer but seek to establish maximum efficiency in the performance of all process of the company. With such optimized procedures, it can provide products of high quality with a minimum effort of time and costs (Werner and Weckenmann, 2012). For all those quality improvements to be happening, the implementation of smart manufacturing is needed. Smart Manufacturing can improve quality management by improving productivity in the production process as well as manufacturing planning (Wang & Wang, 2016).

Further, smart manufacturing can communicate with each other under the quality management system to reconfigure themselves for flexible production with high-quality improvement. Smart manufacturing has the potential advantage in bringing higher integration of the top floor and shop floor and thus more intelligence and flexibility to production. An additional, smart manufacturing will allow the manufacturer to improve the quality system by using data from production, service, and quality control that lead to quality improvement of both product and process.

In relation to the quality perspective, it has conducted several studies to verify the priority and importance of different tools and techniques for quality improvement.

In the previous study conducted by Tari and Sabater (2004) found that the most frequent tools and techniques used within ISO certified firms in Spain are audits, graphs, SPC, and flowcharts. The least used tools and techniques in the firms studied were the basic tools. Meanwhile, another study by Drew and Healy (2006) of Irish organisations highlighted that the most used quality tools were customer surveys, followed by competitive benchmarking.

In the study by Fotopoulos and Psomas (2009), it was found that two-thirds of the organizations used to understand quality tools, which included check sheets, flowcharts, and data collection, while the remaining tools and techniques had the very limited implementation. As such, a study conducted by Lagrosen and Lagrosen (2005) discovered that it generally limited the application of all quality tools and techniques, except for flowcharts, which were used. Although quality tools and techniques were used more often in larger organizations (Fotopoulos & Psomas, 2009), they could be implemented in all organisations, regardless of size or type (Basu & Wright, 2012).

In most recent studies carried out by authors such as Gluck, M., Wolf, J. (2014); Mosconi, (2015) in the areas of quality management and Industrial Revolution 4.0 seems lack to see how current quality tools and techniques need to change, improvise and to be in line with development of the Industrial Revolution 4.0 in smart manufacturing.

Thus, all of the above literature suggests that there is an ample amount of the literature review on quality management tools and techniques, most studies have been conducted to measure or eliciting the view of quality management tools and techniques from customers' perspectives or with the attention given to examining quality tools and techniques practices from managers' and employees' perspectives. Based on relevant quality management review, this book chapter contributes to the quality management literature by fulfilling the following gap:

*"There are very few studies in the field of quality management that have been comprehensively conducted for determining the factors in selecting the appropriate quality tools and techniques in industrial revolution 4.0 particularly in smart manufacturing context".*

In saying that, therefore this book chapter aims to answer, "What are the factors determining which quality tools and techniques are more applicable in the context of the Industrial Revolution 4.0 particularly for smart manufacturing?"

As a result of that, the Northern Corridor Economic Region (NCER) has been selected as a case study for this study is based on their experience which involved in smart manufacturing for several years. A lot of companies in NCER has been involved in smart manufacturing that led to manufacturing networks that are more interconnected, complex and heterogeneous. In conjunction with that, NCER has been appointed as a leading region for driving Malaysia towards becoming the Industry 4.0 hub in South-East Asia through the Malaysia National Policy on Industry 4.0 (Industry4WRD) that was launched back in 2018 by Malaysian Government. Technologies such as the Internet of Things, Advanced Robotics, Artificial Intelligence and Additive Manufacturing are contributing factors to selecting NCER as a pioneer for leading Malaysia into Industry 4.0 hub.

The authors structure the rest of the book chapter as follows: the first section provides the literature review on the quality management tools and techniques, smart manufacturing in Industry 4.0 for quality management and quality tools and techniques of smart manufacturing in Industry 4.0. The second section discusses the methodology of the study. In the third section, the book chapter continues with the findings and discussion. The final section concludes the study.

## BACKGROUND

### Quality Management Tools and Techniques

Even though all quality tools and techniques are helpful, many companies do not use certain quality tools and techniques when applying them (Novak, 2005). According to (Basu, 2004; Charantimath, 2011), there is an increased recognition of the need to identify tools and techniques process improvement, as there are over 400 tools and techniques in the quality management area. Identifying such tools and techniques could use several criteria, including their successful implementation in various circumstances. Thus, whether the tools and techniques selected are required or alternate in other conditions; and whether they apply to the manufacturing industries (Dale, 2003).

There is a need for a thorough investigation as to the reasons or real factors in selecting certain tools over others, and what difficulties they encounter when implementing quality tools and techniques (Bamford & Greatbanks, 2005; Fotopoulos & Psomas, 2009). Among many reasons, the failure of utilizing these tools and techniques stem from the inappropriate selection of the right ones.

With the above background information on quality management tools and techniques, the authors can now turn to the quality management applications in Industry 4.0. In the following sections, the authors will illustrate on the overview of Industrial Revolution 4.0 and how this quality management tools and techniques need to correspond and in line with Industrial Revolution 4.0, particularly in the smart manufacturing context.

## Overview of Industrial Revolution 4.0

Modern industrial development has lasted for several hundred years and has now the era of Industry 4.0 come. The concept of Industry 4.0 was proposed for developing the German economy in 2011 (Roblek, Mesko & Krapez, 2016; Vogel-Heuser & Hess, 2016). According to Lukac (2015), the first industrial revolution began at the end of the 18th century and was represented by mechanical production plants based on water and steam power. The second industrial revolution started at the beginning of the 20th century with the symbol of mass labour production based on electrical energy. The third industrial revolution began in the 1970s with the characteristic of automatic production based on electronics and internet technology. The fourth industrial revolution, Industry 4.0, is ongoing, with the characteristics of cyber-physical systems (CPS) production, based on heterogeneous data and knowledge integration.

The main roles of CPS are to fulfill the ability and dynamic requirements of production and to improve the effectiveness and efficiency of the entire industry. Industry 4.0 encompasses numerous technologies including Radio Frequency Identification (RFID), Enterprise Resource Planning (ERP), Internet of Things (IoT), cloud-based manufacturing, and social product development (Baur & Wee, 2015; Georgakopoulos, et al., 2016; Kube & Rinn, 2014; Lasi et al., 2014; Lin et al., 2016; Lom, Pribyl & Svitek, 2016; Pfeiffer, 2016; Roblek, Mesko & Krapez, 2016; Singer, 2016; Thames & Schaefer, 2016; Thamsen & Wulff, 2016; Vijaykumar, Saravanakumar & Balamurugan, 2015; Wan et al., 2016).

Scholars have defined Industry 4.0 from diverse perspectives. For instance, according to the Lu, (2017) Industry 4.0 is "the integration of complex physical machinery and devices with networked sensors and software, used to predict, control and plan for better business and societal outcomes." Henning and Johannes (2013) define Industry 4.0 as "a new level of value chain organization and management across the life-cycle of products." Hermann, Pentek, and Otto (2016) define Industry 4.0 as "a collective term for technologies and concepts of value chain organization." They note that, within the modular structured Smart Factories of Industry 4.0, Cyber-Physical System (CPS) monitor physical processes, create a virtual copy of the physical world and make decentralized decisions.

Likewise, Industry 4.0 facilitates interconnection and computerization into the traditional industry. According to Shafiq et al., (2015), "the goals of Industry 4.0 are to provide IT-enabled mass customization of manufactured products; to make automatic and flexible adaptation of the production chain; to track parts and products; to facilitate communication among parts, products, and machines; to apply human-machine interaction (HMI) paradigms; to achieve IoT-enabled production optimization in smart factories; and to provide new types of services and business models of interaction in the value chain". While, Schmidt et al. (2015) further claim that Industry 4.0 also brings disruptive changes on supply chains, business models, and business processes.

Further, they also claim that "the principles of Industry 4.0 are interoperability, virtualization, decentralization, real-time capability, service orientation, and modularity. In terms of features, Industry 4.0 can provide more flexibility, reduce lead times, customize with small batch sizes, and reduce costs" (Shafiq et al., 2016). The key fundamental principles of Industry 4.0 include cloud/intranet, data integration, flexible adaptation, intelligent self-organizing, interoperability, manufacturing process, optimization, secure communication, and service orientation (Ji et al., 2016; Vogel- Heuser & Hess, 2016).

In addition, a fifth generation (5G) will be acquired in Industry 4.0 to accomplish latent, long, reliable, and secure communication and to meet the complex demands of emerging business paradigms (Siddiqui et al., 2016; Varghese & Tandur, 2014). Although 5G is still in its infancy, the technology of the 5G is a necessary developmental step for the Machine-to-Machine (M2M) communication associated with Industry 4.0 and with the IoT, as industries are becoming more complex and more knowledge-intensive, massive data appear with Industry 4.0. (Mi & Zolotov, 2016; Zhou, Liu & Zhou, 2015).

In Industry 4.0, the manufacturing procedure will require more sensors, actors, microchips, and autonomous systems due to the quick development of technologies (Lasi et al, 2014; Oses et al., 2016; Roblek, Meško & Krapez, 2016; Rubmann et al., 2015; Sanders, Elangeswaran & Wulfsberg, 2016). Advanced methodologies of analytics, CPS, and energy conservation measures (ECM) will be implemented in manufacturing, as well (Oses et al., 2016). Based on high-frequency energy metering, Oses et al. (2016) propose a model for an injection machine to estimate the adjusted baseline with lower risks and uncertainties in measuring and verifying energy conversation. Shafiq et al. (2016) propose the assimilation of virtual manufacturing at three levels: virtual engineering objects, virtual engineering processes, and virtual engineering factories. The integrated mechanism of the three levels will help build the structure of Industry 4.0 and for achieving a higher level of intelligent machines, industrial automation, and advanced semantic analytics.

Industry 4.0, also known as the fourth industrial revolution, refers to the technical integration of Cyber-Physical Systems (CPSs) in all industrial processes where "components and machines become smart and part of a standardized network based on the well prove internet standards" (Kolberg, & Zühlke, 2015). Driven by the diffusion of ICT (including internet), the concept has been spread through different terminologies such as Smart Manufacturing and Smart Factory. According to (Russmann, M., Lorenz, M., Gerbert, P., Waldner, M., Jastus, J., Hengel, P., & Harnisch, M, 2015), nine key technologies characterize smart manufacturing:

additive manufacturing, augmented reality, big data analytics, cloud computing cyber security, horizontal and vertical integration systems, Internet of Things (IoT), robotics and automation, simulation. The combination of these technologies enables the realization of a smart manufacturing system (Kolberg, & Zühlke, 2015) that consists of five main components which are Smart Product, Smart Operator, Smart Machine, Smart Workstation, and Smart Planner.

In sum, all the above arguments suggest that Industry 4.0 can be summarized as an integrated, adapted, optimized, service-oriented, and interoperable manufacturing process which is correlated with algorithms, big data, and high technologies.

## Smart Manufacturing in Industry 4.0 for Quality Management

Industry 4.0 makes factories more intelligent, flexible, and dynamic by equipping manufacturing with sensors, actors, and autonomous systems (Roblek, Mesko & Krapez, 2016). They further point out that "machines and equipment will achieve high levels of self-optimization and automation. In addition, the manufacturing process has the capacity to fulfil more complex and qualified standards and requirements of products, as expected" (Roblek, Mesko & Krapez, 2016). Thus, intelligent factories and smart manufacturing are the major goals of Industry 4.0 (Sanders, Elangeswaran & Wulfsberg, 2016).

Industry 4.0 makes value-added integration occur horizontally and vertically in the manufacturing process (Shafiq et al., 2016; Stock & Seliger, 2016). The horizontal procedure is integrated with value creation modules from the material flow to the logistics of the product life cycle, whereas the vertical procedure integrates the product, equipment, and human needs with different aggregation levels of the value creation and manufacturing systems. They integrate intelligence and digitization from the raw material acquisition to the manufacturing system, product use, and the end of product life. Lasi et al. (2014) point out that Industry 4.0 drives manufacturing in two directions: the application-pull procedure and the technology-push procedure. The former induces dynamic changes caused by a new generation of industrial infrastructure. The latter requires the higher-level mechanization, digitalization and networking, and miniaturization.

Having reviewed the pertinent of Industrial Revolution 4.0 literature and its characteristic, this allows the authors to further understand how this Industrial Revolution 4.0 context may give the impact of respective quality tools and techniques.

A study conducted by Albers et al. (2016) analysed quality-related production with an intelligent condition monitoring-based quality control system and developed a comprehensive descriptive model. To achieve transparency and productivity of big data, Lee et al. (2014) address the trends of manufacturing service transformation and the readiness of smart predictive informatics tools. The prognostics-monitoring system is a trend of the smart manufacturing and industrial big data environment (Lee, Kao & Yang, 2014; Vijaykumar, Saravana Kumar & Balamurugan, 2015). Cuihua et al. (2016) present a novel approach to simplifying the scheduling problem of job shop scheduling by using RFID to collect real-time manufacturing data.

In turn, Scheuermann, Verclas & Bruegge (2015) describe an agile factory prototype that transfers agile software engineering techniques to the domain of manufacturing; they also propose a framework that depicts the impact and feasibility of customer changes during assembly-time. Paelke (2014) presents an augmented reality system that supports human workers in a rapidly changing production environment. S. Wang et al. (2016) examine the relationship between lean production and intelligent manufacturing and propose a lean intelligent production system (LIPS) to improve product quality and efficiency and to reduce costs, in Industry 4.0.

Although few researchers showed no significant difference associated with tools and techniques between manufacturing industries (Fotopoulos & Psomas, 2009; Sousa et al., 2005), several other studies revealed the difference between the two industries based on the priority selection of different tools and techniques (Antony et al., 2007; Antony & Banuels, 2002; Nicols, 2006).

An example of this, a study conducted by Yau (2000) revealed that "the manufacturing industry frequently used the seven basic quality control tools, acceptance sampling, and process capability, whereas the service industry used benchmarking, Gantt charts, and quality circles the most often". Consistently, a study conducted in the Saudi food industry by Alsaleh (2007), seconded that view by pointing out that control charts, histograms, and run charts were tools and techniques used most often. In general, manufacturing organizations more often apply quality improvement tools and techniques (Tari & Sabater, 2004).

As such, Burcher, Lee, and Waddell (2006) claimed that "although quality managers in Britain and Australia have very limited skills in many quality tools and techniques, they do not pay a major effort to enhance their knowledge in that area. They do not use the most current quality tools and techniques, and they are perhaps not even aware of them. Quality managers in these two countries mostly used a very narrow collection of tools and techniques, which consisted of brainstorming, control charts, and Pareto analysis".

The more experienced an organization associate with applying the quality management, the more tendency it has to use different quality tools and techniques, particularly advanced ones (Revuelto-Taboada, Canet-Giner, & Balbastre-Benavent, 2011); and the more an organization uses quality tools and techniques, the better performance it gains, regardless of its size (Ahmed & Hassan, 2003).

## RESEARCH METHODOLOGY

This book chapter is an exploratory qualitative study. A systematic approach to literature review is based on knowledge that plays a major role in evidence-based practices (Denyer & Tranðeld, 2008; Rousseau, Manning, & Denyer, 2008; Tranfield, Denyer, & Smart, 2003) was adapted in this research. Process in getting literature review that has been conducted include 'Industrial Revolution 4.0', 'Smart Manufacturing', quality tools and techniques in general and as well as quality tools and techniques in Industrial Revolution 4.0.

Essentially, systematic reviews are formulated around the research question. In this study, our key aim is to answer the question of "What are the factors determining which quality tools and techniques are more applicable in specific circumstances related to quality performance in Industrial Revolution 4.0 particularly for smart manufacturing?".

In saying that, the authors have reviewed the particular issues by looking in depth at the literature via an online database journal, such as Emerald, Science Direct, and ABI/Pro-Quest. These online databases cover journals in the area of quality management, namely the Journal of Production and Operations Management, Journal of Total Quality Management and Business Excellence, International Journal of Operation and Production Management, International Journal of Quality and Reliability Management, California Management Review, Managing Service Quality, The TQM Magazine, Journal of Operations Management, as well as other leading general management journals.

Next, after analysing a patent of the literature, the authors have adopted a case study approach to illustrate how this phenomenon–the characteristics are applied to the real-world context. This is supported by Yin (2003, 2012) who claims that for the evaluation research, the case can be used to document and analyse the implementation process.

Moving on from this, the researchers also want to focus and be specific at the highest level possible. As a result, researchers chose Toyo-Memory Technology and Intel Malaysia, as there are one of the companies that can fit well with the Industrial Revolution 4.0 model. These two companies devote a significant amount of time and resources into fostering an Industrial Revolution 4.0 ecosystem for communities that promote the commitment and innovation in practices in their daily operation. Therefore, the key reason for selecting these two companies is based on the premise that they operate successfully in the Industrial Revolution 4.0 context (i.e. The pioneer Malaysian project for Industrial Revolution 4.0), fulfilling the criterion purpose and providing the exceptional case, as they are the stepping stones and benchmarking for the other companies to learn from them.

As a result, in conducting this research, two key data collection methods (qualitative methods) were used: (1) Primary data from face-to-face interviews with Toyo Memory Technology and Intel Malaysia (2) Secondary data from previous studies. Accordingly, this review on the previous study allows the researchers to establish a better understanding of the pertaining issue regarding the appropriate quality tools and techniques in the context of Industrial Revolution 4.0. This review, coupled with the case study analysis, also led to the identification of the real implementation of quality tools and techniques in the industries.

In this study, respondents were selected based on their background of the manufacturer that participate and living in the environment of Industry 4.0 particularly in Smart Manufacturing context. Turner (2010) and Creswell (2007) showed that a researcher should conduct sampling strategies to get qualified respondents that will provide appropriate and valuable information. Respondents were chosen based on certain categories and characteristics that meet the research outcomes. They have; (i) implemented quality tools and techniques; (ii) various experiences in managing issues over quality management; (iii) moving towards digital manufacturing; (iv) and living in the environment of Industry 4.0 context such as smart manufacturing, digital manufacturing, full automation, and others. The respondent's details are shown in Table 1 as follows.

## DISCUSSION

### Northern Corridor Economic Region (NCER) Overview

Northern Corridor Economic Region (NCER) established in 2007 as one of the economic corridors to provide fair growth in the four states in the northern region of Peninsula Malaysia, the state of Kedah, Northern Perak, Perlis, and Pulau Pinang. This region has exhibited strong economic progress, with higher annual gross domestic product (GDP) growth rate of 5.8% compared to Malaysia's 5.4% during the period of 2010–2014, as this illustrates that the GDP growth was driven by the services and manufacturing sectors. Essentially, the services sector is the top GDP contributor for all four states, with government services as the highest subsector contributor.

While the manufacturing sector is the second highest GDP contributor for Kedah, Pulau Pinang, and Perak then the agriculture sector is the second highest GDP contributor for Perlis. In the nine years since introducing NCER, significant changes have occurred on expanding of NCER coverage in 2014, the district of Manjung was incorporated into NCER, and in 2016, NCIA's Council approved for the extension of NCER's boundaries to cover the entire state of Perak. Impacts of NCER in national

*Table 1. Respondents details*

| Respondent | Designation | Years of Experience |
|---|---|---|
| **General Manager 1, Toyo-Memory Technology (TMT)** | General Manager<br>Chief Quality Assurance & Chief Production Officer | 30 Years |
| **Senior Manager 2, TMT** | Senior Manager, Quality Assurance | 20 Years |
| **Senior Manager 3, TMT** | Senior Manager, Internal Quality | 20 Years |
| **Senior Engineer 1, TMT** | Senior Engineer, Quality Assurance | 15 Years |
| **Senior Engineer 2, TMT** | Senior Engineer, Quality Assurance | 12 Years |
| **Senior Engineer 3, TMT** | Senior Engineer, Internal Quality | 8 Years |
| **Senior Engineer 4, TMT** | Senior Engineer, Internal Quality | 8 Years |
| **Manager 1, INTEL** | Manager, Strategic Integration Management (SIM), Intel | 13 Years |
| **Engineer 2, INTEL** | Engineer SIM, Intel | 10 Years |
| **Engineer 3, INTEL** | Engineer SIM, Intel | 10Years |

Source: Originated by authors (2019)

and global economic conditions are dropping in fuel price, depreciating ringgit, the economic slowdown in China, and declining foreign investments.

As such, NCER is strategically located within the Indonesia-Malaysia-Thailand Growth Triangle (IMT-GT). The region has the potential to develop strong international relations with Sumatra, Indonesia, and Thailand. Given their many complementarities, geographically proximity, and close historical and cultural ties. This can help boost the region's economy, creating a natural bloc for economic cooperation that would enable NCER to process, distribute and export goods beyond Malaysia borders.

NCER has a strong manufacturing ecosystem with 40 years of evolution. The region's strong GDP growth is driven by manufacturing, in electrical and electronics, with the industry having been established since the 1970s. Since 1971, Pulau Pinang's Free Industrial Zones (FIZs) has hosted many multinational companies (MNCs). Many local companies have also grown in lockstep with the MNCs. Approximately, RM47.7 billion of investment in manufacturing projects from 2009 to 2016 had been approved in the state.

Further, Kulim Hi-Tech Park (KHTP), Kedah, plays an important role in driving the growth of the manufacturing industry. Established in 1996, it strives to provide world-class infrastructure for hi-tech manufacturing and serves as a strategic gateway to Southeast Asia for business and commercial expansion for various industries, particularly to be the forefront of Industrial Revolution 4.0 key players in Malaysia. To date, the park has attracted more than RM 34 billion of investment along with

MNCs that have brought with them patented, state-of-the-art manufacturing technologies and products.

Intel Malaysia and Toyo-Memory Technology (TMT) are one of the companies operating in Kulim Hi-Tech Park. The overview of these two selected companies is illustrated as follows.

## Overview of Case Study 1: Toyo-Memory Technology

Toyo-Memory Technology (TMT) Sdn. Bhd. was established by Toyo-Kohan Co., Ltd. to manufacture Nickel Plated (NiP) Aluminium Substrates for Hard Disk has started in 1934 to supply plated steel to canning industry. And it began producing NiP (Nickel Plated) Substrates in 1985, a natural step forward for a company already possess of surface treatment, grinding and polishing technology. Then TMT has improved and developed its process and become one of the biggest substrate manufacturers in the world. It equips the plant of one of the most advanced and highest achieved automated production lines in the world. The advanced technology, started, implemented and transferred to Toyo-Memory Technology Sdn Bhd. TMT develops the process and product, and their target is to be a quality leader in the world. Toyo-Memory Technology Sdn Bhd is a certified ISO 9001:2008 (Quality Management System, March 2005) and ISO 14,001:2004 (Environmental Management System, Dec 2007) company.

## Overview of Case Study 2: Intel Malaysia

Intel, Kulim started off as a manufacturer of motherboards in 1995 and has grown from one building to five buildings. The company manufactures and assembles computer and communication components like the microprocessor, chipsets, motherboards, wireless and wired connectivity products, and integrated digital technology platforms. As such, Intel, Kulim is an important site for building mobile modules and also has a research and development unit that focuses on early development.

Original equipment manufacturers (OEMs), original design manufacturers (ODMs), industrial and telecommunication equipment manufacturers are the key buyers for the components manufactured that produced by Intel. In relation to this, there is another customer who buys Intel products through distributors, resellers, retailers and other OEM channels around the world. Intel has three major customers (Hewlett Packard Company, Dell Inc., and Lenovo Group Limited) and many smaller direct and indirect customers.

With the above background information on the selected case study, we can now turn to the key aim of the study in which to investigate and reveal the key factors in selecting the quality tools and techniques used for achieving quality performance in

Industrial Revolution 4.0, in Smart Manufacturing context. Throughout this section, the researchers present the reasoning (i.e. the key factors) behind the selection of tools and techniques that have been implemented in the organization for achieving quality performance. In so doing, the authors have adopted the Thematic Analysis method as the main method to analyse the data.

## Thematic Analysis Method

The purpose of this analysis is to identify common themes that emerged from the study. From the interview conducted, it is revealing that there are five key factors in determining which quality tools and techniques are more applicable and appropriate related to quality performance in Industrial Revolution 4.0 particularly in Smart Manufacturing context, which merit further analysis, namely, knowledge on quality tools and techniques; Industry 4.0 environment; customer satisfaction; continuous improvement and supplier partnership. Therefore, this section focuses on an analysis of the case study, according to the five themes.

*What are the factors to determine which quality tools and techniques are more applicable in specific circumstances related to quality performance in Industrial Revolution 4.0?*

## Knowledge on Quality Tools and Techniques

According to General Manager of TMT, "Here in TMT, we are demanding for the vast knowledge in quality management, quality control, and managing quality tools and techniques that is one of the factors when throughout the new era of Industry 4.0." (General Manager TMT).

The GM also believed that employees with higher knowledge in advanced technology and quality area are a major contributor to their company and economic success for producing, changing and transferring knowledge to the production level. Figure 1 shows that TMT has implemented a smart manufacturing concept by using a cloud server and digital manufacturing in the HDD production process.

## Industry 4.0 Environment

Industry 4.0 is promoting the traditional manufacturing of HDD towards smart manufacturing with advanced IT technology, therefore there is a huge demand of professionals with expertise in advanced technologies, such as IoT, Big Data, Cloud Computing, and Cyber Security to continue updating their employee's knowledge level within the quality management area to match the pace of technology

*Figure 1. TMT process flow of HDD production*
*Source: TMT Quality Control Manual, 2016*

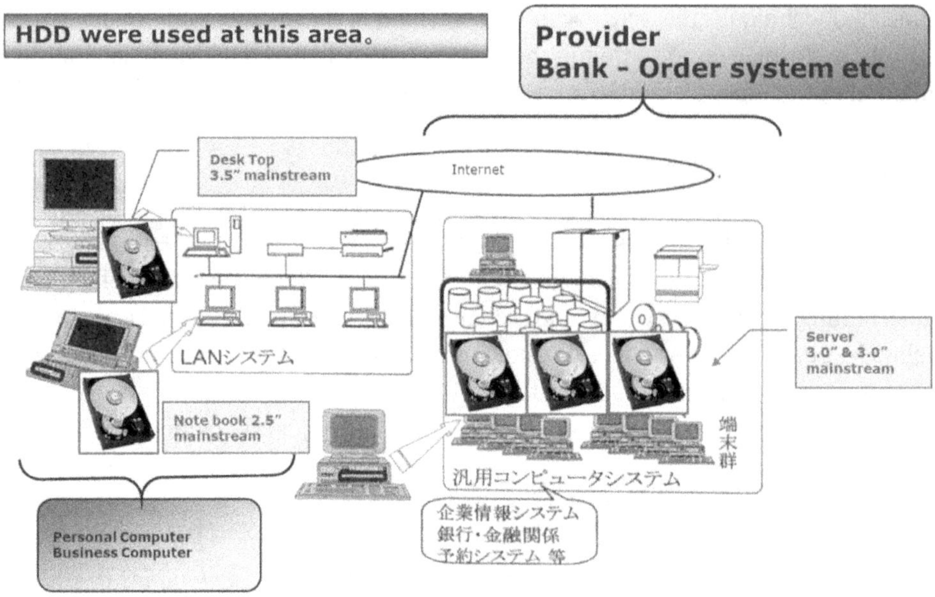


development. In addition, by having various knowledge in the technology itself will give a huge impact to the industries which supported by Kang, Lee et al. (2016) that mentioned, "it is a collection and a paradigm of various technologies that can promote a strategic innovation of the existing manufacturing industry through the convergence of humans, technology, and information".

On the other hand, Manager 4 from Intel point out that, "Intel preferably creates a smart manufacturing environment through applying Industry 4.0. Intel also highlighted in the vision and mission since Industry 4.0 is driving much of this change within industries and emerging are some powerful industrial smart manufacturing environment" (Manager 4, Intel).

Further, Manager 4 also claims that the environment is delivering the service and structuring knowledge based on smart manufacturing, which able to enhance quality performance that will be the frontier of their new competitive positions. Manager 4 further adds that the use of high technology and quality control such as visual simulation, smart machines, smart production and heavy use of sensors is better than through human intervention. All of these are changing work dramatically, which require higher levels of responsiveness, an anticipation, a different problem-solving, correcting skills, significant logic diagnostics and yield management thinking as well as requires this growing environment of support.

## Customer Satisfaction

TMT culture of the business is mainly focused on customer satisfaction. TMT is engaged in a very competitive global marketplace. The business will not grow if the company continues to focus on past accomplishments only. TMT continues to strive to understand the customers' needs for service and support by focusing on customer service. The key factor is to focus on the feedback that TMT gets on the quality of the products and services.

TMT understands very well and is able to expect solutions to products and service needs by the customers, which yet to recognize. Meaning that TMT is listening to customer thoughts about how they can desirable serve them from a total system's perspective, essentially from an ideal introduction to the successful delivery of a product or service. As General Manager TMT mentioned that to determine the external customers perceive in terms of quality and expectation provided by the annual quality survey as follows:

*This can be accomplished by organizing the Annual Quality Survey. The objective that accomplished through the Annual Quality Survey are:*

- *The company determining the customers' current business expectations where from there they will continue strengthening their business operating system.*
- *The customer expectation will be reviewed and provide a baseline measurement against the performance.*
- *An annual review will conduct to feedback on the performance against the customer expectation.*
- *Review and track the changing expectations in order to make changes in the quality system.*
- *Adequately provide a standard consistent set of customer satisfaction metrics that provides a check of the internal quality measurements.*

*Therefore, TMT business should grow customer driven indices by deploy factors established by the customer and set aggressive improvement goals. We will also change in time when customers raise the bar as in order to meet our current expectations. Our Quality Policy states, "We will exceed Customer Expectation with our Superior Products and Services" (General Manager, TMT).*

In line with this, the Manager 1, Intel also seconded the General Manager TMT opinion by saying that "*Our quality statement stated, every Intel employee is personally responsible for ensuring the highest quality in the products and services delivered to internal and external customers. Continuous improvement in the quality of our*

*Figure 2. Customer business process model and structure*
*Source: Intel Quality System Handbook 2014 and Manager 1, Intel*

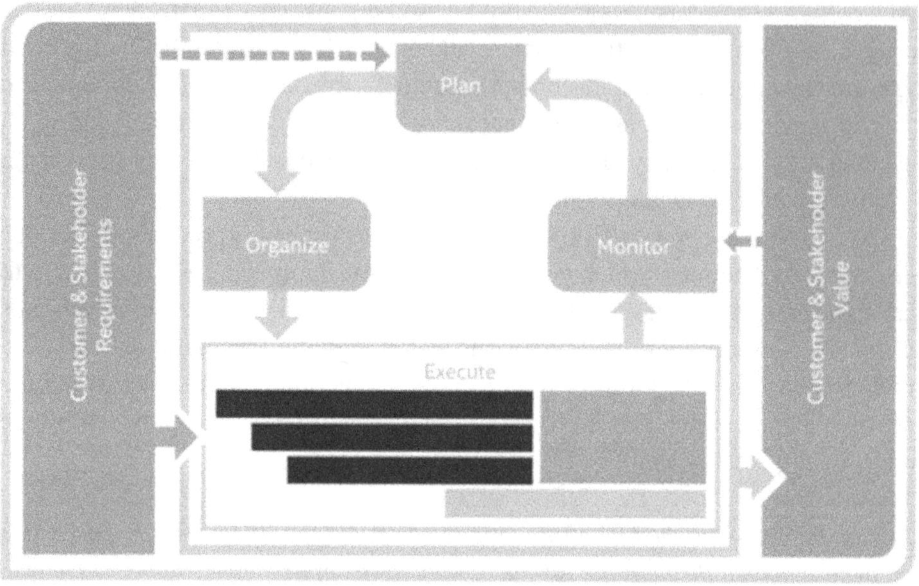


*processes, products, and service is foundational to the achievement of customer satisfaction. We believe that fulfilling customer requirements is the first step in customer satisfaction. Our core business process model starts with the customer and ends with the customer. Our core business processes are linked into our global work processes, ensuring alignment between our business strategy and practice,"* which is depicted in Figure 2 (Manager 1, Intel).

## Continuous Improvement

TMT involves in continuous improvement and focuses on formal problem solving and responsiveness. When customer feedback or claim a problem, the complaints will pass through the TMT sales representative of the company and then followed by the Quality Assurance Department for further verification. The investigation and analysis of the complaint scopes and feedback of these results are both a duty and a service to customers, and provide valuable information for improving product quality, as illustrated in the following Figure 3 as follows.

Figure 3 illustrates an outline of the customer complaint handling flow for TMT. The results of investigations of complaint items and the contents of countermeasures are reported to customers in document form and efforts are made to obtain understanding. However, in some cases, customers may visit to report these results directly. This is

*Figure 3. An outline of the customer complaint handling flow for TMT*
*Source: TMT Quality Control Manual, 2016*

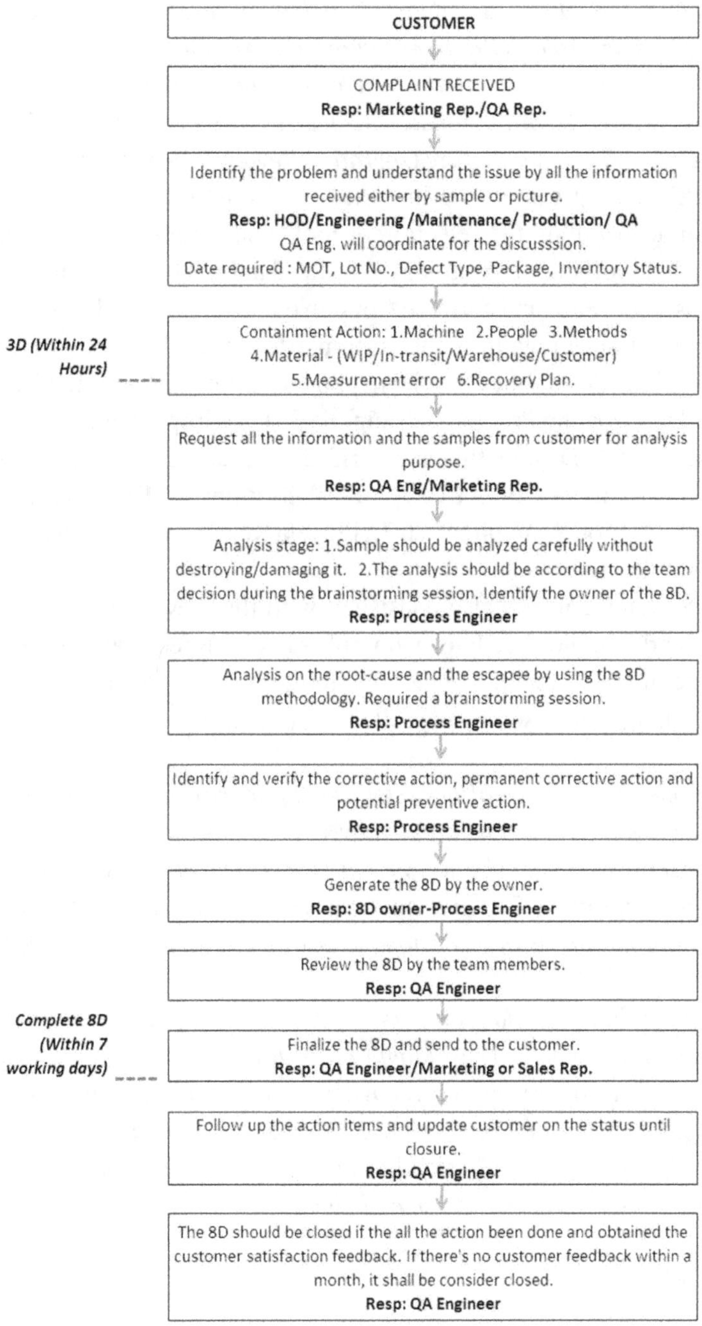

consistent with the view from Senior Manager 2, TMT who claims that "*Customer claims are tracked in our customer claim tracking information system. Monthly customer claim metrics are compiled and distributed to corporate-wide for review. Responsiveness metrics are used to drive continuous improvement in the cycle time arena. Failure mechanism Pareto is used to drive continuous improvement in the Product and Administrative Quality arenas. This metrics are also reviewed in our monthly Business Unit and Manufacturing Operation Review*," (Senior Manager 2).

Manager 1, Intel also agrees on the importance of continuous improvement as the key factor in determining the selection of tools and techniques. He further claims that 8D Problem Solving Methodology is utilized in Intel to determine on the containment actions, root cause and corrective or preventive actions and at the same time to address on the issues regarding the customer feedback for the continuous improvement. The Eight Disciplines are, Discipline 1 (D1): Establish the Team; Discipline 2 (D2): Describe the Problem; Discipline 3 (D3): Implement and verify Containment; Discipline 4 (D4): Define and verify root cause; Discipline 5 (D5): Choose and verify Permanent Corrective Action; Discipline 6 (D6): Implement Permanent Corrective Action; Discipline 7 (D7): Prevent Recurrence; and Discipline 8 (D8): Congratulate the Team.

All of the above statements are also consistent with the view from the Senior Engineer 2, TMT and Engineer 1, Intel who collectively agree that continuous improvement as one of the factors that determine the selection of quality tools and techniques. These can be witnessed by the following quotations:

*Continuous improvement is the desire of the customer confidence in the TMT packaging product. These are the foundation that created by TMT on customer relationships. Quality resolve is deeply embedded in every employee. TMT perceives that for any manufacturer to achieve the objective, the products must meet and consistently greater the stringent demands and needs of its customer base (Senior Engineer 2, TMT).*

*At Intel, quality and reliability monitors are performed on major categories of semiconductor packaging products. These monitors are designed to test the packaging product's design and material as well as to recognize and eliminate potential failure mechanisms. The goal of the ongoing monitor is to provide reliable packaging performance in real-world applications and to identify trends that enable Intel to continuously improve the products. (Engineer 1, Intel).*

## Supplier Partnership

Furthermore, it should be noted that both respondents from TMT and Intel have pointed out that supplier partnership also has become one of the key factors that determine the selection of quality tools and techniques. These are supported by Manager 1, Intel and Engineer 1, Intel who claimed that "*Intel has created a Supplier Development Program that is designed with the goal of aligning suppliers with our corporate, it is called Cycle of Success. At the center of the Cycle of Success is Intel's Core Values, every piece of the cycle of success depicted an area of how Intel's expectations of suppliers restrict into the cycle of success. The Supplier Development Program stimulates constant communication between Intel and our suppliers, which provide the ability to our suppliers to better perceive the role they plan in the success of Intel for our mutual benefit,*" (Manager 1, Intel). "Intel understands the value of recognizing and awarding suppliers for their hard work and dedication. We believe that by recognizing our best suppliers for their superb performances we are setting a standard for our entire supplier to achieve. This is the final step in our Supplier Development Process; Recognition and Award" (Engineer 1, Intel).

Manager 1 and Engineer 1 Intel further claimed that Intel has followed an eight-step of the Supplier Development process for improving the quality of goods and services delivered by their suppliers. The eight steps of the process comprise the identification of supplier, the supplier selection team formed, assess Intel, define the requirement, supplier analysis, risk assessment, final selection and approval and selection, notification, and postmortem/debrief. During the supplier analysis stage, they establish a general expectation of performing the business with Intel and make the supplier selection based on their technology, quality, availability, cost, service, and resourcefulness. This can be summarized in Figure 4 as follows.

Consistent with this, Manager 2 from TMT also states that supplier partnership is one of the key factors needed to consider when selecting quality tools and techniques. He claims that "*Within the global and highly competitive packaging market, TMT believes that a close relationship and alignment with our supply chain partners is a critical differentiator in our success. We rely on our partners to help enable TMT to deliver superior quality, high volume and on time solutions, which allow us to meet the increasingly stringent requirements of our customers. We use the Supplier Day and Supplier Awards to maintain alignment, recognize the critical role and celebrate* the contributions that our supply chain partners make toward the long-term success of TMT," (Manager 2, TMT).

## FUTURE RESEARCH DIRECTIONS

Looking at the most current trend, there are some topics that are dwindling, and others will possibly escalate. TQM, for illustration, is no longer an active research area. Baldrige and ISO are too likely to diminish in their research attention since they have been largely studied in Production and Operations Management and other journals.

*Figure 4. Supplier development process*
*Source: Intel Quality System Handbook 2014*

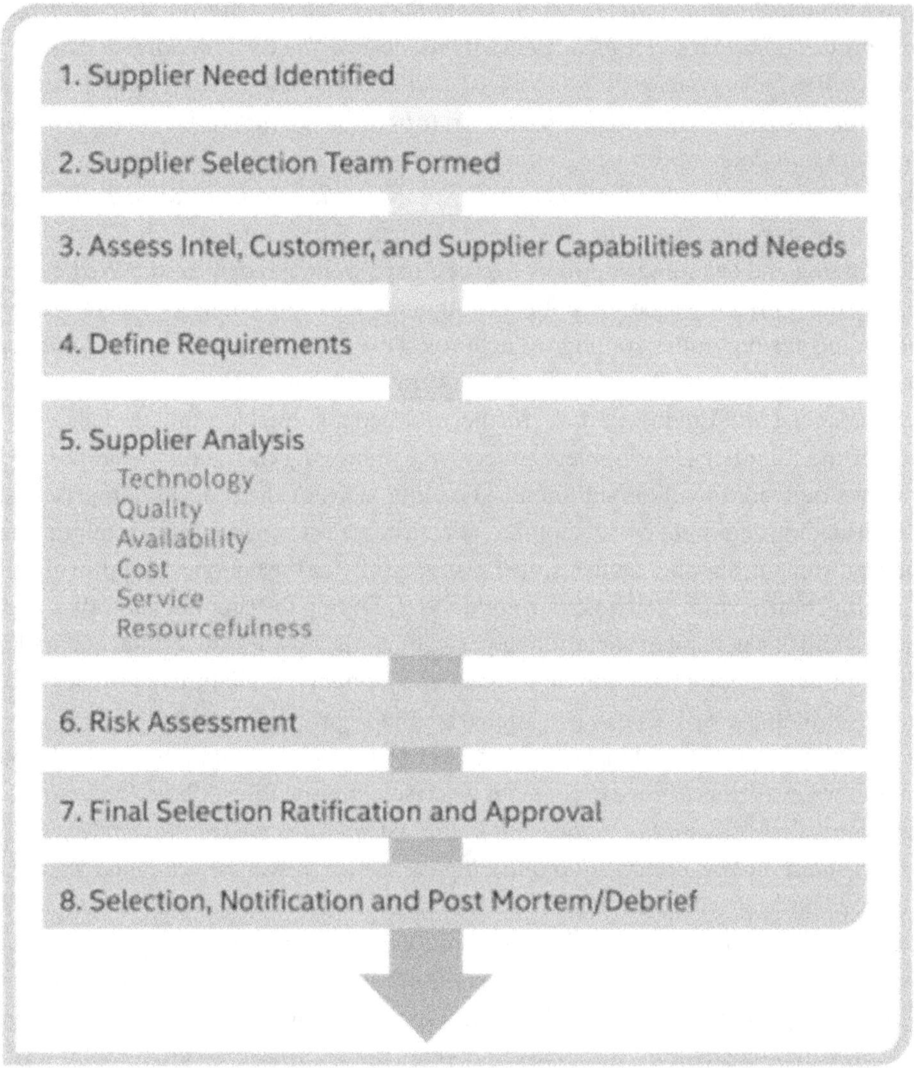


The authors expect research on technical aspects of quality to go on, specifically in the areas of tools and techniques and perhaps there will intensify interest in both human issues and service quality and the most present on the application and the impact of Industrial Revolution 4.0 on the quality management per se.

Further, future research should focus on a specific issue (e.g. continuous improvement for product design) and neglect other issues/factors around it. It should consider the entire system. This means that the future researcher needs to understand the whole picture of the process internally and externally, as the future is not only about dealing with a specific problem in a single company, but what matters is how companies managing and dealing the wide resources of improvements and innovation across the networks with the architecture of participation and collaboration that come from all over the world (i.e. high involvement of communities of practice).

The fact that the future will be more about the network and digitalize, key quality principles such as: Continuous improvement, standards, leadership and partnerships will be managed in a network context (i.e. open source, open innovation, "smart" environment). For example, Sony has moved from lean production to open source, where Sony Corporation and Google Inc. announced an alliance to provide a range of new and rich entertainment experiences that combine Google's open-source Android OS platform with Sony's expertise in technology and product design. The two companies are exploring the joint development of compelling new Android-based hardware products for the home, mobile and personal product categories and are also exploring extending the alliance in connection with Sony's wide range of entertainment assets to establish new forms of cloud-based user experiences (Perakakis, 2017). Through this alliance, Sony aims to leverage the stability, future growth potential and open-source accessibility of Google's Android platform to further optimize its product development processes while also providing consumers with an open, expansive and evolving user experience (See also Sony Official website at https://www.sony.com).

All the above discussion suggests that the collaborators and partners need to think about how to manage the standards comprising open technologies standards, codes of practice and standard for control, and to deal with the issues of managing leadership, continuous improvement and partnerships; internally and externally beyond their boundaries of the companies..

## CONCLUSION

The key aim of this book chapter is to answer, "What are the factors determining which quality tools and techniques are more applicable in specific circumstances related to quality performance in Industrial Revolution 4.0?". In so doing, the researchers have reviewed the pertinent part of Industrial Revolution 4.0 literature and its characteristics, particularly in the smart manufacturing environment in corresponds to the quality tools and techniques implementation and this follows with the case study conducted.

Thus, from the analysis discussed in this study, the conclusion can be reached that on one hand, it is confirmed that there are five key factors in determining which quality tools and techniques are more applicable in specific circumstances related to quality performance in Industrial Revolution 4.0. On the other hand, it also has a significant effect on quality performance in the Industrial Revolution 4.0. The key factors identified, namely, knowledge of quality tools and techniques, industry 4.0 environment, customer satisfaction, continuous improvement, and supplier partnership. The summary of the case study of factors in quality tools and techniques implementation is shown in Table 2.

**Indicators**

**GM1:** General Manager, Chief Quality Assurance & Chief Production Officer, TMT
**SM2:** Senior Manager, Quality Assurance, TMT
**SM3:** Senior Manager, Internal Quality, TMT
**SE1:** Senior Engineer Quality Assurance, TMT
**SE2:** Senior Engineer, Quality Assurance, TMT
**SE3:** Senior Engineer, Internal Quality, TMT
**SE4:** Senior Engineer, Internal Quality, TMT
**M1:** Manager, Strategic Integration Management, Intel
**E2:** Engineer, Strategic Integration Management, Intel
**E3:** Engineer, Strategic Integration Management, Intel

In sum, all the above mentioned suggest that the knowledge of quality tools and techniques is important for the organization in order to be successfully implement quality tools and techniques. General Manager, TMT suggests that employees with higher knowledge in advanced technology and quality area are a major contributor

*Table 2. The summary of the case study (Factors to determine quality tools and techniques implementation)*

| **Research Objectives** | **Interview data from respondents** | | | | | | | | | |
|---|---|---|---|---|---|---|---|---|---|---|
| **Key Factors** | **GM1** | **SM2** | **SM3** | **SE1** | **SE2** | **SE3** | **SE4** | **M1** | **E1** | **E2** |
| Knowledge on Quality Tools and Techniques | ✓ | ✓ | ✓ | ✓ | ✓ | ✓ | ✓ | ✓ | ✓ | ✓ |
| Industry 4.0 Environment | ✓ | ✓ | ✓ | ✓ | ✓ | ✓ | ✓ | ✓ | ✓ | ✓ |
| Customer Satisfaction | ✓ | ✓ | ✓ | ✓ | ✓ | ✓ | ✓ | ✓ | ✓ | ✓ |
| Continuous Improvement | ✓ | ✓ | ✓ | ✓ | ✓ | ✓ | ✓ | ✓ | ✓ | ✓ |
| Supplier Partnership | ✓ | ✓ | ✓ | ✓ | ✓ | ✓ | ✓ | ✓ | ✓ | ✓ |

Summarize by the researchers (2019)

to their company and economic success to producing, changing and transferring knowledge to the production level. He further indicates, that the environment of Industry 4.0 plays an important role in delivering the service and structuring knowledge based on smart manufacturing, which able to enhance quality performance that will be the frontier of their new competitive positions. While, Manager 4, Intel states that the use of high technology and quality control such as visual simulation, smart machines, smart production and heavy use of sensors is better than through human intervention.

Customer satisfaction has become a factor in TMT and Intel in implementing quality tools and techniques. This has been highlighted by General Manager TMT who pointed out that to determine the external customers perceive in terms of quality and expectation provided, TMT will distribute an annual quality survey to the customer for feedback on the result when using the required quality tools and techniques. Furthermore, TMT is strongly involved in continuous improvement, which concentrates on formal problem solving and responsiveness. The investigation and analysis of the complaint scopes and feedback of these results are both become a duty while providing the services to their customers, and at the same time providing the valuable information for improving product quality. In line with this, Manager 1, Intel also affirms on the factor of continuous improvement by mentioning that the 8D Problem Solving Methodology is utilized in Intel to determine on the containment actions, root cause and corrective or preventive actions and at the same time to address on the customer feedback for the overall continuous improvement.

It should be noted that Toyo-Memory Technology and Intel believe that supplier partnership does influence the implementation of quality tools and techniques. The fact that TMT experiences adopted a five-step of the supplier development process for improving the quality of goods and services delivered by their suppliers. The five steps of the process consist of planning, implementation, measurement, improvement, and recognition and award. For illustration, during the planning stage, they form a general expectation of completing the work and the selection of their supplier is based on their Quality System, Cost, Capacity, Value-Added Services, Technical Capability, etc. As such, TMT suppliers' performance will be measured in the states of Quality, Cost, Delivery, Service and Technology. In so doing, they distribute the data among their suppliers both online and during the Business Review Meetings. As this permits them to define clearly upon their expectation on their suppliers and presents a method to follow up and verifies in order for the suppliers to meet their goals.

In terms of methodology, similar studies conducted in organizations similar to these respective companies are likely to yield similar results. The lessons are extracted and therefore, this, on the one hand, may help quality assurance and strategic policymakers to benchmark/evaluate where their organisations are now

(See Morse, 1999; Stierand & Dorfler, 2010). It also means that they do not need to start from scratch in predicting how quality management tools and techniques need to be corresponded or aligned to the Industrial Revolution 4.0 movement, as this study already provides some understanding and insights into this.

As a result of this study, the authors can confirm that the implementation of quality tools and techniques will effectively be solved many quality issues in the industry, particularly by knowing the real/key factors in order to determine the right tools and techniques being used. This observation is consistent with, Revuelto-Taboada, Canet-Giner, and Balbastre-Benavent (2011) who pointed out that, the higher competent an organization with the application of quality management, the better tendency it takes to handle other quality tools and techniques, especially advanced ones. Likewise, this also supported by Ahmed & Hassan (2003) that claims, the better an organization employs quality tools and techniques, the further performance it achieves, nevertheless of its size.

As such, all the above discussion also suggests that although there are almost 400 quality tools and techniques available (See Basu, 2004 and Charantimath, 2011), however, what is more important is to know the right tools and techniques relating to the specific circumstances. Therefore, it is fair to conclude that those key factors revealed from this study in selecting tools and techniques are considered relevant, practical and effective in line with the current movement of Industrial Revolution 4.0, particularly for the smart manufacturing environment.

## ACKNOWLEDGMENT

The authors wish to thank all the respective respondents during the interviews and provide data throughout this study conducted. In addition, the authors acknowledge the support given by Universiti Teknikal Malaysia Melaka (UTeM) for the financial support and facilities provided in completing this research. We will welcome any collaboration for this kind of research with an open arm.

## REFERENCES

Ahmed, S., & Hassan, M. (2003). Survey and case investigations on application of quality management tools and techniques in SMIs. *International Journal of Quality & Reliability Management*, *20*(7), 795–826. doi:10.1108/02656710310491221

Albers, A., Gladysz, B., Pinner, T., Butenko, V., & Stürmlinger, T. (2016). Procedure for defining the system of objectives in the initial phase of an industry 4.0 project focusing on intelligent quality control systems. *Procedia Cirp*, *52*, 262–267. doi:10.1016/j.procir.2016.07.067

Ale Ebrahim, N., Ahmed, S., & Taha, Z. (2003). Virtual R&D teams in small and medium enterprises: A literature review.

Antony, J., Jiju Antony, F., Kumar, M., & Rae Cho, B. (2007). Six sigma in service organisations: Benefits, challenges and difficulties, common myths, empirical observations and success factors. *International Journal of Quality & Reliability Management*, *24*(3), 294–311. doi:10.1108/02656710710730889

Bamford, D. R., & Greatbanks, R. W. (2005). The use of quality management tools and techniques: A study of application in everyday situations. *International Journal of Quality & Reliability Management*, *22*(4), 376–392. doi:10.1108/02656710510591219

Basu, R. (2004). *Implementing quality: A practical guide to tools and techniques*. London, UK: Thomson Learning.

Basu, R., & Wright, J. N. (2012). *Quality beyond six sigma*. Routledge. doi:10.4324/9780080515502

Baur, C., & Wee, D. (2015). Manufacturing's next act. *McKinsey Quarterly, Jun.*

Bayazit, O. (2003). Total quality management (TQM) practices in Turkish manufacturing organizations. *The TQM Magazine*, *15*(5), 345–350. doi:10.1108/09544780310502435

Brady, J. E., & Allen, T. T. (2006). Six Sigma literature: A review and agenda for future research. *Quality and Reliability Engineering International*, *22*(3), 335–367. doi:10.1002/qre.769

Charantimath, P. M. (2011). *Total quality management* (2nd ed.). Boston, MA: Pearson Education.

Clegg, B., Rees, C., & Titchen, M. (2010). A study into the effectiveness of quality management training: A focus on tools and critical success factors. *The TQM Journal*, *22*(2), 188–208. doi:10.1108/17542731011024291

Constantiou, I. D., & Kallinikos, J. (2015). New games, new rules: Big data and the changing context of strategy. *Journal of Information Technology*, *30*(1), 44–57. doi:10.1057/jit.2014.17

Cuihua, C., Sheng, L., Pengfei, L., & Lu, W. 2016. Active Shop Scheduling of Production Process Based on RFID Technology. In *MATEC Web of Conferences* (Vol. 42, p. 04004). EDP Sciences. 10.1051/matecconf/20164204004

Dale, B. (2003). *Managing quality* (4th ed.). Oxford, UK: Blackwell Publishers.

Drew, E., & Healy, C. (2006). Quality management approaches in Irish organizations. *The TQM Magazine*, *18*(4), 358–371. doi:10.1108/09544780610671039

Fotopoulos, C., & Psomas, E. (2009). The use of quality management tools and techniques in ISO 9001: 2000 certified companies: The Greek case. *International Journal of Productivity and Performance Management*, *58*(6), 564–580. doi:10.1108/17410400910977091

Fotopoulos, C. B., & Psomas, E. L. (2009). The impact of "soft" and "hard" TQM elements on quality management results. *International Journal of Quality & Reliability Management*, *26*(2), 150–163. doi:10.1108/02656710910928798

Georgakopoulos, D., & Jayaraman, P. P. (2016). Internet of things: From internet scale sensing to smart services. *Computing*, *98*(10), 1041–1058. doi:10.100700607-016-0510-0

Hagemeyer, C., Gershenson, J. K., & Johnson, D. M. (2006). Classification and application of problem-solving quality tools: A manufacturing case study. *The TQM Magazine*, *18*(5), 455–483. doi:10.1108/09544780610685458

Henning, K., Wolfgang, W., & Johannes, H. (2013). Recommendations for Implementing the Strategic Initiative INDUSTRIE 4.0: Securing the Future of German Manufacturing Industry. *Final Report of the Industrie, 4.*

Hermann, M., Pentek, T., & Otto, B. (2016, January). Design principles for industrie 4.0 scenarios. In *2016 49th Hawaii International Conference on System Sciences (HICSS),* (pp. 3928-3937). IEEE.

Ishikawa, K. (2012). Introduction to Quality Control. *Productivity Press.*

Kube, G., & Rinn, T. (2014). Industry 4.0-The next revolution in the industrial sector.

Kwok, K. Y., & Tummala, V. M. R. (1998). A quality control and improvement system based on total control methodology (TCM). *International Journal of Quality & Reliability Management*, *15*(1), 13–48. doi:10.1108/02656719810197288

Lagrosen, Y., & Lagrosen, S. (2005). The effects of quality management–a survey of Swedish quality professionals. *International Journal of Operations & Production Management*, *25*(10), 940–952. doi:10.1108/01443570510619464

Lam, S. S. (1996). Applications of quality improvement tools in Hong Kong: An empirical analysis. *Total Quality Management*, *7*(6), 675–680. doi:10.1080/09544129610559

Lasi, H., Fettke, P., Kemper, H. G., Feld, T., & Hoffmann, M. (2014). Industry 4.0. *Business & Information Systems Engineering*, *6*(4), 239–242. doi:10.100712599-014-0334-4

Lee, G. L., Burcher, P. G., & Waddell, D. (2008). The challenges for quality managers in Britain and Australia. *The TQM Journal, 20*(1), pp. 45-58.

Lee, J., Kao, H. A., & Yang, S. (2014). Service innovation and smart analytics for industry 4.0 and big data environment. *Procedia Cirp*, *16*, 3–8. doi:10.1016/j.procir.2014.02.001

Lom, M., Pribyl, O., & Svitek, M. (2016, May). Industry 4.0 as a part of smart cities. In *Smart Cities Symposium Prague (SCSP),* 2016 (pp. 1-6). IEEE. 10.1109/SCSP.2016.7501015

Lu, Y. (2017). Industry 4.0: A survey on technologies, applications and open research issues. *Journal of Industrial Information Integration*, *6*, 1–10. doi:10.1016/j.jii.2017.04.005

Lukač, D. (2015, November). The fourth ICT-based industrial revolution" Industry 4.0"—HMI and the case of CAE/CAD innovation with EPLAN P8. In Telecommunications Forum Telfor (TELFOR), 2015 23rd (pp. 835-838). IEEE.

McAfee, A., Brynjolfsson, E., Davenport, T. H., Patil, D. J., & Barton, D. (2012). Big data: The management revolution. *Harvard Business Review*, *90*(10), 60–68. PMID:23074865

Mi, M., & Zolotov, I. (2016). February. Comparison between multiclass classifiers and deep learning with focus on industry 4.0. In 2016 Cybernetics & Informatics (K&I) (pp. 1-5).

Miguel, P. A. C., Satolo, E., Andrietta, J. M., & Calarge, F. A. (2012). Benchmarking the use of tools and techniques in the Six Sigma programme based on a survey conducted in a developing country. *Benchmarking: An International Journal*, *19*(6), 690–708. doi:10.1108/14635771211284279

Mitra, A. (2012). *Fundamentals of quality control and improvement.* Hoboken, NJ: John Wiley & Sons.

Mosconi, F. (2015). *The new European industrial policy: Global competitiveness and the manufacturing renaissance*. Routledge. doi:10.4324/9781315761756

Novak, S. (2005). *The small manufacturer's toolkit: A guide to selecting the techniques and systems to help you win*. Boca Raton, FL: CRC Press.

Oses, N., Legarretaetxebarria, A., Quartulli, M., García, I., & Serrano, M. (2016). Uncertainty reduction in measuring and verification of energy savings by statistical learning in manufacturing environments. [IJIDeM]. *International Journal on Interactive Design and Manufacturing, 10*(3), 291–299. doi:10.100712008-016-0302-y

Paelke, V. (2014, September). Augmented reality in the smart factory: Supporting workers in an industry 4.0. environment. In *Proceedings of the 2014 IEEE emerging technology and factory automation (ETFA)* (pp. 1-4). IEEE. 10.1109/ETFA.2014.7005252

Revuelto-Taboada, L., Canet-Giner, T., & Balbastre-Benavent, F. (2011). Quality tools and techniques, EFQM experience and strategy formation. Is there any relationship?: The particular case of Spanish service firms. *Innovar (Universidad Nacional de Colombia), 21*(42), 25–40.

Roblek, V., Meško, M., & Krapež, A. (2016). A complex view of industry 4.0. *SAGE Open, 6*(2). doi:10.1177/2158244016653987

Rowland-Jones, R., Thomas, P. T., & Page-Thomas, K. (2008). Quality management tools & techniques: Profiling SME use & customer expectations. *The International Journal for Quality and Standards, 1*(1). Retrieved from http://www.bsieducation.org/Education/downloads/ijqs/paper6.pdf

Rubmann, M., Lorenz, M., Gerbert, P., Waldner, M., Justus, J., Engel, P., & Harnisch, M. (2015). *Industry 4.0*. Boston, MA: Boston Consulting Group.

Sanders, A., Elangeswaran, C., & Wulfsberg, J. (2016). Industry 4.0 implies lean manufacturing: Research activities in industry 4.0 function as enablers for lean manufacturing. *Journal of Industrial Engineering and Management, 9*(3), 811–833. doi:10.3926/jiem.1940

Sanders, A., Elangeswaran, C., & Wulfsberg, J. P. (2016). Industry 4.0 implies lean manufacturing: Research activities in industry 4.0 function as enablers for lean manufacturing. [JIEM]. *Journal of Industrial Engineering and Management, 9*(3), 811–833. doi:10.3926/jiem.1940

Scheuermann, C., Verclas, S., & Bruegge, B. (2015, August). Agile factory-an example of an industry 4.0 manufacturing process. In *2015 IEEE 3rd International Conference on Cyber-Physical Systems, Networks, and Applications* (pp. 43-47). IEEE.

Schmidt, R., Möhring, M., Härting, R. C., Reichstein, C., Neumaier, P., & Jozinović, P. (2015, June). Industry 4.0-potentials for creating smart products: empirical research results. In *International Conference on Business Information Systems* (pp. 16-27). Cham, Switzerland: Springer. 10.1007/978-3-319-19027-3_2

Shafiq, S. I., Sanin, C., Toro, C., & Szczerbicki, E. (2015). Virtual engineering object (VEO): Toward experience-based design and manufacturing for industry 4.0. *Cybernetics and Systems*, *46*(1-2), 35–50. doi:10.1080/01969722.2015.1007734

Shahin, A., Arabzad, S. M., & Ghorbani, M. (2010). Proposing an integrated framework of seven basic and new quality management tools and techniques: A roadmap. *Research Journal of International Studies,* (17), 183-195.

Siddiqui, M. S., Parker, M. C., Koczian, G., Adeyemi-Ejeye, F., Quinlan, T., Walker, S. D., ... Habel, K. (2016, June). CHARISMA: Converged heterogeneous advanced 5G cloud-RAN architecture for intelligent and secure media access. In *2016 European Conference on Networks and Communications (EuCNC)* (pp. 240-244). IEEE.

Sousa, S. D., Aspinwall, E., Sampaio, P. A., & Rodrigues, A. G. (2005). Performance measures and quality tools in Portuguese small and medium enterprises: Survey results. *Total Quality Management & Business Excellence*, *16*(2), 277–307. doi:10.1080/14783360500054434

Stock, T., & Seliger, G. (2016). Opportunities of sustainable manufacturing in industry 4.0. *Procedia Cirp*, *40*, 536–541. doi:10.1016/j.procir.2016.01.129

Tarí, J. J., & Sabater, V. (2004). Quality tools and techniques: Are they necessary for quality management? *International Journal of Production Economics*, *92*(3), 267–280. doi:10.1016/j.ijpe.2003.10.018

Thames, L., & Schaefer, D. (2016). Software-defined cloud manufacturing for industry 4.0. *Procedia CIRP*, *52*, 12–17. doi:10.1016/j.procir.2016.07.041

Thamsen, P. U., & Wulff, S. (2016). Industry 4.0 and current Trends in the Pump industry-A Look back on the ACHEMA 2015. *Chemieingenieurtechnik (Weinheim)*, *88*(1-2), 15–19. doi:10.1002/cite.201690002

Timans, W., Ahaus, K., & Van Solingen, R. (2009). A Delphi study on Six Sigma tools and techniques. *International Journal of Six Sigma and Competitive Advantage*, *5*(3), 205–221. doi:10.1504/IJSSCA.2009.028093

Varghese, A., & Tandur, D. (2014, November). Wireless requirements and challenges in Industry 4.0. In *2014 International Conference on Contemporary Computing and Informatics (IC3I),* (pp. 634-638). IEEE.

Vijaykumar, S., Saravanakumar, S. G., & Balamurugan, M. (2015). Unique sense: Smart computing prototype. *Procedia Computer Science*, *50*, 223–228. doi:10.1016/j.procs.2015.04.056

Vogel-Heuser, B., & Hess, D. (2016). Guest editorial Industry 4.0–prerequisites and visions. *IEEE Transactions on Automation Science and Engineering*, *13*(2), 411–413. doi:10.1109/TASE.2016.2523639

Walker, H. F., Elshennawy, A., Gupta, B., & McShane-Vaughn, M. (2012). *The certified quality inspector handbook*. Milwaukee, WI: ASQ Quality Press.

Wan, J., Wang, S., Li, D., & Zhang, C. (2016). Implementing smart factory of industrie 4.0: An outlook. *International Journal of Distributed Sensor Networks*, *12*(1). doi:10.1155/2016/3159805

Wang, Z. Z., Nie, D. X., Chen, X., & Huang, G. Q. (2016). IoT-based real-time production logistics synchronization system under smart cloud manufacturing. *International Journal of Advanced Manufacturing Technology*, *84*(1-4), 147–164. doi:10.100700170-015-7220-1

Werner, T., & Weckenmann, A. (2012). Sustainable quality assurance by assuring competence of employees. *Measurement*, *45*(6), 1534–1539. doi:10.1016/j.measurement.2012.02.025

## KEY TERMS AND DEFINITIONS

**Cyber Physical System:** A mechanism that is controlled or monitored by computer-based algorithms, tightly integrated with the Internet and its users. In cyber-physical systems, physical and software components are deeply intertwined, each operating on different spatial and temporal scales, exhibiting multiple and distinct behavioral modalities, and interacting with each other in a lot of ways that change with context.

**Gross Domestic Product:** A monetary measure of the market value of all the final goods and services produced in a specific time period, often annually.

**Interoperability:** A characteristic of a product or system, whose interfaces are completely understood, to work with other products or systems, at present or in the future, in either implementation or access, without any restrictions.

**Modularity:** The degree to which a system's components may be separated and recombined, often with the benefit of flexibility and variety in use.

**Prognostics:** An engineering discipline focused on predicting the time at which a system or a component will no longer perform its intended function.

**Smart Manufacturing:** A broad category of manufacturing that employs computer-integrated manufacturing, high levels of adaptability and rapid design changes, digital information technology, and more flexible technical workforce training.

**Virtualization:** An act of creating a virtual (rather than actual) version of something, including virtual computer hardware platforms, storage devices, and computer network resources.

# Chapter 9
# Ethnicity and Household Savings in Indonesia

**Shochrul Rohmatul Ajija**
*Universitas Airlangga, Indonesia*

**Muhamad Abduh**
https://orcid.org/0000-0002-1918-6525
*School of Business and Economics, Universiti Brunei Darussalam, Brunei*

**Wasiaturrahma Wasiaturrahma**
*Universitas Airlangga, Indonesia*

**Ahmad Hudaifah**
*Universitas Internasional Semen Indonesia, Indonesia*

## ABSTRACT

*Household saving is very important, not only for securing the future spending of the family but also for the country's economy. Using the logit analysis on data of The Indonesia Family Life Survey (IFLS) wave three, four, and five, this chapter analyzes factors influencing, especially the role of ethnicity, upon the household savings in Indonesia. The result indicates that gender, location, and level of education are the consistent variables affecting the household saving behaviour in Indonesia across the three wave surveys. Meanwhile, as for the ethnic group variable, there are only Sunda, Batak, and Bima-Dompu that can significantly influence the people's saving behavior across the three wave surveys.*

DOI: 10.4018/978-1-7998-2257-8.ch009

## INTRODUCTION

Saving is believed to be one of the engines driving the economy of a country. Previous studies have shown that savings are able to boost economic growth in many countries such as Nigeria (Adelakun, 2011), Malaysia (Abduh, Omar, & Duasa, 2011), as well as Bostwana (Jagadesh, 2015). The growth of the economy for countries with high capital accumulation, especially through savings, will be more sustain and higher compared to countries with low capital (Chow, 1993). The low level of capital accumulation, one of the reasons is due to insufficient savings, is the common problem faced by developing countries (Wollasa, 2011).

To date, Indonesia is still classified as a developing country and grouped under low and midlle income countries (World Bank, 2017). Similar to other developing countries in this world, Indonesia is facing challenges on how to improve its capital accumulation, especially through the improvement of household savings which currently still in a considerably low level. It is interesting to see that at the Association of Southeast Asian Nations (ASEAN) level, the amount of household savings in Indonesia that have been collected relatively higher and even better than Singapore and Brunei Darussalam as a high-income country, i.e around 300 trillion US$ a year. However, it is not surprising because the population of Indonesia is much greater than those two countries. The average percentage of savings to GDP from 2010 to 2015 shows that Indonesia is in the fourth position in ASEAN with only 34.4 percent (World Bank, 2017).

Unlike other low- and middle-income countries in ASEAN region such as Thailand, Cambodia and Laos, the growth of domestic savings in Indonesia is likely to decline since 2013 (World Bank, 2017). After a fantastic increase of 44 percent in 2010, the level of savings in Indonesia continue to fall with the rate of 0.3 percent in 2015. On the other hand, the same report said that domestic savings of Laos, Thailand, and Cambodia had increased dramatically by 34, 12, and 10 percent respectively. Since domestic saving is one of the main components in developing the economy, it is then very important to investigate the determinant of domestic savings behavior in Indonesia especially at the private level since 91.97 percent of domestic savings in Indonesia are private savings (Vibriyanti, 2014).

However, according to (Scott, 2014), there is a link between ethnic group and economic behaviour including saving. Furthermore, (O'Connor, 2017) evidences that ethnicity greatly affects people's savings behaviour in the three countries of Australia, Canada and China, where Chinese descent can save more than Caucasians.

Since Indonesia is a country with more than 100 ethnic groups live together, it is interesting and important to know the saving behaviour of households in Indonesia with regard to their ethnicity. Hence, this study attempts to analyse factors, especially the ethnicity, influencing the households' saving behaviour in Indonesia using nationwide Indonesian Family Life Survey (IFLS) wave 3, 4, and 5 data.

The rest of this paper is structured as follows. In the second section, this study quotes literature reviews about savings, concepts of ethnicity, and how ethnicity can influence the households' saving behaviour. Section 3 presents data and research methods utilized in this study while section 4 describes research finding and analysis. Lastly, Section 5 summarises the main findings and their implications.

## LITERATURE REVIEW

Generally, saving is defined as money not spent (Popovici, 2012). According to (Akram & Akram, 2015), the determinants of savings are including demographic factors, macroeconomic variables, and financial variables. The Classical Theory stated that savings have a positive relationship with interest rate (Vieneris, 1977; Mishkin, 2010). The high interest rate encourages people to save because they will earn more interest income through savings. According to Keynesian, savings are highly determined by the disposable income or current income (Crouch, 1972). However, Post-Keynesian argued that savings depended on income ambiguously, but they stressed that savings are more influenced positively by one's income and affected negatively by the consumption at the same time (Grigoli, Herman, & Herbel, 2014).

According to (Grigoli, et al., 2014), the starting point of theoretical research on savings is defined by the permanent income hypothesis (PIH) and the life cycle hypothesis (LCH). Unlike Keynesian hypothesis, (Hall, 1978) stated that PIH concerns on a representative, infinitely lived consumer who equalizes the consumption to the permanent income net of the present value of taxes. Ricardian equivalence hypothesis (REH), the variant of the PIH, defines permanent income as net of the present value of the government spending (Barro, 1974). The REH estimates that the permanent government consumption will be fully compensated by the lower of private consumption if a huge number of stringent conditions has been fulfilled (Seater, 1993).

The PIH assumption of homogeneous consumers seems to contradict with the heteroginity of some consumer dimensions, such as age, income, and access to borrow the money. Therefore, according to (Attanasio & Weber, 2010), the LCH had proposed that the age-related consumer heterogenity stated that aggregate savings indicates the addition of savings by different age. Furthermore, saving habits seem to be also influenced by the level of one's financial literacy. One of the reasons of suboptimal saving and investments was the suffering of financial literacy (Hastings & Mitchell, 2011). In addition, (Lusardi & Mitchell, 2007) and (Hasting & Tejeda-Ashton, 2008) had mentioned that the lack of financial literacy also make people to experience lack of saving for retirement, stuck in a lot of debt, take the wrong decision in the housing loan, and face many problems in the current sophisticated financial era.

Ethnicity is something that is not given but as a result of social construction so that ethnicity itself is flexible and dynamic (Yang, 2000). Differences in ethnic groups are judged to influence different mindsets in terms of saving. Honig (1996) argues that ethnic and gender differences influence a person's behavior in planning for retirement. Meanwhile, someone who is ready to face retirement must have a more planned savings since his youth. In addition, (Scott, 2014) stated that the difference in retirement savings behaviour based on race and ethnicity is due to cultural differences in the degree of financial interdependence expected by family members and one's social network. The group will usually save more because there is a more independent set of cultural assumptions in which everyone is responsible for his or her own pension outcomes and financial decisions more generally. A person with a relatively similar level of wealth but coming from different ethnic groups can even have a degree of readiness to welcome a different retirement (Shapiro, 2004).

One of the causes of differences in saving habits between ethnic groups is usually due to differences in cultural norms governing each group (Scott, 2014). For example, there are some ethnic groups who believe that real estate is the best source of wealth. As a result, people with these ethnic groups began to save funds in the form of a house or property at a young age. This belief is born due to the prevailing norm around them, the ethnic group where they reside, so it also affects the way a person thinks in determining the technique of saving or investment.

## DATA AND RESEARCH METHOD

In order to measure the impact of the ethnic group upon household's saving behaviour in Indonesia, this study utilizes the longitudinal socioeconomic and health panel data of Indonesia Family Life Survey (IFLS) wave 3, 4, and 5 with household samples from 13 provinces in Indonesia conducted by the RAND Foundation in 2000, 2007/2008, and 2014/2015 respectively. IFLS data used in this study is the data where respondents surveyed on wave 3, 4, and 5 are the same person. The goal is to see the development of savings character of respondents, whether it is true that ethnic variables affect them consistently or not.

This study focuses upon the influence of demographic and cultural factor, such as ethnicity, upon the formal savings ownership among Indonesian. Therefore, the ownership of formal saving becomes the dependent variable, whereas, ethnicity, gender, location, marital status, and years of school set as the independent variables. Furthermore, since the dependent variable is in nominal outcome; that is 1 if the respondent has a formal household savings and 0 otherwise, so the binary logit model can be attained (Williams, 2017; Anderson, Hernande, Jessup, & North, 2018). The following binary logit equation is utilized to determine the probability of discharge (1) which indicates the respondent has household savings:

$$P_i = E\left(Y = 1 \mid X_i\right) = F\left(Z_i\right) = F\left(\alpha + \sum_{i=1}^{n} \beta_i X_i\right) = \frac{1}{1 + e^{-z}}$$

where,

$$Z_i = \alpha + \sum_{i=1}^{n} \beta_i X_i + \varepsilon_i;\ P_i = \frac{e^{Z_i}}{1 + e^{Z_i}}\ and\ \left(1 - P_i\right) = \frac{1}{1 + e^{Z_i}}$$

The odds ratio is:

$$\frac{P_i}{1 - P_i} = e^{Z_i}$$

The natural logarithm of the odds ratio becomes:

$$Z_i = \ln\left(\frac{P_i}{1 - P_i}\right) = \alpha + \sum_{i=1}^{n} \beta_i X_i + \varepsilon_i = L_i$$

where $P_i$ is the probability of a household to have a formal household savings (the value of outcome $Y_i$ is 1); $1–P_i$ is the probability that $Y_i$=0 when the household does not have a formal household savings; $\beta_i$ was the coefficients of the independent variables to be estimated; $X_i$ were the explanatory variables (i.e., age of head of household; marital status of head of family; the gender of head of family; residential locations (rural or urban), year of school, and discrete data for ethnic groups in IFLS data); *e* denotes the base of the natural logarithm; $e_i$ indicates the stochastic error term; $\ln \frac{P_i}{1 - P_i} = L_i$ was logit, that is the log odds ratio of the probability that a household has a formal saving.

To measure the impact of a variable, this research uses marginal effect analysis (Fountas, Sarwar, Anastasopoulos, & Blatt, 2018). It measures the impact of changes in independent variables on the likelihood of respondents having savings in the bank. It is computed as follows (Greene, 2012: 674):

$$\frac{\partial E\left[P\left(y_i\right)\right]}{\partial X_i} = M'\left(\beta' X\right)\beta_i = f\left(\beta' X\right)\beta_i$$

and

$$f\left(\beta' X\right) = M\left(\beta' X\right)\left[1 - M\left(\beta' X\right)\right]$$

where, $e[P(y_i)]$ indicates the expected value of the logit probability, $\frac{\partial E\left[P\left(y_i\right)\right]}{\partial X_i}$ denotes the change of the overall expected value, $f\left(\beta' X\right)$ and $M\left(\beta' X\right)$ are the density functions and probability of the general conditional mean function $E[y_i|x]$, respectively.

This study also utilizes a random effect binomial logit model on panel data to analyse the impact of demography and ethnicity variables to household savings ownership.

$$y_{it}^* = \gamma' X_{it} + \varepsilon_{it}; \quad \varepsilon_{it} = \upsilon_{it} + \mu_i; \quad y_{it} = 1\left(y_{it}^* > 0\right)$$

The assumption of the random effects model is that the global error term ($\varepsilon_{it}$) consists of two independent components, i.e., $\upsilon_{it}$ for each individual and time period and $\mu_{it}$ for individual.

## EMPIRICAL RESULTS AND DISCUSSIONS

### Overview of Respondents

The respondents of this study are originated from 24 different tribal origins, such as Jawa, Sunda, Bali, Batak, Bugis, Tionghoa, Madura, Sasak, Minang, Banjar, Bima-Dompu, Makassar, Nias, Palembang, Sumbawa, Toraja, Betawi, Dayak, Melayu, Komering, Ambon, Manado, Aceh, et cetera. After going through the data cleaning, the number of respondents of IFLS wave 3, 4, and 5 involved in this study 8,890; 9,693; and 10,773 respectively.

Most of respondents in this study are from Jawa, Sunda, Minang, Bali, Sasak, Betawi, Bugis, Batak, Banjar, and Madura respectively. With regard to these ethnics, Jawa is the largest ethnic group in Indonesia that live at the central and east part of

*Table 1. The distribution of respondents according to the tribes*

| No | Ethnicity | 2000 | | 2007 | | 2014 | | Total | |
|---|---|---|---|---|---|---|---|---|---|
| | | Freq. | % | Freq. | % | Freq. | % | Freq. | % |
| 1 | Jawa | 3,920 | 44.1% | 4,482 | 46.3% | 4,996 | 46.6% | 13,398 | 45.7% |
| 2 | Sunda | 1,245 | 14.0% | 1,288 | 13.3% | 1,324 | 12.3% | 3,857 | 13.2% |
| 3 | Minang | 466 | 5.2% | 509 | 5.3% | 575 | 5.4% | 1,550 | 5.3% |
| 4 | Bali | 456 | 5.1% | 505 | 5.2% | 531 | 5.0% | 1,492 | 5.1% |
| 5 | Sasak | 314 | 3.5% | 358 | 3.7% | 540 | 5.0% | 1,212 | 4.1% |
| 6 | Betawi | 408 | 4.6% | 351 | 3.6% | 390 | 3.6% | 1,149 | 3.9% |
| 7 | Bugis | 344 | 3.9% | 370 | 3.8% | 385 | 3.6% | 1,099 | 3.8% |
| 8 | Batak | 273 | 3.1% | 349 | 3.6% | 428 | 4.0% | 1,050 | 3.6% |
| 9 | Banjar | 296 | 3.3% | 367 | 3.8% | 366 | 3.4% | 1,029 | 3.5% |
| 10 | Madura | 282 | 3.2% | 323 | 3.3% | 326 | 3.0% | 931 | 3.2% |
| 11 | Bima-Dompu | 145 | 1.6% | 184 | 1.9% | 240 | 2.2% | 569 | 1.9% |
| 12 | Makassar | 115 | 1.3% | 134 | 1.4% | 156 | 1.5% | 405 | 1.4% |
| 13 | Melayu | 26 | 0.3% | 111 | 1.1% | 81 | 0.8% | 218 | 0.7% |
| 14 | Other South Sumatera | 197 | 2.2% | - | 0.0% | - | 0.0% | 197 | 0.7% |
| 15 | Manado | 4 | 0.0% | 107 | 1.1% | 67 | 0.6% | 178 | 0.6% |
| 16 | Sumbawa | 49 | 0.6% | 46 | 0.5% | 78 | 0.7% | 173 | 0.6% |
| 17 | Tionghoa | 62 | 0.7% | 64 | 0.7% | 41 | 0.4% | 167 | 0.6% |
| 18 | Palembang | 52 | 0.6% | 41 | 0.4% | 68 | 0.6% | 161 | 0.5% |
| 19 | Toraja | 48 | 0.5% | 46 | 0.5% | 45 | 0.4% | 139 | 0.5% |
| 20 | Ambon | 104 | 1.2% | 7 | 0.1% | 3 | 0.0% | 114 | 0.4% |
| 21 | Nias | 34 | 0.4% | 23 | 0.2% | 42 | 0.4% | 99 | 0.3% |
| 22 | Komering | 30 | 0.3% | 12 | 0.1% | 35 | 0.3% | 77 | 0.3% |
| 23 | Dayak | 8 | 0.1% | 12 | 0.1% | 6 | 0.1% | 26 | 0.1% |
| 24 | Aceh | 8 | 0.1% | - | 0.0% | - | 0.0% | 8 | 0.0% |
| | Total | 8,886 | 100.0% | 9,689 | 100.0% | 10,723 | 100.0% | 29,298 | 100.0% |

Java island. Sunda is the indigenous population in the western part of Java island and becomes the second largest ethnic group in Indonesia (Candramila, Sumarsono, Suryobroto, & Moeis, 2015). Minangkabau people, also known as Minang, is one of the biggest ethnic group in Indonesia and originally from Minangkabau Highlands of West Sumatera. Balinese people are living mostly in Bali and Lombok Island as well as in Banyuwangi. It is the most eastern region of Java Island and most of them live in village called as desa tradisional (traditional village) in Lombok Island. Sasak

*Table 2. Descriptive statistics of discrete variables*

| | | 2000 | | 2007 | | 2014 | |
|---|---|---|---|---|---|---|---|
| | | Frequency | Percentage | Frequency | Percentage | Frequency | Percentage |
| Gender | Male | 2,160 | 24.31 | 2,131 | 21.99 | 1,854 | 17.29 |
| | Otherwise | 6,726 | 75.69 | 7,558 | 78.01 | 8,869 | 82.71 |
| Marital Status | Married | 8,881 | 99.94 | 9,689 | 100.00 | 10,720 | 99.97 |
| | Otherwise | 5 | 0.06 | - | - | 3 | 0.03 |
| Location | Urban | 3,998 | 44.99 | 4,937 | 50.95 | 6,085 | 56.75 |
| | Otherwise | 4,888 | 55.01 | 4,752 | 49.05 | 4,638 | 43.25 |

people are the native inhabitants of Lombok Island. Betawi people are ethnic group native to the Jakarta, the capital city of Indonesia. Bugis people are originally from South Sulawesi, Indonesia. Batak people are the indigenous tribe of North Sumatra Island, Indonesia, one of the significant tribes in Indonesia. Banjar people are native ethnic group that live in South Kalimantan, Indonesia. Madura, the third largest ethnic group by population in Indonesia, are originally from Madura Island, East Java. The distribution of respondents according to their tribes is shown in Table 1.

Demographically, there is no significant different on the character of respondents of each period. Most of the respondents of each period are women and married. Furthermore, around half of respondents live in the city. The demography profile of the respondents of each period is tabulated in Table 2 as follows:

According to Table 3, it can be asserted that the level of education of the respondents has been improved gradually over periods. In 2000, the mean of years of school is 6.49 meaning that on average, the respondents complete their education until elementary school but do not finish their first stage in junior high school.

*Table 3. Descriptive statistics of continuous variables*

| Variables | 2000 | | | | 2007 | | | | 2014 | | | |
|---|---|---|---|---|---|---|---|---|---|---|---|---|
| | Mean | Std. Dev | Min | Max | Mean | Std. Dev | Min | Max | Mean | Std. Dev | Min | Max |
| Years of School (old school, in years) | 6.49 | 4.47 | 0 | 18 | 7.72 | 4.45 | 0 | 21 | 8.60 | 4.34 | 0 | 21 |
| Age (years) | 37.68 | 13.75 | 11 | 105 | 37.52 | 13.02 | 15 | 96 | 37.99 | 12.43 | 14 | 93 |

*Table 4. Saving ownership of respondents*

| Saving Ownership | 2000 | | 2007 | | 2014 | |
|---|---|---|---|---|---|---|
| | Number | % | Number | % | Number | % |
| Yes | 2,484 | 27.95 | 2,402 | 24.79 | 3,313 | 30.90 |
| No | 6,402 | 72.05 | 7,287 | 75.21 | 7,410 | 69.10 |
| Total | 8,886 | 100.00 | 9,693 | 100.00 | 10,723 | 100.00 |

Meanwhile in 2014, the education level of respondent increases because on average, they almost can complete their junior high school.

In addition, the average of age of IFLS's respondents is steadily same from 2000 to 2014. However, the oldest age in the IFLS survey declined, from 105 years in 2000 to 93 years in 2014.

The inactivity of savings in Indonesia is also reflected in the IFLS data. Most respondents from all period do not have savings in the bank. There are only around one third of respondents owning saving account in the bank. This condition is tabulated as follows:

## Empirical Result

The logit coefficient shown in the result indicates the impact of changes in the independent variables towards the dependent variable, while the coefficient cannot be directly interpreted. Therefore, the meaning of the estimation can be asserted from the odds ratio and marginal effect. The odds ratio is the ratio between two opportunities, i.e. having household savings or not. Meanwhile, marginal effects indicate predicted probability changes in household saving ownership due to changes in independent variables.

From the results of logit estimation in Table 5, it can be seen that age has a significant effect to the probability that someone has a savings account in the bank. The older a person, the greater the probability of having savings. The odd ratio stated that the older a person, then the possibility of having savings is double from the younger person. The impact of age upon saving behaviour can be explained from elderly perspectives whereby older people requires more spending. Therefore, to manage financial planning for family, saving remains very good solution to secure future spending.

The education background of respondents seems to have a consistent impact to the probability of owning the formal savings in Indonesia. The logit estimation from all three periods shows that the higher the education level of the respondent, the greater the chance of having a savings account in the bank. From the odds ratio it can

*Table 5. The logit estimation, odds ratio, and marginal effects results*

| Variables | 2000 | | 2007 | | 2014 | |
|---|---|---|---|---|---|---|
| | Logit Est. | Odds Ratio | Logit Est. | Odds Ratio | Logit Est. | Odds Ratio |
| Constanta | -3.271845 | .0379364 | -2.968988 | .0513552 | -2.578913 | .0758564 |
| | 1.16445*** | .044175*** | .1226834*** | .0063004*** | .1132983*** | .0085944*** |
| age | .0067802 | 1.006803 | .0086909 | 1.008729 | .0076572 | 1.007687 |
| | .0021411 *** | .0021557*** | .0022405*** | .0022601*** | .0020182*** | .0020337*** |
| Gender | -.4332406 | .6484044 | -.3065939 | .7359494 | -.2727505 | .7612827 |
| | .0618184*** | .0400833*** | .0613653*** | .0451618*** | .0592536*** | .0451087*** |
| Year of School | .186598 | 1.205143 | .1776443 | 1.1944 | .1658167 | 1.180357 |
| | .0069823*** | .0084146*** | .0070919*** | .0084706*** | .0062303*** | .0073539*** |
| Location | .366811 | 1.443125 | .3268783 | 1.386633 | .2420336 | 1.273837 |
| | .0548376*** | .0791375*** | .0550702*** | .0763622*** | .048314*** | .0615442*** |
| Sunda | -.1708183 | .8429747 | -.465879 | .6275832 | -.1656544 | .847339 |
| | .0776361** | .0654453** | .0821306*** | .0515438*** | .0706661*** | .0598782*** |
| Bali | .0820778 | 1.08554 | .1282134 | 1.136796 | -.1695038 | .8440835 |
| | .1187501 | .128908 | .1127014 | .1281184 | .1045707 | .0882664 |
| Batak | -.7529156 | .4709913 | -.7313796 | .4812446 | -.6461834 | .524042 |
| | .1564906*** | .0737057*** | .1483597*** | .0713973*** | .119364*** | .0625518*** |
| Bugis | .2211047 | 1.247454 | .3647989 | 1.440224 | .0160498 | 1.016179 |
| | .1300909* | .1622824* | .1288146*** | .1855219*** | .1206085 | .1225598 |
| Tionghoa | -.5340862 | .5862047 | .2114484 | 1.235466 | .3729499 | 1.452012 |
| | .2951097* | .1729947* | .2722447 | .3363491 | .3275265 | .4755722 |
| Madura | .0239659 | 1.024255 | .0857734 | 1.089559 | .1173877 | 1.124555 |
| | .1613487 | .1652623 | .1538848 | .1676666 | .1368626 | .1539095 |
| Sasak | -.1643032 | .8484848 | -.4168824 | .6590984 | -.1803111 | .8350104 |
| | .1502312 | .1274689 | .1564909*** | .1031429*** | .1070367* | .0893767* |
| Minang | -.2187699 | .8035066 | -.367144 | .6927099 | -.4759269 | .6213089 |
| | .1151971* | .0925616* | .1142063*** | .0791119*** | .1007749*** | .0626123*** |
| Banjar | -.3185345 | .727214 | .0500454 | 1.051319 | -.2990575 | .7415167 |
| | .1523974** | .1108255** | .133001 | .1398265 | .130739** | .0969451** |
| Bima-Dompu | -.5159655 | .596924 | -.4192392 | .6575469 | -.9955983 | .3695023 |
| | .2371015** | .1415316** | .2065656** | .1358266** | .183229*** | .0677035*** |
| Makassar | -.8858852 | .412349 | .2657344 | 1.304389 | -.0613509 | .9404931 |
| | .2826851*** | .1165649*** | .2023853 | .2639891 | .1820865 | .1712511 |
| Nias | -2.080715 | .124841 | -1.431438 | .238965 | -1.362519 | .2560151 |
| | 1.029738** | .1285535** | 1.042237 | .2490582 | .6208527** | .1589477** |

*Table 5. Continued*

| Variables | 2000 | | 2007 | | 2014 | |
|---|---|---|---|---|---|---|
| | Logit Est. | Odds Ratio | Logit Est. | Odds Ratio | Logit Est. | Odds Ratio |
| Palembang | -.2842601 | .7525709 | -.5985885 | .5495868 | -.6546722 | .5196124 |
| | .3101118 | .2333811 | .3961437 | .2177153 | .2890527** | .1501954** |
| Sumbawa | -.2095149 | .8109775 | .1453626 | 1.156459 | -.2886641 | .7492639 |
| | .384231 | .3116027 | .3570626 | .4129281 | .2692231 | .2017191 |
| Toraja | -.4347159 | .6474486 | -.3801953 | .6837279 | -.1195459 | .8873233 |
| | .3882472 | .2513701 | .3774957 | .2581043 | .3305583 | .2933121 |
| Betawi | -.2329418 | .7921997 | .1080184 | 1.114068 | -.042749 | .9581519 |
| | .1217748* | .0964699* | .1263806 | .1407966 | .1176025 | .112681 |
| Dayak | .0214852 | 1.021718 | -.0152207 | .9848946 | .0477434 | 1.048901 |
| | .8099933 | .8275844 | .6587665 | .6488156 | .8382052 | .8791947 |
| Melayu | -.1094909 | .8962903 | .2373097 | 1.267834 | -.3180043 | .7275996 |
| | .4220392 | .3782696 | .2308434 | .2926711 | .2518996 | .1832821 |
| Komering | .756091 | 2.129934 | .2602096 | 1.297202 | -.3904894 | .6767256 |
| | .399912* | .8517861* | .6152888 | .7981538 | .3844403 | .2601606 |
| Ambon | -.5438382 | .5805158 | .9231985 | 2.517329 | 1.360754 | 3.899133 |
| | .2634453** | .1529342** | .7923318 | 1.99456 | 1.242069 | 4.842993 |
| Manado | -.9405155 | .3904265 | -.1876173 | .8289318 | -.2243222 | .7990577 |
| | 1.177901 | .4598839 | .2559661 | .2121784 | .2937105 | .2346917 |
| Aceh | -.6697572 | .5118328 | | | | |
| | .7456963 | .3816718 | | | | |
| Other (South Sumatera) | .0299899 | 1.030444 | | | | |
| | .1690951 | .174243 | | | | |
| Prob > chi2 | 0.0000 | | 0.0000 | | 0.0000 | |
| Pseudo R2 | 0.1167 | | 0.1014 | | 0.0823 | |

be estimated that when a respondent has a one level higher of education level, then the chances of having savings increased 1.2 times more than others. The findings are interestingly consistent through all waves.

Savings behaviour in Indonesia was leveraged by gender. Men are more likely to have saving than women consistently in all waves with the odds ratio exemplified that the probability of women to save are less than one, or only 0.65 to 0.76 times than men. However, getting closer to the year 2014, women's chances to have savings are also getting bigger although the addition is not really significant. The inclination of female's educational background has reshaped the saving behaviour in Indonesia. After completion of school, female is more aware of future generation of her children by saving more money for education cost, healthcare insurance and gold to be pawned or sold back in case of emergency.

In addition, the respondents' residence (whether in the city or village) also consistently influence saving behavior consistently. The respondents residing in cities have a greater probability to have savings at formal financial institutions than those living in the village. The odds ratio also evidences that respondents who reside in the city initially have a chance to have savings about 1.2 times bigger than those living in the village.

Regarding the influence of ethnic backgrounds upon saving behaviour of households in Indonesia, it can be seen that the influence started from wave 3 survey. From the logit estimation it can be asserted that there are some ethnic groups that significantly and positively influencing their people to save money in formal financial institutions. Those are:

**2000:** Sunda, Batak, Makassar, Banjar, Bima-Dompu, Nias, Ambon, Bugis, Tionghoa, Minang, Betawi, and Komering
**2007:** Sunda, Batak, Bugis, Sasak, Minang, and Bima-Dompu
**2014:** Sunda, Batak, Minang, Bima-Dompu, Banjar, Nias, Palembang, and Sasak

Therefore, ethnic groups that consistently affect the probability of owning a formal saving account on the three waves analyzed are Batak, Sunda, and Bima-Dompu. Interestingly, as the most dominant tribe in IFLS respondents, Jawa ethnic does not have a significant effect on savings ownership opportunities.

The difference in terms of geographical location between urban and rural area influences saving behavior among the respondents. Location of living and urban residential settlement are often surrounded by public facilities particularly banks and investment agent companies. Therefore, people living in urban areas can easily save and invest their money into financial institutions and productive investment products. The world trend of preferable living location has moved into urban dwelling. Around 50 percent of world population, including in Indonesia, has chosen to reside in urban areas (World Bank, 2017). Several countries are experiencing urbanisation which more citizens are living in cities and metropolitan. The result of study mostly indicates that geographical location has significant impacts upon saving behaviour.

## CONCLUSION AND RECOMMENDATION

The outcome of study establishes a solid conclusion that several important determinants could prompt the saving behaviour. The results from logit estimation indicate that the age has a significant effect to the probability of someone has a savings account in the bank. The education background of respondents also appears to lead a consistent impact to the probability of owning the formal savings in Indonesia. In addition, savings behaviour in Indonesia is also stimulated by gender characteristic where women are more likely to save their money in formal financial institutions than men. The odds ratio interpreted from the logit model has exemplified that the probability of women to have a saving account is less than men. It can also be asserted from the logit model that there are some ethnic groups that have most significant impressions on the probability of savings in bank, namely Batak, Sunda, and Bima-Dompu. Interestingly for Jawa, as the most dominant tribe in IFLS respondents, does not have a significant consciousness on savings ownership opportunities.

The recommendations from this study is to provide financial literacy programmes for people living in villages and from the lower middle-income groups so that they understand the importance of financial planning and at the same time to boost the country's capital accumulation for better economic growth. Meanwhile for the upper high-income family, policy makers could encourage them through many initiatives or programmes which can enhance their awareness upon saving proportion as internal source of investment within the country.

## REFERENCES

Abduh, M., Omar, M., & Duasa, J. (2011). The Impact of Crisis and Macroeconomic Variables towards Islamic Banking Deposits. *American Journal of Applied Sciences*, *8*(12), 1413–1418. doi:10.3844/ajassp.2011.1378.1383

Adelakun, O. J. (2011). The Nexus of Private Savings and Economic Growth in Emerging Economy: A Case of Nigeria. *Journal of Economics and Sustainable Development*, *2*(6), 31–45.

Akram, N., & Akram, M. I. (2015). Savings Behaviour in Muslim and Non Muslim Country in Context to the Interest Rate. *Pakistan Journal of Applied Economics*, *25*(2), 161–177.

Anderson, J. C., Hernande, S., Jessup, E. L., & North, E. (2018). Perceived Safe and Adequate Truck Parking: A Random Parameters Binary Logit Analysis of Truck Driver Opinions in the Pacific Northwest. *International Journal of Transportation Science and Technology*, *7*(1), 89–102. doi:10.1016/j.ijtst.2018.01.001

Attanasio, O. P., & Weber, G. (2010). Consumption and Saving: Models of Intertemporal Allocation and Their Implications for Public Policy, *Journal of Economic Literature. American Economic Association*, *48*(3), 693–751.

Barro, R. J. (1974). Are Government Bonds Net Wealth? *Journal of Political Economy*, *82*(6), 1095–1117. doi:10.1086/260266

Candramila, W., Sumarsono, S. H., Suryobroto, B., & Moeis, M. R. (2015). Face Shape Variation Among Sundanese People form Western Java, Indonesia. *Hayati Journal of Biosciences*, *22*(1), 34–40. doi:10.4308/hjb.22.1.34

Chow, G. C. (1993). Capital Formation and Economic Growth in China. *The Quarterly Journal of Economics*, *108*(3), 809–842. doi:10.2307/2118409

Crouch, R. L. (1972). Macroeconomics. New York: Harcourt Brace Javanovich.

Fountas, G., Sarwar, M. T., Anastasopoulos, P. C., & Blatt, A. (2018). Analysis of Stationary and Dynamic Factors Affecting Highway Accident Occurrence: A Dynamic Correlated Grouped Random Parameters Binary Logit Approach. *Accident; Analysis, and Prevention*, *113*, 330–340

Greene, W. H. (2002). *Econometric Analysis*. New York: Prentice Hall.

Grigoli, F., Herman, A., & Hebbel, K. S. (2014). World Saving. *IMF Working Paper*, *204*(14), 1–55. doi:10.5089/9781498393454.001

Hall, R. E. (1978). Stochastic Implications of the Life Cycle-Permanent Income Hypothesis: Theory and Evidence. *Journal of Political Economy*, *86*(6), 971–987. doi:10.1086/260724

Hasting, J., & Tejeda-Ashton, L. (2008). Financial Literacy, Information and Demand Elasticity: Survey and Experimental Evidence from Mexico, *NBER Working Paper, 14538*.

Hasting, J. S., & Ashto, L. T. (2008). Financial Literacy, Information, and Demand Elasticity: Survey and Experimental Evidence from Mexico, *Working Paper* 14538.

Hastings, J. S., & Mitchell, O. S. (2011). How Financial Literacy and Impatience Shape Retirement Wealth and Investment Behaviors, *National Bureau of Economic Research Working Paper Series, 16740*, 1-26

Honig, M. (1996). Retirement Expectations: Differences by Race, Ethnicity, and Gender. *The Gerontologist*, *36*(3), 373–382. doi:10.1093/geront/36.3.373 PMID:8682335

Jagadeesh, D. (2015). The Impact of Savings in Economic Growth: An Empirical Study Based on Botswana. *International Journal of Research in Business Studies and Management*, *2*, 10–21.

Lusardi, A., & Mitchell, O. S. (2007). Baby Boomer Retirement Security: The Roles of Planning, Financial Literacy, and Housing Wealth. *Journal of Monetary Economics*, *54*(1), 205–224. doi:10.1016/j.jmoneco.2006.12.001

Mishkin, F. S. (2010). The Economic of Money, Banking, and Financial Markets. New York: The Addison-Wesley.

O'Connor, T, (2017, April 18). Retrieved February 9, 2018, from IntheBlack: https://www,intheblack,com/articles/2017/04/18/religion-and-ethnicity-drive-savings-habits

Popovici, G. (2012). *Understanding the Factors Affecting Savings of Dutch Households,* Groningen: University of Groningen and "Alexandru Ioan Cuza" University of Iasi.

Scott, A. C. (2014). *Ethnic Differences in Reliance On Family Versus Personal Savings in the Face of a Financial Shock,* Unpublished Master's Thesis of University of Colorado.

Seater, J. J. (1993). Ricardian Equivalence, Journal of Economic Literature, 31, 142-190

Shapiro, T. M. (2004). The Hidden Cost of Being African American: How Wealth Perpetuates Inequality. *Regional Science and Urban Economics, 30,* 238.

Vibriyanti, D. (2014). The Effect of Socio-Demographic Variables on Household Saving: The Analysis of the 2007 IFLs Data. Developing Country Studies, 4(1), 73–84.

Vieneris, Y. P. (1977). Macroeconomics Model and Policy. New York: Wiley & Sons.

Williams, R. (2016). Understanding and Interpreting Generalized Ordered Logit Models. *The Journal of Mathematical Sociology*, *40*(1), 7–20.

Wollasa, L. K. (2011). *Investment Efficiency, Savings and Economic Growth in Sub Saharan Africa.* Retrieved July 18, 2017, from http://www,politicalarticles, net/blog/ 2011/09/05/ investment- efficiency-savings-and-economic-growth-in-sub-saharan-africa/

World Bank. (2017). *World Bank Open Data*, Retrieved March 10, 2017, from http://data,worldbank,org/

Yang, P. Q. (2000). *Ethnic Studies: Issues and Approaches.* New York: State University of New York Press.

## ADDITIONAL READING

Choudhury, S. (2002). Racial and Ethnic Differences in Wealth and Asset Choices. Retrieved November 17, 2018, from https://www.ssa.gov/policy/docs/ssb/v64n4/v64n4p1.html

Dal Borgo, M. (2018). Ethnic and Racial Disparities in Saving Behavior. Banco de Mexico Working Papers No 2018-02 (January 2018). Retrieved November 17, 2018, from https://www.banxico.org.mx/publications-and-press/banco-de-mexico-working-papers/%7BC6DA7FDC-C774-D061-0894-CAA06CCC2E31%7D.pdf

## KEY TERMS AND DEFINITIONS

**Ethnicity:** the fact or state of belonging to a social group that has a common national or cultural tradition.

**Logistic Regression:** the appropriate regression analysis to conduct when the dependent variable is dichotomous (binary).

**Saving:** the money one has saved, especially through a bank or official scheme.

# Chapter 10
# Strengthening Islamic Finance in South-East Asia Through Innovation of Islamic FinTech in Brunei Darussalam

**Abdurrahman Raden Aji Haqqi**
*Universiti Islam Sultan Sharif Ali (UNISSA), Brunei*

## ABSTRACT

*Fintech solutions can revolutionize Islamic financial services and leverage on the so-called 'Fourth Industrial Revolution' which is the movement towards combining everyday aspects of our lives, such as finance, into the digital realm that will help increase speed, efficiency, and convenience. The most significant challenge for all countries pursuing Fintech is regulating the industry. Following the issuance of the Financial Sector Blueprint, the Fintech Unit was established under Autoriti Monitori Brunei Darussalam (AMBD). AMBD envisions a vibrant economy powered by ICT through ICT-Smart Citizens as well as being a connected and efficient nation. This chapter discusses the application of Fintech specifically in Islamic finance sector based on the descriptive method of research by concentrating on its regulations. At the end, the research found that though Fintech in Islamic finance sector has been done since it's emerging through Guidelines Fintech Regulatory Sandbox Guidelines Islamic financial Fintech will be strengthened and developed and more diversified.*

DOI: 10.4018/978-1-7998-2257-8.ch010

## INTRODUCTION

Within Islamic finance, as stated by McCaw (2018), money in and of itself cannot be used to generate profit. That is, those involved in Islamic banking cannot lend or borrow money primarily for the purposes of earning interest. While the objective of Islamic finance is not profit maximization, but rather purely to facilitate Sharia-compliant trading, leasing, fee-based transactions and investment activities, Islamic Fintech is rapidly growing in significance and scale. Across the globe, Fintech sandboxes instigated by regulatory bodies have helped bring new players into regulatory scope while making regulators aware of growing trends within the industry. In the US, the Commodity Futures Trading Commission's Lab CFTC works closely with Fintech innovators, while the UK's Financial Conduct Authority's FCA Innovate offers support to market participants.

Although Islamic Fintech (financial technology) is still very limited in number, scope and size, it may grow rapidly into disruptive technology, especially in the growing number of jurisdictions where Islamic banking has achieved systemic importance. Among the technological innovations of recent years, distributed ledger technology (DLT) is often seen as the innovation with the greatest potential disruptive power for traditional banking and beyond.

No Islamic financial institution (IFI) can afford to ignore the march of technology particularly in an environment of thinning margins, low global growth and increasing cost of compliance and doing business. Cheaper, simpler and more efficient financial solutions which do not necessarily require banks or any forms of intermediation are becoming commonplace.

The bigger momentum of Fintech development especially as observed by Abdullah (2017) is in the following areas:

1) Rise of Fintech in Asia Pacific region. Now Asia Pacific is already second biggest in Fintech investment after North America which are mainly driven by Fintech hubs in Mumbai, Bangalore, Beijing and Tokyo.
2) Emergence of newer Fintech segments such as Insurtech (targeting Insurance space), Risktech (focusing on risk management solutions) and Regtech (focusing on regulatory aspect of financial services).
3) Most importantly, there will be more collaborations between banks and Fintech companies as banks seem to have accepted that fact that Fintech disruptions are real and begun to realize the potential of collaborating with Fintech companies to accelerate their evolutions.

The financial industry covers a wide range of activities including financing, payments and infrastructure, operation and risk management, data security and monetization, and customer interface. And Fintech as combination of the words finance and technology, broadly refers to the application of technology within the financial industry. Thus, Fintech applies to the segment of the technology start-up that is disrupting sectors such as mobile payments, money transfers, loans, fundraising and asset management.

The Fintech revolution has been emerged recently. It started after 2007-2008 financial crisis. At that time, policy makers were busy supposedly making finance safer while financial institutions were investing heavily in the solutions for the newly introduced compliance requirements. In between, information technology "geeks" partnered with venture capitalists to introduce a solution that was set to disrupt traditional financial services. The financial solution was technology-based, more convenient, more accessible and more cost effective. Since then, Fintech has been growing rapidly with a global investment reported to be US$12 billion (RM46.92 billion) in 2014 compared to only US$4 billion the year before (Abdullah, 2017; Malaysia World's Islamic Finance Marketplace, 2016).

The main types of Fintech services are peer-to-peer (P2P) lending, crowdfunding, money transfer, mobile payments and trading platforms. There are also Fintech services for other sub-sectors such as wealth management, insurance, etc. Some names involved in Fintech are Funding Circle, FundedByMe, TransferWise, TradeCrowd and Kantox (Abdullah, 2016).

Fintech has also penetrated the Islamic finance space. A few prominent Fintech companies that offer *Shariah*-compliant financial solutions are Dubai-based Beehive, Jakarta-based Blossom Finance, and Singapore-based KapitalBoost and ClubEthis. These Fintechs are in the segments of P2P lending and crowdfunding (Abdullah, 2016).

According to *ASEAN Today*, 5th June 2018, experts believe Brunei has enormous growth potential. Brunei could harness Islamic finance to boost its economy and meet development goals. Innovation, and particularly Fintech development, is critical.

Despite only having a population of 0.42 million, Brunei holds a strong position. By 2020, Islamic finance will account for as much as 50% of Brunei's financial sector. It is one of four countries that can issue Halal certificates for financial products. With this certificate, foreign and local companies can penetrate other Islam markets (*ASEAN Today,* 2018).

Brunei launched its Fintech office in 2017, after other ASEAN nations. At the same time, it put in place regulatory guidelines. Fintech development is one option Brunei is exploring. The Autoriti Monetari Brunei Darussalam (AMBD) committed to Fintech development. The authorities see Fintech as a tool to help stabilize Brunei's banking industry (*ASEAN Today,* 2018).

The government included Fintech development as part of *Brunei Wawasan 2035*. Brunei's financial sector (FSBP) released its 2016-2025 blueprint earlier in 2016.

The FSBP wants to create a competitive and forward-thinking financial sector. It cannot meet that goal without establishing and nurturing Fintech. If Brunei is to compete with countries which capitalize on Fintech, it must do so by innovating. It must develop its own Fintech ecosystem. Furthermore, Brunei wants to leverage its flourishing Islamic finance sector. Fintech in Islamic finance is still new. Brunei could gain an advantage by establishing this now (*ASEAN Today,* 2018).

This article aims to observe the development of Fintech in Brunei Darussalam to what extent it strengthens Islamic finance in the Country through innovation. It concentrates in the regulatory field as occur in the sandbox.

## RESEARCH METHODOLOGY

This article uses library research method in which it gathers some references in the issue in order to attract understanding of Fintech in Islamic financial industry in Brunei Darussalam especially its regulatory framework and implementation. After discussion on Islamic Fintech, the chapter highlight regulatory framework of Islamic Fintech in Brunei Darussalam.

## FINDING

Brunei had clear goals when it pursued Fintech. Companies developing Fintech solutions can help Brunei achieve its development goals. It could help the country reduce its dependence on oil and gas. Brunei could yet become a center for Islamic Fintech and finance.

The most significant challenge for Brunei Darussalam in pursuing Fintech is regulating the industry. Currently, there is something of a vacuum which fraudsters could exploit. Those predicting the growth of Islamic Fintech stressed the need for proper regulation.

Brunei can now play a role in regulating the industry. The country participated at a high-level Asian financial meeting. Brunei implemented its regulatory framework. Therefore, it must focus on regulatory innovations, such as facial recognition technology.

## LITERATURE REVIEW

Alsayed (2017) observed that Fintech, or financial technology may still be in its early stages, but 2016 was nonetheless a whirlwind year for the world of Fintech.

According to PwC's annual Global Fintech Report, cumulative investment globally is set to exceed US$150 billion in 2017. Experts predict that in the near future, no enterprise will succeed and flourish without the right Fintech services in place. For its newly stage, Fintech in Brunei Darussalam also in its newly touched. For its regulatory framework the chapter highlights the issue.

In EFICA Fintech Roundtable 2017 (Thomson Reuters, 2017), the traditional financial sector has been slow to react to the growth of Fintech in many areas but one of the most striking is in changing the perception of how social impact fits within the banking business model. At its most simple, the innovation embedded in Fintech offers a revolution in the cost to reach and service a single customer. This change can have profound consequences in terms of financial inclusion which opens up many more possibilities for Fintech to deliver meaningful social impact. The same technology that can make traditional banking more efficient and accessible can also integrate areas of social finance such as *waqf*, *sadaqa*, and *zakat* to ensure the funds reach the intended beneficiaries as well as offering a tool to measure the impact which can encourage more resources to flow through these channels. To answer this issue, this chapter discusses regulatory angel of Fintech in Brunei Darussalam.

Omar (2017) stated that the financial industry today is confronted with a new normal – rapid advances in technology and an increasingly tech-savvy demographic are presenting both opportunities and challenges to the industry. Indeed, as financial technology or Fintech is disrupting the industry, it is also emerging as a major game changer with unique value propositions. The nascent yet growing Fintech space has large ambitions. This chapter discusses only its sandbox in Brunei Darussalam.

As written in *Islamic Finance Technology & Innovation* (Malaysia World's Islamic Finance Marketplace, 2016), the digital technology has expanded to include more innovation in the financial sector, such as innovations in financial literacy and education, retail banking, and investment. Thus far, the financial technology industry has grown exponentially since 2011, and in 2015, the financial technology industry saw a USD16.5bln of funding, with a 22.2 percent y-o-y funding growth. To date, there are over 600 IFIs operating in about 75 countries across the globe ranging from banking, *takaful* to capital market. Therefore, as Islamic finance progresses, technology is becoming a key enabler for future business. IFIs offering *Shariah*-compliant products need a dedicated end-to-end Islamic banking system that facilitates and automates *Shariah*-compliant banking operations and enables banks to scale up their operations to meet global competition, grow market share, retain the loyalty of their customers and of more importance, enhance their profitability. As an appraisal to Brunei effort in enhancing her Islamic financial industry that accommodate its need this chapter is written.

Today more than two billion adults still do not have a bank account. There are also more than million micro, small and medium size businesses with unmet ðnancing needs. The demand for a responsible *Shariah*-compliant ðnancial system is huge. Every year, EY Global Islamic Banking Center (GIBC) shares insights shaping the future of the industry. This year it is about the ðnancial technology (Fintech) industry focusing on the Gulf Cooperation Council (GCC) region. It provides an overview of the global Islamic banking sector and highlight the business opportunities offered by Fintech innovations while taking into consideration the GCC banking sectors views on Fintech. For both participation (Islamic) and traditional ðnancial institutions across emerging markets the risk of disruption is real. And the ðnance function of banks is at the center of this disruption. Advances in new technologies such as in-memory computing, the cloud, analytics mobility, artiðcial intelligence block chain and robotic - over CFOs an opportunity to reimagine what the ðnance function should look like. Many CFOs are now key players in driving adoption of these technologies more broadly in the organization and in leading the transformation that ensues from technology innovation (EY, 2016). This chapter focused on Fintech regulatory in Brunei Darussalam.

## FINTECH: REGULATING ISLAMIC FINANCE INDUSTRY

Fintech, or financial technology, may still be in its early stages, but 2016 was nonetheless a whirlwind year for the world of Fintech. According to PwC's annual Global Fintech Report, cumulative investment globally is set to exceed US$150 billion in 2017. Experts predict that in the near future, no enterprise will succeed and flourish without the right Fintech services in place. (Alsayed, 2017)

In the fast-paced changing regulatory environment, policy makers face continuous pressure to develop strong regulations to support a robust regulatory eco-system. At the same time, there is a widening gap in the implementation of regulations between developed and emerging markets, which poses a key challenge to the development of a strong financial system. Should regulators focus on closing this gap, or should they be proactive and forward looking in developing more regulatory infrastructures?

As Islamic finance continues to play a bridging role in effective development of financial and regulatory infrastructures, regulators are looking at enhancing their regulatory frameworks.

Fintech is a buzzword. It is a mantra indicating 'innovation is future'. There are intense debates and coverage of Fintech on social media, for instance, Twitter, LinkedIn, Facebook, and blogs. Having seen rapid growth over the last few years, it is no more a nascent financial technology industry. There are international banks and regions competing for being new financial technology hubs (Chatta, 2017).

Fintech is a broad category that refers to the innovative use of technology in the design and delivery of financial services and products. Fintech is one of the most promising industries in 2016. The application of Fintech cuts across multiple business segments, including lending, advice, investment management and payments. The rise of Fintech is due to the fact that many customers at the moment are on mobile solutions for example smartphones. Smartphones are cheaper and more popular than ever, with 1.9 billion users estimated in 2015 (Abdul Rahim, 2016)

This innovation has not only enticed but also engaged all walks of professionals and market participants from software developer to entrepreneur, companies to financial institutions, and banks (including Islamic banks) to regulators. As a result, we have seen various developments over the last couple of years reflecting Fintech. This article shares the thought on one dimension of it, that is, potential regulatory issues and implications arising out of Fintech, although, many regulators differ in their respective approach to Fintech.

In the 21st century, the global financial services industry is facing a wave of digital disruption with Fintech, which is a combination of financial technology and innovation. It has mainly two purposes:

a. to compete with traditional financial approaches in the delivery of financial services;
b. to make financial services more accessible to the general public.

Within these aims, Fintech has echoed various implications for risk management in financial institutions (e.g. banking, insurer) and supervisors regulating financial and non-financial institutions (Chattha, 2017).

Developments in Fintech have taken the financial industry by storm, covering the field of disruptive technologies that deliver innovative financial products and services, adding that it includes the novel payment methods and financial software and hardware services that are seen today.

Significant growth has been seen in Islamic financial services in recent years. This growth is expected to continue at a rapid pace, particularly in the Middle East and Asia Pacific regions. There has been an increase in the number of Islamic financial institutes being established, with over 600 operating in about 75 countries across the globe.

The growth of Islamic finance is evident with a move by large international banks and other private sector financial institutions now offering various Islamic financial services and products, ranging from banking, Islamic insurance (*Takaful*) to capital market that comply with the basic principles of *Shariah*. Market interest in Islamic bonds or *Sukuk* has also risen, with many being issued and bought even outside the Islamic world.

According to *the Gulf Times*, which in 2016 declared Fintech to be a game changer for Islamic finance, and further reported that new ventures are combining *Shariah*-

compliant financing principles with new technologies, such as web-based Islamic crowd funding; peer-to-peer lending; as well as other forms of IT-based financing options such as Bitcoin-based and *Shariah*-compliant micro-lending. Hence Fintech solutions can revolutionize Islamic financial services and leverage on the so-called 'Fourth Industrial Revolution' which is the movement towards combining everyday aspects of our lives, such as finance, into the digital realm that will help increase speed, efficiency and convenience. Technologies will help drive the change include the Internet of things (IoT), artificial intelligence (AI) and data analytics. (*Borneo Bulletin*, 11 November 2016)

Islamic finance advisors agree that there is an urgent need to push for necessary legislation and regulation, infrastructure support and technology enablement for Islamic Fintech. So far, Islamic startups are on their own, presenting complex explanations why their Fintech innovations are halal, while other Fintech are endorsed by specific fatwas. The common stance seems to be that innovations in Fintech become impermissible only if there is clear evidence that they are in conflict against the basic finance rules of Islamic law.

What regulations/laws have been put into place to support IF Fintech? What are the BNM regulations for IF Fintech? And what are the other ASEAN and global IF regulations? There is no IF Fintech specific regulations or laws. IF Fintech will have to comply with whatever regulations/laws out there that Fintech in general will have to comply. From *Shariah* compliance perspective, the financial services provided by IF Fintech will have to comply with the prevailing *Shariah* ruling of

*Figure 1. Fintech and regulatory concerns*
*Source: Chatta (2017)*

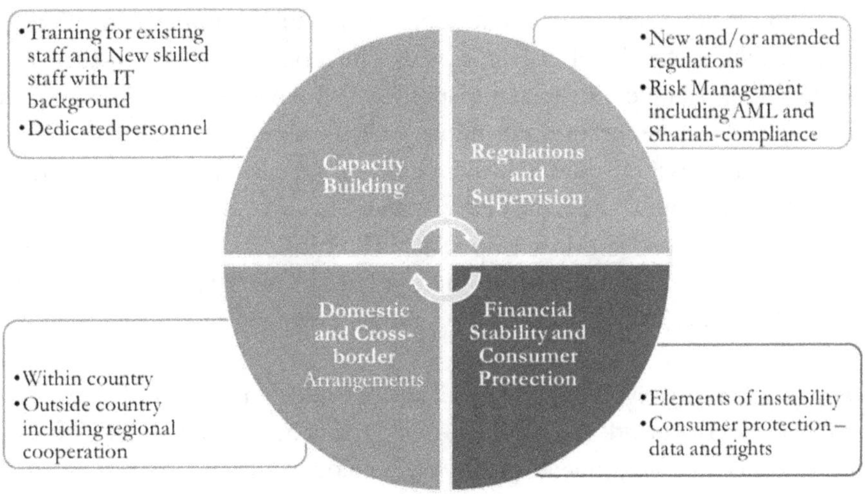

the jurisdictions that the IF Fintech is operating in. For example, the BNM Fintech regulatory sandbox issued in July this year stated that one of the intended outcomes was to ensure innovative solutions for Islamic financial services are consistent with the prevailing *Shariah* standards (Abdullah, 2017).

## Regulations and Supervision

Regulators are mindful that Fintech has the potential to deliver economic benefits, by lowering the cost of operations and enhancing competition, and societal benefits, by boosting financial inclusion and delivering more convenient financial services.

However, risk and failure are an integral part of innovation in Fintech solution. It is, therefore, vital for regulators to ensure availability of appropriate safeguards to manage the risks (such as institution-specific micro-financial risks and system-wide macro-financial risks). Hence, providing parameters and regulatory clarity through a set of framework (for Fintech business models) is critical for Fintech's mass adoption in order to ensure the financial stability of the system.

The bigger challenge of Islamic finance is ensuring that innovative solutions for Islamic financial services are consistent with prevailing *Shariah* rules and principles not only domestically but also internationally. The larger issue is the role of the *Shariah* supervisory board (SSB) in the oversight of the product innovation at the financial institution level and ultimate responsibility for *Shariah* compliance issues for consolidated supervision. In this respect, the CIBAFI has recently suggested (in its comments submitted to the BCBS's consultative document) that Islamic banks will:

a. need to consider how they can ensure that the end to end transactions are in line with *Shariah*, including the rights and ownership at each stage;
b. need to consider not only whether there is a valid contractual relationship between the parties involved, but how that relationship is to be characterized in terms of Islamic financial jurisprudence. Likewise, the IFSB has also highlighted in its report the innovations related to Fintech and a corresponding set of challenges it raises for the Islamic finance in particular. Having said that the *Shariah* compliance issues have sparked massive debate in the industry at different forums (e.g. ISRA Fintech, CIBAFI, IFSB, a thorough guidance covering all the modalities of the Fintech issues from Islamic finance, is not readily available.

To this end, rapidly evolving developments of Fintech necessitates supervisors to provide a new framework or guidelines to the financial institutions as a forward-looking guidance to accommodate positive technological development. One of the ways this can be achieved is through creating a unit responsible for Fintech, where this unit should be well diversified, having a skilled set of innovators, IT Security, and financial stability. (Dr. Jamshaid Anwar Chattha, Chief Financial Analyst at the Central Bank of Kuwait, 2017) highlighted the foregoing issues by adding:

## Financial Stability and Consumer Protection

The second consideration is the extension of the first. In Fintech, what supervisors will need to ensure is that financial institutions including banks have in place robust plans for scenarios that could threaten their own stability or the interests of customers.

Under financial stability, consumer protection including data security is one of the issues regulators should be concerned about. The threat of hacking, as well as the need to protect sensitive consumer and corporate financial data, is very critical. It is argued that any data breach, no matter how small, can result in severe financial and reputation consequences for a Fintech company.

Moreover, at the banking supervisory level, the coordination between banking supervision departments (On-site and Off-site) and IT department is pivotal in ensuring the financial safety and soundness of banking institutions. The inclusion of more IT graduates with financial skills will be an added advantage to the supervisory authorities in addressing the risks emerging from Fintech (Chatta, 2017).

## Domestic and Cross-Border Arrangements

Both domestic and cross-border considerations are important for supervisors. At domestic level, for Fintech developments, there has to be a coordination among the supervisory agencies regulating financial institutions. A common approach and strategy needs to be in place to address Fintech issues at country level.

Regulators are generally focused on how Fintech is affecting the domestic financial landscape; cross-border issues (such as cross-border payments through licensing of foreign-based service providers) are generally not being discussed. Regional cooperation is a relevant factor for Fintech. Furthermore, innovations in cross-border lending, trading and payment transactions, including via smart contracts, raise questions about the cross-jurisdictional compatibility of national legal frameworks (Chatta, 2017).

## Capacity Building

Lastly, capacity building is one of the areas, which is receiving less attention, but have a critical role to play. Though traditionally for supervisors, this has not been a key concern, there are serious challenges for building staff capacity in new areas of required expertise. No matter what the size of the Islamic bank is, proper planning for capacity building has to be part of the overall strategy.

Supervisors should consider placing greater emphasis on ensuring that they have the adequate resources and skill-sets (whether in-house or outsourced) to deal with Fintech. One way to ensure is having regulators and financial institutions to put concerted efforts in capacity building and development of IT Infrastructure.

The academic business schools or universities should also enhance training of next-generation talent through updating their current curriculum by adding courses that focus on Fintech, Design Thinking, Coding and Product Development, Risk Management and Prudential Supervision of the Fintech (Chatta, 2017).

## BRUNEI DARUSSALAM POSITION

The most crucial challenge facing Islamic financial institutions (IFIs) is the full compliance of the IFIs in its product and activities with *Shariah* rules and principles. As Islamic finance continues to attract global attention, the area of regulatory framework of its product including Fintech becomes increasingly analyzed and scrutinized by stakeholders across the industry (Haqqi, 2014).

Technological developments in the financial industry, used under the umbrella term ‘Fintech’, are increasingly affecting the entire financial landscape. Fintech did not emerge on its own, however—it was the financial crisis of the last decade that caused a revolution in innovation to occur.

Islamic Fintech is an area through which Brunei can find fresh avenues for international collaboration and investment. This was highlighted by Dato Paduka Awang Haji Abdul Mokti bin Haji Mohd Daud, the Deputy Minister of Religious Affairs, while delivering a keynote speech at a seminar on ‘Exploring Islamic Fintech’ in November 2016. According to him, “Islamic Fintech is a good example of where we can find avenues for international collaboration and investment that will enhance and strengthen our niche.” For “It promotes the importance of *aqad* or mutual agreement which is clearly understood by users in order to validate the process.

He added, “Most importantly, it provides security, transparency, a *Shariah*-compliant system and adopts the principality of the *Shariah* higher objectivity that is the preservation of wealth.” And “This can, in turn, create and generate capital, spinoffs in the local market employment opportunities and, ultimately, diversify and boost the Brunei economy.

Reflecting on the topic of the seminar, the Deputy Minister noted that it marries together two unique concepts – financial technology or ‘Fintech’ and Islamic values. “The merging of the two into a single field of Islamic Fintech is symbolic of where our aspirations for Brunei Darussalam lie, that is to hold fast to and enrich our lives with Islamic values while also being unafraid of taking strides forward in an ever-advancing global society." (*Borneo Bulletin*, 11 November 2016)

## FINTECH REGULATION IN BRUNEI DARUSSALAM

Regulatory sandbox is only one of the approaches to manage Fintech and may not fit circumstances in different jurisdictions. Supervisors will have to ensure that financial institutions or firms have robust governance frameworks and are cultivating the right culture including ongoing engagement on the evolution of Regtech. This should be complemented by the increasingly intense and data-driven supervision.

Fintech revolution promises to accrue notable beneðts to the ðnancial sector in general and the user of ðnancial services in particular. For the incumbent players in the ðnancial sector, some Fintech innovations will result in shorter transaction chain, reduced operational cost, enhanced resilience of operational processes, ability to access new customer segments to increase revenue and improved capital efðciency. This will reinforce their strategic position and improve the bottom line. But the real beneðciary of Fintech innovations will be the user of ðnancial services. Fintech laser like focus on consumers is redeðning the consumer journey while conducting ðnancial transactions by improving ease of use simplifying transaction flow and enhancing the look and feel to introduce a bit of "delight" in the consumer journey. Fintech innovations promise to reduce the transaction cost, increase the choice, improve the transaction speed and empower the customers by moving control over conducting a ðnancial transaction from the ðnancial institution to the customer. Above all, Fintech innovations and high penetration of mobile technology promise to enhance ðnancial inclusiveness by bringing in a large swathe of less well-off individuals, who currently remain unserved by the legacy ðnancial sector because of its reliance on the "physical" distribution structure and the resulting high cost of intermediation. (*Banking in emerging markets GCC Fintech play 2017*, p. 13)

The regulatory sandbox will enable industry players to apply innovative Fintech products while maintaining the overall safety and soundness of the financial system.

In Brunei Darussalam, Fintech is guided by guidelines NO. FTU/G-1/2017/1, Fintech Regulatory Sandbox Guidelines which is under the supervision of Autoriti Monetari Brunei Darussalam (AMBD).

## AMBD

Brunei Darussalam's banking system is characterized by a dual banking system consisting of Islamic banks and conventional banks. The banking system consists of eight banks comprising one Islamic Bank and seven conventional banks, as well as an Islamic Trust Fund which is set up under its own statute. Out of the eight banks, three are international, three regional and two domestic. In addition, there are three licensed finance companies, two are conventional and one is Islamic. The three finance companies are wholly owned subsidiaries of three licensed banks in Brunei Darussalam.

There are four offshore banks operate within the framework of the International Banking Order, 2000. There is only one licensed pawnbroker in Brunei Darussalam.

In cognizant with the country's *Malay Islamic Monarchy* (MIB) philosophy, Islamic banking and finance has become one of the primary sectors of focus in the financial services industry. At present, the Islamic financial services sector covers banking, takaful, asset management, mutual funds and trusts services.

Islamic Banking was first introduced in Brunei Darussalam in the early 1990s and has since seen tremendous growth. In 2010, it held a significant role in Brunei Darussalam's banking industry with total assets of B$6.36 billion and deposits totaling B$5.167 billion which accounted for 37% and 34.6% of the total market share. Similarly the takaful industry has been able to penetrate the insurance market with a sizeable market share of 42% (gross premiums) and 20% (assets) as of the end of 2010 (http://www.ambd.gov.bn).

His Majesty the Sultan and Yang Di-Pertuan Negara Brunei Darussalam consented to the Autoriti Monetari Brunei Darussalam Order, 2010 (http://www.ambd.gov.bn) which commenced on 1st January 2011. The Autoriti Monetari Brunei Darussalam Order 2010, amongst other things, introduced the establishment of AMBD, its Board and matters connected to the objects, operations, administration, functions, powers and duties of AMBD that includes relations between AMBD and the Government; relations between AMBD and the banks and financial institutions; and consequential and related amendments to other written laws that govern the activities supervised by AMBD.

His Royal Highness Prince Haji Al-Muhtadee Billah ibni His Majesty Sultan Haji Hassanal Bolkiah Mu'izzaddin Waddaulah, the Crown Prince and Senior Minister at the Prime Minister's Office in his capacity as the Chairman of AMBD consented to officiate the Establishment of AMBD and chaired the First Meeting of the AMBD Board of Directors, on Monday 5 Safar 1432 corresponding to 10th January 2011 at AMBD Head Office, Level 14, Ministry of Finance, Commonwealth Drive, Bandar Seri Begawan.

The establishment of AMBD signifies yet another important milestone in the development of the financial sector in Brunei Darussalam. It also accentuates the commitment of the Government of His Majesty the Sultan and Yang Di-Pertuan Negara Brunei Darussalam in achieving and maintaining a sound and dynamic financial system; by continuously implementing appropriate measures and embarking on necessary financial sector reforms in support of the national economic development objectives.

AMBD is a statutory body, acting as the central bank of Brunei Darussalam, which undertakes several core functions, chief of which is the formulation and implementation of monetary policies, the regulation and supervision of financial institutions as well as currency management.

AMBD serves to provide a supporting role towards developing Brunei Darussalam as an Islamic Financial hub in the region comparable to other global and regional peers.

The four main objectives of AMBD as prescribed under the Autoriti Monetari Brunei Darussalam Order, 2010 are as follows:-

- To achieve and maintain domestic price stability
- To ensure the stability of the financial system, in particular by formulating financial regulations and prudential standards
- To assist in the establishment and functioning of efficient payment systems and to oversee them; and
- To foster and develop a sound and progressive financial services sector

According to the Guidelines, AMBD has recognized several key areas of development for Brunei Darussalam's financial sector and it envisions a vibrant economy powered by ICT through ICT-Smart Citizens as well as being a connected and efficient nation. Hence, the movement towards being an E-Payment economy is also a focus, i.e. moving away from being paper-based in favour of electronic methods. This move is intended to improve financial institutions operational efficiency and costs, as well as to provide new services and greater convenience to the customers. In other words, AMBD recognizes that the evolution of Financial Technology (Fintech) has given rise to innovations that allow more sophisticated financial services to be offered to customers. Similarly, these innovations may also give rise to ambiguity on whether compliance to regulatory requirements are being met. However, the ambiguity that might arise from the need to comply with legal and regulatory requirements may discourage financial institutions or potential Fintech startups from implementing innovative solutions. This situation would be undesirable as missed opportunities may arise if innovation is stifled.

The Guidelines interpreted:

- "applicant" means any financial institution or Fintech company which intends to apply or has applied for AMBD's approval to participate in the regulatory sandbox;

- "Fintech" means technological innovation to be utilised in the provision of financial services;
- "Fintech companies" means any company registered under the Companies Act (Chapter 39) or business registered under the Business Names Act (Chapter 92) that utilises or plans to utilise Fintech but excludes a financial institution;
- "financial services" means regulated activities under any of the following:-
  i. Banking Order, 2006
  ii. Islamic Banking Order, 2008
  iii. Insurance Order, 2006
  iv. Takaful Order, 2008
  v. Securities Market Order, 2013
  vi. Payment and Settlement Systems (Oversight) Order, 2015
  vii. Money Changing and Remittance Business Act (Chapter 174)
  viii. Moneylenders Act (Chapter 62)
  ix. Pawnbroker Order, 2002
- "financial institution" refers to all institutions licensed under any of the following:–
  i. Banking Order, 2006
  ii. Islamic Banking Order, 2008
  iii. Insurance Order, 2006
  iv. Takaful Order, 2008
  v. Securities Market Order, 2013
  vi. Payment and Settlement Systems (Oversight) Order, 2015
  vii. Money Changing and Remittance Business Act (Chapter 174)
  viii. Moneylenders Act (Chapter 62)
  ix. Pawnbroker Order, 2002
- "regulatory sandbox" refers to the framework that enables qualified companies or businesses to experiment with innovative Fintech solutions in a relaxed regulatory environment, for a limited period of time and boundaries
- "sandbox entity" refers to the financial institution or Fintech company which has been given approval by AMBD to participate in the regulatory sandbox.

What are the approaches of Fintech regulatory sandbox in regulating the industry? The sandbox clearly states:

1. In an effort to provide an environment that is conducive for innovation, AMBD will adopt the Fintech Regulatory Sandbox Approach to encourage safe and responsible experimentation.

2. Interested parties may apply to enter a regulatory sandbox to experiment and test their solutions in.
3. AMBD recognizes that risk and failures are fundamental elements of innovation and so a regulatory sandbox should contain all the safeguards necessary to contain the consequences of these elements, with the overall safety and soundness of the financial system being a prime consideration.
4. AMBD will work together with the applicant, and depending on the financial service involved, specific legal and regulatory requirements will be identified, which may be relaxed or maintained for the duration of the regulatory sandbox.
5. Upon obtaining approval of their application from AMBD, the applicant will be responsible for deploying and operating the regulatory sandbox while AMBD will provide the regulatory support, for example, in the form of relaxing the appropriate legal and regulatory requirements for the duration of the regulatory sandbox.
6. Upon the successful completion of the experiment, the sandbox entity must fully comply with all relevant legal and regulatory requirements if it wishes to proceed with deployment on a wider scale.

Regarding the purpose of the Guideline, it is said: "The Fintech Regulatory Sandbox Guidelines (the "Guidelines") aims to provide clarity on the objectives and principles of the regulatory sandbox. This document will also serve as a guide for applicants on the application process".

And the target audience, the guidelines declared: "The Guidelines may interest any party that wishes to offer financial services that are or likely to be regulated by AMBD using technology in an innovative manner. This may include but is not limited to licensed financial institutions and Fintech companies".

In order to be clear in giving the objective and principles of the regulatory sandbox, the sandbox explains by stating:

1. To provide the target audience with the rationale for deploying a regulatory sandbox. A regulatory sandbox should not be used to circumvent existing legal and regulatory requirements.
2. By encouraging the adoption of innovative and safe technologies through Fintech experimentation in a well-defined environment, customers will be able to enjoy the benefits associated with this technology.
3. It should be emphasized that since the regulatory sandbox operates in a live environment, the consequences of failure should be contained by defining the space and duration of the regulatory sandbox.
4. Applicants should be able to show that they have done their due diligence before applying, including testing the proposed solution in a laboratory environment,

as well as have knowledge on the relevant legal and regulatory requirements for deploying it.

On the other hands, the sandbox also mention the evaluation criteria which are:

1. AMBD will use to assess applications submitted. APPENDIX A shows the supporting information that an application should contain.
2. This supporting information should explain how the regulatory sandbox evaluation criteria below will be fulfilled:
   a. The proposed financial service is innovative (e.g. is new or emerging technology or uses existing technology in an innovative way) and there are no comparable offerings in Brunei, with clear potential to:
      i. Improve accessibility, efficiency, security and quality in the provision of financial services;
      ii. Enhance the efficiency and effectiveness of risk management; and/or
      iii. Lead to a better deal for consumer directly or indirectly;
3. The applicant has the intention as well as the ability to deploy the proposed financial service on a broader scale after exiting the regulatory sandbox;
4. Clear test scenarios and expected outcomes;
5. Clear and appropriate parameters or boundaries of the regulatory sandbox for the protection of consumers as well as the safety and soundness of the financial industry;
6. Identification, assessment and mitigation of the risks arising from the experimentation of the proposed financial service;
7. A clear and suitable exit and transition strategy in the event that the proposed financial service has to be discontinued or if it proceeds for deployment on a broader scale.

Relating to reporting and information requirements, the Guidelines provided:

1. During the regulatory sandbox period, AMBD requires the sandbox entities to submit information relating to the test.
2. In order to meet this requirement, the sandbox entity must ensure proper maintenance of records during the sandbox period to support reviews of the test by AMBD.
3. The sandbox entity must submit interim reports to AMBD on the progress of the test, which may include information on the following:
   a. key performance indicators, key milestones and statistical information;

b. key issues arising as observed from fraud or operational incident reports; and
c. actions or steps taken to address the key issues referred to in paragraph 8.3(b).

4. The frequency and specific details to be included in interim reports will be agreed between AMBD and the sandbox entity, taking into account the duration, complexity, scale and risks associated with the test.
5. A final report containing the following information to AMBD within 30 calendar days from the expiry of the testing period:
   a. Key outcomes, key performance indicators against agreed measures for the success or failure of the test and findings of the test;
   b. a full account of all incident reports and resolution of customer complaints; and
   c. in the case of a failed test, lessons learnt from the test.
6. All reports must be confirmed by the CEO, or in situations of joint testing where more than one sandbox entity of the regulatory sandbox is involved, both CEOs confirmation is required.

How to apply and what is the process, the Guideline stated:

1. Applicants should ensure that the objective, principles and criteria specified under Section 6 (Objective and Principles of the Regulatory Sandbox) and Section 7 (Regulatory Sandbox Evaluation Criteria) are satisfied before submitting the application in APPENDIX A to AMBD at Fintech@ambd.gov.bn. Applicants may and should clarify any questions regarding applying for the regulatory sandbox by contacting AMBD at Fintech@ambd.gov.bn.

*Table 1*

| |
|---|
| **Application phase**<br>AMBD will assess the application and will endeavour to inform the applicant of the potential suitability or otherwise for a sandbox within 10 working days of receiving all information necessary for making the assessment. |
| **Evaluation and Preparation Phase**<br>AMBD will take the necessary amount of time to assess the application, this is dependent on the complexity of the application, the completeness of the information and the specific legal and regulatory requirements involved. AMBD will work together with the applicant on any further refinements that might need to be made to the application during this phase. Applicants will be informed in writing whether to proceed with the sandbox. |
| **Testing and Experimentation Phase**<br>Once approved the sandbox is launched and the sandbox entity may begin testing. AMBD and the sandbox entity will be in constant communication on the progress of the testing. |

2. Applicants will be informed if their applications are rejected. Applicants may re-apply when the reasons for their rejection have been addressed.
3. At the beginning of the Experimentation and Testing Phase the sandbox entity shall notify its customers that they are offering their services in a regulatory sandbox, explain key risks associated with it, as well as obtain customer acknowledgement that these risks have been understood.
4. If the sandbox entity intends to make material changes to the service that is under experimentation an application should be made to AMBD at least 30 days in advance with reasons for the change. The sandbox entity may continue with the existing service while AMBD reviews the request.
5. AMBD will publish all relevant information regarding sandbox entities onto the AMBD website for the purposes of informing the general public.

The regulatory framework in addressing consumer protection and market conduct issues as well as the technological impact on the orderly functioning of financial markets that promotes *Maslahah* to the general public as desired by the *Shariah* must be there. A firm that operates within the framework must also commit to observing reasonable standards of service, transparency to customers, appropriate funding and reporting requirements.

A proper *Shariah* governance framework would also ensure the operations of Fintech are in total compliance with the *Shariah* to minimize *Shariah* noncompliance risk to firms who utilize Fintech and reduce dispute and conflict.

## Bank Islam Brunei Darussalam Experience in Fintech

According the a statement released by the bank, BIBD NEXGEN harnesses the latest innovations in artificial intelligence, virtual reality, machine learning, data analytics and customer insights, symbolising BIBD's position as a pioneer in the digital space to bring more convenience and connectivity to its customers (http://www.bibd.com.bn)

BIBD NEXGEN creates a futuristic banking concept that is mobile-led and customer-centric, whilst providing financial inclusion for the unbanked and underserved segments. Banking services will be more accessible to the public through the platforms powered by BIBD NEXGEN which will de-cash the economy with emphasis on mobile-led digital transactions through enhanced interconnectivity and project multi-industry alliances.

Aligned with Brunei Wawasan 2035, BIBD NEXGEN showcases the bank's intent to transform traditional banking to the fintech age, creating a branchless banking proposition. At the same time, BIBD NEXGEN promotes key alliances among different industries, going beyond our shores with its local, regional and international partnerships to create synergies through inter-operability and open infrastructures. Not only will it support national priorities to make Bruneians highly skilled in the digital space, it will also benefit the entire ecosystem with higher digital adoption among the society for better interconnectivity to progress the economy towards a documented, secured, and digitised nation.

BIBD has seen an almost 400% growth in transactions made on its digital banking platforms since 2014. This galaxy of BIBD NEXGEN technology will complement its physical infrastructure such as its award-winning digital application, branches and contact-centre.

The first steps: BIBD NEXGEN Branch and BIBD NEXGEN Mobile

The launch of BIBD NEXGEN includes the unveiling of our first truly digital branch located at the Mall, Gadong. A first of its kind in Brunei Darussalam, the BIBD NEXGEN branch showcases cutting-edge technologies that will provide superlative experiences using next-generation devices to allow instant account openings and registration for BIBD NEXGEN Mobile.

At the same time, our popular BIBD NEXGEN Mobile app have also been upgraded with cutting edge updates including:

- Biometric and facial log in.
- Instant remittance services to several countries across Asia.
- eCredit: Purchase of gift cards from a variety of online international service providers that such as Google play, iTunes, Amazon and others.
- Direct Push Messaging to replace SMS service for better interactivity.

## BIBD NEXGEN Mobile

BIBD NEXGEN Mobile offers a convenient and safe way to perform everyday banking needs direct from an Android or iOS smartphone.

**Features:**

- Secure and fast login via biometrics (fingerprint or face ID).
- Account balances in your Current, Savings, Investment, Financing and Credit Card accounts.
- Subscription to Certificate of Deposit (BIBD Aspirasi).
- Temporarily block your BIBD Cards.
- Transfer money between BIBD accounts, locally within other banks in Brunei and also internationally.
- Mobile remittance.
- Send funds to other users of BIBD vCard (Virtual Prepaid Mastercard) via a mobile number.

- Purchase eVouchers and eCredits.
- Scan to pay with BIBD QuickPay.
- Instant Electricity (DES) and Mobile (DST & PCSB) Top-ups.Latest foreign currency exchange rates.
- Live status update of ATMs.
- Operating times and branch locations.
- Talk directly to our Contact Centre via Mobile Chat.
- Generate PIN for cardless cash withdrawals at BIBD ATMs.
- Check Hadiah Points balance.

### BIBD vCard

A prepaid card that gives flexibility and control. To be used for online shopping, pay bills, top-up prepaid mobile and electricity credits, transfer and receive funds too. All these and with worldwide acceptance at Mastercard on-line merchants. Simply registration, activation and load of BIBD vCard via BIBD NEXGEN Mobile.

### Policy Recommendations

The article recommends that there is more Fintech innovation going on outside on the banks than inside, the opportunity is for participation Islamic banks in Brunei to win trough collaboration. Investment Account Platform in Malaysia and mWallet Platform in the GCC region are encouraging signs. It will not be a surprise if the bank of the future will be an amalgamation of Fintech boutiques under a single brand.

## CONCLUSION

In conclusion, the bank's business model and technology infrastructure were based on pre-internet era, mass expensive branch opening where product sets delivered through branches, manual processes and bold marketing campaigns. In addition, the bank engaged head to head competition with other banks in price cutting. From the above discussion, if banks fail to adapt into the Fintech then the banks might lose the customers especially segment of the younger and bankable future customers. Concrete actions must be taken to ensure the survival of the bank in this era of Fintech.

Digital start-ups, companies and ventures recognize that there are great opportunities to be explored by enhancing and reshaping traditional Islamic financial services with these technologies.

The Islamic finance world desperately needs to keep up with the technological trends of the era, which are moving faster than ever. In fact, the opportunity for Islamic banks to take advantage of Fintech may be greater than conventional banks because the key themes of Fintech – democratizing capital – is the same as ethical Islamic banking. These are compatible with the ethical foundation of Islamic banking.

Therefore, Fintech application and practices, as in traditional Islamic finance, should follow the principles of the *Shariah* by avoiding the prohibited elements in the transactions such as interest (*Riba*), gambling (*Maysir*), uncertainty (*Gharar*), harms (*Darar*), cheating (*Tadlis*), etc. It must be transparent with no hidden cost, irresponsible or unethical financing (Laldin, 2017).

The idea of financial technology as a force for good in society can be harnessed by bringing together like-minded people from across the financial industry, from regulators and *Shariah*-compliant institutions, from long-established banks, and from Fintech start-ups.

## REFERENCES


Abdul Rahim, F. (2016). Fintech Pitch for Islamic Bank: Three New Areas of Services. Paper submitted to meet course requirements IB5013 Islamic Banking Practices, Masters In Islamic Finance Practice (MIFP) INCEIF, September 2016 Semester.

Abdullah, O. (2016). Impact of Fintech to Islamic finance. Retrieved from https://www.islamicfinance.com/2016/04/impact-Fintech-islamic-finance/

Alsayed, K. (2017). Fintech: The new barrier to entry in Islamic finance, *Islamic Finance News*, August 23, 2017.

*Asean Today*. (2018). Better late than never? Brunei and its role in the Fintech revolution. Retrieved from https://www.aseantoday.com/2018/06/better-late-than-never-brunei-and-its-role-in-the-Fintech-revolution/

Autoriti Monetari Brunei Darussalam. (n.d.). *Autoriti Monetari Brunei Darussalam.* Retrieved from http://www.ambd.gov.bn/

Borneo Bulletin. (2016, Nov. 11).

Chatta, J. A. (2017). Fintech and Islamic finance: A regulatory perspective. *Global Halal Investing Journal*, December, 2017. Retrieved from https://journal.wahedinvest.com/Fintech-and-islamic-finance-a-regulatory-perspective/

Easy access savings accounts. (n.d.). Retrieved from http://www.bibd.com.bn/

EY. (2016). *Banking in emerging markets GCC Fintech play* 2017.

Fintech And Islamic Finance. (2017). Retrieved from https://islmFintech.com/Fintech-and-islamic-finance/

Guidelines, N. O. FTU/G-1/2017/1, Fintech Regulatory Sandbox Guidelines. AMBD, Brunei Darussalam. Retrieved from https://www.ambd.gov.bn/SiteAssets/fintech-office/FTSG%20v1_final.pdf

Islamic Fintech can take Brunei to new heights. (2016, Nov. 11). Retrieved from http://www.business.gov.bn/Lists/News/DispItem.aspx?ID=683

Malaysia World's Islamic Finance Marketplace. (2016). Islamic Finance Technology & Innovation. Kuala Lumpur: Bank Negara Malaysia, April 29, 2016.

McCaw, M. (2018). Islamic Finance Embraces Fintech. Retrieved from http://www.bobsguide.com/guide/news/2018/Apr/5/islamic-finance-embraces-fintech/

Omar, M. (2017). "Fintech & entrepreneurship" at the Islamic Fintech Dialogue 2017, Fintech & Entrepreneurship, Kuala Lumpur, Oct. 11, 2017.

Thomson Reuters and EFICA Fintech Roundtable. (2017). *Fintech: A Source of Positive Change*, in collaboration with White Paper Media. UAE.

## ADDITIONAL READING

Accenture (2015), "The Future of Fintech and Banking: digitally disrupted or reimaged?", available at: www.accenture.com/_acnmedia/Accenture/ConversionAssets/DotCom/Documents/Globa l/PDF/Dualpub_11/Accenture-Future-Fintech-Banking.pdf

Arner, D. W., Barberis, J. N., & Buckley, R. P. (2015), "The Evolution of Fintech: A New Post-Crisis Paradigm?", (2015/047). Hong Kong.

2016. Blurred lines: How FinTech is shaping Financial Services – Global FinTech Report":http://www.pwc.com/gx/en/advisoryservices/FinTech/PwC%20 FinTech%20Global%20 Report.pdf

Chishti, S., & Barberis, J. (2016). *The FinTech Book: The Financial Technology Handbook for Investors, Entrepreneurs and Visionaries*. Chichester, UK: John Wiley & Sons Ltd. doi:10.1002/9781119218906

Drummer, D., Jerenz, A., Siebelt, P., & Thaten, M. (2016). *'FinTech: Challenges and Opportunities -How digitization is transforming the financial sector*. Dusseldorf: McKinsey.

Ernst and Young Global Ltd. (2015), "Fintech: are banks responding appropriately?", available at: www.ey.com/Publication/vwLUAssets/EY-Fintech-are-banks-respondingappropriately/$FILE/EY-Fintech-are-banks-responding-appropriately.pdf

Ernst and Young Global Ltd. (2017), "Banking in emerging markets: GCC FinTech play 2017", available at: http://www.ey.com/Publication/vwLUAssets/EY-banking-inemerging-markets-gcc-fintech-play-2017/$FILE/EY-banking-in-emerging-markets-gccfintech-play-2017.pdf

2016. Fintech and the evolving landscape: landing points for the industry", available at: www.Fintechinnovationlabapac.com/media/1157/Fintech_Evolving_Landscape_2016.pdf

Gulamhuseinwala, I., Bull, T., & Lewis, S. (2015). FinTech is gaining traction and young, high-income users are the early adopters. *The Journal of Financial Perspectives*, *3*(3).

Haqqi, A. R. A. (2014) "Shariah Governance in Islamic Financial Institution: An Appraisal", US-China Law Review, Volume 11 Number 1, January 2014, USA.

Hochstein, M. (2015), "Fintech (the Word, That Is) Evolves", http://www.americanbanker.com/bankthink/fintech-the-word-that-isevolves-10770981.html

Hochstein, M. (2015)," Friday Flashback: Did Citi Coin the Term 'Fintech'?", http://www.americanbanker.com/bankthink/friday-flashback-did-citi-coin-thetermfintech-1076875-1.html

Laldin, M. A. (2017). *Fintech and Shariah governance*. Islamic Finance News.

PWC. (2016), "Developing a FinTech ecosystem in the GCC Let's get ready for takeoff", https://www.strategyand.pwc.com/media/file/Developing-a-FinTech-ecosystem-in-theGCC.pdf

https://www.islamicfinancenews.com/Fintechand*Shariah*governance.html/print/ 2/2

## KEY TERMS AND DEFINITIONS

**AMBD:** AMBD is abbreviation of Autoriti Monetari Brunei Darussalam. It is a statutory body, acting as the central bank of Brunei Darussalam which undertakes several core functions, including the formulation and implementation of monetary policies, the regulation and supervision of financial institutions as well as currency management.

**BIBD NEXGEN:** BIBD NEXGEN harnesses the latest innovations in artificial intelligence, virtual reality, machine learning, data analytics and customer insights, symbolising BIBD's position as a pioneer in the digital space to bring more convenience and connectivity to its customers.

**Fintech:** "Fintech" refers to the use of technology for delivering financial services, specifically through Internet-based crowdfunding platforms and mobile payment systems. In other word, it refers to the application of technology within the financial industry. It covers a wide range of activities including financing, payments and infrastructure, operation and risk management, data security and monetization, and customer interface.

**Islamic Finance:** Islamic finance is a financial system that operates according to *Shariah* (Islamic law) and is, therefore, *Sharia*h-compliant. Just like conventional financial systems, Islamic finance features banks, capital markets, fund managers, investment firms, and insurance companies. However, these entities are governed both by Islamic law and the finance industry rules and regulations that apply to their conventional counterparts.

**MIB:** MIB (*Melayu Islam Beraja*) or Malay Muslim Monarchy is Brunei national ideology that fuses Islamic values and Brunei Malay culture.

**Regulatory Sandbox:** Regulatory sandbox is a framework set up by a financial sector regulator to allow small scale, live testing of innovations by private firms in a controlled environment. It is a bridge between the people trying to solve problems and the people trying to prevent those problems from ever repeating.

# Chapter 11
# Opportunities and Challenges of Social Media to the Islamic Banks in Indonesia

**Ahmad Rafiki**
*Universitas Medan Area, Indonesia*

## ABSTRACT

*The Islamic banks in Indonesia have a serious issue of a low market share of 5%. This emerged due to the limited/unvaried product range, low literacy and inclusion level of Islamic finance, unfavorable perception for Islamic banking, and limited distribution networks and outreach. All of these causes could be resolved by using social media, which will bring several opportunities such as transparency and openness, effective marketing channels, stakeholders' relationship, social media content, brand image and reputation, shariah compliance activity, learning and knowledge, and greater personalization. Meanwhile, in using social media, the Islamic banks face few challenges such as network infrastructure, negative comments, information risk management, privacy, and deception. This chapter can be a reference to any institutions, particularly the Islamic banks which associated with digital interfaces and interactions in their daily businesses. Thus expectedly, the Islamic banks could enhance the public trust and establish a good Islamic identity.*

## INTRODUCTION

Islamic banks are obligated to conduct their activities in accordance with shariah principles, which strictly forbid any receipts or payments of interest. Other prohibited

DOI: 10.4018/978-1-7998-2257-8.ch011

activities include having or taking usury, *gharar* (uncertainty) and *maysir* (gambling). All the guidelines are written clearly in *Al-Qur'an* and *Hadith*.

Islamic banking still takes a large portion of 75% on global Islamic finance total asset. Meanwhile, in Indonesia, the largest portion of Islamic finance belongs to the Islamic capital market contributed up to 93% of government sukuk issuance. The total assets of Islamic banks in Indonesia reach US$29.94 billion, which is far behind the total assets of Islamic banks in Malaysia with US$181 billion (GIFR, 2017). Moreover, the Islamic banks in Indonesia have a low market share of 5% which ironically contrasts with the potential as the most Muslim population of 265 million in the world. Among the problem emerged are limited/unvaried product range, low literacy and inclusion level of Islamic finance, unfavorable perception for Islamic banking, lack of talent and qualified employees, limited distribution networks and outreach, and only focus on the retail segment (Bappenas, 2015).

There are initiatives had been started and taken to resolve the above constraints, one of them is through continuous socialization. By then, public awareness is increasing and followed with the creation of public trust among the Islamic banks. These actions are purposely to be done to stimulate the public to use Islamic banks' financial solutions and promotethe Islamic banking sector in Indonesia.

In promoting products and services, the Islamic banks need to find the best and effective tool to achieve their aim that is to increase its market share. The latest and commonly used is social media. It is a low-cost channel which will enable the Islamic banks to reach a broader audience and then communicate widely their products and services' offerings. Other uses of this social media are expanded to the recruitment of highly talented employees, and support networks and outreach.

## LITERATURE REVIEW

### The Social Media

Social media can be defined as internet-based applications that foster creations and exchange user-generated content (Kaplan & Haenlein, 2010). Its rapid global growth is influenced by its ability to allow users to personalize their social media accounts and to interact with other users across the globe (Zolkepli & Kamarulzaman, 2015).

Social media classified into two key dimensions: social presence/media richness and self-presentation/self-disclosure (Kaplan & Haenlein, 2010). It also can be grouped into two broad categories depending on their main purpose; a) expressive social media where users express themselves by sharing text, video, picture, music; and b) collaborative social media where users share knowledge or content and work

*Table 1. Types of social media*

| No | Main Usage | Example | Function |
|---|---|---|---|
| 1 | Blogs and microblogs | Twitter | Provide freedom for users to express their feelings, experiences, statements, and criticism on the platforms |
| 2. | Content communities | YouTube | Enable users to share multimedia content, such as e-books, videos, photos, images, and more |
| 3. | Social networking sites | Facebook | Allow users to connect by creating personal or social information that can be accessed by others |
| 4. | Social networking app | Instagram | Allow to share and update of photos and videos. |

Source: Kaplan and Haenlein (2010)

together for a common goal (Kotler, Kartajaya, & Setiawan, 2010). There are types of social media which designed to meet various needs of users as shown in Table 1:

The above types of social media are among the largest and fastest-growing social media platforms. For example, Facebook and Twitter platforms have been fundamentally used as marketing tools by most of the US companies (Joyce, 2011; Barnes, Lescault, & Wright, 2013). Facebook has a massive increase of users by 25 percent in one year (Hockenson & Molla, 2013), while, Twitter has 36 percent of the annual increase (Edwards, 2013). Both platforms have millions of active users as the potential consumers that can get updates of information easily. Pan, Vorvoreanu, and Zhou (2014) mentioned that Facebook provides extensive content with relatively longer information, which is significant for influencing an audience by sharing experience and delivering values. Meanwhile, Twitter enables prompt, brief, and more on superficial discourses. Its simplicity is imperative for the public to understand news easily.

Other social media platforms are Youtube and Instagram. Youtube creates the opportunity for the provider of content to target a niche market which is focused on their similar interest and need. Youtube is now the world's 2nd biggest search engine for more than 1,8 billion people registered on the site. Meanwhile, Instagram is seen as the "rising star" which has a visual-sharing platform that allows users to post photos and videos. Instagram is considered more follower-friendly in terms of post visibility, tendency to comment, and share ability which allows Instagram users to be more engaged with their followers (DeMers, 2017). In 2016, it had approximately 500 million users, and this number has been continually increasing since 2015. The user engagement level on Instagram brand posts reaches about 4% of total followers, much higher than the figure for Facebook and Twitter of less than 0.1% (Vendramin, 2016).

## Social Media in Indonesia

Islamic banks can take advantage of the usage of social media in Indonesia. In 2019, over 150 million Indonesian are the users of social media, increased by 15-20% compared in 2018. Below Table presents the figures related to social media users:

As presented in the below chart, there are more than 100 million users of social media in Indonesia that potentially access the Islamic banks' content. Assumably, they like to see attractive and creative content that able to convince them to switch from other content.

Other facts of social media in Indonesia which can be used as opportunities and challenges for the Islamic banks as presented below:

*Table 2. Figures related to social media users*

| Social Media Platform | User Monthly Worldwide (Million Users) - April 2019 | | | Penetration of leading social networks in Indonesia (%) |
|---|---|---|---|---|
| | Worldwide Users (Million Users) | Indonesia Users (Million Users) / Share Percentage (%) | Indonesia Rank in the World | |
| Instagram | 1000* | 56 / 12.3% | 4th | 80 |
| Facebook | 2375 | 120 / 40.88% | 4th | 81 |
| YouTube | 1900** | 50***/ 19.3% | - | 88 |
| Twitter | 330 | 22.8 /17.23% | 3rd | 52 |

*June 2018; **Sept 2018; *** Dec 2017
Source: Statista Internet (2018)

*Figure 1. Digital in Indonesia*
*Source: McKinsey Asia PFS Survey (2017); We Are Social (2017); GSMA Intelligence (2017)*

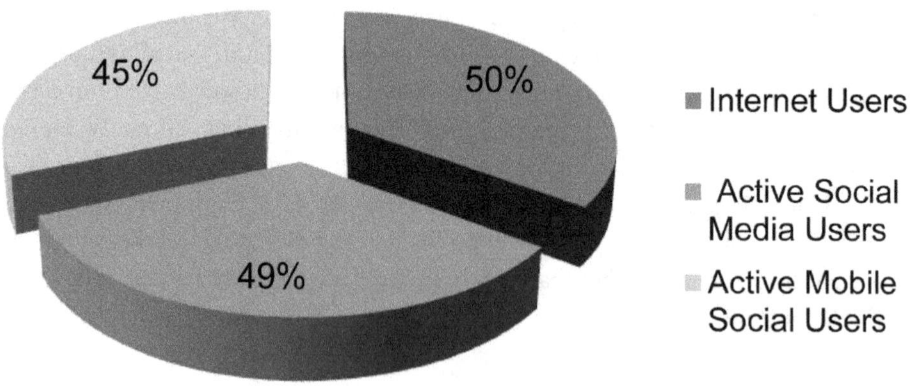

*Table 3. Social media in figures in Indonesia*

| Facts | Numbers |
|---|---|
| Average Daily Time Spent Using Social Media | 3 Hours 23 Minutes |
| Believe that New Technologies offer More Opportunities than Risks | 71% |
| Believe Data Privacy and Protection are very important | 79% |
| Has a Bank Account | 36% |
| Searched Online For a Product or Service to Buy | 45% |
| Mobile Network Infrastructure | 41.39<br>(Out of a Maximum Score of 100) |
| Digital banking penetration has doubled in the last 5 years | 58% |
| Frequency of digital channel usage in 2017 | 42% |

Source: Google Consumer Barometer (January, 2018); Global WebIndex (2017); World Bank Global Financial Inclusion (2015); GSMA Intelligence (2017); McKinsey Asia PFS Survey (2017).

## The Islamic Principle of Using Social Media in Islamic Banks

All activities in the Islamic banks have to comply with the shariah principles. This is aligned with the verse in the Holy *Qur'an* of Al Baqarah (2): 208 as follows:

*O you who have believed, enter into Islam completely [and perfectly] and do not follow the footsteps of Satan. Indeed, he is to you a clear enemy. (Al Baqarah (2): 208)*

This verse explained that Allah the Almighty commanded His servants to embrace Islam in its entirety and to avoid abandoning any part of it. All guidance have been written as well as rules to be obeyed. Hence, in relation to social media, the Islamic banks should act according to the shariah by means of maintaining a good image as one of the Islamic institutions which they could consider as doing *da'wah* to all customers (Muslim and non-Muslim).

Da'wah can be done in many ways including writing in the form of books, articles, and other short messages or videos, in this case; Instagram, Twitter, Facebook, and Youtube. This rapid growth of social media can be used by the Islamic banks for disseminating the truth of information or news.

Moreover, the content of social media in Islamic banks must be right which can be a reliable reference in helping adherents to be more obedient to Allah the Exalted, able to avoid any controversies and any violations. Allah the Almighty will raise the degrees of whoever informing others as he/she teaches others for some knowledge.

The role of social media in Islamic banks can be used to respond to any comments particularly on negative issues, thus the truth can be explained. It is a *'tabayyun'* platform for any misunderstood matters. This is in accordance with the verse of *Al-Qur'an* in An-Nisa' (4): 83 as follows:

*And when there comes to them information about [public] security or fear, they spread it around. But if they had referred it back to the Messenger or to those of authority among them, then the ones who [can] draw correct conclusions from it would have known about it. And if not for the favor of Allah upon you and His mercy, you would have followed Satan, except for a few. (An-Nisa' (4): 83)*

Some consumers need pictures, photos and videos to understand the content of social media easily. This is an opportunity for the Islamic banks to present a good content and prepare verified materials which accordance with Islamic principles to get consumers' attentions. The Islamic banks should understand their limits and responsibilities in creating any contents on social media, thus need to protect and aware of not to reveal any inappropriate images or contain of unnatural meanings. With this, the aim of increasing awareness and encouraging more interests in Islamic banks' products and services by the public can be attained.

## METHODOLOGY

This chapter was conducted using a qualitative method of descriptive and content analysis based on a review of literature from academic research journals, websites, socia media platforms, electronic databases (secondary data), and other relevant sources. From the sources of previous studies, the arguments and discussions are created.

### The Use of Social Media in Islamic Banks

The fact is, only 7.39% of the total social media users are accessing banking-related matters (APJII, 2017). While none of studies analysing the adoption of social media by the Islamic banks particularly in Indonesia. Although the following figures are uncomparable with the figures of the conventional banks, the growing interest in the Islamic banks' contents is gradually significant via social media. Below are the Tables of Islamic banks' figures on Instagram, Twitter, YouTube, and Facebook:

The number of followers and posts on Instagram indicating potential responses by the public on Islamic banks' products and services. As it is depicted in the above Table, Bank BNI Syariah has the most followers with 51,100, followed with Bank Syariah Mandiri, Bank BRI Syariah, and Bank Muamalat Indonesia. In fact, BNI

*Table 4. Islamic banks with it's Instagram usage*

| No. | Islamic Banks | Instagram Account | Posts | Followers |
|---|---|---|---|---|
| 1 | Bank Muamalat Indonesia | bank.muamalat | 5,426 | 28,800 |
| 2 | Bank Syariah Mandiri | banksyariahmandiri | 1,101 | 44,200 |
| 3 | Bank BRI Syariah | Brisyariah | 2,307 | 36,300 |
| 4 | Bank Mega Syariah | bankmegasyariah | 757 | 5,890 |
| 5 | Bank Syariah Bukopin | bank_syariahbukopin | 792 | 2,906 |
| 6 | Bank BNI Syariah | bni.syariah | 759 | 51,100 |
| 7 | Panin Dubai Syariah Bank | Panindubaisyariah.bank | 111 | 268 |
| 8 | Bank Aceh Syariah | hababankaceh | 579 | 5,752 |
| 9 | Bank Sinarmas Syariah | banksinarmas_syariah | 841 | 6,407 |
| 10 | Bank BJB Syariah | bankbjbsyariah | 662 | 9,280 |
| 11 | Bank Syariah Al Salaam | banksyariahalsalaam | 556 | 4,258 |

Sources: Retrieved on 3th May 2019

*Table 5. Islamic banks with it's Twitter usage*

| No. | Islamic Banks | Twitter Account | Following | Followers |
|---|---|---|---|---|
| 1 | Bank Muamalat Indonesia | @BankMuamalat | 121 | 33,100 |
| 2 | Bank Syariah Mandiri | @syariahmandiri | 5,819 | 260,000 |
| 3 | Bank Mega Syariah | @Mega_Syariah | 11 | 295 |
| 4 | Bank Syariah Bukopin | @BsyariahBukopin | 8,639 | 20,200 |
| 5 | Bank BNI Syariah | @BNISyariah | 634 | 274,000 |
| 6 | Panin Dubai Syariah Bank | @panin_syariah | 280 | 2,876 |
| 7 | Bank Sinarmas Syariah | @BankSinarmas_iB | 26 | 2,299 |
| 8 | Bank BJB Syariah | @bankbjbsyariah | 9 | 626 |

Sources: Retrieved on 3th May 2019

Syariah won the Satisfaction, Loyalty and Engagement (SLE) award in 2019 which held by Marketing Research Indonesia (MRI) collaborated with Info bank. It can be assumed that BNI Syariah, as the most followers, able to grow emotional bound feelings with their customers, one of them through social media.

Twitter sends a short message to the audience/public and it would be a sufficient way to remind and give comments. It is also could nominate the trending topic with its hashtag (#) which indicates as a popular topic to be discussed. Both Bank BNI Syariah and Bank Syariah Mandiri are the most followers with 274,000 and 260,000 respectively.

*Table 6. Islamic banks with it's YouTube usage*

| No. | Islamic Banks | YouTube Channel | Subscriber | Video |
|---|---|---|---|---|
| 1 | Bank Muamalat Indonesia | Bank Muamalat | 1,641 | 42 |
| 2 | Bank Syariah Mandiri | Bank Syariah Mandiri | 1,920 | 91 |
| 3 | Bank BRI Syariah | BRI Syariah | 1,108 | 14 |
| 4 | Bank BNI Syariah | BNI Syariah | 777 | 56 |
| 5 | Bank BJB Syariah | Bank BJB Syariah | 109 | 17 |

Sources: Retrieved on 3th May 2019

*Table 7. Islamic banks with it's Facebook usage*

| No. | Islamic Banks | Facebook Account | Like |
|---|---|---|---|
| 1 | Bank Muamalat Indonesia | Bank Muamalat | 24,369 |
| 2 | Bank Syariah Mandiri | Bank Syariah Mandiri | 76,161 |
| 3 | Bank BRI Syariah | BRI Syariah | 56,542 |
| 4 | Bank Mega Syariah | Bank Mega Syariah | 2,397 |
| 5 | Bank Syariah Bukopin | Bank Syariah Bukopin | 2,143 |
| 6 | Bank BNI Syariah | PT Bank BNI Syariah | 51,931 |
| 7 | Panin Dubai Syariah Bank | Panindubai Syariahbank | 4,610 |
| 8 | Bank BJB Syariah | bank bjb syariah | 14,805 |
| 9 | Bank Syariah Al Salaam | Bank Syariah Al Salaam | 16,696 |

Sources: Retrieved on 3th May 2019

Both numbers of subscribers and videos are important signs to see the growing interest of Islamic banks' customers to their content via YouTube. Currently, Bank Syariah Mandiri as the most subscribers (1,920) and videos (91) compare to other Islamic banks. Some customers that like to see the full video to learn and get the pictures of Islamic banks' products and services. It is an easy, quick, and convenient way to absorb things. With these facts of YouTube channels owned by the Islamic banks, the information can be disseminated effectively and efficiently.

Meanwhile, Facebook offers complete features that everyone could interact through chat, messages, pictures or videos. It is expected can attract more customers from various interfaces. Based on its 'like' means at least that an individual has attention to the content, Bank Syariah Mandiri has the most likes on its content on Facebook, followed with Bank BRI Syariah and Bank BNI Syariah.

Below is a comparison of Instagram followers of top three conventional and Islamic banks. It is also shows that the three of Islamic banks represent 18% of the

*Table 8. A summary of social media by top five conventional banks*

| Banks | Instagram | | Twitter Followers | YouTube Subscriber | Facebook Like |
|---|---|---|---|---|---|
| | Followers | Posts | | | |
| Bank Mandiri | 162000 | 1037 | 126000 | 16815 | 279461 |
| Bank Negara Indonesia | 178000 | 3755 | 1100000 | 5151 | 333603 |
| Bank Rakyat Indonesia | 211000 | 1014 | 138000 | 7683 | 560735 |
| Bank Cental Asia | 209000 | 890 | 76300 | 22957 | 162508 |
| Bank CIMB Niaga | 191000 | 1406 | 69600 | 6396 | 1176812 |

*Figure 2. Instagram followers of Islamic banks versus conventional banks*

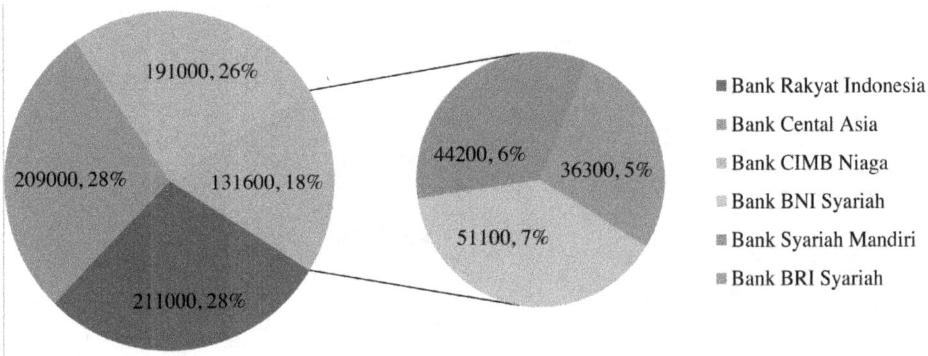


number of Instagram followers, whereby the number of Instagram followers of Bank CIMB Niaga alone exceeds by 8% than those three Islamic banks.

Below is a comparison of Twitter followers of top three conventional and Islamic banks. It is also shows that the three of Islamic banks represent 29% of the number of Twitter followers, while the two conventional banks; Bank Mandiri and Bank Rakyat Indonesia have less Twitter followers than the two of Islamic banks' followers; Bank Syariah Mandiri and Bank BNI Syariah.

Below is a comparison of YouTube subscribers of top three conventional and Islamic banks. It also shows that the three of Islamic banks represent 9% of the number of YouTube subscribers, whereby the number of Youtube subscribers of Bank Rakyat Indonesia alone exceeds by 6% than those three Islamic banks.

Below is a comparison of Facebook likes of top three conventional and Islamic banks. It also shows that the three of Islamic banks represent 8% of the number of Facebook likes, whereby the number of Facebook likes of Bank Negara Indonesia alone exceeds by 7% than those three Islamic banks.

*Figure 3. Twitter followers of Islamic banks versus conventional banks*

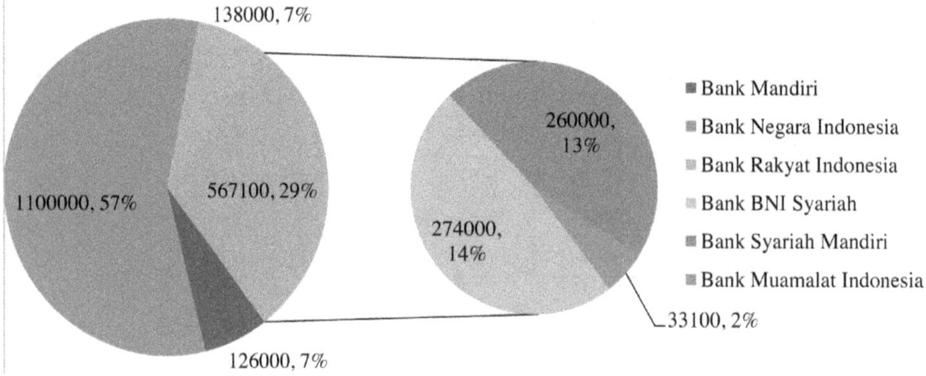


*Figure 4. YouTube subscribers of Islamic banks versus conventional banks*

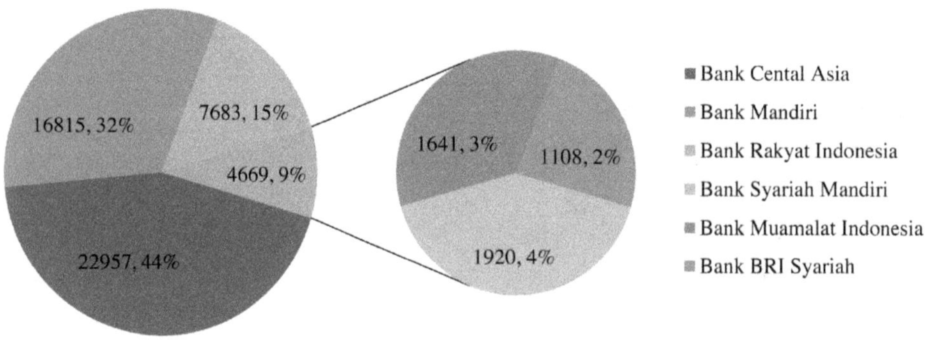


*Figure 5. Facebook likes of Islamic banks versus conventional banks*

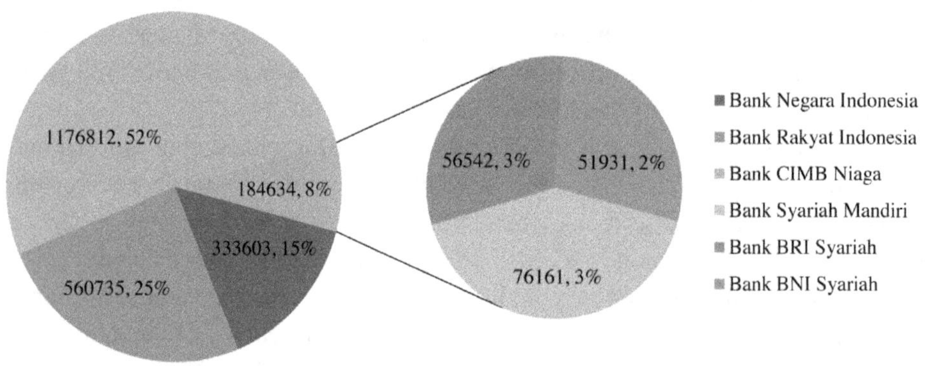

Based on the tables and figures presented above, there are important points to be highlighted as follows:

§ The Islamic banks are aware ofthe crucial role of social media, thus, they open their accounts and actively presented attractive content to persuade customers.
§ The Islamic banks have the potential of a huge number of active users using social media in Indonesia
§ The Islamic banks realized to gain competitive advantage through social media

## Opportunities in Social Media

With the elaborated use of social media, there are opportunities that can be exploited by Islamic banks as follows:

### a. Transparency and Openness

Both transparency and openness are interrelated. The social media's active presence can lead to further transparency and openness to the customers. Customers who doubted the details of Islamic banking products, now they can see it and have all the information needed. Some of the Islamic banks' concepts are related to Islamic jurisprudence which exposes debates and arguments. Through social media, everyone can ask and give any explanation based on their understandings. In particular, for non-Muslims, they might have the interest to know the Islamic banks' products and services, thus the social media is a suitable platform for them to learn.

With the new concepts of fintech and big data, social media can play a role in distributing complete data, figures or content that can be accessed by customers openly. Additionally, Harris and Rae (2009) explained that social media can help to facilitate transparency where trust can be established between two parties. Trust is one of the Islamic banks' principles and related to *amanah*, which means to cooperate or deal with the permitted parties according to the *amanah* given by customers. Trust generates closer relationships with the consumers, which then consumers can feel that the Islamic banks are friendlier, more real and more gracious towards them. By emphasizing transparency, the banks' employees can respond to negative comments. When the Islamic banks' systems are performed honestly and with an emphatic manner, thus the followers' trust can be regained and increased (Duncan, 2016; Shukle, 2015).

## b. An Effective Marketing, Communication, and Promotion Channel

Many financial institutions including Islamic banks have started to utilize this social media platform as one of the efficient channels, to communicate, reach out and provide consumers with updated information including discounts on the products and services, and other vital news. Social media also enables open communication that helps companies to understand better their customers' needs and motivates them to proactively and efficiently respond to them (Parveen, et al., 2016).

For the millennials, the online interfaces and transactions bring easiness and convenience, thus any marketing approaches can be used to attract their attentions. Social media is less costly than mainstream media advertising, means able to reduce marketing and communication expenses (Parveen, Jaafar, & Ainin, 2016). It enables to identify key influencers of the audiences and respond it in a timely manner (Weinberg & Pehlivan, 2011). With regards on costs matter, a consulting company known as NM Incite which has a partnership with Nielsen and McKinsey did a survey and found that social customer care costs around $1 per interaction while using phone support costs at least $6, and further interaction per e-mail costs $2.50 to $5 (BenMark, 2014).

Previously, the banks have widely used the TV or direct sales marketing/email marketing to reach out their consumers but today the social media offers a unique way to promote the products, thus it called as a very effective marketing tool (Mitic & Kapoulas, 2012). The promotional activities can be accessed 24 hours a day and 7 days a week by consumers. In fact, 45% of the users in Indonesia are using online platforms to buy products or services. With social media, the Islamic banks can do a research on customer data, create customized advertising in a simple method, and widen the coverage of markets through a deepening partnership that offers financial services to customers anywhere in the world; eliminating geographical constraints.

## c. Stakeholders' Relationship

The Islamic banks use social media as an efficient platform to improve the relationship between the company and other stakeholders such as government, suppliers, distributors, customers, etc and then could figure out the needs of the stakeholders and addressing its expectations. Constant interactions via social media may generate effective relationships among stakeholders. Social media offers a unique opportunity to reform the relationship between stakeholders from a mono or bi-directional information exchange into a many-to-many communication process (Agostino, 2013) which considered as a medium to increase engagement with potential customers by publishing quizzes or rewards etc., that can help to improve services of the banks (Kumar, Rajan, Gupta, & Pozza, 2017). These various benefits may explain why about 79% of Fortune 100 companies use social media to communicate with their stakeholders (Dekay, 2012).

Social media can be interpreted as a multi-directional communication between parties where accurate and important data of the Islamic banks can be distributed to the customers immediately. A relationship with stakeholders is created through interactions with the absence of physical presence, offers flexibility to accommodate various types of tasks and increases the individuals' access to companies' websites (Stern & Ibarra, 2011; Tajvidi & Karami, 2017). The increase in social media's role and presence, will open ways to plan for future communication strategies and enables businesses to build sustainable relationships by engaging their audiences through exchanges of ideas (Ang, 2011; Ray & Singh, 2010).

## d. Social Media Content

Refers to Instagram's posts, the Islamic banks have a significant number of posts, it is slightly lesser than the conventional banks. The content indicates that the banks are having initiatives and efforts to introduce or promote their products. An attractive content consists of information that can be read, see and understand easily. The social media content allows creativity in presentations and aggressiveness in conveying the news on products and services. As most of the consumers prefer to have flexibility in uploading or updating the content, thus the Islamic banks must deliver the ultimate customer experience through its content.

Nowadays, the number of followers of Islamic banks is increasing and received positive comments from the consumers which often presented in attractive content, thus the awareness of the Islamic banks' products is increasing. This means, the content plays an important role in the development of Islamic banks. Meanwhile, the followers' inputs through social media content can be analyzed to predict and monitor customers' trends, understand customers' interests, emotions and behavior, find and identify the priorities for future plans, and useful information for further investigation and evaluation for the banks' products and services.

The continuous improvement of the social media content is required to accommodate the fact that users are spending 3 Hours 23 Minutes on an average of their daily time of using social media. The audience attention is increasing because social media store kinds of information which give various ideas. Additionally, with 42% frequency of digital channel usage in 2017 in Indonesia, there is a potential of engaging more on social media content and more access to the Islamic banks' products. Furthermore, a study of Deutsche Bank Research shows that social media users have a stronger demand for financial information which contrasts with the less desire to see a bank consultant face to face, i.e. to this user the personal contact is slightly less important (Thomas, 2011).

## e. Brand Image and Reputation

Studies show that social media communications strongly influence brand image (Bruhn, Schoenmueller, & Schäfer, 2012). Through social media, the brands of products appear and pop up daily with attractive content. Once the number of likes or followers is increasing, it means the reputation is strengthened. Any differentiations which notified by social media are associated with brand equity that influences consumer's brain. This asserted by Tajvidi and Karami (2017) that social media is strengthening company branding, while Parusheva (2017) mentioned that another role of social media in companies' management practice is to build a brand image, brand equity and to improve brand awareness. Most importantly, the Islamic banks could promote Islamic identity and reputation through its products' characteristics. Thus, no reason for Islamic banks to not exploiting social media to grab these opportunities.

In fact, the image of financial sectors is negatively perceived by the consumers after the global financial crisis in 2008, where now the consumers' trust need to be rebuilt by capitalizing the social media (Parusheva, 2017).

## f. Shariah Compliance Activity

The activity of using social media is permitted by the *shariah*. It meant that the activities related to social media could be encouraged, enhanced and developed to attract more customers and create awareness. Through social media, the Islamic values and principles are exposed and will be known by the audience, which is called *da'wah*. This is considered as an effective and efficient *da'wah* of reaching wider coverage and having lower costs.

Through social media, the disputes and disagreements of financial products can be discussed. For example, the issue of e-money product or cashless transactions which explained by the contemporary *fiqh muamalah* to do not lead to *riba*. This open argument will be responded by the social media users or at least get their attention to the principles of the products/concepts.

## g. Learning and Knowledge

The educational level impacts the understanding level of consumers on the products' offerings. The products and services of the banks related to financial literacy in which not familiar with, the public has the opportunity to learn via social media.

This knowledge and willingness to learn are able to resolve an issue of consumer awareness that becomes a classic constraint faced by the Islamic banks. Parusheva (2017) mentioned that digital channels allow people to go through Facebook, Twitter,

YouTube, Instagram and other social networks to gain the necessary education and information regarding the services, products and financial institutions. This asserted by Weinberg and Pehlivan (2011) that social media helps companies educate audiences about their services. Even it can use to recruit qualified employees (Madia, 2011).

No doubt that social media channels have become a very significant source of information in our world today. Companies including the Islamic banks rely on social media purposely to get the latest news. Thus, they did efforts to make social media as a medium of transfer of knowledge in which will bring the invaluable return to the businesses for the long term. Additionally, with evidence of 58% digital banking penetration has doubled in the last 5 years in Indonesia, it opens possibilities for the audience to learn the Islamic banks' products or at least can cultivate the consumers' interests to know about the Islamic banks' products.

## h. Greater Personalization and Support

Personalization is an opponent of privacy. A partnership between banks and social media users will open up new doors in terms of personalizing customer experiences where data are shared and exchanged between the two parties. Some customers looking for privileges or they want faster and accurate information for all questions being asked, thus the Islamic banks must prepare with sufficient materials through social media.

Personalization creates a sustainable relationship by knowing and understanding each other better. The social media tries to build strong communication which consumers may ask questions without any limits. Through personalization, Islamic banks are creating customer satisfaction and loyalty. Moreover, social media is already being used for customer support by most of the banks, but a deeper partnership with social media platforms will empower the banks to offer more support services. This will help in establishing better relationships with customers to further improve the response time. This asserted by Shankar & Khan (2012) that the bank institutions are aware of the power of social media and actively used the social platforms because they want to meet the rising customer expectations for personalization, demonstrating value to them and positive social care.

As 36% of the social media users have a bank account, they might need additional services related to the products. The supports to customers consist of account information, cards' promotions or applications, updates on profit and loss offers, important dates and events. Personalization and support made every consumers feel that they are treated professionally and proportionally.

*Figure 6. Opportunities of social media to Islamic banks*

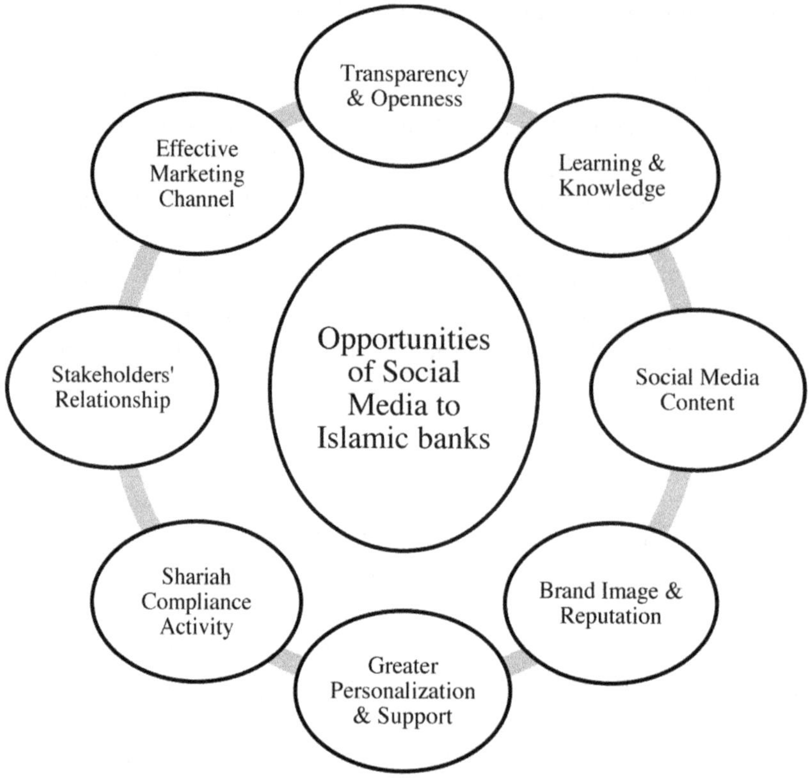


## Challenges of Social Media

Despite having opportunities in using social media, there are challenges for the Islamic banks as follows:

### a. Network Infrastructures

The technology infrastructures may differ in each country particularly for the Internet network. As many of the social media users are mobile users, they expect to access the content of Islamic banks' products and services anywhere and anytime, thus the Internet network must be supported especially in the suburban or rural areas.

With the fact of a score of 41.39 out of 100 for the network infrastructure in Indonesia, it is quite slow, which may discourage the interactions of two parties. The Islamic banks have to find other alternatives to get a reliable network and faster, to be able to reach the customers in real-time. Moreover, 71% of social media users in

Indonesia believe that new technologies offer more opportunities than risks, which means that a network is required to support of using new technologies.

### b. Negative Comments and Unresponsiveness Queries

The social media offers direct replies and comments from the public or customer, some of them are negative comments. The Islamic banks need to have full-time personnel to control and counter those nagged comments. The personnel must have capabilities to be actively switching, managing and answering those inappropriate comments. This is considered as a serious challenge for the banks.

An interaction is an important part of social media. One of the ways to boost such interactions is by responding comments left on the relevant posts. Data generated from gramwiki.com showed that only five out of the nine Indonesian Islamic banks (namely Bank Syariah Mandiri, Bank Mega Syariah, BRI Syariah, Bank Syariah Bukopin, and BNI Syariah) which were sufficiently responsive in addressing their followers' comments. However, it seems those Islamic banks do not use social media particularly Instagram to monitor customer trends. This indicates the encouragement of capitalizing the use of social media still low.

### c. Information Risk Management

There is possibly sensitive information that may disclose intentionally through the Islamic banks' content where the public can access it instantly. Thus the Islamic banks have to manage and concern on the safety and security of the social media pages as a platform related to the financial transactions. To anticipate this case, the Islamic banks may appoint a manager/supervisor that specialized in managing these risks associated with IT (information technology) compliances and functions. Meanwhile, social media sites pose an equal threat to the security of personal information and other concerned data. The hacking of the websites is the most common feature and considered an immediate threat to the audience of social media.

As Islamic banks carry the identity of Islam, it should be noted that every aspect/item posted in social media must be compliance with Islamic values stated in *Al-Qur'an* and *Hadiths*. Therefore, every posts made on social media must avoid conflicts with *shariah* principles. An example of making promotions, which include giving gifts to customers. This issue must be carefully posted because it needs further review as guided in *fiqh muamalah.* Consultation to the experts or advisory board is required to ensure the posted items comply with *shariah*, however, it has to go through a certain process and will take times.

### d. Privacy

The primary challenge posed by social media is privacy. Many people restrain themselves from taking part in a dialogue with a fear of losing their privacy. Some banks' employees are disclosed by negative comments from customers without going through a proper channel on how to criticize the products' contents, systems or procedures. At the same time, the Islamic banks' employees have to carefully upload or create captions that oppose certain tribe, race, religion, nationality or other personal matters. It is a direct message that can be seen by the audience in real-time, thus any misinterpretation or misunderstanding may emerge. Based on the users' profile that 79% of users believe that data privacy and protection are very important elements associated with social media content.

### e. Deception

The identity of the individual who joins the social networking sites may either original or fake. This is due to the identity disclosures which are shared with unknown users. Nowadays, there are many cases of deception around the world that have been registered. Social media turns out to be an easy way of deceiving people using technology. For the Islamic banks, they may face or interact with unknown users who could copy or imitate some content.

## CONCLUSION

To achieve the expected outcomes, Islamic banks need to ensure that social media helps to increase their engagement with their 'likes' and followers. The Islamic banks have no choice except to manage optimally the social media with its attractive content. Those opportunities can be exploited and resulted in the best outcomes for the development of Islamic banks. The Islamic banks should develop multi-ways of communications and respond directly all comments from the audience, thus creating emotional attachment and better relationships with customers. As it is mentioned by Kumar et al (2017) that companies can retain a higher level of client satisfaction and emotional attachment if they focus their efforts on maintaining positive service experiences for their clients.

Islamic banks have to collaborate with associated parties or authorities to find a solution for the mentioned challenges. A thorough evaluation of the level of social media adoption is crucial in order to know how effective social media is helping the Islamic banks to disseminate information to the public and identify areas that need improvements.

*Figure 7. Challenges of Social Media to Islamic banks*

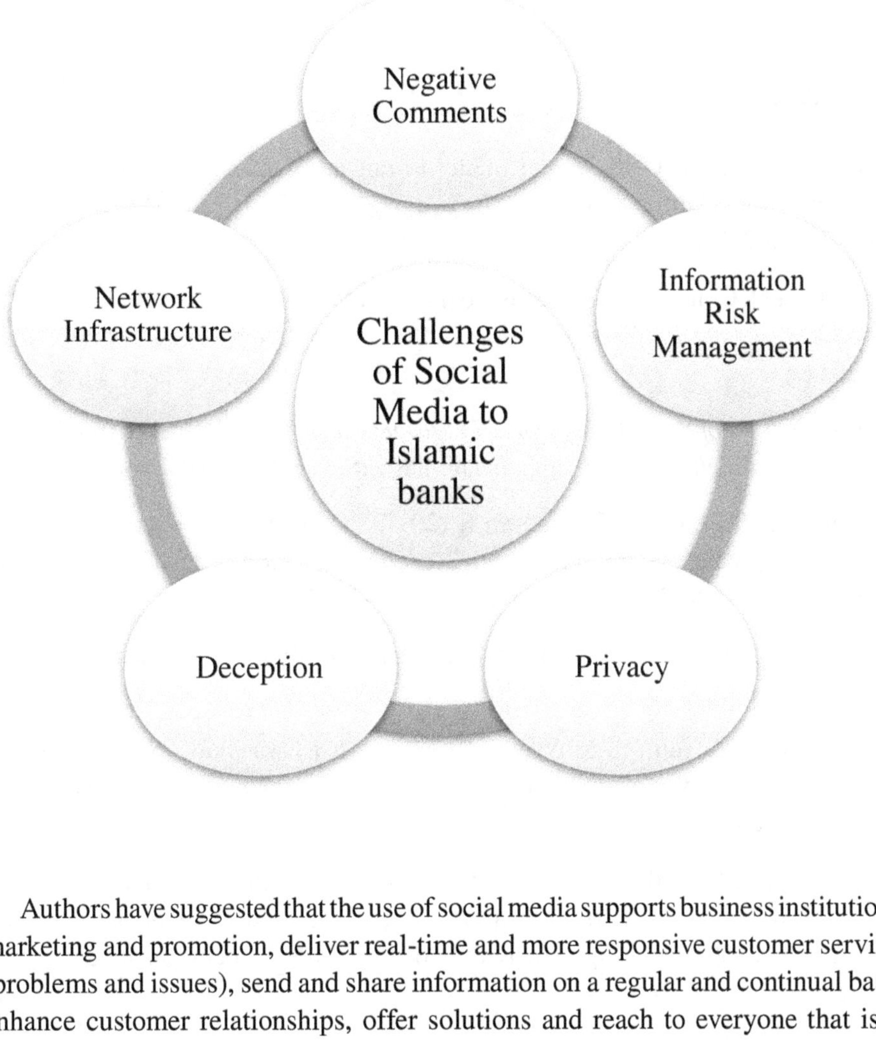


Authors have suggested that the use of social media supports business institutions' marketing and promotion, deliver real-time and more responsive customer services (problems and issues), send and share information on a regular and continual basis, enhance customer relationships, offer solutions and reach to everyone that is in need, improve an organization's reputation, provide public access to information, create product innovations, participate and collaborate in providing shared social values, and develop customer loyalty and trust (Arnaboldi, Busco, & Cuganesan, 2017; Castells, 2011; Deloitte, 2013; Smith & Sanderson, 2015; Harris & Rae, 2009; Parveen et al, 2016; Tajvidi & Karami, 2017; Etter, Ravasi, & Colleoni, 2017; Parusheva, 2017). However, to maintain Islamic banking's reputation in upholding Islamic values, the useof social media at Islamic banks should be managed to avoid conflict with the principles of *shariah*.

It is found that the listed Islamic banks still have difficulties in creating two-way interactions with the public through social media. An increasing number of followers and get constructive comments may encourage Islamic banks to improve their business performance.

## REFERENCES

Agostino, D. (2013). Using social media to engage citizens: A study of Italian municipalities. *Public Relations Review, 39*(3), 232–234. doi:10.1016/j.pubrev.2013.02.009

Ang, L. (2011). Community relationship management and social media. *Journal of Database Marketing and Customer Strategy Management, 18*(1), 31–38. doi:10.1057/dbm.2011.3

APJIII. (2017). *Indonesia Internet Usage for Business Sector 2017*. Retrieved from https://apjii.or.id/downfile/file/SurveiPenggunaanInternetSektorBisnis2017versienglish.pdf

Arnaboldi, M., Busco, C., & Cuganesan, S. (2017). Accounting, accountability, social media, and big data: Revolution or hype? *Accounting, Auditing, & Accountability Journal, 30*(4), 762–776. doi:10.1108/AAAJ-03-2017-2880

Bappenas. (2015). *Masterplan Arsitektur Keuangan Syariah Indonesia*. Jakarta: Bappenas Press.

Barnes, N. G., Lescault, A., & Wright, S. (2013). *2013 Fortune 500 are bullish on social media*. Retrieved May 2, 2019 from www.umassd.edu/cmr/socialmediaresearch/2013fortune500/

BenMark, G. (2014). *Why the COO should lead social-media customer service*. Retrieved July 16, 2019 from http://www.mckinsey.com/business-functions/marketing-and-sales/our-insights/why-the-coo-should-lead-social-media-customer-service

Blackshaw, P. (2006). *The consumer-generated surveillance culture*. Retrieved June 28, 2019 from http://www.clickz.com/showPage.html?page=3576076

Bruhn, M., Schoenmueller, V., & Schäfer, D. (2012). Are social media replacing traditional media in terms of brand equity creation? *Management Research Review, 35*(9), 770–790. doi:10.1108/01409171211255948

Castells, M. (2011). *The Rise of the Network Society* (3rd ed.). Oxford, UK: John Wiley & Sons.

Dekay, S. H. (2012). How large companies react to negative Facebook comments. *Corporate Communications, 17*(3), 289–299. doi:10.1108/13563281211253539

Deloitte. (2013). *Who says banks can't be social? Become a social bank, inside and out*. Ontario, Canada, Deloitte LLP.

DeMers, J. (2017). *Why Instagram Is The Top Social Platform For Engagement (And How To Use It)*. Retrieved August 20, 2019 from https://www.forbes.com/sites/jaysondemers/2017/03/28/why-instagram-is-the-top-social-platform-for-engagement-and-how-to-use-it/

Duncan, S. (2016). *Brands, Handle Negative Criticism on Social Media Like a Champ*. Retrieved August 11, 2019 from https://www.salesforce.com/blog/2016/03/brands-handle-negative-criticism-social-media-champ.html

Edwards, J. (2013). *Twitter's "dark pool": IPO doesn't mention 6541 million users who abandoned Twitter*. Retrieved May 26, 2019 from www.businessinsider.com/twitter-total-registered-users-v-monthlyactive-users-2013-11

Etter, M., Ravasi, D., & Colleoni, E. (2017). *Social Media and the Formation of Organizational Reputation. Academy of Management Review*. In-Press.

GIFR. (2017). *Global Islamic Finance Report*. Retrieved July 10, 2019 from http://www.gifr.net/gifr_2017.htm

Global WebIndex. (2017). *GWI Social*. Retrieved August 18, 2019 from https://cdn2.hubspot.net/hubfs/304927/Downloads/GWI%20Social%20Summary%20Q3%202017.pdf

Google Consumer Barometer. (2018). *Trended Data*. Retrieved September 10, 2019 from https://www.consumerbarometer.com/en/trending/?countryCode=ID&category=TRN-NOFILTER-ALL

Harris, L., & Rae, A. (2009). Social networks: The future of marketing for small business. *The Journal of Business Strategy*, *30*(5), 24–31. doi:10.1108/02756660910987581

Hockenson, L., & Molla, R. (2013). *Facebook grows daily active users by 25 percent, mobile users by 45 percent*. Retrieved May 29, 2019 from http://gigaom.com/2013/10/30/facebook-grows-dailyactive-users-by-25-percent-mobile-users-by-45-percent/

Joyce, S. (2011). *2011 UMass study of Fortune 500 companies and social media: 23% blog, 62% use Twitter, 58% Facebook*. Retrieved May 8, 2019 from www.q4blog.com/2011/10/27/2011-umassstudy-of-fortune-500-companies-and-social-media-23-blog-62-use-twitter-58-facebook/

Kaplan, A. M., & Haenlein, M. (2010). Users of the world, unite! The challenges and opportunities of *Social Media*. *Business Horizons*, *53*(1), 59–68. doi:10.1016/j.bushor.2009.09.003

Kotler, P., Kartajaya, H., & Setiawan, I. (2010). *From Products to Customers to the Human Spirit: Marketing 3.0*. Hoboken, NJ: John Wiley & Sons. doi:10.1002/9781118257883

Kumar, V., Rajan, B., Gupta, S., & Pozza, I. D. (2017). Customer engagement in service. *Journal of the Academy of Marketing Science*.

Madia, S. A. (2011). Best practices for using social media as a recruitment strategy. *Strategic HR Review*, *10*(6), 19–24. doi:10.1108/14754391111172788

McKinsey Asia, P. F. S. Survey (2017). *Asia's digital banking race: Giving customers what they want*. Retrieved September 22, 2019 from https://www.mckinsey.com/~/media/McKinsey/Industries/Financial%20Services/Our%20Insights/Reaching%20Asias%20digital%20banking%20customers/Asias-digital-banking-race-WEB-FINAL.ashx

Mitic, M., & Kapoulas, A. (2012). Understanding the role of social media in bank marketing. *Marketing Intelligence & Planning*, *30*(7), 668–686. doi:10.1108/02634501211273797

Pan, J., Vorvoreanu, M., & Zhou, Z. (2014). Social media adoption in disaster restoration industry. *Construction Innovation*, *14*(3), 346–369. doi:10.1108/CI-03-2013-0014

Parusheva, S. (2017). Social Media Banking Models: A case study of a practical implementation in banking sector. Икономически изследвания, *3*, 125-141.

Parveen, F., Jaafar, N. I., & Ainin, S. (2016). Social media's impact on organizational performance and entrepreneurial orientation in organizations. *Management Decision*, *54*(9), 2208–2234. doi:10.1108/MD-08-2015-0336

Ray, S. K., & Singh, S. (2010). Blog content based recommendation framework using wordnet and multiple ontologies. *Proceedings of the International Conference on Computer Information Systems And Industrial Management Applications*, 432-437. Cracow, Poland, 10.1109/CISIM.2010.5643502

Shankar, R., & Khan, S. (2012), The Next Generation Social Banking Ecosystem: A Road Map for Banks, Happiest Minds Technologies. 1-13. Retrieved August 01, 2019 from http://www.happiestminds.com/whitepapers/The-Next-Generation-Social-Banking-Ecosystem--A-Road-Map-for-Banks.pdf

Shukle, R. (2015). How to Handle Customer Complaints via Social Media. Retrieved June 03, 2019 from https://www.socialmediaexaminer.com/how-to-handle-customer-complaints-via-social-media/

Smith, L. R., & Sanderson, J. (2015). I'm Going to Instagram It! An Analysis of Athlete Self- Presentation on Instagram. *Journal of Broadcasting & Electronic Media*, *59*(2), 342–358. doi:10.1080/08838151.2015.1029125

Statista Internet. (2018). *Mobile Internet & Apps*. Retrieved August 28, 2019 from https://www.statista.com/markets/424/topic/538/mobile-internet-apps/

Stern, S., & Ibarra, P. (2011). Digital government: Creating the social media game plan. *Government Finance Review*, *27*(5), 8–14.

Tajvidi, R., & Karami, A. (2017). (in press). The effect of social media on firm performance. *Computers in Human Behavior*. doi:10.1016/j.chb.2017.09.026

Thomas, M. (2011). *Social media in finance: Users want tangible benefits, not friendship, Deutsche Bank Research, E-Banking Snapshot 37*, pp. 1-4. Retrieved July 16, 2019 from http://www.dbresearch.com/PROD/DBR_INTERNET_EN-PROD/PROD0000000000273185.pdf

Vendramin, S. (2016). *Why Banks Need Instagram*. Retrieved May 12, 2019 from https://medium.com/@stefanovendramin/why-banks-need-instagram-3b66747093b7

We are Social. (2017). *Digital in 2017*. Retrieved September, 26 2019 from https://www.juancmejia.com/wp-content/uploads/2017/03/Digital-2017-WeAreSocial-y-HootSuite.pdf

Weinberg, B. D., & Pehlivan, E. (2011). Social spending: Managing the social media mix. *Business Horizons*, *54*(3), 275–282. doi:10.1016/j.bushor.2011.01.008

World Bank Global Financial Inclusion. (2015). *Global Financial Inclusion (Global Findex) Database*. Retrieved August 10, 2019 from https://datacatalog.worldbank.org/dataset/global-financial-inclusion-global-findex-database

Zolkepli, I. A., & Kamarulzaman, Y. (2015). Social media adoption: The role of media needs and innovation characteristics. *Computers in Human Behavior*, *43*, 189–209. doi:10.1016/j.chb.2014.10.050

## ADDITIONAL READING

Al-Kandari, A. A., Gaither, T. K., Alfahad, M. M., Dashti, A. A., & Alsaber, A. R. (2019). An Arab perspective on social media: How banks in Kuwait use instagram for public relations. *Public Relations Review*, *45*(3), 101774. doi:10.1016/j.pubrev.2019.04.007

Cannell, S., & Travis, B. (2018). *YouTube Secrets: The Ultimate Guide to Growing Your Following and Making Money as a Video Influencer*. Lioncrest Publishing.

De Veirman, M., Cauberghe, V., & Hudders, L. (2017). Marketing through Instagram influencers: The impact of number of followers and product divergence on brand attitude. *International Journal of Advertising*, *36*(5), 798–828. doi:10.1080/02650487.2017.1348035

Hjorth, L., & Hinton, S. (2019). *Understanding social media*. SAGE Publications Limited.

Kane, B. (2018). *One Million Followers: How I Built a Massive Social Following in 30 Days*. BenBella Books.

Kerpen, D. (2015). *Likeable social media*. McGraw-Hill.

Kusumasondjaja, S. (2018). The roles of message appeals and orientation on social media brand communication effectiveness: An evidence from Indonesia. *Asia Pacific Journal of Marketing and Logistics*, *30*(4), 1135–1158. doi:10.1108/APJML-10-2017-0267

Macarthy, A. (2018). *500 Social Media Marketing Tips: Essential Advice, Hints and Strategy for Business Facebook, Twitter, Pinterest, Google+, YouTube, Instagram, LinkedIn, and More!* CreateSpace Independent Publishing Platform.

Rahmawati, T. Y., Dewi, M. K., & Ferdian, I. R. (2019). Instagram: Its roles in management of Islamic banks. *Journal of Islamic Marketing*, *ahead-of-print*(ahead-of-print). doi:10.1108/JIMA-11-2018-0213

Weintraub, M., & Litwinka, L. (2013). *The complete social media community manager's guide: essential tools and tactics for business success*. John Wiley & Sons.

## KEY TERMS AND DEFINITIONS

**Al-Qur'an:** literally meaning "the recitation" which is the central religious text of Islam, which Muslims believe to be a revelation from God (*Allah*). It is the sacred writings of Islam revealed by God to the Prophet Muhammad during his life at Mecca and Medina.

**Challenges:** (The situation of being faced with) something that needs great mental or physical effort in order to be done successfully and therefore tests a person's ability.

***Da'wah*:** an Arabic word which has the literal meaning of "issuing a summons" or "making an invitation".

**Deception:** is an act or statement which misleads, hides the truth, or promotes a belief, concept, or idea that is not true. It is often done for personal gain or advantage.

**Hadith:** A collection of traditions containing sayings of the prophet Muhammad which, with accounts of his daily practice (Sunnah), constitute the major source of guidance for Muslims apart from the *Al-Qur'an*.

**Islamic Banks:** known as non-interest banking, is a system based on the principles of Islamic or *Shariah* law and guided by Islamic economics. Islamic banks make a profit through equity participation which requires a borrower to give the bank a share in their profits rather than paying interest.

**Opportunities:** A favorable or advantageous circumstance or combination of circumstances.

**Privacy:** is the ability of an individual or group to seclude themselves, or information about themselves, and thereby express themselves selectively.

***Shariah*:** an Islamic religious law that governs not only religious rituals but also aspects of day-to-day life in Islam. It is literally translated as "the way."

**Social Media:** are interactive computer-mediated technologies that facilitate the creation and sharing of information, ideas, career interests and other forms of expression via virtual communities and networks.

**Transparency:** is an element used in science, engineering, business, the humanities and in other social contexts, operating in such a way that it is easy for others to see what actions are performed.

# Chapter 12
# The Loan Shark in ASEAN:
## Can Nanofinance With Qardhul Hassan Deal With It? Lesson Learned From Bank Wakaf Mikro in Indonesia

**Khairunnisa Musari**
*IAIN Jember, Indonesia*

## ABSTRACT

*Loan shark is a humanitarian problem faced by many countries in the world, including in Asia, even in the Association of Southeast Asian Nations (ASEAN)'s countries. Loan shark activities are found not only in Myanmar and Cambodia, which has the lowest per capita income in ASEAN but also in Indonesia, Thailand, Malaysia, Brunei, and even Singapore, which are the five countries with the highest gross domestic product (GDP) per capita in ASEAN. How are loan shark practices in ASEAN countries? Can nanofinance overcome the microfinance gap to fight the loan shark? How the practice of Bank Wakaf Mikro (BWM) in Indonesia to nanofinance with qardhul hassan contract? Find the answers in this chapter.*

## INTRODUCTION

Loan shark evolves in almost every country. Investopedia defines a loan shark as *"a person who – or an entity that – charges borrowers interest above an established legal rate. Often loan sharks are members of organized groups offering short-term loans who use threats of violence for debt collection"*. Cambridge Dictionary underlines as *"a person who charges very large amounts of money for lending*

DOI: 10.4018/978-1-7998-2257-8.ch012

*money to someone"*. Haller & Alviti (1977) highlight as *"the lending of money at an illegal rate of interest and without holding claim to some physical possession of the borrower as collateral."*

Packman (2014), Mayer (2012, 2010) explain that loan shark originated from land sharks, a name for unscrupulous traders who hiding around ports in 19th-century America. It is estimated that the first mention of moneylenders was made in a copy of the Chicago Tribune in 1888 in an article about the condition of Minnesota farmers who were victims of moneylenders. This epithet is an Americanism popular discourse, one of a family of slang metaphors to the predatory behavior of the shark. Though any sharp lender may be described disparagingly as a loan shark, from the beginning this particular phrase was associated with a set of expensive small-loan products that had come into existence around the Civil War.

Leong, Li, & Xu (2018), Musari (2016d, 2017, 2019), Coy (2017), Mayer (2010), Haller & Alviti (1977) mention the practice of loan shark is categorized as social ill, illegal moneylending market, illegal lenders, informal financial institution, and racketeer lender. It serves an unmet need, unbanked people, low income and desperate families, who do not have enough financial resources or credit profile to access the formal banking system, even if often in a heartless and exploitative way. The loan shark is brave enough to provide cash in very fast service and flexible for them but with high interest. They could seem friendly at first but borrowing from them will bring consequences and many risks of high-interest lending.

As a humanitarian problem faced by many countries in the world, loan shark flourishes in both developed and developing countries. In England, loan shark in Glasgow who charged people interest rates of more than 719,000% faces having his assets seized under proceeds of crime legislation. In Leicester, Police hunt loan sharks riding Britain's rising tide of debt. In South America, a Colombian loan shark network is operating in more than three-quarters of Mexico's states marking its growing presence throughout Latin America. Mexican authorities found a Colombian loan shark network of over 1,800 foreigners dispersed throughout Latin America. In Kentucky, a woman who was a victim of loan shark reminds, *"You don't have to be poor to be a victim of payday loans... They were everywhere."*

Although there's never been consensus on what's a limit for interest rates by the loan shark, generally it is exorbitant. At least, refer to Mallick (2009, 2012), Hossain (2002), Hossain & Knight (2008), Irfan, Arif, Ali, & Nazli (1999), Tiwary (2017), Khandelwal (2010), Deshpande & Arora (Eds.) (2010), the loan shark's interest rates in Bangladesh, Pakistan, and India charge very high than formal financial sector, particularly in rural areas. The victims in some areas even to suicide.

## THE PRACTICE OF LOAN SHARK IN ASEAN'S COUNTRIES

The existence of loan shark is happening also in ASEAN. Loan shark activities are found not only in Myanmar and Cambodia, which has the lowest per capita income in ASEAN but also in Indonesia, Thailand, Malaysia, Brunei, and even Singapore, which are the five countries with the highest GDP per capita in ASEAN. In the absence of banking services and also the MFIs, the poor frequently borrow money from relatives and acquaintances. If the available loans do not exist, they come to the nonformal financial institutions. The target of nonformal financial institutions is usually a lower-middle-class society, namely a community that often require emergency funds to maintain its economy.

Association of Southeast Asian Nations (ASEAN) Secretariat (2018) notes that ASEAN has made tremendous economic progress over recent decades. With current combined gross domestic products (GDP) of almost US$2.8 trillion in 2017, ASEAN is collectively ranked as the world 5th largest and Asian 3rd largest economy. Figure 1 highlights the trends in GDP per capita by ASEAN member states from 2000 to 2017. ASEAN Key Figures 2018 shows GDP per capita in Singapore and Brunei Darussalam were considerably higher than the other ASEAN member states, reaching US$57,772 and US$28,986 respectively, in 2017. The 2017 GDP per capita of other ASEAN member states stood at US$9,899 for Malaysia, US$6,736 for Thailand, US$3,872 for Indonesia, US$2,992 for Philippines, US$2,531 Lao PDR, US$2,390 for Viet Nam, US$1,421 for Cambodia, and US$1,229 for Myanmar. While GDP per capita increased significantly in all ASEAN member states during 2000-2017, very rapid increases were mainly recorded in Lao PDR (with an increase of 662.0%), Myanmar (502.3%), Viet Nam (492.3%) and Cambodia (394.0%).

**Myanmar** has a long history with a loan shark. Refer to Foerch, Ki, Thein, & Waldschmidt (2016), from the mid-19th century until the end of British colonial rule, *Chettiars*, people of a mercantile caste originally from India, successfully operated as professional but largely informal moneylenders, particularly for Myanmar's agricultural sector. They often offered additional financial services, such as bills of exchange used for advancing credit or for remitting funds – so called *hundis*. A study by Finmark Trust & UNCDF (2013) finds that more people in Myanmar use informal loans than formal loans. Duflos, Luchtenburg, Ren, & Chen (2013) illustrate a survey of 4,000 households conducted by Livelihoods and Food Security Trust Fund (LIFT) which found that only 16% of households used formal financial services. According to the survey, the most common sources of loans were family, friends, and loan shark. Kaino (2006), Foerch et al (2016) states that borrowing from a loan shark who charge usurious rates is categorized as informal credit and filling a gap in the current financial sector. However, lending money without holding a license in Myanmar is illegal and may be punished with a fine or imprisonment.

*Figure 1. GDP per Capita by the ASEAN Member States from 2000 to 2017*
*Source: ASEAN Secretariat (2018), modified*

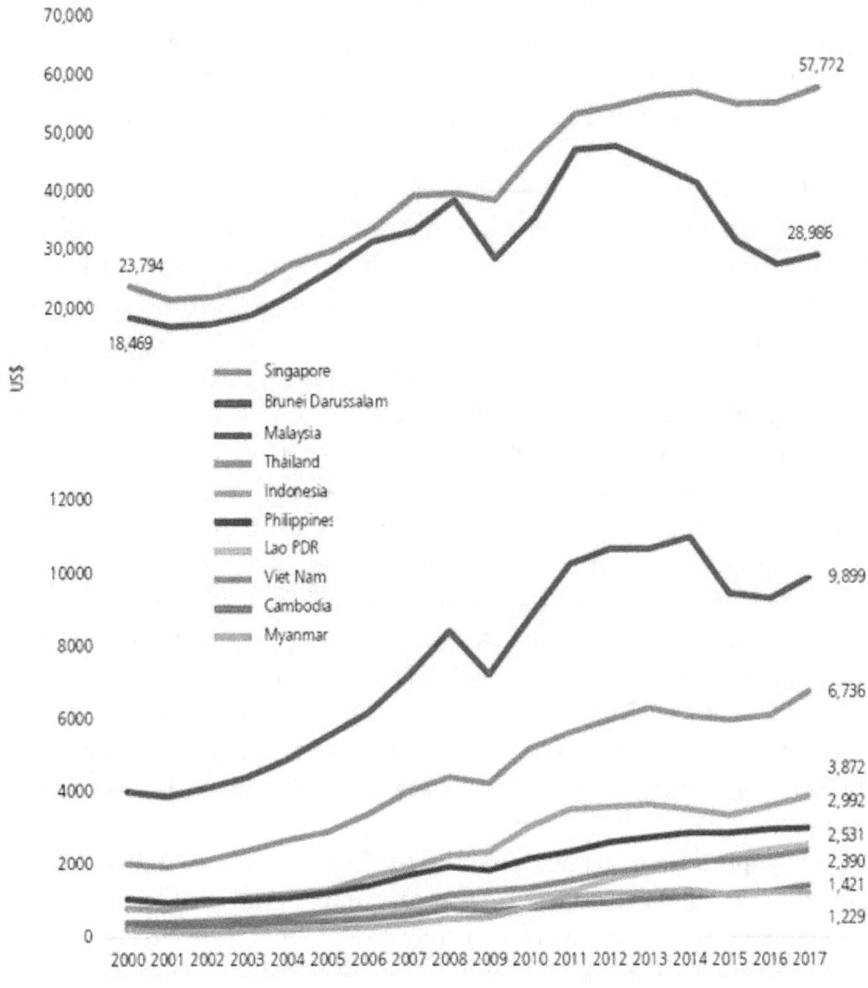


In **Cambodia,** microfinance for alleviating poverty is a very debated issue. Study by Ovesen & Trankell (2014) show microfinance in formal financial institution coexists with loan shark because loan shark also needs a loan. The study result indicates a loan either from microbanks and private lenders have malicious economical consequences for the most vulnerable people because of high-interest rates. However, study by Vathana, Dalis, Bopharath, & Dorina (2016) show the presence of competition between formal financial institution and loan shark either in urban and rural areas of developing countries also occurs in Cambodia. Murakami

(2013) clarifies that the government has efforted to limit on high-interest rates and restrictions on financial services. The government diminishes the enthusiasm of people for investing in microfinance services. But it implicates poor people going back to the loan shark. This also brings a problem. In reality, interest rates by the loan shark is higher than microfinance services. The annual percentage rate charged by the loan shark is around 120-180%, compared to only 18% charged by banks and about 45% by MFIs.

In **Viet Nam,** 'black credit' is available at a number of places, including pawn shops, as a market for the practices of a loan shark. Borrowers of 'black credit' have to pay daily interest with super-high rates. For the loan over 40 days, the borrower had to pay 30% the interest rate per month or 1% per day. Moreover, a loan shark has applied an interest rate of 500% per year. Barslund & Tarp (2008) explain that the informal sector has a higher share of loans than the formal sector. This sector also has a higher interest rate. Households depend on loans from the informal sector to cover shocks and incidental events because of lower transaction costs and more supple terms of lending. As a note, more than 50% of the high-interest loans from the informal sector is for production aims, showing the importance of this loan segment for the economic growth of Viet Nam. Vuong (2014) elucidates that the impact of the economic crisis and the tightened of banking credits on mounting bad debts had triggered the thrive of informal credits and hyperactivity of loan sharks. This underground finance was estimated to be equivalent to roughly 30% of total formal credit. Loan sharks caused the financial frauds that could potentially trigger serious economic consequences and even social unrest. Frauds are conditioned in the transitioning society where many households and individuals tend to act as rent-seekers.

In **Lao People's Democratic Republic (PDR),** Chaleunsinh, Akihiko, Koichi, & Fumiharu (2015) elucidate that rural people rely on informal lenders such as relatives, friends, loan shark, and so forth for loans. Rural people feel difficult to access formal financial markets. Seibel & Kunkel (1999) explain that informal financial institutions do not appear as an important part of the social fabric. Their place is largely taken by small local networks of reciprocal relations and mutual obligations among relatives, friends and neighbours. There is a small number of moneylenders who provide microloans at around 20% interest per month. This is supplemented by a very limited volume of supplier credit. Moneylending seems to be a female domain. Yes, women in Laos is the key of moneylender. One of the most striking aspects of the emerging landscape of microfinance is the key role of women within the cultural traditions. Beside they hold the family purse, they are the small traders and microentrepreneurs, they produce cash crops, they are the innovators in urban informal finance, they are in charge of saving for investments and emergencies, and they are also the moneylenders.

As a developing country, the **Philippines** has a large informal sector comprised of micro-enterprises. Kondo (2003) describes many of micro-enterprises are severely resource-constrained small vendors operating in public markets, whose survival in business relies heavily on access to financing. The access to financing usually comes from the informal sector as well in the form of informal financiers called "5-6". Two types of 5-6 financiers are found in public markets, each with a distinctive lending mechanism, Filipinos and Indians. Seibel et al (2000) mention the informal sector like loan shark as an ingredient of the financial system. As an informal financial institution, the loan shark is unregistered and unsupervised. In most rural areas, there is a phenomenon the increasing of the dependence of the farmer on subsidized credit and loan shark because of deposit facilities by formal institutions were mainly absent. By using a sample of 108 entrepreneurs, study of Zapata (2006) showed that those who are less-educated, married, and/or have large household size are easy prey for the informal lenders. Even if government microfinance programs provide funds with favorable terms, they are still inclined to get their funds from informal lenders. They are enticed by the low nominal rate quoted by the informal lenders. They are not aware of the high effective cost implied by the nominal rate. Informal lenders also have less stringent requirements.

In **Indonesia,** historically, Schrader (1994) believes the lower level of credit consisted of the traditional credit relations in kind within the village and of commercial credit relations of merchants-cumlenders and pure moneylenders, not much different from India. One form was credit in cash or kind, to be repaid in kind after the harvest. Typical were advances by Chinese merchants to farmers on standing crops (*ijon*). The professional moneylenders were mainly aliens: Chinese and to a lesser extent Arabs, *Chettiars,* and Europeans. Awirya, Rahmayani, & Prirayani (2012) assert commercial moneylenders are still working in rural areas and catering to the short-term needs of the poorest, although they are not flourishing as in the past. Some moneylenders are disguising their activities under the name of cooperatives. Characteristics of moneylenders in Indonesia are similar to other informal MFIs. The easiness of lending to the borrower still remains as the main reason for this activity to still exist in society. Musari (2016d, 2019) notes the loan shark in Indonesia charged 10-30% interest rate per month. Those who have the profession as loan shark or become accomplices of loan shark are not only done individually, but also group, even institution. The fact shows that the loan shark continues to flourish. Some call as *Bank Kredit, Batak Kredit (Bakri), Bank Harian, Bank Plecit, Bank Thitil, Bank Keliling,* etc. The participants are housewives, street vendors, small traders, and other micro community who are mostly low in savings and assets and thus have to seek external loans to meet emergency needs.

In **Thailand,** the government give attention to against the loan shark. Since 1932, the enactment of Thailand's Interest Overcharging Law had existed. The government prohibited any person from loaning money to another person and subsequently charging them interest at a rate that exceeded the rate prescribed by the law. According to Sakai (2008), lending costs used unlimited, even though lending rates were terminated at 15%. In 2005, however, lending rates including costs were limited to a maximum of 28%. Meyer (2002) claims the existence of village bank membership had no significant impact on household physical assets, expenses, sales, production, labor time or expenditures on health care and education. Paradoxically, village bank membership appeared to increase the women's high-interest debt and lending out at interest. A study by Coleman (2006) finds the Bank for Agriculture and Agricultural Cooperatives (BAAC) services over 80% of rural households. The BAAC is a state-owned bank established to provide loans primarily for agricultural infrastructure. Hence, it is possible that the rural poor in Thailand are not credit constrained. However, the BAAC's outreach in the Northeast, the country's poorest region, is smaller than the rest of the country. At the time of the study, BAAC's annual interest rate varied from 3% to 12%, whereas moneylenders charged between 60% and 120% per year. There is evidence that women in Northeast Thailand may be credit constrained and may benefit from access to lower-cost institutional credit.

In **Malaysia,** Arif (2009) explains that moneylending affair is a longstanding industry that has served consumers from diverse backgrounds. The industry is ruled by the Moneylenders Act 1951, which in 2003 has undergone major amendments. The history of a loan shark in Malaysia has occurred since the British era with the advent of *Chettiars* as professional moneylenders. Suppiah (2014), Suppiah & Raja (2013) confirm that pressure from the British to *Chettiars* in South India makes them did a migration to Southeast Asia and then expansion to Malaya. Nadaraja (2016) also addresses that one of the important sources of money for Malay farmers in the past were *Chettiars.* The farmers could be obtained the loans easily and quickly from them. However, borrowing money from *Chettiars* requires a guarantee, for example, a land grant.

Further, study of Abdullah & Hanafi (2007) find the illegal financial institutions, otherwise known as *Ah Long*, also widespread into the society in Malaysia. *Ah Long* is another form of credit facility which offers loan service to the society, especially those who are in dire need of money. They are viewed as illegal moneylender because have no licensed or authorized. There is not any Malay law authorize *Ah Long* and *Chettiars.* If the moneylender is not authorized, it might be categorized as a loan shark.

**In Brunei,** loan shark activities may occur and that certainly happens to the black market because the population in Brunei is not large and the country is relatively calm, when there is an activity that harms others, the state will know and will intervene to solve it. Hassan (2010) mentions that after the further restrictions to credit introduced in 2010 may push consumers to desperation and force them to borrow from illegal predatory lenders, especially loan sharks, which impose excessive interest rates that can be dangerous to consumers. In the recent development related to increased consumer debts, CIKL (2011) clarifies that there is no report of consumers obtaining loans from unlicensed moneylenders in Brunei Darussalam. Regarded to loan shark activities, Laws of Brunei (Revised Edition 1984) has Moneylenders Act in Chapter 62 to provide for the registration of moneylenders and to restrict the practice of charging exorbitant interest. In this Act, moneylenders mean any person who habitually lends money at interest or a person who is proved to have lent money at interest on one occasion shall until the contrary be proved to be deemed to have habitually lent money at interest.

In **Singapore,** Gardner (2015) mentions that moneylending in there is complex, diverse, and an important area. The moneylending regulator has been active in this area. Since 2011, there have been 35 licensed moneylenders convicted for breaches of the Moneylender Act and fines in excess of $1.5 million. There has also been an increased focus on the prosecution and criminal conviction of unlicensed moneylenders by the Singapore Police Force, resulting in a 21% reduction in loan shark's harassment cases in 2011. Ho (2010) in Leong et al (2018) states that *"the loan shark scourge persists because loan sharks enjoy good profits. They charge exorbitant interest rates and recycle their ill-gotten gains to fund more loans, thereby accruing even more profits. It is a vicious cycle."*

## CAN NANOFINANCE OVERCOME THE MICROFINANCE GAP TO FIGHT THE LOAN SHARK?

### Nanofinance: Theory and Practice

No many literature reviews about nanofinance. Most literatures explain about microfinance as a powerful device to alleviate poverty. Obaidullah (2008), Obaidullah & Khan (2008) confirm, microfinance means the provision of financial services to poor and low-income people who exclude from formal financial systems. Unfortunately, as stated by Mitra (2009) that the interest rate on loan of MFIs are kept at an exorbitant level and additional costs in the form of margin money, compulsory savings, and insurance premium are being imposed on borrowers in order to improve the profitability. Kar & Swain (2013) argue controversies regarding the high-interest rates being charged by MFIs have been justified in the name of financial sustainability. However, Ali (2011) reminds that microfinance and Islamic finance actually have the same goals and objectives to some extent. Both aim to reduce poverty and income disparities and encourage equitable distribution of income and sustainable income growth for the poor. Similarly, Ali (2007) mentioned that

*Table 1. The generic concept of (Islamic) nanofinance*

| ASPECTS | DESCRIPTION |
|---|---|
| Mission | 1. To avoid the very poor to go to the loan shark;<br>2. To fill the (Islamic) microfinance gap;<br>3. To encourage the very poor to be independent and have the minimum necessities to live a decent life;<br>4. To build sufficient internal financial and human resources and to use them to leverage resources from external sources; |

microfinance and Islamic finance objectives are socially oriented and intended to promote economic development and cooperation.

Referring to Deb, Sengupta, & Ray (Eds.) (2008), nanofinance is another concept distinct from microfinance in order to address the serious problems of the extremely poverty. Nanofinance creates community within the community. On one count microfinance constructs the community and on another count breaks it and throws the community into the fold of nanofinance. Mahanti (2008) mentions nanofinance as a small interest free loans could be given to women for their emergency needs. Nanofinance institution (NFIs) in India are established truly help the poorest of the poor women of the society. Chonlaworn & Pongpirodom (2015) emphasize that the aims of nanofinance scheme to reduce the loan shark problem and promote better access to capital that would expand occupational chance of the borrowers. Nanofinance is a flexible credit process designed to meet the financial needs of customers, such as new business owners. According to Musari (2016a), the generic concept of nanofinance, must based on the Islamic perspective, can be constructed as shown by Table 1.

The practice of nanofinance may differently in some countries. Musari & Simanjuntak (2016), Musari (2016a, 2016b, 2016c, 2019) claim most MFIs in Indonesia, Cambodia, Thailand, and India which doing nanofinance play a key role in providing financial services to the very poor, very low income, and very micro enterprises. Unfortunately, most of MFIs charge such high interest rates despite it looks relatively low and regarded not burden to the borrowers. But its interest rates are higher than bank's interest rates because the costs of producing a small loan are higher in percentage terms than the costs of producing a larger loan. It is also believed to occur in the Islamic MFIs.

Musari & Simanjuntak (2015, 2016) claim some MFIs now give attention to the very micro society. They introduce a new term 'nanofinance' to provide opportunities of financial service for the very poor, very low income, and very low enterprises. Actually, there are 'very poor' (and also very low income and very low enterprises) that should be a target of microfinance, but most banks do not yet cover them. Referring to Microcredit Summit, microfinance is programs extend small loans

*Table 2.*

| ASPECTS | DESCRIPTION |
|---|---|
| | 5. To reduce the humanitarian cases as impact of the extremely poverty and loan shark. |
| Funding Source | NFIs/MFIs must have low cost fund to finance the very poor to avoid interest rate. Funding source may be obtained mostly from grants, donations, corporate social responsibility (CSR), philanthropy institutions, crowdfunding, *zakah, infaq, shadaqa, waqf, waqf* linked sukuk, sukuk linked *waqf, esham,* etc. |
| Market Target | The very poor people; the very micro enterprises that may not have a constant income, monthly, paycheck, or have limited financial history; The very low-income groups/individuals that do not meet financial institutions' borrowing criterion. |
| Credit Needs | Emergency needs |
| Loan Size | US$1-100 (This number is an approximate figure. Each country may have different level for the amount span of nanofinance). |
| Interest Rate | 0% (using *qardhul hassan* contract for the emergency needs (for food, healthcare, education, death, wedding, daily livelihood) or *musharaka/mudharaba* (for small trading or very micro enterprises). |
| Lending Procedures | People do not have to go through paperwork and/or rigid rules and regulations for getting small financing for their emergency needs. For business, people can be submitted orally. Funds can be directly liquid after a survey conducted at a glance toward the business. |
| Disbursement | 1 day |
| Repayment Periods | Time agreed together, but must < 1 year. |
| Collateral/ Guarantees | - |

Source: Musari (2016a, 2016c, 2019), modified

to very poor for self-employment projects that generate income, allowing them to care for themselves and their families. So, there are 'very poor' not only 'poor' that should be an object of microfinance too. In Indonesia, microfinance is also classified into a type of bank financing, but in the fact, most of banks do not cover the needs of very micro society.

In **Indonesia,** one of MFIs which serve nanofinance for the poor is MFI for Society that initiated by Department of Cooperative and Micro Small Medium Enterprises (MSMEs) since 2005 and has deployed to various sub-districts. Study of Musari & Simanjuntak (2015, 2016), Musari (2016b) explain this institution, Bank for Poor Family or Bank Keluarga Miskin (Gakin), become a good alternative financing for the very poor, very low income, and very micro enterprises rather than formal banks or laon shark. Although inspired by Grameen Bank, Bank Gakin in Jember works like self-help groups (SHGs). Another lesson learned from nanofinance in Indonesia is *Kredit Melati (Melawan Rentenir)* by the Government of Bandung City. Musari (2016b, 2016c) affirm that for avoiding the Bandung's residents from the moneylender, the local government ask the Rural Bank (BPR) to release nanofinance with a name *Kredit Melati*. By this program, the Bandung's residents obtain the credit by 0% interest. In the term of Islamic finance, what *Kredit Melati* do is referring to the practice of *qardhul hassan*. However, the BPR cuts 8% of total funds as administration fee. For residents who late paying the loan installments, the BPR also impose interest 0.2% per day of the total installments.

In the beginning of 2017, the Indonesian government through Ministry of Cooperatives (Kemenkop) and Small Medium Enterprises (UKM) released *Kredit Ultra Mikro* (UMi). *Kredit* UMi is a hope for the realization of financial inclusion for all parties, especially for those who have limited access to banking facilities. Previously, the low-cost credit that became the mainstay of the government is *Kredit Usaha Rakyat* (KUR) about IDR10-25 million. Now, *Kredit* UMi brings the mission to serve the business sector with a ceiling below IDR10 million and also without collateral. The existence of *Kredit* UMi is in line with the spirit of nanofinance. *Kredit* UMi is a hope for micro groups to access financing that match their capacity and capability. This small credit value is rational to be reached by them.

In **Thailand,** refer to Karaivanov & Kessler (2013, 2016), households resort more often to loan shark or to the BAAC. In order to prevent people who have already been in the formal loan system to additionally seek informal finances, the government and Bank of Thailand (BOT) released nanofinance as the tool to reduce the loan shark's problem and promote better access to capital. Nanofinance is a flexible credit process designed to meet the financial needs of customers, such as new business owners. Each borrower may borrow not more than Bt100,000 at an interest rate up to 36% p.a without any collateral. Parpart (2014), Chonlaworn & Pongpirodom (2015) clarify the smallest form of loan through microfinance has a maximum loan amount of Bt200,000, at an interest rate of 28%, while the nanofinance offers Bt100,000-120,000 with higher interest rate at 30-36%.

Overall, the practices of nanofinance in Indonesia and Thailand can be viewed in Table 3. There are some differences. Nanofinance in Thailand tends to the microfinance in Indonesia because the value is higher than the nanofinance in Indonesia.

Absolutely, the practice of nanofinance should avoid the usury. This is not only in order to comply the *shari'a* principles, but also in the name of humanity, because the benefit recipients of nanofinance is the poor, even the poorest of the poor. Musari (2016c, 2017, 2019) argue that for an emergency behalf, the loans must refund by according to the amount borrowed through *qardhul hassan* contract. Also for a business behalf in nanofinance and/or picofinance must using *qardhul hassan.* In Thailand, the term of picofinance has introduced to the public. It is viewed as a tool to a final solution to the longstanding problem of moneylenders, in addition to earlier suggested nanofinance. The Thai government employ picofinance and

*Table 3. The profile of nanofinance in Indonesia and Thailand*

| | INDONESIA | THAILAND |
|---|---|---|
| The Concept of Financial Institution | Cooperative/MFI (under Department of Cooperative and MSMEs) | Non-Bank, Limited Company or Public Company (under BOT as regulator) |
| Mission | Avoid the people to go to the moneylenders and encourage the people to have (small) business. | Allow the grassroots to have easier access to obtain credits, to tackle the problem of informal loans, ease the loan shark problem and promote better access to capital that would expand occupational opportunities of the borrowers. |
| Funding Source | Grant from Department of Cooperative and SMEs, the savings of group members. | Can mobilize funds from retail investors by promissory note (private placement) and issue corporate bonds and minimum registered capital of Bt50 million. |
| Market Target | Women for micro businesses that have no access to capital from financial institutions because have no collateral or guarantee. | 1. Current borrowers of informal loans.<br>2. Bank borrowers that are classed as special mention group.<br>3. New business owners that may not have a constant income, monthly paycheck, or have limited financial history.<br>4. Low income groups/individuals that do not meet financial institutions' borrowing criterion. |
| Loan Target | Business, but also for emergency | 1. Promote better access to capital<br>2. Increase occupational opportunities<br>3. Alleviate illegal lending |
| Loan Size | IDR50 thousand-1million | Up to Bt100,000 |
| Interest Rate | 0.5% per week; 0%, but there is administration fee | Not exceeding 36% per year |

*Table 4.*

| | INDONESIA | THAILAND |
|---|---|---|
| Interest Calculation | Fixed/effective interest rate | Effective interest rate |
| Repayment Periods | 10 weeks | 2-3 years |
| Collateral | - | - |

Source: Musari (2016a, 2016c, 2017, 2019), Musari & Simanjuntak (2016), developed and improved

nanofinance to handle loans at rural level. Picofinance will handle smaller funds and with loans not exceeding Bt50,000 whereas nanofinance handle larger loans up to Bt100,000. So, any return on capital in the form of interest is completely prohibited in Islam, there is no objection to getting a return on capital if the provider of capital enters into a partnership with a worker or entrepreneur and is prepared to share in the risks of the business.

## *Qardhul Hassan*: Theory and Practice

*Qardhul hassan* (also written as *qard hassan; qard-ul-hassan*) is an example of a unique instrument offered by Islamic economics and finance. *Qardhul hassan* is often referred to as a zero-return loan, benevolent loan, voluntary loan, soft loan, charitable loan or beautiful loan. According to Febianto & Ashany (2012), ISRA (2010, 2015), Iqbal & Mirakhor (2008, 2011), Askari, Iqbal, & Mirakhor (2009), Obaidullah & Khan (2008), Chapra & Khan (2008), *qardhul hassan* is one of social-welfare contracts in form of interest-free loan to make available to the needy people. Overall, there are some verses of the *Qur'an* and *Hadits* addressing the *qardhul hassan* as shown at Table 5.

In Islamic economics, *qardhul hassan* is one of *tabarru'* contract that can be advanced for microfinance purposes and poverty alleviation. MFIs can provide this contract to the people who are in need of small start-up capital and/or have no business experience and/or have an emergency needs. Then, the MFIs may charge only a service or administration fee. The term of repayment will be on installment basis for an agreed period. As *tabarru'* contract, *qardhul hassan* is performed in order to improve the economic life of the financing participants. Through *qardhul hassan,* the MSEs and/or the poorest of the poor can be helped to improve and enhance the income, particulary can be avoided from the moneylender.

# LESSON LEARNED FROM BANK WAKAF MIKRO IN INDONESIA

Poverty and inequality are Indonesia's problems that have been going on for years. The poor people are often trapped by the loan shark. According to Statistics Indonesia (BPS, 2018), currently the number of poor people in Indonesia was 25.67 million or around 9.66% in September 2018. This is followed by an inequality level, in March 2019, as measured by the Gini Ratio was 0.382 (BPS, 2019). The Gini Ratio in urban areas was recorded as the bigger contributor than in rural areas.

Today, the Financial Services Authority (OJK) in Indonesia develops ultra-micro financing through the establishment of Islamic microfinance institutions (IMFI) with a brand "Bank Wakaf Mikro (BWM)". The BWM was first present in October 2017. Two months lapse, in December 2017, the BWM managed to collect 827 customers. Its growth continues rapidly after it was inaugurated in early 2018. This was seen in March 2018, as many as 20 waqf banks managed to obtain business licenses from OJK and managed to have 3,876 customers. At the end of December 2018, there have been 41 licensed BWM from OJK and registered as many as 8,000 customers.

*Table 5. Legitimacy to qardhul hassan in the qur'an and hadits*

| *QUR'AN* AND VERSES | THE MEANING |
|---|---|
| QS. Al Baqarah [2]: 245 | "Who is it that would loan Allah a goodly loan so He may multiply it for him many times over? And it is Allah who withholds and grants abundance, and to Him you will be returned". |
| QS. Al Baqarah [2]: 273. | "[Charity is] for the poor who have been restricted for the cause of Allah, unable to move about in the land. An ignorant [person] would think them self-sufficient because of their restraint, but you will know them by their [characteristic] sign. They do not ask people persistently [or at all]. And whatever you spend of good - indeed, Allah is knowing of it." |
| QS. Al Maa'idah [5]: 12 | "And Allah had already taken a covenant from the Children of Israel, and We delegated from among them twelve leaders. And Allah said, "I am with you. If you establish prayer and give *zakah* and believe in My messengers and support them and loan Allah a goodly loan, I will surely remove from you your misdeeds and admit you to gardens beneath which rivers flow. But whoever of you disbelieves after that has certainly strayed from the soundness of the way." |
| QS. Huud [11]: 57 | "But if they turn away, [say], "I have already conveyed that with which I was sent to you. My Lord will give succession to a people other than you, and you will not harm Him at all. Indeed my Lord is, over all things, Guardian." |
| QS. Al Israa' [17]: 64 | "And incite [to senselessness] whoever you can among them with your voice and assault them with your horses and foot soldiers and become a partner in their wealth and their children and promise them." But Satan does not promise them except delusion." |
| QS. Al Kahfi [18]: 57 | "And who is more unjust than one who is reminded of the verses of his Lord but turns away from them and forgets what his hands have put forth? Indeed, We have placed over their hearts coverings, lest they understand it, and in their ears deafness. And if you invite them to guidance - they will never be guided, then - ever." |
| QS. Al Hadid [57]: 11 | "Who is it that would loan Allah a goodly loan so He will multiply it for him and he will have a noble reward?" |
| QS. Al Hadid [57]: 18 | "Indeed, the men who practice charity and the women who practice charity and [they who] have loaned Allah a goodly loan - it will be multiplied for them, and they will have a noble reward." |
| QS. At Taghaabun [64]: 17 | "If you loan Allah a goodly loan, He will multiply it for you and forgive you. And Allah is Most Appreciative and Forbearing." |
| QS. Al Muzzammil [73]: 20 | "Indeed, your Lord knows, [O Muhammad], that you stand [in prayer] almost two thirds of the night or half of it or a third of it, and [so do] a group of those with you. And Allah determines [the extent of] the night and the day. He has known that you [Muslims] will not be able to do it and has turned to you in forgiveness, so recite what is easy [for you] of the *Qur'an*. He has known that there will be among you those who are ill and others traveling throughout the land seeking [something] of the bounty of Allah and others fighting for the cause of Allah. So, recite what is easy from it and establish prayer and give *zakah* and loan Allah a goodly loan. And whatever good you put forward for yourselves - you will find it with Allah. It is better and greater in reward. And seek forgiveness of Allah. Indeed, Allah is Forgiving and Merciful." |
| Anas bin Malik reported that Allah's Messenger (may peace be upon him) saying: *"I saw in the night of Isra', at the door of heaven is written: Shadaqah is given ten times and qardh 18 times. I asked, O Jibril, why qard greater than sadaqa? He answered: because the beggar asks something and he had, while the borrower will not borrow except for purposes."* (HR. Ibn Majah and Baihaqi). | |
| Abu Usama reported that the Holy Prophet (may peace be upon him) said: *"A person woul be taken to a gate of the Paradise. When he would raise his head he would find inscribed there: The reward for shadaqa is ten times and for a loan it is eighteen times, because whoever comes for a loan is in (real) need. But when shadaqa is given by you,the receiver may not be (really) needy."* | |
| It is reported that the Prophet (saw) said, "in the night of the journey, I saw on the gate of heaven written, 'reward for *shadaqa* is ten times and reward for *qard al-hassan* is eighteen times'. So, I asked the angel, how is it possible? The angel replied, "Because beggar who asked had already had something but a loanee did not ask for loan unless he was in need." (HR. Ibn Hisham and Ibn Majah). | |
| Reported by Abu Hurairah Ra., the Prophet (saw) said, "whoever relieves a believer from a difficulty in this world, Allah will relieve him from his difficulty and Allah will facilitate him in this world and world hereafter." (HR. Muslim). | |

Source: *Askari et al (2009), Zauro, Saad, & Sawandi (2016), Najeeb & Lahsasna (2016), Khan (2008), Hossain (2002), Khan (1989), Musari (2016c),* Febianto & Ahsany (2012)

*Table 6. The profile of BWM in Indonesia*

| | |
|---|---|
| Background | The establishment of BWM is based on the poverty and inequality which becoming as the problems of the nation has been going on for years, believe about the importance of conducting economic empowerment, and believe that one element of society that has a strategic function in mentoring to encourage the economy of the community is *pesantren*. |
| Institutional Status | The legality as a cooperative with business license as IMFIs |
| Business Model | Providing financing, mentoring/assistance, entrepreneurship training, nondeposit taking, group or joint responsibility based, low yield or equal to 3%. |
| Vission | Avoiding the poor from the loan shark and empowering the community economic as a solution in alleviating poverty and inequality. |
| Mission | Become a quick solution in providing capital or financing access for people who are not yet connected with formal financial institutions, especially in *pesantren*, which currently number more than 28 thousand Islamic boarding schools in various parts of Indonesia. |
| Funding Source | A profit-sharing of Islamic deposits, returns on financing, and other service revenues, and also donations from all Indonesian people who have excess funds, especially entrepreneurs and/or large companies that have a concern for the empowerment program of the poor and alleviating inequality in Indonesia. Each BWM will be given IDR4.2 billion in funds with a distribution of IDR1.2 billion for micro business financing and IDR3 billion for BWM deposits. |
| Market Target | Productive poor people who have difficulty accessing formal financial institutions as well as those live in rural or remote area. |
| Market Strategy | Establish based on a group or a community, particularly in *pesantren*. |
| Costumer Criteria and Requirement | 1. Poor people who have been able to fulfill basic needs for their survival.<br>2. Poor people who already have productive businesses or have the willingness and enthusiasm to work.<br>3. Poor people who are committed to participate in empowerment programs. |
| Loan Size | A maximum value of IDR 3million and a profit-sharing margin equal to 3%. |
| Interest Rate | - |
| Lending Procedures and Disbursement Process Duration | 1. Survey of prospective customers around *pesantren.*<br>2. Selection of prospective customers through Group Compulsory Training (PWK) for five days with material discipline, cohesiveness, solidarity and courage to try. This is the initial stage of the mentoring process.<br>3. Selected one group that has passed PWK under the name Indonesian Productive Micro Business Group (KUMPI) consisting of five people. |
| | 4. Conformed groups with the name Weekly *Halaqoh* (HALMI) which consisting of 3-5 KUMPI.<br>5. The first meeting of HALMI will be disbursed financing.<br>6. The second and next meeting of HALMI are held with the following activities: payment of weekly instalments, religious services, business development, household economics, etc. |
| Repayment Periods | IDR20 thousand/week for financing package IDR1 million. |
| Collateral/ Guarantees | - |

Source: OJK (2018) and from any sources, developed

As of June 2019, there have been 51 licensed BWM with 15,236 customers and the disbursed financing was IDR18.54 billion.

BWM is actually an effort to realize financial inclusion to reduce inequality and poverty in Indonesia, especially for people who have no access to formal financial institutions. More specifically, the existence of BWM is actually also a manifestation of Islamic economic mainstreaming in the national economy. The main goal of the establishment of BWM is to avoid the poor from the loan shark by providing a financing for society who have no access to the formal financial institutions, particularly in the rural and remote area, by focusing the society around the *pesantren* (Islamic boardings). Related to the scope of BWM's work, nanofinance has a close relationship with BWM. The profile of BWM can be shown in Table 6.

Overall, it can be concluded that BWM is not permitted to take deposits from the society because it has a focus on community empowerment through financing along with business assistance. To reach the market target, BWM concerns to *pesantren* as the main facilitator. *Pesantren* is chosen because its existence is always there in rural and remote areas. The environment of *pesantren* tends to close among people so that the dissemination and distribution of loan funds becomes easier. BWM is managed directly by people who are part of a *pesantren.* Although BWM is run directly by *pesantren*, it does not mean that the loan application is only limited by certain religious groups and does not mean that other religious groups cannot establish the same institution.

To avoid the misuse of loan funds, BWM requires the borrowing funds in the form of a business group containing five people, with the aim of reminding each other. Even though it was in the form of a group, the funds did not immediately run out, there were other coaching that the group had to go through for five days first. After successfully becoming a business group, these customers must hold intense meetings every week to increase solidarity and this activity will be supervised directly by the BWM as the place to submit loans.

The next question is 'Has it been proven that BWM is effective against loan shark? Has it been proven that BWM is effective to reduce the poverty and inequality? How many and how long BWM will survive'? These questions will not be found in this chapter. It needs the investigation and further research in the future. But, absolutely, the answer depends on how capable the BWM's social capital is to make it effective and survive to serve the society.

However, the important message to be conveyed in the BWM's story is how Islamic finance is also present in very poor communities through the ultra-micro financing. Islamic finance should not be an ivory tower. In the Indonesian context, Islamic finance is actually talking about how to help MSMEs that become the backbone of the national economy. In the context of Indonesia, true Islamic finance is how to be present for the very poor people. Not by giving, but by financing and assistance that suits their needs and abilities. Musari (2018) claims, BWM through *qardhul hassan* can be an empirical study of how the best practice of nanofinance in Indonesia as *ikhtiar* to avoid the poor from the trap of the loan shark by focusing on community empowerment through nano financing along with business assistance. *Wallahua'alam bish showab.*

## REFERENCES

Abdullah, N., & Hanafi, H. (2007). *A comparative approach of money lending activities practiced by the financial institution and "Ah Long" in Malaysia. Law Conference 2007*, April 18th-20th, Sintok, Kedah, 257-267.

Ahmed, H. (2002). Financing microenterprises: An analytical study of Islamic microfinance institutions. *Islamic Economic Studies, 9*(2), March.

Arif, A. M. M. (2009). The licensing system under the Malaysian moneylenders act 2003. *International Journal of Economics and Management*, *3*(1), 1–21.

Askari, H., Iqbal, Z., & Mirakhor, A. (2009). New issues in Islamic finance and economics, progress and challenges. Singapore: John Wiley & Sons (Asia).

Awirya, A. A., Rahmayani, K., & Prirayani, J. (2012). The opportunity of profit-sharing scheme implementation on moneylender in expanding Islamic banking service, evidence from traditional market in Surabaya, Indonesia. In Jurnal BPPK, 4, 1-17. Jakarta: Badan Pendidikan dan Pelatihan Keuangan (BPPK) Kementerian Keuangan Republik Indonesia (Kemenkeu RI).

Barslund, M., & Tarp, F. (2008). Formal and informal rural credit in four provinces of Vietnam. *The Journal of Development Studies, 44,* 4, 485-503. DOI: 798 doi:10.1080/00220380801980

BPS. (2018). *Berita Resmi Statistik No. 07/01/Th. XXII, 15 Januari: Profil kemiskinan di Indonesia September 2018.* Jakarta: Badan Pusat Statistik (BPS).

BPS. (2019). *Berita resmi statistik no. 57/07/Th. XXII, 15 Juli: Tingkat ketimpangan pengeluaran penduduk Indonesia maret 2019.* Jakarta: Badan Pusat Statistik (BPS).

Chaleunsinh, C., Akihiko, O., Koichi, F., & Fumiharu, M. (2015). An analysis on borrowing behavior of rural households in Vientiane municipality: Case study of four villages. *Southeast Asian Studies, 3,* Supplementary Issue, March, 113–133.

Chandadarot, K., & Liv, D. (2011). *Impact of micro finance services in Cambodia.* Phnom Penh: Cambodia Microfinance Association.

Chandararot, K. (2002). The development of micro finance in Cambodia. *Cambodia Development Review*, *6*(3), 1–4.

Chapra, M. U., & Khan, T. (2008). *Regulasi dan pengawasan bank syariah*. Jakarta: Bumi Aksara.

Chonlaworn, P., & Pongpirodom, P. (2015). *Can Nano Finance unleash The Grassroots from Loan Shark Problems?* EIC Analysis. April. 1. Retrieved from https://www.scbeic.com/ en/detail/product/1255

CIKL. (2011). *Roadmapping capacity building needs in consumer protection in ASEAN, country report: Brunei Darussalam (final)*. Revised 3 June. Project under the Special Services Agreement between the ASEAN Secretariat and Consumers International Kuala Lumpur (CIKL) Office.

Coleman, B. E. (2006). Microfinance in Northeast Thailand: Who benefits and how much? *World Development, 34*(9), 1612–1638. DOI: dev.2006.01.006 doi:10.1016/j.world

Coy, P. (2017). When Does a Lender Become a Loan Shark? In *Bloomberg Businessweek, April* 15. Retrieved from https://www.bloomberg.com/news/articles/2017-04-05/when-does-a-lender-become-a-loan-shark

Daley, S., & Sautet, F. (2005). *Microfinance in action: The Philippine experience*. Mercatus Policy Series, Mercatus Center's Global Prosperity Initiative, George Mason University. February.

Deb, B. J., Sengupta, K., & Ray, B. D. (Eds.). (2008). *Globalization and north east India*. New Delhi, India: Ashok Kumar Mittal.

Deshpande, R. S., & Arora, S. (Eds.). (2010). *Agrarian crisis and farmer suicides: Land reforms in India* (Vol. 12). New Delhi, India: Sage.

Duflos, E., Luchtenburg, P., Ren, L., & Chen, L. Y. (2013). *Microfinance in Myanmar, sector assessment*. IFC Advisory Services in East Asia and the Pacific. January.

Dusuki, A. W. (2008). Banking for the poor: The role of Islamic banking in microfinance initiatives. *Humanomics*, *24*(1), 49–66. doi:10.1108/08288660810851469

Duvall, A. (2004). *The impact of interest rate ceilings on microfinance. Donor Brief No. 18, May. CGAP Donor Information Resource Centre*. DIRECT.

Febianto, I., & Ashany, A. M. (2012). The impact of qardhul hasan financing using zakah funds on economic empowerment (Case study of Dompet Dhuafa, West Java, Indonesia). *Asian Business Review*, *1*(1), 15–20. doi:10.18034/abr.v1i1.139

Finmark Trust & UNCDF. (2013). *Survey highlights, finscope Myanmar 2013. A survey by Finmark Trust and The United Nations Capital Development Fund*. UNCDF.

Foerch, T., Ki, O., Thein, S., & Waldschmidt, S. (2016). Myanmar's financial sector a challenging environment for banks, 3rd Edition, October. Yangon: The Deutsche Gesellschaft für Internationale Zusammenarbeit (GIZ).

Gardner, J. (2015). *Regulating moneylending in Singapore: Looking at Alla sides*. Research Policy Report CBFL-Rep-JG1, July. Centre for Banking and Finance Law (CBFL), Faculty of Law, National University of Singapore.

Glasgow loan shark 'charged 719,000% interest'. (2011, April 6). Retrieved from https://www.bbc.com/news/uk-scotland-glasgow-west-12991640

Haller, M. H., & Alviti, J. V. (1977). Loansharking in American cities: Historical analysis of a marginal enterprise. *The American Journal of Legal History*, *21*(2), 125–156. doi:10.2307/845211

Hassan, P. H., & Binti, D. N. H. (2010). *Everyday finances and consumption in Brunei Darussalam.* (Doctoral Thesis), University of Southampton.

Hossain, F. (2002). Small loans, big claims. *Foreign Policy*, (132), 79–82. doi:10.2307/3183463

Hossain, F., & Knight, T. (2008). *Financing the poor: Can microcredit make a difference? Empirical observations from Bangladesh.* Brooks World Poverty Institute (BWPI) Working Paper 38. University of Manchester, Manchester.

Hossain, M. D. (2002). *Al-Qard al-Hasan: A Practical Approach.* Retrieved from sarjoon.weebly.com/uploads/3/4/7/9/3479157/al-qarz.doc

Iqbal, Z., & Mirakhor, A. (2008). *Pengantar keuangan Islam: Teori dan Praktik.* Jakarta: Kencana.

Iqbal, Z., & Mirakhor, A. (2011). An introduction to Islamic finance: Theory and practice, 2nd Edition. Singapore: John Wiley & Sons (Asia). doi:10.1002/9781118390474

Irfan, M., Arif, G. M., Ali, S. M., & Nazli, H. (1999). *The structure of informal credit market in Pakistan.* Pakistan Institute of Development Economics (PIDE) Research Report No. 168. Islamabad: PIDE.

ISRA. (2010). ISRA conpendium: For Islamic finance terms, Arabic-English. Kuala Lumpur: International Shari'ah Research Academy for Islamic Finance (ISRA).

ISRA. (2015). *Sistem keuangan Islam: Prinsip dan operasi*. Jakarta: Rajawali Pers.

Kagan, J. (2019, October 6). Loan Shark Definition. Retrieved from https://www.investopedia.com/terms/l/loansharking.asp

Kaino, T. (2006). Rural credit markets in Myanmar: A study of formal and non-formal lenders. *Asian Journal of Agriculture and Development, 3*(1,2), 1-15.

Karaivanov, A., & Kessler, A. (2013). *A friend in need is a friend indeed: Theory and evidence on the (dis)advantages of informal loans.* Simon Fraser University, Department of Economics Working Papers. Retrieved from http://www.sfu.ca/econ-research/RePEc/sfu/ sfudps/dp13-03.pdf

Karaivanov, A., & Kessler, S. (2017). *(Dis)Advantages of Informal Loans – Theory and Evidence.* May. Retrieved from http://www.sfu.ca/~akaraiva/KKpaper_current.pdf

Khan, A. A. (2008). *Islamic microfinance: Theory, policy and practice.* Birmingham: Islamic Relief Worldwide.

Khan, M. A. (1989). *Economic teachings of prophet Muhammad.* Islamabad: International Institute of Islamic Economics and Institute of Policy Studies.

Khandelwal, P. (2010). Money lender drives man to commit suicide. In *Hindustan Times*, August 12. Retrieved from http://www.hindustantimes.com/delhi/money-lender-drives-man-to-commit-suicide/story-KSixMHviIbkhvUTcoiqZ1H.html

Kondo, M. (2003). The "bombay 5-6": Last resource informal financiers for Philippine micro-enterprises. *Kyoto Review of Southeast Asia*, Issue 4, October.

Lakic, V. (n.d.). Colombia Loan Shark Network Booming in Mexico. Retrieved from https://www.occrp.org/en/daily/6910-colombia-loan-shark-network-booming-in-mexico

Leong, K., Li, H., & Xu, H. (2018). *Exploiting the unbanked: Evidence from Singapore's unlicensed moneylending market.* Discussion Paper Series IZA DP No. 11786. IZA Institute of Labor Economics. August.

Llanto, G. M., & Fukui, R. (2003). *Rural finance and microfinance development in transition countries in Southeast and East Asia.* PIDS Discussion Paper Series, No. 2003-12, Philippine Institute for Development Studies (PIDS), Makati City.

LOAN SHARK. meaning in the Cambridge English Dictionary. (n.d.). Retrieved from https://dictionary.cambridge.org/dictionary/english/loan-shark

Loan sharks trap poor people. (n.d.). Retrieved from http://vietnamnews.vn/society/482580/loan-sharks-traps-poor-people.html#259EbmV0HFO01xAX.99

Mahanti, J. (2008). *Women Helping Women Through Nano Finance Institution.* Retrieved from http://www.ashanet.org/detroit/Projects/BISWA/Nano_Finance_Report_ Jan2008.pdf

Mallick, D. (2009). Microfinance and moneylender interest rate: Evidence from Bangladesh. Munich Personal RePEc Archive (MPRA). May. Retrieved from http://mpra.ub.uni-muenchen.de/17800/

Mallick, D. (2012). Microfinance and moneylender interest rate: Evidence from Bangladesh. *World Development, 40*(6), 1181–1189. doi:10.1016/j.worlddev.2011.12.011

Mayer, R. (2010). *Quick cash: The story of the loan shark.* Illinois: Northern Illinois University Press.

Mayer, R. (2012). Loan sharks, interest-rate caps, and deregulation. *Washington and Lee Law Review, 69*(2), Article 10, Spring 3-1, 807-845.

Meyer, R. L. (2002). *Track record of financial institutions in assisting the poor in Asia.* Asian Development Bank (ADB) Institute Research Paper 49, December. Tokyo: ADB.

Mitra, S. K. (2009). Exploitative microfinance interest rates. *Asian Social Science, 5*(5). doi:10.5539/ass.v5n5p87

Murakami, S. (2013). Social capital in Vietnam, Cambodia and Laos. *The Senshu Social Capital Review* No. 4, 65-110.

Musari, K. (2016a). *Nanofinance, redefine the microfinance for the very micro society.* A poster was presented at the 13th Indonesian Regional Science Association International Institute (IRSA) and was hosted by Department of Economics, Faculty of Economics and Business, Brawijaya University, at Atria Hotel, Malang. July 25-26.

Musari, K. (2016b). Economic sustainability for Islamic nanofinance through sukuk-waqf linkage program (Case study in Indonesia). [IJISEF]. *International Journal of Islamic Economics and Finance Studies, 2*(3), 83–94.

Musari, K. (2016c). *Redefining the Islamic nanofinance and its institutional strengthening: Lesson learned from Asian countries.* A paper was presented at 11th International Conference on Islamic Economics and Finance (ICIEF) "Rethinking Islamic Economics and Finance: Paving The Way Forward for Inclusive and Sustainable Development" with Organizer and Host Institution Kulliyyah of Economics and Management Sciences International Islamic University Malaysia (IIUM) and Co-Organizers Islamic Research and Training Institute (IRTI), Islamic Development Bank (IDB) and International Association of Islamic Economics (IAIE), Kuala Lumpur. October 11-13.

Musari, K. (2016d). Yuk, Perangi Riba, & Rentenir! In Jawa Pos Radar Jember Daily Newspaper, Perspektif. July 18. pp. 1, 11.

Musari, K. (2017). *Nanofinance, addressing the Islamic microfinance gap through global Islamic humanitarian institution.* E-Proceedings of Conference on Philanthropy for Humanitarian Aid 2017 "Philantrophy for Humanitarian Aid as Mechanism to Alleviate Poverty and Maintain Human Dignity" held by International Research Centre of Islamic Economics and Finance (IRCIEF) International Islamic University College Selangor (KUIS) in collaboration with Islamic Research and Training Institute (IRTI) International Islamic Development Bank (IDB) and Sultan Sharif Ali Islamic University (UNISSA) at UNISSA, Brunei Darussalam, May 23-24, 170-183.

Musari, K. (2018). Menyambut BUMDes Center dan Bank Wakaf Mikro. In Jawa Pos Radar Jember Daily Newspaper, Perspektif. September 14, pp. 21 and 31.

Musari, K. (2019). Promoting qard al-hasan in nanofinance to counter the moneylender in Southeast Asia. *Studia Islamica, 26*(1), 1–16. doi:10.15408di.v26i1.5990

Musari, K., & Simanjuntak, R. (2015). *Reconstruction the bank for poor family through Islamic linkage program (Case study in Indonesia).* A paper was presented at 4th International Conference on "Inclusive Islamic Financial Sector Development" held by Islamic Research and Training Institute Islamic Development Bank (IRTI-IDB) and International Islamic University (IIU) Islamabad at Faisal Mosque, IIU Islamabad, Pakistan. November 17-18.

Musari, K., & Simanjuntak, R. (2016). Nanofinance, redefinition of microfinance for the very micro society through philanthropy linkage program (Case study in Indonesia, Cambodia, Thailand, India). [AARJSH]. *Asian Academic Research Journal of Social Science and Humanities, 3*(4), 455–463.

Nadaraja, K. (2016). Malay reaction to the 1930s economic depression in Malaya. *Jebat: Malaysian Journal of History, Politics, & Strategy, 43*(1), 46–64.

Najeeb, S. F., & Lahsasna, A. (2016). Qard hasan: Its shari'ah rules and applications in Islamic finance. In H. Khalid, M. N. Barom, & N. S. Shirazi. (2016). Essential Perspectives in Islamic Economics and Finance. Kuala Lumpur: Kulliyyah of Economics and Management Sciences, International Islamic University Malaysia (IIUM).

Obaidullah, M. (2008). Introduction to Islamic microfinance. India: The Islamic Business and Finance Network (IBF Net) and Islamic Relief Worldwide.

Obaidullah, M., & Khan, T. (2008). Islamic microfinance development: Challenges and initiatives. Policy Dialogue Paper No. 2. Jeddah: Islamic Research and Training Institute (IRTI) Islamic Development Bank (IDB).

OJK. (2018). *Bank wakaf mikro, program pemberdayaan masyarakat melalui pendirian bank wakaf mikro - LKM Syariah.* A public socialization material by Financial Services Authority (OJK) in Forum Merdeka Barat 9, March 27.

Ovesen, J., & Trankell, I. (2014). Symbiosis of microcredit and private moneylending in Cambodia. *The Asia Pacific Journal of Anthropology, 15*(2), 178–196. doi:10.1080/14442213.2014.894116

Packman, C. (2014). *Payday lending: Global growth of the high-cost credit market.* New York: Palgrave Macmillan. doi:10.1057/9781137361103

Parpart, E. (2014). BOT Considers 'Nano-Financing' for Grass-Roots People. *Nation (New York, N.Y.), 25*(October). Retrieved from http://www.nationmultimedia.com/business/BOT-considers-nano-financing-for-grass-roots-peopl-30246202.html

Robinson, M. S. (2001). The microfinance revolution: Sustainable finance for the poor. Washington: International Bank for Reconstruction and Development (IBRD)-World Bank. doi:10.1596/0-8213-4524-9

Sakai, K. (2008). Headwinds lashing Japan's moneylenders. In *Finance, Japan Spotlight,* November/December. pp. 50-51. Retrieved from https://www.jef.or.jp/journal/jef_contents_ pdfloader.asp?c=3547andt=

Sandman, J. (n.d.). The New Loan Sharks: Payday Lenders Have More Tricks Up Their Sleeves - AARP ... Retrieved from https://www.aarp.org/money/scams-fraud/info-12-2012/the-new-loan-sharks.html

Schrader, H. (1994). Money Lenders and Merchant Bankers in India and Indonesia. In F. J. A. Bouman, & O. Hospes (Eds.), Financial landscapes reconstructed: The fine art of mapping development. Colorado and Oxford: Westview Press. pp. 341-356.

Secretariat, A. S. E. A. N. (2018). *ASEAN key figures 2018, December*. Jakarta: ASEAN Secretariat.

Seibel, H. D., Llanto, G., & Quiñones, B. (2000). *How values create value: Social capital in microfinance - the case of the Philippines*. Working Paper, No. 2000,2, Universität zu Köln, Arbeitsstelle für Entwicklungsländerforschung (AEF), Köln. May.

Seibel, H. D., & Kunkel, C. R. (1999). *Microfinance in Laos: A case for women's banking?* Working Paper, No. 1999,3, Universität zu Köln, Arbeitsstelle für Entwicklungsländerforschung (AEF), Köln.

Suppiah, U. (2014). *History of moneylending during British era: A case study of chettiars as the major money lenders*. A conference paper in 23th International Conference of Historians of Asia 2014 (IAHA2014) held by Universiti Utara Malaysia and Malaysian Historical Society, August 23-27, in Alor Setar, Kedah, Malaysia, 850-867.

Suppiah, U., & Raja, S. S. (2013). Sejarah asal-usul dan kegiatan ekonomi chettiar di Tanah Melayu. *Jebat: Malaysian Journal of History, Politics, and Strategy*, *40*(1), 63–90.

Tiwary, D. (2017). In 80% farmer-suicides due to debt, loans from banks, not moneylenders. In *Indian Express,* January 7. Retrieved from http://indianexpress.com /article/india/in-80-farmer-suicides-due-to-debt-loans-from-banks-not-moneylenders-4462930/

Turnell, S. (2005). A Survey of Microfinance Institutions in Burma. *Burma Economic Watch*, *1*, 26–50.

Vathana, R. T. M. S., Dalis, P., Bopharath, S., & Dorina, P. (2016). *Credit access, multiple sources of borrowings and household wellbeing: The case of eleven villages in Cambodia*. Final Report for Partnership for Economic Policy (PEP) with funding from the Department for International Development (DFID) of the United Kingdom (or UK Aid), and the Government of Canada through the International Development Research Center (IDRC). May.

Vuong, Q. H. (2014). *Vietnam's political economy: A discussion on the 1986-2016 period*. Centre Emile Bernheim (CEB) Working Paper No. 14/010, May. Solvay Brussels School of Economics and Management, Université Libre de Bruxelles. Brussels, Belgium.

White, L. (2018, September 4). Police hunt loan sharks riding Britain's rising tide of debt. Retrieved from https://www.reuters.com/article/us-britain-lending-loansharks/police-hunt-loan-sharks-riding-britains-rising-tide-of-debt-idUSKCN1LK1LX

Zapata, N. R. (2006). Credit decision and rationing rules: A study of informal lenders in the Philippines. *Philippine Management Review, 13*, 117–126.

Zauro, N. A., Saad, R. A. J., & Sawandi, N. (2016). The moderating effects of financial inclusion on qardhul hassan financing acceptance in Nigeria: A proposed framework. *International Journal of Economics and Financial Issues, 6*(S7), 143–148.

## ADDITIONAL READING

Gay, S. (2001). *The moneylenders of late medieval Kyoto*. Honolulu: University of Hawai'i Press.

Madestam, A. (2014). Informal finance: A theory of moneylenders. *Journal of Development Economics* 107, Elsevier B.V., 157-174.

Pardieck, A. M. (2008). Japan and the moneylenders - Activist courts and substantive justice. *Pacific Rim Law & Policy Journal Association, 17*(3), 529–568.

Rosenberg, R. (2010). Does microcredit really help poor people? Focus Note 59. Washington: The Consultative Group to Assist the Poor (CGAP).

Rosenberg, R., Gaul, S., Ford, W., & Tomilova, O. (2013). *Microcredit interest rates and their determinants 2004-2011. Access to Finance Forum Reports by The Consultative Group to Assist the Poor (CGAP) and Its Partners No. 7, June*. Washington: CGAP.

Rosenberg, R., Gonzalez, A., & Narain, S. (2009). *The new moneylenders: Are the poor being exploited by high microcredit interest rates?* Occasional Paper The Consultative Group to Assist the Poor (CGAP) No. 15. February. Washington: CGAP.

## KEY TERMS AND DEFINITIONS

***Ah Long***: A Cantonese phrase; An informal term for illegal moneylenders in Malaysia and Singapore.

***Chettiars***: A Cantonese phrase; The main reputable moneylenders during the British era since the late 19$^{th}$ century.

**Nondeposit Taking:** Not managing public funds, in the form of deposits, savings, and similar products.

**Self-Help Group (SHG):** The initiative was developed by India several decades ago in order to alleviate poverty and improve women's ability to achieve rights and well-being. It carries out all the same functions as those required by the Grameen system but they do this on their own behalf, since the SHG is effectively a micro-bank, carrying out all the familiar intermediation tasks of savings mobilisation and lending.

**Social-Welfare Contracts:** Contracts between individuals and the society to promote the well-being and welfare of the less privileged. Although facilitation of such contracts is beyond the scope of intermediation, an intermediary can certainly offer community services by institutionalizing social-welfare contracts.

# Chapter 13
# Factors That Influence Retail Equity Investors to Patronize Islamic Stockbroking in Malaysia:
## An AHP Approach

**Muhamad Abduh**
https://orcid.org/0000-0002-1918-6525
*School of Business and Economics, Universiti Brunei Darussalam, Brunei*

**Faizal Asfan**
*Independent Researcher, Malaysia*

## ABSTRACT

*This study investigates factors that influence retail equity investors to patronize Islamic stockbroking in Malaysia and ranks their level of importance using Analytical Hierarchy Process. Data are collected using questionnaire via online and offline survey among clients, individuals who work in the stockbroking industry and stockbroking related industry such as fund managers, unit trust managers, and mutual funds. The results show that religiosity and product awareness significantly influence the patronizing behavior of Malaysian retail equity investors. On the other hand, economic motives, convenience, social influence, and attractiveness of stock investment ranked below religiosity and product awareness. In view of the findings, stockbroking industry players such as investment bank, stockbroking firm, or participating organization should take advantage of the religiosity and product awareness factors as a main focus to develop Islamic stockbroking service in Malaysia. Sales, marketing and business development strategies can be designed according to the said criteria.*

DOI: 10.4018/978-1-7998-2257-8.ch013

## INTRODUCTION

A stockbroking service is an agency service which buys and sells shares on behalf of clients (principal) and is paid brokerage or commission for the service (Securities Commission, 2007). In other words, a stockbroking service provides a platform or an avenue for investors to trade securities listed in stock market. Besides the main broking service, Stockbroking Company also provides related or value-added services like placement of trust monies into investment instruments, collateralized trading, custodian services, research, underwriting, and e-broking.

Back in 1994, BIMB Securities Sdn Bhd, the first full-fledged Islamic Stockbroking in Malaysia was incorporated in order to provide stockbroking and related activities based on *Shariah* principles. In September 2007, Bursa Malaysia released its 'Best Practices in Islamic Stockbroking Services Undertaken by Participating Organizations' (Securities Commission, 2007) and as a result, from 2008 onwards, most of the top stockbroking companies in Malaysia have answered the call by the government to establish Islamic Stockbroking windows. Among the Participating Organizations who have established Islamic Stockbroking windows are AmInvestment Bank Berhad, Affin Investment Bank Berhad, CIMB Investment Bank Berhad, Maybank Investment Bank Berhad and Jupiter Securities Sendirian Berhad. In total, there are 15 licensed Participating Organizations offering Islamic Stockbroking (Shah, 2018).

Islamic scholars had confirmed that there are prohibited elements in Conventional Stockbroking such as trading and pledging of non-halal shares, *riba* (interest) in the forms of contra service charge and interest charge for late and default in payment, conventional ways of banking, borrowing and placement, mixing of halal and non-halal funds in transactions and records. Hence, Islamic Stockbroking service which can defined as *wakalah* (agency) service which buys and sells shares on behalf of *muwakkil* (client) and is paid brokerage or commission for the service based on *Shariah* Principles was introduced. The main *Shariah* principles applied in Islamic stockbroking service are *wakalah* (agency) which is applied on stock broking service and on arrangement and placement of client's trust monies, *Rahn* (collateral) which is applied on collateralized trading, *kafalah* (guarantee) which is on remisier's indemnity and *bai'* which is incorporated on the purchase and sale of shares activity.

Islamic stockbroking services have some benefits over the conventional counterpart. First, the lower *ta'widh* (compensation) and *gharamah* (penalty) rate to be charged on default and late payment (Malaysian ICM, 2013). The *ta'widh* rate may range from 2% to 8% per annum based on the Islamic Interbank Money Market rate or any rate used by respective stockbroking companies while in conventional stockbroking, the rate may range from 8% to 12% per annum. Secondly, the absence of contra service charge. Contra trading exist when seller sells his shares before payment has been made for his purchase of the shares earlier within the settlement due date, currently on T+3, where T is the transaction days and 3 represents the number of trading days. The conventional stockbroking contra service charge may range from 8% – 12% per annum on the transaction value. Thirdly, the activities of Islamic stock broking service are free from non-*Shariah* compliant issues. All *Shariah* controls have been put in place, from the opening of the trading account, settlement and until the tail end.

Islamic capital market has expanded in many areas covering wide range of products and services, bigger number and diversity of stakeholders, infrastructures, geographical reach and human capital development. Malaysia's Islamic capital market offers wide range of products and services such as *Shariah*-compliant securities, *sukuk* (Islamic bond), unit trusts, exchange traded fund, real estate investment fund, fund management and stock broking services. In view of the fast growth and extensive Malaysia's Islamic capital market development, it is important to conduct researches which can support the efforts. Hence, this study is aimed at exploring one of the most important topics in the industry i.e. factors influencing investors to patronize Islamic capital market, specifically in Islamic stockbroking industry.

The structure of the paper is as follows. Section two describes related studies on Islamic capital market products' selection criteria and section three discuss the data and methods used in the analysis. Findings and discussion will be elaborated in section four and conclusion is presented in section five.

## LITERATURE REVIEW

(Karim, 2010) investigates the relationship between investors' characteristics and their choices upon Islamic funds in Malaysian markets. The study has confirmed that economic-related reasons i.e. profit maximization, enhancing competitive advantage and marketing strategy are the main motives in selecting the fund. Meanwhile, religious reason is placed as secondary motive behind fund management companies offering Islamic funds. As an additional point, with regards to economic factor, (Mahfouz, 2012) confirms that non-financial socially responsible, ethics, and beliefs screening criteria do not influence the investment decision which implies that there is no investment restrictions considered by the investors. Rational investors aim to achieve highest profit with the lowest risk.

(Hassan, 2005) evidences that Islamic ethical investors consider both Islamic ethical and financial motivation when they evaluate investments. This ensures that the securities chosen provides them profit while meeting their value system and beliefs. The study also marks that *Shariah* screening do not necessarily have an adverse impact on the funds' performances. In fact, most of the Islamic screened portfolios are able to show higher expected returns than the conventional portfolios. (Jamaludin, Smith, & Gerrans, 2012) explores the mutual fund selection criteria for Malaysian Muslims and non-Muslims who are members of EPF (Employees Provident Fund). The Malaysian EPF permits its members to invest part of their retirement savings into external mutual funds. The results have shown that non-Muslims retail investors look into past performances of the funds while Muslims investors prefer funds that are *Shariah*-compliant.

Managing one's own stocks portfolio can be cheaper than paying a mutual fund manager and is also tax efficient as the timing of trading stocks is within the owner's control (Burton, 1998). This signifies that saving cost of investment is also an important factor in stock investment. Investors are in control and the timing of trading i.e. buying and selling shares is up to the investors themselves. These are components of convenience that investors may be looking for in stock investment. With regard to this convenience issues, (Gopi & Ramayah, 2007) studies the applicability of theory planned behavior in predicting the intention to trade online and found that e-trading being convenience and referent group or individuals increases the favorable attitude towards internet stock trading.

In relation to investors' risk perception upon investing in stock market, (Chen, Cheng, & Lee, 2011) investigates Taiwanese investors' asset preferences and investment criteria. The study has found that Taiwanese investors' focus on risk tolerance factor and they prefer mutual funds when they consider market environment and risk tolerance. Few years ago, Bursa Malaysia found that 61.0% potential retail investors did not know how to invest in the stock market and about 48.0% of non-investors perceived that stock market investment is highly risk (Wan Omar & Mohd Ali, 2010).

Since 2005, retail participation is only in the range of 24 per cent to 37 per cent. The rest was heavily participated by institutional funds. Out of the individual investors, 40% are investors with age below 35, 37% are investors with age between 35 and 45, and other groups are about 23% (Securities Commission, 2017). (Yang & Fang, 2005) investigates customers' review upon securities brokerage services and confirms that ease of use is the major driver for customer satisfaction.

The aforementioned studies had confirmed that factors influence equity investors to patronize fund management and stock broking industry includes economic motives like profits and losses, convenience issues, awareness on values of religion, social influence or the influence of people perceived importance, product awareness like risks involved with the product offered, and attractiveness of stock investment. These factors will be tested in the next section and eventually ranked based on the importance level revealed by respondents.

## DATA AND METHODS

### Data

The primary data are collected via online and offline survey. More than five hundreds questionnaires were distributed to the clients, individuals who work in the stock broking industry and stock broking related industry such as fund managers, unit trust managers, research houses, mutual funds, members of the public who trade shares, alumni groups, employees of listed companies which have issued IPO (Initial Public Offering) before, share investment groups in Facebook and other platforms. Respondents will be screened whether they have or used to have a share trading account in Malaysia and the type of their main share trading account i.e. Islamic, Conventional or both main Islamic and Conventional trading account. The respondents who do not have any share trading account will be excluded as they are not our relevant or target respondents.

The questionnaire was developed purposely to extract information on retail investors' stockbroking selection criteria. It is divided into four sections. Section one incorporated the demographic information of the respondents such as gender, age, marital status, ethic, religion, highest education, employment and total annual income. Section two covers questions on share investment background that can provide a better understanding on investors' patronizing behavior. Section three is the most important section where it is divided into six sub-sections i.e. Criterion one - economic reasons, criterion two – convenience, criterion three – religiosity, criterion four – social influence, criterion five – product awareness and criterion six – attractiveness of stock investment.

Subsection – criterion one – economic motives may assist us to understand investors' patronizing behavior relating to the influence of economic factors such as profit expected et cetera. Next on convenience, it helps us to understand whether the convenience factors influence investors in choosing stockbroking service. Third, religiosity part was designed to understand the respondents' *Shariah* awareness (knowledge) and *Shariah* compliance readiness (willingness to support, follow, abide and commit) to *Shariah* principles. Then criterion four on social influence, this subsection provides the information upon the influence of people perceived importance on the investors' investment decision. Next, product awareness – may tell us if investors are aware of the existence of Islamic stock broking and understand the risks involved of the said products. Last, subsection – criterion six – attractiveness of stock investment will help us ascertain whether direct stock market investment (not via fund manager or mutual fund manager) is still attractive to investors. The fourth section of the questionnaire has two questions only i.e. whether or not respondents will choose to open and/or maintain Islamic trading account.

## Methods

Basically, customers or investors' patronizing behavior involve very complex decisions. There are many criteria, alternatives, and options that need to be considered at multiple levels to make the best decision. In view of that, this paper decided to employ Analytical Hierarchical Process (AHP) developed by Thomas Saaty in the 1970s. AHP can be used for complex decision-making process and be applied in many areas such as strategic planning, allocation of resources, selection of sources, policies, selection of program et cetera (Alexander, 2012).

AHP assesses, prioritizes, ranks and evaluates decision choices. Through certain steps that will be discussed below, the geometric means shall be assigned to each criterion as criteria weights. These criteria weights represent significance values for each criterion and can be ranked based on the respective weights assigned. Hence, AHP can assist to achieve research objective that is to identify and rank the significant factors influencing investors' selection.

Data collected will be analyzed using AHP spreadsheets programmed in Microsoft Excel. Microsoft Excel is used to replace the AHP software developed by Expert Choice because Expert Choice is programmed with pairwise comparison. On the other hand, the Likert 5-scale questionnaire developed earlier do not incorporate pairwise comparison. Therefore, a transformation of Likert scale data has to be made to fit into AHP requirement. Hence, a modified AHP programming is developed in Microsoft Excel for data analysis purposes (Kallas, 2010). The following steps are incorporated to analyze the data using a modified AHP:

**Step 1.** Scores given by the respondents in Likert 5-scale questionnaires are being averaged according to respective criteria. For question 17 to 21, the scores are being averaged to get a score for Economic reasons criteria, score criteria number one, Sc1. Then, averaging scores for questions 22 to 26 will give an average score for convenience criteria, score criteria number two, Sc2. Next, an average score for criteria number three, Sc3, religiosity criteria, questions 29 – 34 will be considered. Then, score for Sc4 on social influence criteria, scores of questions 37 to 40 to be averaged. For Sc5 product awareness, scores of questions 41, 43 to 49 to be averaged and for score Sc6 attractiveness of stock investment respectively, scores of questions 50, 51 to 57 were counted.

**Step 2.** As mentioned earlier, pairwise comparison was not incorporated into the questionnaires distributed to the respondents. So, for replacement, Likert Scale comparison is introduced that will show the difference of relative importance. To simulate the traditional AHP pairwise comparison between criteria i and criteria j, this formula, $a_{ij}$ = [Sci – Scj] + 1 will be incorporated into a matrix to find the difference of relative importance for the criteria as seen in Table 1.

*Table 1. Step 2 – Formula of difference of relative importance of Likert scale comparison*

| | Econ | Conv | Rel | Soc | PrAw | Att |
|---|---|---|---|---|---|---|
| Econ | =(Sc1-Sc1)+1 | =(Sc1-Sc2)+1 | =(Sc1-Sc3)+1 | =(Sc1-Sc4)+1 | =(Sc1-Sc5)+1 | =(Sc1-Sc6)+1 |
| Conv | =(Sc2-Sc1)+1 | =(Sc2-Sc2)+1 | =(Sc2-Sc3)+1 | =(Sc2-Sc4)+1 | =(Sc2-Sc5)+1 | =(Sc2-Sc6)+1 |
| Rel | =(Sc3-Sc1)+1 | =(Sc3-Sc2)+1 | =(Sc3-Sc3)+1 | =(Sc3-Sc4)+1 | =(Sc3-Sc5)+1 | =(Sc3-Sc6)+1 |
| Soc | =(Sc4-Sc1)+1 | =(Sc4-Sc2)+1 | =(Sc4-Sc3)+1 | =(Sc4-Sc4)+1 | =(Sc4-Sc5)+1 | =(Sc4-Sc6)+1 |
| PrAw | =(Sc5-Sc1)+1 | =(Sc5-Sc2)+1 | =(Sc5-Sc3)+1 | =(Sc5-Sc4)+1 | =(Sc5-Sc5)+1 | =(Sc5-Sc6)+1 |
| Att | =(Sc6-Sc1)+1 | =(Sc6-Sc2)+1 | =(Sc6-Sc3)+1 | =(Sc6-Sc4)+1 | =(Sc6-Sc5)+1 | =(Sc6-Sc6)+1 |

Note: $a_{ij} = (Sc_i - Sc_j)+1$

**Step 3.** Upon getting the difference of relative importance from the matrix, the geometric mean for each criterion is then calculated. Two options to estimate the weights namely the geometric mean and the main eigenvector. The calculated geometric means are then normalized to get the normalized weight for each criterion (Perera & Sutrisna, 2010).

**Step 4.** Final step is to insert the criteria weights into the goal hierarchy. Afterwards, the weights supporting the super goal that is selecting a stockbroking service can be found. The larger the rating, the more the preference given.

## FINDINGS AND DISCUSSION

AHP shows the weights of the demand factors and ranks those factors by showing the priority of the factors influencing the respondents. Frequency distribution tables were also used to show some categories of the data such as demographic characteristics of the respondents, share investment background, and some additional information such as education, product awareness and investment preference. The information with regard to respondents' demography is provided in Table 2.

Table 2 shows that male respondents represent more than 70% while female respondents cover nearly 29%. The biggest age group are those in the range of 36 – 45 years old and those in the range of 18 – 35 and 46 -55 represented 31.4% and 12.4% respectively. Only 3.3% of the participants are more than 55 years old. Furthermore, about 78.5% of the respondents are married while nearly 20% of them are singles

*Table 2. Respondents' demography*

| Characteristics | | Frequency | % | Cumulative (%) |
|---|---|---|---|---|
| Gender | Male | 86 | 71.1% | 71.1% |
| | Female | 35 | 28.9% | 100.0% |
| Age | 18 - 35 | 38 | 31.4% | 31.4% |
| | 36 - 45 | 64 | 52.9% | 84.3% |
| | 46 - 55 | 15 | 12.4% | 96.7% |
| | >55 | 4 | 3.3% | 100.0% |
| Marital | Single | 24 | 19.8% | 19.8% |
| | Married | 95 | 78.5% | 98.3% |
| | Other | 2 | 1.7% | 100.0% |
| Ethnic | Malay | 105 | 86.8% | 86.8% |
| | Chinese | 14 | 11.6% | 98.3% |
| | Indian | 0 | 0.0% | 98.3% |
| | Other | 2 | 1.7% | 100.0% |
| Religion | Islam | 101 | 83.5% | 83.5% |
| | Buddhism | 9 | 7.4% | 90.9% |
| | Christianity | 4 | 3.3% | 94.2% |
| | Hinduism | 0 | 0.0% | 94.2% |
| | Others | 7 | 5.8% | 100.0% |
| Highest Education | Certificate | 19 | 15.7% | 15.7% |
| | Diploma | 5 | 4.1% | 19.8% |
| | Bachelor | 68 | 56.2% | 76.0% |
| | Master | 22 | 18.2% | 94.2% |
| | Professional | 1 | 0.8% | 95.0% |
| | Phd | 1 | 0.8% | 95.9% |
| | Pondok | 2 | 1.7% | 97.5% |
| | Other | 3 | 2.5% | 100.0% |
| Employment | Self-Employed | 8 | 6.6% | 6.6% |
| | Salaried / Commissioned / Waged etc | 105 | 86.8% | 93.4% |
| | Investment Income | 2 | 1.7% | 95.0% |
| | Allowance - student, family, govt etc | 2 | 1.7% | 96.7% |
| | Retired | 1 | 0.8% | 97.5% |
| | Unemployed | 1 | 0.8% | 98.3% |
| | Other | 2 | 1.7% | 100.0% |

*continued on following page*

*Table 2. Continued*

| Characteristics | | Frequency | % | Cumulative (%) |
|---|---|---|---|---|
| Total Annual Income* | < RM25,000 | 10 | 8.3% | 8.3% |
| | RM25,000 - RM50,000 | 30 | 24.8% | 33.1% |
| | RM50,000 - RM100,000 | 33 | 27.3% | 60.3% |
| | > RM100,000 | 36 | 29.8% | 90.1% |
| | Other | 12 | 9.9% | 100.0% |
| * US$ 1 =RM 3 (Malaysian Ringgit) | | | | |

and a small portion may have other marital status reasons. In terms of ethnicity, Malay represented the largest group with a percentage of 86.8%. The Chinese on the other hand cover 11.6% and other races represented only 1.7%.

As majority of the respondents are Malay, it is not surprised that majority of them are also Muslims. About 7.4% of them are Buddhists, 3.3% are Christians, 0% Hindus and about 5.8% represented the "Others" group. The largest group had completed their bachelor degree (56.2%) and the Master holders represented the second largest group with 18.2%. Next, 15.7% of the respondents are certificate holders, 4.1% are diploma holder and 1 one them completed the professional accounting exam and another one a PhD holder. About 1.7% went to Pondok (informal Islamic school).

Most of the respondents earn salary, commission or wage. That made up close to 87%. About 6.6% of the respondents are self-employed and the remaining groups ie. Investment income, allowance-student, family, government etc., retired, unemployed and other covered less than 2%. The data shows that most of the respondents (about 81.8%) earn their annual income in the range of RM25,000 – RM50,000 (24.8%), RM50,000 – RM100,000 (27.3%) and more than RM100,000 (29.8%). Approximately

*Table 3. Difference of relative importance of Likert scale comparison*

| | Econ | Conv | Rel | Soc | PrAw | Att |
|---|---|---|---|---|---|---|
| Econ | 1 | 0.9074 | -0.4441 | 1.0442 | -0.3184 | 0.5422 |
| Conv | 1.0926 | 1 | -0.3515 | 1.1368 | -0.2258 | 0.6348 |
| Rel | 2.4441 | 2.3515 | 1 | 2.4883 | 1.1257 | 1.9863 |
| Soc | 0.9558 | 0.8632 | -0.4883 | 1 | -0.3626 | 0.498 |
| Pr.Aw | 2.3184 | 2.2258 | 0.8743 | 2.3626 | 1 | 1.8606 |
| Att | 1.4578 | 1.3652 | 0.0137 | 1.502 | 0.1394 | 1 |

Note: $a_{ij} = (Sc_i - Sc_j)+1$

*Table 4. Geometric mean for all criteria*

| Criteria | Geometric Mean | Normalized Weights |
|---|---|---|
| Econ. | 0.4173 | 0.0572 |
| Conv. | 0.3970 | 0.0545 |
| Rel. | 3.1740 | 0.4353 |
| Soc. | 0.4175 | 0.0573 |
| Pr.Aw. | 2.7068 | 0.3712 |
| Att. | 0.1787 | 0.0245 |

Normalized weight i = (Geo.mean for Criteria i) / (Sum of Geo.mean)

one-fifth of the respondents earn less than RM25,000 (8.3%) and earn in other annual income range (9.9%).

Table 3 displays the matrix of difference of relative importance of Likert scale comparison and Table 4 exhibits calculated Geometric means for all criteria. Results from the AHP shows that religiosity and product awareness are the two main factors representing the selection criteria of the 121 respondents. Religiosity and product awareness cover more than 80% of the selection criteria.

Interestingly, Table 5 shows that retail equity investors in Malaysia consider religiosity as the main selection criteria. Religiosity scored 0.4353 and placed at the top of the criteria ranking. Religiosity here does not measure the *Shariah* belief but the *Shariah* awareness and the readiness to comply with *Shariah* requirement and prohibition. This implies majority of the respondents are aware and have basic knowledge on *Shariah* principles. Referring to Table 2, this could be happened due to majority of the respondents are Muslim (83.5%).

The score for product awareness is 37.12% and thus, product awareness is considered the second most influencing factor in selecting the stockbroking service. The result shows that adequate disseminated information regarding the product in

*Table 5. Results of criteria ranking using AHP*

| | Criteria Ranking | |
|---|---|---|
| 1 | Religiosity | 0.4353 |
| 2 | Product Awareness | 0.3712 |
| 3 | Social Influence | 0.0573 |
| 4 | Economic Motives | 0.0572 |
| 5 | Convenience | 0.0545 |
| 6 | Attractiveness | 0.0245 |

financial markets which is reflected by product awareness criteria plays an important role on the respondents' decision-making.

Social influence i.e. recommendation from family and friends; economic motives i.e. profit, rate of return, cost, switching costs, subsidies; and convenience i.e. branch offices, parking space, ATM machines and online services criteria almost have the same weights where social influence factor lead with 5.73%, economic motive factor scored 5.72% and convenience factor with 5.45%. Those three factors have approximately the same level of influence on the respondents' decision-making process in stockbroking selection and these three factors are considered far less important than religiosity and product awareness in stockbroking selection. Finally, the attractiveness of direct stock market investment has the lowest weight of 0.0245. This means attractiveness of direct stock market investment is far less important than the other five criteria in the decision-making hierarchy of investors in choosing a stockbroking service.

## CONCLUSION

This study analyzes factors influencing retail investors to patronize Islamic stockbroking in Malaysia through a survey which was conducted online and offline. Analytic Hierarchy Process was used to statistically rank those factors or criteria influencing the decision in selecting the service. The study reveals that awareness upon *shariah* principles (religiosity) and product awareness significantly influenced the patronizing behavior of Malaysian retail equity investors on Islamic stockbroking. On the other hand, economic motives, convenience, social influence and attractiveness of stock investment ranked below religiosity and product awareness. Interestingly, though religiosity was found to be the main factor, only 25.6% of the respondents own Islamic share trading accounts only and 49.6% own conventional share trading accounts only. The remaining 24.8% own both Islamic and conventional share trading accounts. This shows that even if only 25.6%, these investors are very consistent and committed to invest only in *shariah* approved stocks while remaining investors may have dynamic decision following the situation.

Insufficient literatures available pertaining to the issue of demand on Islamic stockbroking in Malaysia is one of the limitations in this study. Perhaps, this could be due to the participation of Islamic stockbroking in Malaysian's stock market is considered to be new and far behind the well-established conventional stockbroking. Even though, BIMB Securities was long established back in 1994, Islamic stockbroking was not so popular until recently when the top investment banks began to set-up their respective Islamic stockbroking windows.

Second limitation could be on the variables selected in this study which may only be applied for the Islamic stockbroking in Malaysia. Furthermore, in order to obtain more comprehensive results, sampling can be extended to different types of clients like those supporting conventional stockbroking, foreign investors, Government-Linked Companies, et cetera. Further breakdown on the clients can also be made based on different trading techniques or methods of clients like investors, traders and punters.

In view of the possible implication of the findings, stock broking industry players such as investment bank, stockbroking firm or participating organization should take advantage of the religiosity and product awareness factors as a main focus to develop Islamic stock broking service in Malaysia. Sales, marketing and business development strategies can be designed according to the said criteria.

## REFERENCES

Alexander, M. (2012). *Decision-Making using the Analytic Hierarchy Process (AHP) and SAS / IML* (pp. 1–12). Baltimore, MD: Social Security Administration.

Burton, J. (1998). How, When, And Why To Buy Stocks. *Medical Economics*, *75*(13), 86–94.

Chen, A. H.-L., Cheng, K., & Lee, Z.-H. (2011). The behavior of Taiwanese investors in asset allocation. *Asia-Pacific Journal of Business Administration*, *3*(1), 62–74. doi:10.1108/17574321111116405

Gopi, M., & Ramayah, T. (2007). Applicability of theory of planned behavior in predicting intention to trade online: Some evidence from a developing country. *International Journal of Emerging Markets*, *2*(4), 348–360. doi:10.1108/17468800710824509

Hassan, A. (2005). *Evaluating the performance of managed funds: The cases of equity, ethical funds and Islamic index*. Durham Theses, Durham University, 1–293. Retrieved November 8, 2018 from http://etheses.dur.ac.uk/2731/

Jamaludin, N., Smith, M., & Gerrans, P. (2012). Mutual fund selection criteria: Evidence from Malaysia. *Asian Review of Accounting*, *20*(2), 140–151. doi:10.1108/13217341211242187

Kallas, Z. (2010). Butchers' Preferences for Rabbit Meat; AHP Pairwise Comparisons Versus a Likert Scale Valuation. Retrieved from https://www.semanticscholar.org/

Karim, M. R. A. (2010). *Analysing The Characteristics And Performance Of Islamic Funds: A Critical Review Of The Malaysian Case*. Durham Theses, Durham University, 1–366. Retrieved November 8, 2018 from http://etheses.dur.ac.uk/521/

Mahfouz, S. S. (2012). *Investment Characteristics Of Islamic Investment Portfolios: Evidence From Saudi Mutual Funds And Global Indices*. Durham Theses, Durham University, 1–277. Retrieved November 8, 2018 from http://etheses.dur.ac.uk/4440/

Malaysian, I. C. M. (2013). New Shariah Advisory Council Resolutions. *Bulletin on the Islamic Capital Market*, *8*(2), 3–6.

Perera, N., & Sutrisna, M. (2010). The Use of Analytic Hierarchy Process (AHP) in the Analysis of Delay Claims in Construction Projects in the UAE. *The Built & Human Environment Review*, *3*(1), 29–47.

Securities Commission. (2007). *Best Practices in Islamic Stockbroking Services undertaken by Participating Organisations*. Kuala Lumpur: Securities Commission.

Securities Commission. (2011). *List of Shariah-compliant Securities by the Shariah Advisory Council of the Securities Commission Malaysia*. Kuala Lumpur: Securities Commission.

Securities Commission. (2017). *Annual Report 2017*. Kuala Lumpur: Securities Commission.

Shah, S. A. (2018, November 26). Bursa includes UOB Kay Hian Securities in Islamic stockbroking list. *The Malaysian Reserve*. Retrieved from https://themalaysianreserve.com/

Wan Omar, M., & Mohd Ali, M. N. (2010). Brand Loyalty and Relationship Marketing in Islamic Banking System. *Canadian Social Science*, *6*(1), 25–32.

Yang, Z., & Fang, X. (2005). Online service quality dimensions and their relationships with satisfaction: A content analysis of customer reviews of securities brokerage services. *International Journal of Service Industry Management*, *15*(3), 302–326. doi:10.1108/09564230410540953

## ADDITIONAL READING

Abduh, M., & Omar, M. A. (2012). Islamic-Bank Selection Criteria in Malaysia: An AHP Approach. *Business Intelligence Journal*, *5*(2), 271–281.

Ali, S., Zani, R. M., & Kasim, K. (2014). Factors Influencing Investors' Behavior in Islamic Unit Trust: An Application of Theory of Planned Behaviour. *Journal of Islamic Economics, Banking, and Finance*, *10*(2), 183–201.

Nathie, M. (2009). Islamic Equity Investments: Determinants of Investment Behaviour of Malaysian Islamic Equity Investors under Conditions of Competing Alternatives. Griffith University Theses, 1-402.

## KEY TERMS AND DEFINITIONS

**Islamic Stockbroking:** a business in securities carried out by an Islamic participating organization on the stock market of Bursa Securities, whether on a fully ñedged basis or via an Islamic window service.

**Kafalah:** a contract made between the Bank and another party whereby the Bank agrees to discharge the liability of a third party in the case of default by the third party.

**Sukuk:** an Islamic financial certificate, similar to a bond in Western finance, that complies with Islamic religious law.

**Ta'widh:** all types of compensation or remuneration ('iwadh) charged or paid in relation to a commutative transaction or against damages inflicted on a contracting party due to a wrongdoing or negligence or carelessness by the counterparty.

**Wakalah:** an agency contract, where one party appoints another to conduct a defined legal action on his behalf, for a specified fee or commission.

# Chapter 14
# Post-Crisis Interdependence Between Islamic Unit Trust Funds and Islamic Stock Market in Malaysia

**Muhamad Abduh**
https://orcid.org/0000-0002-1918-6525
*School of Business and Economics, Universiti Brunei Darussalam, Brunei*

**Ruzanna Ramli**
*City University Malaysia, Malaysia*

## ABSTRACT

*This chapter evaluates short- and long-term relationships between 34 Islamic unit trusts and the Islamic stock market after the global financial crisis. The study collects data from Bloomberg's database from 2009 until 2012 and employs J-J cointegration to identify the long-term relationship while Granger causality test is used to investigate how the changes in Islamic stock market can influence the changes in Islamic unit trusts in the short term. The finding indicates that 61.76 percent out of the 34 Islamic unit trusts tested do not have long-term equilibrium with the Islamic stock market. Furthermore, only a few Islamic trusts responded to the changes in the Islamic stock market. This study is important for at least two reasons: its role in filling the gap in the literature of unit trust—stock markets nexus in Islamic finance; and its findings provide relevant information that can benefit investors and fund managers.*

DOI: 10.4018/978-1-7998-2257-8.ch014

## INTRODUCTION

Unit trust is defined as the pool of savings of many investors which is invested in collection of assets, such as stock and bonds managed by investment managers to achieve certain objectives (such as income and growth) with more efficient and slightly easier than picking directly from stocks or bonds market (Omar, Abduh, & Sukmana, 2013). The unit trust is beneficial especially for small or moderate investor that wish to prosper from financial markets but lack the knowledge, skill, time or expertise to invest directly in the financial markets. In Malaysia, the net asset value (NAV) of unit trust funds keep increasing from RM15.72 billion in 1992 to RM338.337 billion in November 2013, which is indicating the tremendous increase in demand for both the Islamic and conventional unit trusts.

During the subprime mortgage crisis in 2008, the Malaysian unit trust industry is holding up relatively well. As at the end of 2008, the total NAV of the unit trust industry was fell by RM34 billion as compared to RM169 billion in 2007. However, this decline is far less severe if compared to 40 percent drop in the market capitalization of Bursa Malaysia. As the end of 2009, NAV of unit trust industry decline from 19.65 percent to 19.18 percent but increase to 20.24 percent of Bursa Malaysia market capitalization at the end of November 2013.

As an alternative indirect investment product in financial markets, it is expected that the price movement of unit trust will reflect the changes in direct stock market investment. With regard to this, numerous studies had been done to investigate the price linkages between unit trust and stock markets in certain countries. However, none is found to be done within the Islamic financial market framework.

Therefore, this paper intends to investigate the price linkages between Islamic unit trusts and the Islamic stock market, particularly in Malaysia and after the global financial crisis. This paper will enrich the existing literature upon unit trust and stock markets nexus. The paper is organized as follows. The second section discusses the literature review and the third section explains the methods of analysis used in his study. The findings and discussion of the research and the conclusion are presented in section four and five respectively.

## LITERATURE REVIEW

In earlier study, (Bailey & Lim, 1992) investigated the correlation between country funds and foreign funds with the U.S. stock market. The result indicated the significant correlation between the return on country fund and US market index. Although the country funds have higher diversification level, the result revealed that the funds' pricing are more reflected on domestic US stock rather than foreign equity portfolios.

In the case of Australia, (Allen & MacDonald, 1995) investigated the relationship of stock index with 15 countries from year 1971 to 1992 using cointegration test. The results presented that there is no cointegration between Australia market with markets in Belgium, Austria, Italy, Malaysia, Japan, USA, Spain, Norway, Sweden and Singapore. The findings suggested that investors in Australia could diversify their portfolio investment into these countries to gain more benefit.

The price linkages between country funds listed in New York Stock Exchange (NYSE) with market indices in Germany, Japan and UK from December 1987 to February 1990 was examined by (Ben-Zion, Choi, & Hauser, 1996). The study used cointegration test and revealed that ther country funds are not cointegrated with local market indices in the three countries tested. This suggested that country funds are not perfectly reflecting national markets in the long run. However, Granger causality test for short-run dynamic showed that interdependence relationship exists between the country funds and the local market indices except with US market index.

In Spain, (Matallin & Nieto, 2002) found out only 11 out of 63 unit trust funds have cointegration with local stock markets Ibex 35, over the period 1995 to 1998. This is because most of the funds have been manage through market timing and security selection which leads to deviate from market index over time. Moreover, (Chu, 2010) said that the actively managed funds must diversify their investments in order to meet legal requirements, cash reimbursements or new stock applications which may increase the possibility of lack cointegration.

(Low & Ghazali, 2007) examined the price linkages between unit trust funds and the stock market index from 1996 to 2000 in Malaysia. The results indicated that there is no cointegration between the price of Malaysian unit trusts including two index funds significantly and the stock market in the long run. However, in the short run, the Granger causality test reported that changes in the local stock market Granger causes changes in the unit trust funds.

(Chu, 2010) evaluated the short and long run price linkages between Hong Kong Mandatory Provident Fund (MPF) and nine difference benchmark indices over the period of 2001 until 2008. The findings presented that some funds have both short and long run relationship with stock market indices. Furthermore, cointegration analysis between foreign equity fund and the local stock market index (Hang Seng Index) revealed that MPF may have global diversification benefit by investing in US and Japanese equity funds. (Chu, 2011) extended the study by examining the cointegration and causality of MPF price with Hang Seng Index (HIS) and other macroeconomic variables including the inflation rate, money supply and short-term interest rate from the period of 2001 until 2009. The bi-variate cointegration indicated that MPF have responded to stock market and inflation rate while multivariate cointegration displayed the cointegration between MPF with all the macroeconomic variables. The changes in MPF were Granger caused by HSI, inflation and money supply. Furthermore, the multivariate error correction model (ECM) of each fund on all macroeconomic variables reported that the funds price was not causal related with HIBOR. These findings suggested that any movements in selected macroeconomic variables can be used to predict the movement of MPF price except the changes in interest rate when reallocate the distribution between equity funds and other types of funds.

In Jordan, (Al-Jafari, Salameh, & Al-Asil, 2013) examined the relationship between unit trust funds and Amman Stock Exchange Index by using ECM and Granger causality tests. The data used were from March 2005 until November 2009. Similar to (Low & Ghazali, 2007), the findings revealed a significant long run influence of Amman Stock Index upon the unit trust funds but not vice versa.

(Alexakis, Dasilas, & Grose, 2013) scrutinized the dynamic interdependence between unit trust funds and stock index prices in Japan. The study had employed hidden cointegration analysis and crouching ECM to capture varied fund flow reaction upon the changes in stock index prices and. Similar to (Al-Jafari et al., 2013), the results evidenced that stock index prices and unit trust funds are cointegrated in the long run.

In Thailand, (Pojanavatee, 2013) investigated short run and long run price linkage between Thailand unit trust funds and local stock market from May 2005 to 31 December 2010. Based on Johansen cointegration test, there was no evidence of long run relationship between unit trust funds and Stock Exchange of Thailand SET100 Index. This indicated that the investors can benefit from diversifying in equity unit trust funds that managed by the eight major asset management companies. On the other hand, Granger causality test evidenced some dual causal link between equity unit trust funds and stock market. As unit trust funds companies are dominated by SET100 Index, investors can predict the price direction by observe the price movement in stock market.

The above literatures have shown various conclusion of the relationship between stock market index and unit trust funds in the conventional framework. However, as far as the author's know, studies investigating the linkages between Islamic stock markets index and Islamic unit trust funds are not yet in the literature.

This study is aimed at fulfilling the gap by investigating the price linkages between Islamic unit trust and Islamic stock market in Malaysia after the global financial crisis period, especially from the year of 2009 to 2012.

## DATA AND METHODS

### Data

This study uses daily closing price of 34 Islamic unit trusts which represent 17 management companies in Malaysia. FTSE Bursa Malaysia Emas Shariah Index is served as proxy for market returns from 2009 till 2012. All data were obtained from Bloomberg's database. The study employs cointegration test and Granger causality test to analyze the long run and short run price linkage between Islamic unit trust funds and the Islamic stock market represented by FTSE Bursa Malaysia Emas Shariah Index respectively.

### Methods

Augmented Dickey-Fuller (ADF) and Phillips-Perron (PP) will be delivered to test the stationarity of Islamic unit trust and market index to avoid spurious regression. A common non-stationary series (random walk) is denoted as:

$$y_t = y_{t-1} + \varepsilon_t$$

where $\varepsilon$ is a stationary random disturbance term. The series $y$ has a constant forecast value on time $t$, while the variance increases over time. The series at I(0) is stationary at the level form. However, the problem of non-stationarity can be eliminated by taking differences in the series. Therefore, the series is characterized by I(d) which means that the series need to be difference d times before becoming a stationary series. Typically, the series is tested at I(1)which means first-difference is required to achieve stationarity in the series as follows:

$$y_t - y_{t-1} = (1\text{-L})\, y_t = \varepsilon_t$$

The null hypothesis of unit root indicates the time series is non-stationary will be tested against the alternative hypothesis. If reject null hypotheses means any shock to the variable will temporarily deviate from its long run mean values. However, if accept the null hypotheses shows the deviation of the variable from long run mean values will be permanent.

The cointegration test between Islamic unit trusts and Islamic market index suggests that in the long run, their movement will be equilibrium although they have reacted differently in the short run. Each Islamic fund will be tested for possible existence of cointegration with Islamic index. Based on cointegration analysis, if the error term, $\varepsilon_t$ is stationary, the variables have long run equilibrium although they deviate each other during the short run. Thus, the deviations of Islamic unit trust funds can be dictated by Islamic market and will intersect in long run. The cointegration relationship can be represented by an error correction model (ECM) in the following equation:

$$\Delta FUND_t = \gamma\varepsilon_{t-1} + \sum_{j=1}^{\rho}\delta_J \Delta FUND_{t-J} + \sum_{j=1}^{q}\varphi_j \Delta SHARIAH\ INDEX_{t-j} + \nu_t$$

This study employs the VAR model which is developed by (Johansen, 1991). Based on (Akaike, 1971), it is necessary to determine the optimal lag length by using the Akaike's Information Criteria (AIC) in the VAR model. This study uses also trace statistic to report the existence of cointegration between two variables.

(Granger, 1969) introduced Granger causality to investigate the short run relationship between Islamic unit trust and Islamic stock market index. Besides that, the test also measure how much the current value of Islamic funds can be explained by its past values and stock market index as shown in the following equation:

$$\Delta FUND_t = \propto_0 + \sum_{j-1}^{J} \propto_J \Delta FUND_{t-J} + \sum_{k-1}^{k}\tau_k \Delta SHARIAH\ INDEX_{t-k} + \nu_t$$

In the one-way causality test, the null hypothesis is the independent does not Granger-cause dependent. Based on (Akaike, 1971), it is necessary to select the optimal lag structure in the regression and AIC will be used to select the optimal lag structure in this study. Furthermore, chi-squared value on the estimated lagged coefficients $\tau_k$ provides whether changes in Shariah index Granger causes changes in Islamic unit trust funds in the short run.

## FINDINGS AND DISCUSSION

The prerequisite of J-J cointegration test is to ensure all the series are stationary at first difference by using ADF and PP unit root tests. Table 1 provides the ADF and PP unit root tests for 34 Islamic unit trusts and stock market index at I(0) and I(1) form. The result shows that the null hypotheses for all series are rejected which means the series are all in stationary in first difference form. This indicates that there is possibility of long run equilibrium between Islamic unit trusts and stock market index.

*Table 1. Augmented Dickey Fuller (ADF) and Philip Perron (PP) unit root tests at level and first differences of fund prices and stock market index*

| Fund | ADF | | PP | |
|---|---|---|---|---|
| | I(0) | I(1) | I(0) | I(1) |
| ABMLTII | -1.809042 | -27.99894*** | -1.960806 | -28.12214*** |
| ALLADIB | -1.802263 | -27.67041*** | -1.992509 | -27.72703*** |
| APXISIF | -2.337368 | -18.81060*** | -2.467254 | -27.83450*** |
| APXSCAP | -2.411894 | -27.47022*** | -2.501674 | -27.60582*** |
| ASMBMPA | -1.016171 | -26.19486*** | -1.217062 | -26.24591*** |
| ASMBPEI | -2.130250 | -29.72341*** | -2.087618 | -29.74541*** |
| ASMBPSI | -1.633676 | -26.91136*** | -1.801364 | -26.91136*** |
| ASMDAAI | -2.159662 | -28.08982*** | -2.380834 | -28.10778*** |
| ASMEBPI | -1.937552 | -18.52456*** | -2.053335 | -28.29619*** |
| ASMFBPI | -2.233632 | -19.15228*** | -2.285448 | -29.20039*** |
| ASMPRFI | -1.573757 | -27.37823*** | -1.765585 | -27.41326*** |
| BBMBDPI | -2.099058 | -19.96242*** | -2.575225 | -28.86691*** |
| BHLPDA2 | -2.138535 | -29.43878*** | -2.183555 | -29.47530*** |
| BHLPDAI | -1.692524 | -29.60814*** | -1.787013 | -29.74546*** |
| BHLPDAZ | -1.597241 | -19.08084*** | -1.659434 | -28.09537*** |
| BIMASBI | -0.890880 | -28.27407*** | -0.977157 | -28.19835*** |
| BIMPEND | -2.444141 | -32.68196*** | -2.415117 | -32.68507*** |
| CMSISLA | -0.970429 | -26.63080*** | -1.124872 | -26.60503*** |
| HIJASWI | -2.071233 | -32.95146*** | -2.245443 | -55.24184*** |
| HLBMAKM | -2.209773 | -28.21409*** | -2.375614 | -28.28916*** |
| HWAIZDI | -1.853589 | -28.13005*** | -1.980724 | -28.23039*** |
| INGEISL | -1.315482 | -28.09926*** | -1.514870 | -28.25245*** |
| INGSSCM | -0.986797 | -28.60302*** | -1.174082 | -28.64446*** |
| KLITTFI | -0.986797 | -28.60302*** | -1.174082 | -28.64446*** |
| KUTEQIS | -2.426452 | -30.53906*** | -2.454884 | -30.53998*** |
| MAAFAID | -2.228232 | -28.57590*** | -2.397086 | -29.04302*** |
| MAAFAUZ | -2.066629 | -29.40821*** | -2.064439 | -29.40817*** |
| MAYDANA | -1.258310 | -27.63703*** | -1.428413 | -27.62699*** |
| OSKDANA | -1.651349 | -28.27471*** | -1.725976 | -28.26692*** |
| PRUALIL | -1.893953 | -29.58738*** | -1.875333 | -29.60332*** |
| PRUDMIK | -0.664377 | -30.81109*** | -0.654338 | -30.81502*** |
| PUBISEF | -1.897944 | -29.39016*** | -1.908239 | -29.40101*** |
| PUBISOP | -2.524439 | -28.28664*** | -2.687743 | -28.65926*** |
| PUBPBIE | -2.383816 | -28.98984*** | -2.392497 | -28.98626*** |
| PUBPIDF | -1.434697 | -29.42175*** | -1.439965 | -29.42175*** |
| FBMS_INDEX | -1.515031 | -27.92606*** | -1.809217 | -27.98885*** |

Notes: *** indicates significance at the 1 percent.

*Table 2. Johansen cointegration test*

| Fund | Trace statistic | Coefficient |
|---|---|---|
| ABMLTII | 22.05481*** | -4.02E-05*** |
| ALLADIB | 12.66156 | -4.27E-05*** |
| APXISIF | 6.854154 | -5.30E-06 |
| APXSCAP | 8.179984 | -4.18E-05*** |
| ASMBMPA | 16.32217** | -8.89E-05*** |
| ASMBPEI | 18.77692** | -2.04E-05*** |
| ASMBPSI | 10.18953 | -1.56E-05*** |
| ASMDAAI | 21.31637*** | -1.83E-05*** |
| ASMEBPI | 13.33920 | -1.46E-05*** |
| ASMFBPI | 9.078703 | -1.20E-05 |
| ASMPRFI | 17.83906** | -2.28E-05*** |
| BBMBDPI | 22.88461*** | -6.07E-05*** |
| BHLPDA2 | 7.674197 | -3.02E-05 |
| BHLPDAI | 44.70488*** | -0.000110*** |
| BHLPDAZ | 10.78921 | -7.59E-05*** |
| BIMASBI | 28.59588*** | -2.65E-05*** |
| BIMPEND | 30.42093** | -3.46E-05 |
| CMSISLA | 7.585838 | -6.98E-05*** |
| HIJASWI | 10.52810 | -3.12E-05*** |
| HLBMAKM | 10.53984 | -3.18E-05*** |
| HWAIZDI | 19.64826** | -7.10E-05*** |
| INGEISL | 6.920556 | -5.61E-05*** |
| INGSSCM | 7.233564 | -7.86E-05*** |
| KLITTFI | 22.55302 | -0.000112*** |
| KUTEQIS | 16.17228** | -0.000131*** |
| MAAFAID | 7.793732 | 3.79E-06 |
| MAAFAUZ | 6.609192 | -1.17E-05 |
| MAYDANA | 26.98491*** | -5.42E-05*** |
| OSKDANA | 5.234725 | -4.67E-05*** |
| PRUALIL | 27.87355*** | -0.000101*** |
| PRUDMIK | 10.32167 | -6.50E-05*** |
| PUBISEF | 14.04786 | -1.95E-05*** |
| PUBISOP | 8.239756 | -4.16E-06 |
| PUBPBIE | 7.575268 | -4.62E-06 |
| PUBPIDF | 19.03533** | -2.82E-05*** |

Notes: ** Indicates significance at the 5 percent; *** indicates significance at the 1 percent

Table 2 shows the results of cointegration tests run upon each of the Islamic unit trusts with the Islamic stock market. Interestingly, the trace statistic values indicate that 14 out of 34 Islamic unit trusts are cointegerated with Islamic stock market index at 1 percent and 5 percent level of significant. This implies that most of the Islamic unit trust funds do not have long run equilibrium with Islamic stock markets. In other words, the prices for Islamic unit trust and the Islamic stock market do not converge and thus, Islamic unit trust can be a good alternative for the Islamic stock market. Therefore, the fund managers can be very active in constructing the investment portfolio through market timing and security selection which are not in line with the parallel movement with Islamic stock market index in the long run. However, the fund managers need to ensure that the asset allocation must not deviate from the objective of shariah.

Similar to (Matallin & Nieto, 2002) and (Pojanavatee, 2013), the absence of long-run cointegration between Islamic unit trust and Islamic stock market index is interestingly surprising. This is because selected components in Islamic unit trust's portfolio came from the Islamic stock market index and thus the performance of Islamic unit trust should mimic that of Islamic stock markets. The findings imply that most of the Islamic unit trust funds have been manage through market timing and security selection which leads to deviate from market index over time.

With regard to short-run relationship, this study focuses only upon one-way causality by assuming that the Islamic fund managers will change their asset allocation as a response to the changes in the Islamic stock market, not otherwise. Table 3 reports the Granger causality test for Islamic unit trust funds and the Islamic stock market index in short run. The findings show that 26 Islamic funds are found to have no short-run causal relationship with the changes in Islamic stock market and only 8 Islamic funds have it at 1 percent, 5 percent or 10 percent level of significance. The significant relationship indicates that the fund manager will adjust the composition of their portfolio when there are changes in the Islamic stock market index.

Overall, there are five funds namely Kenanga Shariah Growth Fund (INGSSCM), Hwang Aiiman Growth Fund (HWAIZDI), BIMB i-Growth Fund (BIMASBI), CIMB Islamic Dali Growth Fund (BHLPDAI) and CIMB equity Aggressive Fund (BBMBDPI) that have short-run and long-run relationship with the Islamic stock market index which indicates that the price of Islamic unit trust will be affected by the changes in Islamic stock market index in both the short- and long-run as also reported by Chu (2010). One of the reasons of the short-run and long-run co-movement is that abovementioned five funds include blue chips stocks as part of their portfolio and these stocks are very likely to be index-based component stocks in Islamic stock market index.

*Table 3. Granger causality test*

| Market index (FTSE Bursa Malaysia Emas Shariah) | ΔMarket Index does not Granger cause ΔFund | |
|---|---|---|
| | Funds | Chi-sq |
| FTSE BMES | ABMLTII | 4.371148 |
| FTSE BMES | ALLADIB | 0.636304 |
| FTSE BMES | APXISIF | 2.647028 |
| FTSE BMES | APXSCAP | 2.449731 |
| FTSE BMES | ASMBMPA | 0.345212 |
| FTSE BMES | ASMBPEI | 4.309893 |
| FTSE BMES | ASMBPSI | 1.057590 |
| FTSE BMES | ASMDAAI | 3.067232 |
| FTSE BMES | ASMEBPI | 1.482098 |
| FTSE BMES | ASMFBPI | 0.706289 |
| FTSE BMES | ASMPRFI | 1.443790 |
| FTSE BMES | BBMBDPI | 15.80173*** |
| FTSE BMES | BHLPDA2 | 0.793510 |
| FTSE BMES | BHLPDAI | 33.50499*** |
| FTSE BMES | BHLPDAZ | 3.431129 |
| FTSE BMES | BIMASBI | 5.773859* |
| FTSE BMES | BIMPEND | 2.984456 |
| FTSE BMES | CMSISLA | 0.784484 |
| FTSE BMES | HIJASWI | 11.22030*** |
| FTSE BMES | HLBMAKM | 3.777831 |
| FTSE BMES | HWAIZDI | 8.045923** |
| FTSE BMES | INGEISL | 6.557128** |
| FTSE BMES | INGSSCM | 1.521397 |
| FTSE BMES | KLITTFI | 0.125628 |
| FTSE BMES | KUTEQIS | 12.26661*** |
| FTSE BMES | MAAFAID | 1.152069 |
| FTSE BMES | MAAFAUZ | 3.699341 |
| FTSE BMES | MAYDANA | 1.150072 |
| FTSE BMES | OSKDANA | 3.336178 |
| FTSE BMES | PRUALIL | 3.023797 |
| FTSE BMES | PRUDMIK | 2.729660 |
| FTSE BMES | PUBISEF | 5.337476* |
| FTSE BMES | PUBISOP | 2.390036 |
| FTSE BMES | PUBPBIE | 2.510981 |
| FTSE BMES | PUBPIDF | 1.032356 |

Notes: * indicates significant at the 10 percent;** indicates significance at the 5 percent; *** indicates significance at the 1 percent

## CONCLUSION

The objective of this paper is to examine the dynamic short-run and long-run relationship between Islamic unit trust funds and Islamic stock market index in Malaysia using J-J cointegration and Granger causality test. ADF and PP unit root tests are employed to test the stationarity of the data and the result shows that all funds are stationary at first difference form.

The result reveals that 61.76 percent or 20 Islamic unit trust funds have no long run equilibrium with the Islamic stock market. This situation indicates that the fund managers were able to outperform the market. The divergence of Islamic unit trusts from the Islamic index in the long run shows the fund managers' successful strategies in stock selection criteria and timing the market to construct the portfolio. On the other hand, Granger causality test shows that only 23.53 percent or 8 Islamic unit trust funds have dynamic short-run relationship with Islamic market index.

There are only 5 Islamic unit trusts that statistically proven to have short-run and long-run relationship with Islamic market index. One of the reasons is that those funds include blue chip index-based component stocks in their portfolio. In conclusion, this study is important firstly due to its role in fulfilling the gap in the literature of the linkages between unit trusts and stock market index in the Islamic finance perspective. Secondly, the findings provide some relevant information to the investors and fund managers on the magnitude of the linkage and thus, they could benefit from the situation by diversifying their portfolio investments.

## REFERENCES


Akaike, H. (1971). Autogressive Model Fitting for Control. *Annals of the Institute of Statistical Mathematics*, *23*(1), 163–180. doi:10.1007/BF02479221

Al-Jafari, M. K., Salameh, H., & Al-Asil, K. (2013). An Empirical Investigation of the Price Relationship between Open-end Mutual Funds and Amman Stock Exchange Index. *Advances in Management & Applied Economics*, *3*(5), 1–20.

Alexakis, C., Dasilas, A., & Grose, C. (2013). Asymmetric Dynamic Relations between Stock Prices and Mutual Fund Units in Japan. An Application of Hidden Cointegration Technique. *International Review of Financial Analysis*, *28*, 1–8. doi:10.1016/j.irfa.2013.02.001

Allen, D. E., & Macdonald, G. (1995). The Long-run Gains from International Equity Diversification: Australian Evidence from Cointegration Tests. *Applied Financial Economics*, *5*(1), 33–42. doi:10.1080/758527669

Bailey, W., & Lim, J. (1992). Evaluating the Diversification Benefits of the New Country Funds. *Journal of Portfolio Management, 18*(3), 74–80. doi:10.3905/jpm.1992.409405

Ben-Zion, U., Choi, J. J., & Hauser, S. (1996). The Price Linkages between Country Funds and National Stock Markets: Evidence from Cointegration and Causality Tests of Germany, Japan and UK Funds. *Journal of Business Finance & Accounting, 23*(7), 1005–1017. doi:10.1111/j.1468-5957.1996.tb01037.x

Chu, P. K. K. (2010). The Price Linkages between the Equity Fund Price Levels and the Stock Markets: Evidences from Cointegration Approach and Causality Analysis of Hong Kong Mandatory Provident Fund (MPFs). *International Review of Financial Analysis, 19*(4), 281–288. doi:10.1016/j.irfa.2010.08.001

Chu, P. K. K. (2011). Relationship between Macroeconomic Variables and Net Asset Values (NAV) of Equity Funds: Cointegration Evidence and Vector Error Correction Model of the Hong Kong Mandatory Provident Funds (MPFs). *Journal of International Financial Markets, Institutions and Money, 21*(5), 792–810. doi:10.1016/j.intfin.2011.06.003

Granger, C. W. (1969). Investigating Causal Relations by Econometric Models and Cross Spectral Methods. *Econometrica, 37*(3), 424–438. doi:10.2307/1912791

Johansen, S. (1991). Estimation and Hypothesis Testing of Cointegration Vectors in Gaussian Vector Autoregressive Models. *Econometrica, 59*(6), 1551–1580. doi:10.2307/2938278

Low, S.-W., & Ghazali, N. A. (2007). The Price Linkages between Malaysian Unit Trust Funds and the Stock Market: Short run and Long run Interrelationships. *Managerial Finance, 33*(2), 89–101. doi:10.1108/03074350710715827

Matallin, J. C., & Nieto, L. (2002). Mutual Funds as an Alternative to Direct Stock Investment: A Cointegration Approach. *Applied Financial Economics, 12*(10), 743–750. doi:10.1080/09603100110038693

Omar, M. A., Abduh, M., & Sukmana, R. (2013). *Fundamentals of Islamic Money and Capital Markets*. Singapore: John Wiley & Sons.

Pojanavatee, S. (2013). The Price Linkage between Stock Market and Equity Mutual Funds of Thailand. *The Macrotheme Review, 2*(5), 128–137.

## ADDITIONAL READING

Aloui, C., Hammoudeh, S., & Hamida, H. B. (2015). Co-movement between Sharia Stocks and Sukuk in the GCC Markets: A Time-Frequency Analysis. *Journal of International Financial Markets, Institutions and Money*, *34*, 69–79. doi:10.1016/j.intfin.2014.11.003

Dewandaru, G., Rizvi, S. A. R., Masih, R., Masih, M., & Alhabshi, S. O. (2014). Stock Market Co-Movements: Islamic versus Conventional Equity Indices with Multi-Timescales Analysis. *Economic Systems*, *38*(4), 553–571. doi:10.1016/j.ecosys.2014.05.003

Wahyudi, I., & Sani, G. A. (2014). Interdependence between Islamic Capital Market and Money Market: Evidence from Indonesia. *Borsa Istanbul Review*, *14*(1), 32–47. doi:10.1016/j.bir.2013.11.001

## KEY TERMS AND DEFINITIONS

**Financial Crisis:** is any of a broad variety of situations in which some financial assets suddenly lose a large part of their nominal value.

**Islamic Stock Market:** is where sharia-compliant stocks are traded.

**Islamic Unit Trusts:** a group of specialized collective investment funds which offer investors the opportunity to invest in a diversified portfolio of securities that are managed and selected by professional portfolio managers in accordance to *Shariah* principles.

# APPENDIX

*Table 4. List of Islamic unit trusts in Malaysia included in this study*

| TICKER FUND | FUND NAME |
|---|---|
| ALLADIB | Alliance Dana Adib fund |
| APXISIF | Apex Dana Al Sofi I Fund |
| APXSCAP | Apex Dana Aslah |
| ASMBMPA | ASM Kumpulan Modal Bumiputera - Dana Pertumbuhan |
| ASMBPEI | ASM Kumpulan Modal Bumiputera Yang Kesebelas |
| ASMBPSI | ASM Syariah Aggressive Fund |
| ASMDAAI | ASM Dana Al Aiman |
| ASMEBPI | ASM Dana Bestari |
| ASMFBPI | ASM Dana Mutiara |
| ASMPRFI | ASM Premier Fund |
| BBMBDPI | CIMB Islamic Equity Aggressive Fund |
| BHLPDA2 | CIMB Islamic Dali Equity Fund |
| BHLPDAI | CIMB Islamic Dali Equity Growth Fund |
| BHLPDAZ | CIMB Islamic Small Cap Fund |
| BIMASBI | Bimb I Growth Fund |
| BIMPEND | Bimb Amanah Saham Bank Islam Dana Al Falah |
| CMSISLA | Kenanga Islamic Fund |
| HIJASWI | Libra Amanah Saham Wanita |
| HLBMAKM | Hong Leong Dana Makmur |
| HWAIZDI | Hwang Aiiman Growth Fund |
| INGEISL | Kenanga Ekuiti Islam Fund |
| INGSSCM | Kenanga Shariah Growth Opportunities Fund |
| KLITTFI | Public Mutual Public Ittikal Fund |
| KUTEQIS | Kenanga Syariah Growth Fund |
| MAAFAID | Public Mutual Public Ittikal Fund |
| MAAFAUZ | Maakl Al Fauzan |
| MAYDANA | Amanah Mutual Berhad Dana Yakin |
| OSKDANA | Rhb Osk Dana Kid Save |
| PRUALIL | Eastspring Investments Dana Al Ilham |
| PRUDMIK | Eastspring Investments Dana Dinamik |
| PUBISEF | Public Mutual Public Islamic Equity Fund |
| PUBISOP | Public Mutual Public Islamic Opportunities Fund |
| PUBPBIE | Public Mutual Pb Islamic Equity Fund |
| PUBPIDF | Public Mutual Public Islamic Dividend Fund |

# Chapter 15
# Financial Accessibility and Small-Medium Enterprises (SMEs) in Malaysia:
## The Role of Crowdfunding and Islamic Finance

**Mohamed Asmy Bin Mohd Thas Thaker**
*International Islamic University Malaysia, Malaysia*

**Hassanudin Bin Mohd Thas Thaker**
*Sunway University, Malaysia*

**Choong Pai Wei**
*Sunway University, Malaysia*

## ABSTRACT

*One of the common problems faced by worldwide SMEs including Malaysia is accessing external financial services. Given this fact, this chapter offers a sustainable model of source of financing for Malaysian SMEs in meeting their financial need, which is known as Islamic Crowdfunding-Small and Medium Enterprises (ICSMEs) model. Authors review comprehensive literature by focusing on the issues of financial accessibility faced by Malaysian SMEs, and the existing studies relating to SMEs, crowdfunding, and Islamic finance in support to construct ICSME model. Authors discuss the modus operandi of the proposed ICSME model and offer several significances of the model.*

DOI: 10.4018/978-1-7998-2257-8.ch015

*Table 1. Number of establishments in Malaysia by firm sizes and by economic sectors.*

| Year | 2015 | | | 2010 | | |
|---|---|---|---|---|---|---|
| **Sector** | **SME** | **Large Firms** | **Total** | **SME** | **Large Firms** | **Total** |
| Services | 809126 | 9185 | 818311 | 580985 | 10898 | 591883 |
| Manufacturing | 47698 | 1403 | 49101 | 37861 | 1808 | 39669 |
| Agriculture | 39158 | 1400 | 40558 | 6708 | 2121 | 8829 |
| Construction | 10218 | 1410 | 11628 | 19283 | 2857 | 22140 |
| Mining and quarrying | 865 | 161 | 1026 | 299 | 119 | 418 |
| **Total** | **907065** | **13559** | **920624** | **645136** | **17803** | **662939** |

*Source*: SME Annual Report, various issues.

## INTRODUCTION

Small Medium Enterprises (SMEs) in Malaysia accounted for more than 90 percent of the total number of business establishments in the years 2010 and 2015 as presented in Table 1. Of this, the services sector consisted of about 90 percent share, which was followed by the manufacturing and agriculture sectors. SMEs in Malaysia participate in almost all business activities of various economic sectors. SME Malaysia is classified based on the annual sales turnover of a business or the number of employees working in SMEs and by different economic sectors. Drawing on SME Annual Report 2015-2016 (2016), from the year 2014 onwards, the annual sales turnover of not exceeding RM50 million or full-time employees of not exceeding 200 workers employed for the manufacturing sector is defined as SME Malaysia. While, for services, primary agriculture and other sectors, annual sales turnover of not exceeding RM20 million or full-time employees of not exceeding 75 workers are categorized under SME Malaysia.

## ECONOMIC PERFORMANCE OF SMEs MALAYSIA

SMEs are increasingly important to the Malaysian economic activities in terms of its contribution to value-added, employment and exports. Since the year 2004, SMEs in Malaysia charted gross domestic product (GDP) growth of 7.4 percent per annum over the period of 2012 – 2017 as compared to its overall GDP growth of 5.2 percent, drawing on authors' calculation based on data obtained from NSDC (2018). SME employment grew by an average annual rate of 7.3 percent, which exceeded the total employment growth rate of 4.7 percent over the period. On average, SME Malaysia contributed 62.4 percent share of total employment. SME's labor productivity, measured by the real value-added per worker, only recorded a marginal annual growth rate of 0.4 percent over the period which was so much lower than the 3.5 percent growth of large firms' labor productivity. Moreover, SME's labor productivity was three times lower than the labor productivity of large firms. Of the Malaysian total exports, SME contributed about 17.8 percent share over the period of 2012 – 2017 as compared to 16.4 percent share in 2010. Its exports expanded by a compounded annual growth rate of 5.3 percent over the years of 2011 – 2017, which was higher than the 4.4 percent of overall export growth (NSDC, 2016).

Table 2 shows the Malaysian SMEs' value-added activities by various economic sectors over the years of 2014 – 2017. SMEs contributed about 37 percent share of the Malaysian GDP over the period, which was largely supported by services and manufacturing sectors. Of the total GDP contributed by SMEs, service and manufacturing sectors consisted of 70 percent and 20 percent share, respectively. In addition, the average annual growth rate of total SME real value-added was 6.2 percent over the years of 2015 – 2017, which exceeded the growth rate of 5.1 percent for the overall GDP in Malaysia. The mining and quarrying sector and construction sector showed an average annual growth rate of 8.7 percent and 7.1 percent, respectively, over the period, albeit their contribution to SME value added was relatively small in absolute value.

Drawing on the sectoral performance of SMEs, about 50 percent share of total value added in the agriculture sector was led by SMEs in Malaysia; while 47 percent and 40 percent share of its total value-added were driven by SMEs in construction and service sectors, respectively. In general, about 40 percent share of value-added activities by each economic sector is contributed by the Malaysian SMEs except for the mining and quarrying sector, which can be due to the highly intensive use of technology and capital for producing at scale economies.

Table 3 shows the sub-sector of Malaysian SME value-added by economic activities over the period 2014 – 2017. SMEs' contribution to value-added activities in the services sector was on wholesale and retail trade, restaurants and accommodation which accounted for 62 percent of the total share. Its participation in the manufacturing sector was largely driven by petroleum, chemical, rubber and plastic products, and food which consisted of 24 percent share, while beverages and tobacco accounted for 22 percent. In the agriculture sector, SMEs are largely involved in the production of rubber, oil palm, livestock and other agriculture products, which comprised of 80 percent share of the total value added over the period.

*Table 2. SME value added by economic activity at constant 2010 prices*

| Kind of economic activity | 2014 | 2015 | 2016 | 2017 |
|---|---|---|---|---|
| *RM million* | | | | |
| Agriculture | 45220 | 46255 | 45359 | 48656 |
| Mining and quarrying | 1480 | 1612 | 1745 | 1900 |
| Manufacturing | 78888 | 83571 | 87554 | 93483 |
| Construction | 20571 | 22184 | 23683 | 25255 |
| Services | 213197 | 227345 | 242039 | 259678 |
| **Total** | **363420** | **385854** | **405752** | **435126** |
| *Annual percentage growth* | | | | |
| Agriculture | 2.7% | 2.3% | -1.9% | 7.3% |
| Mining and quarrying | 9.6% | 8.9% | 8.3% | 8.9% |
| Manufacturing | 8.6% | 5.9% | 4.8% | 6.8% |
| Construction | 12.8% | 7.8% | 6.8% | 6.6% |
| Services | 8.3% | 6.6% | 6.5% | 7.3% |
| **Total** | **7.9%** | **6.2%** | **5.2%** | **7.2%** |
| *The percentage share of overall GDP* | | | | |
| Agriculture | 49% | 49% | 51% | 51% |
| Mining and quarrying | 2% | 2% | 2% | 2% |
| Manufacturing | 34% | 34% | 34% | 35% |
| Construction | 48% | 47% | 47% | 47% |
| Services | 39% | 40% | 40% | 41% |
| **Total** | **36%** | **36%** | **37%** | **37%** |
| *The percentage share of SME GDP* | | | | |
| Agriculture | 12% | 12% | 11% | 11% |
| Mining and quarrying | 0.4% | 0.4% | 0.4% | 0.4% |
| Manufacturing | 22% | 22% | 22% | 21% |
| Construction | 6% | 6% | 6% | 6% |
| Services | 59% | 59% | 60% | 60% |
| **Total** | **100%** | **100%** | **100%** | **100%** |

*Source:* Authors' calculation based on data obtained from the Department of Statistics Malaysia's Official portal except for the annual percentage growth rate in 2014, which was obtained from SME Annual Report 2014 (2015).

*Table 3. The components of SME value added by selected economic activities*

| | % Share | | | |
|---|---|---|---|---|
| | **2014** | **2015** | **2016** | **2017** |
| **Agriculture** | | | | |
| Rubber, oil palm, livestock, and other agriculture | 78% | 79% | 78% | 81% |
| Fishing | 17% | 17% | 17% | 16% |
| Forestry and logging | 5% | 4% | 4% | 3% |
| **Manufacturing** | | | | |
| Petroleum, chemical, rubber and plastic products | 24% | 24% | 24% | 24% |
| Food, beverages and tobacco | 22% | 21% | 21% | 22% |
| Non-metallic mineral products, basic metal and fabricated metal products | 18% | 18% | 19% | 19% |
| Other manufacturing | 36% | 36% | 36% | 36% |
| **Services** | | | | |
| Wholesale & retail trade, restaurants and accommodation | 62% | 62% | 62% | 62% |
| Finance, insurance, real estate, and business services | 21% | 20% | 20% | 20% |
| Transportation & storage and information & communication | 10% | 10% | 10% | 10% |
| Other services | 7% | 7% | 7% | 7% |

*Source:* Authors' calculation based on data obtained from the Department of Statistics Malaysia's Official portal.

## ISSUES AND CHALLENGES FACED BY SMEs MALAYSIA

In 2004, the National SME Development Council (NSDC) was set up mainly to enhance SME contribution to the Malaysian economy, which was then renamed as SME Corporation Malaysia in 2009 (NSDC, 2012a). SME Corporation Malaysia started to conduct a survey on the firm-level performance of SME development in Malaysia, the challenges faced by SMEs and to seek SMEs' feedback on government policy and their views on the way forward (NSDC, 2014). To enhance the importance of SMEs to the Malaysian economy, the major issues confronting SMEs are the costs of doing business and the access to financing, human capital and productivity as well as the access to international markets.

Raw material and other input costs comprise about half of the total operating costs of SME Malaysia while employees' salaries, wages and training expenses consist of 18 percent share (NSDC, 2013, 2014). Since 2013, the rising cost of fuel, electricity tariff, labor costs as well as imported raw materials and other inputs costs increased the operating costs of SME business, which were largely attributable to a series of government reforms such as subsidy rationalization, implementation of minimum wage law and goods and services tax as well as the depreciation of Ringgit Malaysia against major currencies. The rising costs of operation created liquidity problems in sustaining SME businesses. At this stance, financial institutions were cautious in giving away loans to SMEs and the SMEs' demand for financing decreased mainly due to their reluctance to widen their debts further. Based on SME Annual Report 2017-2018 (NSDC, 2018), the approval rate for business financing remained high at about 90 percent over the period of the first quarter of 2014 to the third quarter of 2017, but the demand from SME financing application decreased. The access to business financing is still a challenge to SMEs due to their inability to comply with the terms and conditions set by conventional financial system and there is a lack of alternative mechanism such as angel investors and crowdfunding to assist them in the growth and development of their businesses as well as the access to international market (Ministry of Economic Affairs Malaysia, 2018).

Albeit SMEs contributed about 60 percent share of employment opportunities to the Malaysian labor market, but the growth of their labor productivities remained low at less than 1 percent and their labor productivity was three times lower than large firms' labor productivity. Based on World Bank Entrepreneur Survey, inadequate educated and skilled labor force are the major constraint to the growth and operation of Malaysian SMEs (NSDC, 2012b). The reliance on a low skilled workforce and foreign labors, the low utilization of automation machine and equipment and, the lack of required specific skilled workforce for technological advancement remain a concern for SME Malaysia to participate in higher value-added activities (Ministry of Economic Affairs Malaysia, 2018). Over the years of 2012 – 2017, SME Malaysia only contributed 37 percent share of overall GDP in Malaysia and its share of total exports was meager at 17 percent. The Malaysian SMEs face challenges to access to domestic and international markets due to limited production capacity to undertake large orders which also limit their bargaining power, limited resources and financial access for commercialization and research and development activities, marketing and branding as well as limited knowledge and resources to venture into targeted markets (Ministry of Economic Affairs Malaysia, 2018).

Given the fact above, this paper attempt to offers a viable solution to handle the financial accessibility problem facing by Malaysian SMEs by introducing an alternative model such as an Integrated Islamic Crowdfunding Small Medium Enterprises Model (ICSME). The engineering of the model and significances are critically discussed in this paper.

# LITERATURE REVIEW

## Crowdfunding Concepts

In the last years, the concept of crowdfunding has gained acceptance as an alternative source of financing for innumerable ventures globally. Crowdfunding is an initiative to fund a project across industries such as journalism, technology, music, film, and others, through crowd-sources. For instance, projects exhibit on the Kickstarter which based in the United States is known as one of the largest platforms for crowdfunding. In fact, one of the three nominated for Oscar award movie projects funded by crowd investor won the award in Oscar 2013 for the short documentary category (Lu et al., 2014). Unlike the conventional investor in venture capital firms where the enterprises receive a small number of major investments, in crowdfunding, the enterprise receives supports through a large number of small contributions from investors. Therefore, crowdfunding presents a mixture of entrepreneurship and social network participation. In addition, the investor in the crowdfunding projects can keep track of their campaign and obtain useful insight in real-time which ordinarily shared through crowdfunding websites or even in social media.

*Figure 1.*
*Source: (Lu et al., 2014)*

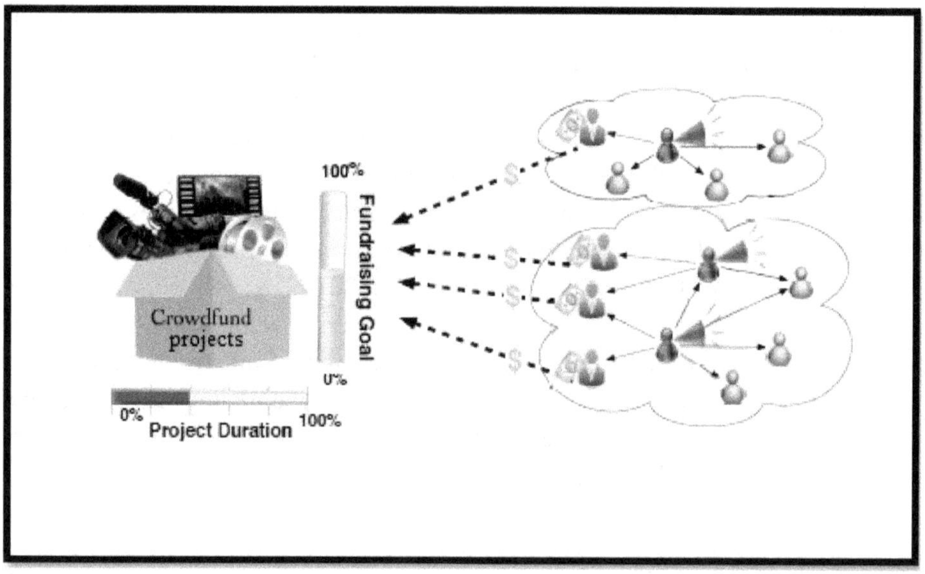

The figure 1 illustrates the example of the crowdfunding process where the red persons act as promoters of the projects, the person in blue are the backers, while the green is the potential target investors. Generally, the investor has the liberty to choose projects according to their priority to contribute. If the fundraising goal is achieved, the funds are awarded to the proposer or the crowdfunding project specified (Mollick, 2013). Initially, the crowdfunding has dominantly cast for funding artists from different sectors (Agrawal et al., 2013). Subsequently, other artistic and creative areas such as film and journalism adopted the idea. The crowdfunding platform was seen as the way to reduce the funding gap in the early stages of new ventures, then only venture capitalist and banks would be available in later development phrases of startups (Robb & Robinson, 2014). Diverse areas of the globe have known to have a different word of reference for the crowdfunding activities. Another term for crowdfunding also known as social-lending (Hulme & Wright, 2006), peer-to-peer (Freedman & Jin, 2014) and crowd-investing (i.e.: in Germany) which is to distinguish the equity-based form of crowdfunding (Moritz & Block, 2016).

## Categories of Crowdfunding

Generally, four crowdfunding models are found with different in analysis among countries which is based on equity, lending, donation, and reward (Brüntje & Gajda, 2016). Kuppuswamy & Bayus (2018) research demonstrate that crowdfunding could be categorized such the Sellaband; where the investors anticipate an interest in the profit-sharing oriented venture, Prosper; crowdlending activities in which the investor expects the original principal is repaid along with some interest, JustGiving; the funder voluntarily donate their money with no expectation of any tangible reward, and Kickstarter; where project backers receive nonfinancial rewards for their contributions (Agrawal et al.,2015; Zhang et al., 2012; Smith et al., 2014; Mollick, 2014). Further explanation on categories of crowdfunding (extracted from Thaker et al. 2018) are given below:

### Donation Crowdfunding

Donation crowdfunding is where the collection of funds takes place for the purpose such as social, artistic, philanthropic and others. Basically, this type of crowdfunding is not based on any exchangeable of tangible value. For example, in the United States, Kickstarter, Indiegogo, etc. are among the platforms supporting donation-based crowdfunding.

## Reward Crowdfunding

Reward crowdfunding is the collection of funds, where the investors or donors receive some tangible reward (such as a membership rewards scheme) as a token of appreciation. Most of the websites which support donation crowdfunding are also managing reward-based crowdfunding, such as Kickstarter, Rockethub, Indiegogo, etc.

## Lending Crowdfunding

Lending crowdfunding is a platform that matches lenders or investors with borrowers or issuers to provide loans with a lower interest rate, which is set by the platform. There are some platforms arrange loans between individuals, while other platforms collect funds and then lent to small and medium enterprises. Some of the leading examples from the US are Lending Club, Prosper, etc. and from the UK are Zopa, Funding Circle, etc. Some of the platforms charge a fee based on the loan.

## Equity-Based Crowdfunding

Equity-based crowdfunding refers to the fund raised through online by a business, particularly early-stage funding, by offering equity interests in the business to investors. Businesses that are looking to raise capital through this mode typically advertise online through a crowdfunding platform website, which serves as an intermediary between investors and start-up companies. In the United Kingdom two platforms namely Crowdcube and Seedrs have dominated the narrative for investment crowdfunding from the equity side.

On the other note, Gleasure & Feller (2016) on study of crowdfunding patterns of behavior classified dominant categories of crowdfunding endeavors known as crowdlending (investing in return for repayment at some agreed-upon rate of interest), crowd equity (investing in return for equity/securities), crowd patronage (investing in return for benefits from a proposed product/service) and crowd charity (investing without expectation of any financial or return in any form). The figure 2 below depicts the categories of crowdfunding system.

The crowdfunding platforms eventually are seen to advantage the funding mechanism including; minimal cost and effort involved, multiple transactions could be pooled together to fund less risky projects, and it also could mitigate the asymmetry information between funders and fund seekers.

*Figure 2. Categories of crowdfunding system*
*Source: (Gleasure & Feller, 2016)*

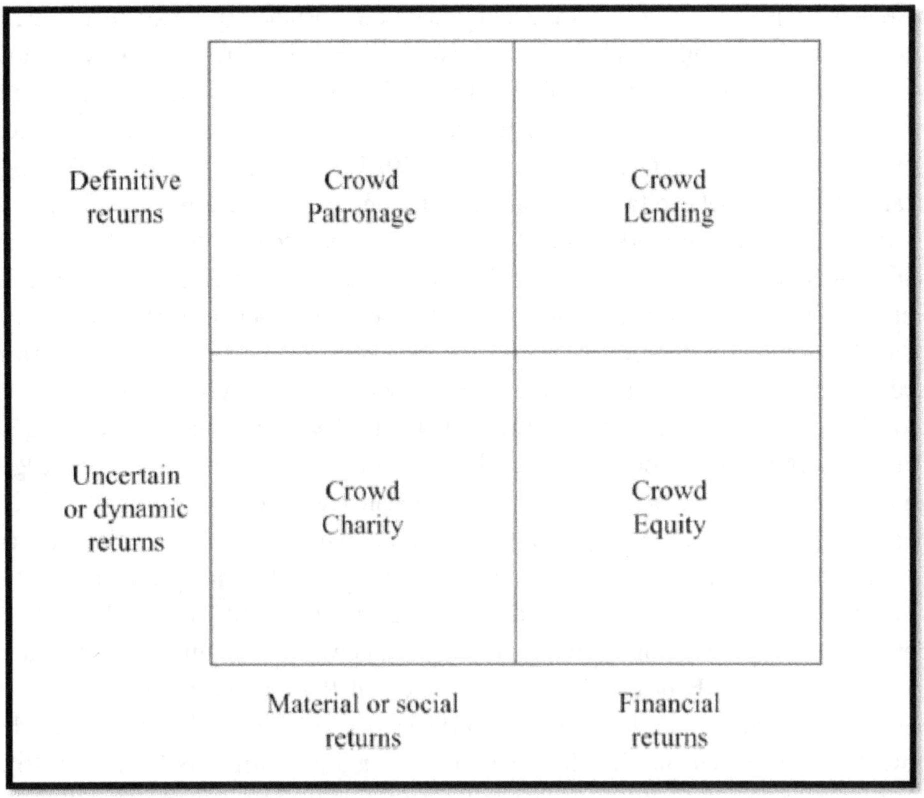


## DEVELOPMENT OF CROWDFUNDING PLATFORM AROUND THE GLOBE

The development of crowdfunding discussion was mainly focused on legal issues. Later, restrictions on the concept dominated the literature vastly on the legislative concern (Belleflamme et al., 2010). Subsequently, a number of scientific contributions began to emerge on the notion of descriptive exploration and concept-based or explanatory approach, frequently with case studies from a particular national context (Ingram et al., 2014). Entrepreneurs opted for crowdfunding concept found to get motivated due to few reasons such as the collection of funds itself, to attain the public attention, receive feedbacks for their goods and services, self-affirmation, replication of success stories and increase awareness of the goods and services provided (Belleflamme et al., 2013a; Gerber et al.,2012).

Kuppuswamy & Bayus (2018) claimed that to date, mainstream empirical research on crowdfunding focuses to identify the project and entrepreneur characteristics associated with successful funding outcomes. For instance, number of research shows that the funding completion is positively associated to project quality signals such as preparedness (Mollick, 2014), chronical in project depiction (Herzenstein et al., 2011); (Allison et al.,2015), individual quality signals such gender, race, personal characteristics (Gorbatai & Nelson, 2015); (Marom et al., 2016), (Zhang et al., 2012), internal capital accumulated from supporting other projects (Colombo et al.,2015), social networks, and the geographic distance between entrepreneur and their contributors (Agrawal et al., 2015). Nevertheless, studies by (Gleasure & Feller, 2016) identifies that two fundamentally novel and under-researched variables related to funding behaviors are an erosion of organizations' financial boundaries and paying to participate variables. Due to overwhelming and promising growth in crowdfunding endeavor, many countries such as Malaysia, Indonesia, UK, the US, Australia, China, Singapore, and others have eventually taken steps to acknowledge and amend their regulatory system to accommodate the operation of crowdfunding. Particularly the crowdfunding operation with the expectation of financial returns for crowdlending and crowd equity (Abdullah, 2016). In Malaysia, the equity crowdfunding gains its regulatory acknowledgment when SCM issued a public consultation paper to propose the regulatory framework for equity crowdfunding operation. Later in February 2015, Guidelines on Regulation of Markets under Section 34 of the Capital Markets and Services Act 2007 was released to provide governance arrangements for the operation of such platforms (Abdullah, 2016). Singapore advanced further to root their crowdfunding activities on the *Shariah* principle especially for the equity-based platforms, named Islamic crowdfunding.

## ISLAMIC FINANCE

The Islamic banking beliefs are based on two basic principles that are the sharing of profit and loss and the prohibition of the collection and payment of interest (*Riba*) as well as other activities that involve gambling (*Maysir*) and speculative trading (*Gharar*). The Islamic banking is set out in line with the *Shariah* law which is enshrined in the *Qur'an*, and the *Sunna*. Today, these principles form the basis of contemporary Islamic banking's range of Islamic financial products. The financial institutions providing a great deal of flexibility, creativity, and choice with the offering of various products using various Islamic financial concepts such as *Ijarah* (leasing), *Mudharabah* (profit sharing), *Musharakah* (partnership), *Murabahah* (price deferred sale contract), *Salam* (object deferred sale contract) and *Istisna* (object and price sale contract) (IOSCO,2004). These principles are also supported by Islamic banking's core values (Bank Negara Malaysia, 2016). The appearance of the Islamic banking system has provided a new aspect of the current economic models and real economic activities (Fazlan & Mohammad, 2007).

The key principles or features in the Islamic finance system emphasize on the need of sharing the risk, equity, and stakes with the customers. The sharing aspect as the main requirement in the Islamic banking system suggests that the outcome of a project, whether it is profitable or otherwise, will be shared in an equitable manner (Dusuki & Abdullah, 2007). The essence of Islamic principles is to achieve a fair distribution of wealth. The main aim of the Islamic banking system is to shield the benefits and interests of all parties who are involved in the economic transaction and to promote the welfare of the whole society as well (Erol et al., 1990).

Islamic finance should act as an impact-oriented mechanism and play a role in developing capabilities and empowering individual and societal development. However, given its current form of adopting the role of conventional commercial banks, an Islamic bank is not there to provide such activities (Asutay, 2007). Thus, there is a need to develop a non-banking Islamic financial instrument and respond to the need of societies with regards to the development of entrepreneurship. One of the non-banking Islamic financial instrument is known as Islamic crowdfunding.

## ISLAMIC CROWDFUNDING

The objective of crowdfunding is to lessen the financial difficulty to a particular group of people or entrepreneurs who need financial assistance. This mechanism is a noble exercise and reflects the principles of *Muamalat* (facilitating transactions) in Islam. The real essence of *Muamalat* in Islamic commercial law promotes dealings between two or more parties to buy or, and sell products or services with reference to *Shariah* principles and emphasizes on being just and fair to each other in the deals made. Nevertheless, there are three main differences between conventional and Islamic crowdfunding namely (i) *Shariah*-compliant crowdfunding invests in halal socially responsible projects/products, (ii) shares the risks of the investment, and (iii) the absence of interest or *Riba* (Marzban, Asutay, & Boseli, 2014).

This paper is an attempt to present a conceptual framework of an alternative model such as ICSME Model. The present paper is purely qualitative in nature, using content analysis. Before proposing an appropriate model, this paper effectively analyses various relevant literature from academic research journals, websites, and electronic databases. In addition to the journal paper, the present study also refers to working paper, government report and websites as they provide very useful information to the researchers or practitioners. But, the refereed academic research journals epitomize the premier level of research in this paper to develop the model.

## PROPOSED INTEGRATED ISLAMIC CROWDFUNDING SMALL MEDIUM ENTERPRISES MODEL (ICSME)

There are several alternative instruments being developed around the world to address the needs of low-income households and to give them a chance to get out of the poverty trap. These include mostly financing as well as social development mechanisms. The instruments developed to finance the needs of the poor and to give them an opportunity to sustain their livelihoods are concentrated around SME programs. However, households with low-income levels, particularly in Muslim communities, continue to face numerous challenges despite the alternative mechanisms being offered to them. The resources provided to them are usually not sufficient and usually, do not require to have a solid project/business to be delivered.

Thus, given these challenges, an Integrated Islamic Crowdfunding Small Medium Enterprises Model (ICSME) is proposed that can address the particular practical challenge of SME faced in Muslim communities, specifically in Malaysia. In this model, Islamic crowdfunding together with SME is practiced in compliance with *Shariah* to address the multi-dimensional aspects of poverty and empowering the poor in order to enhance the socio-economic development and hence the wellbeing of the Ummah. With this aspiration, the ICSME model aims to tackle the main challenge related to the scarcity of capital or financial resources in an integrated approach. The conceptual framework of the proposed ICSME model is illustrated in Figure 3:

*Figure 3. Integrated Islamic crowdfunding small medium enterprises model (ICSME)*

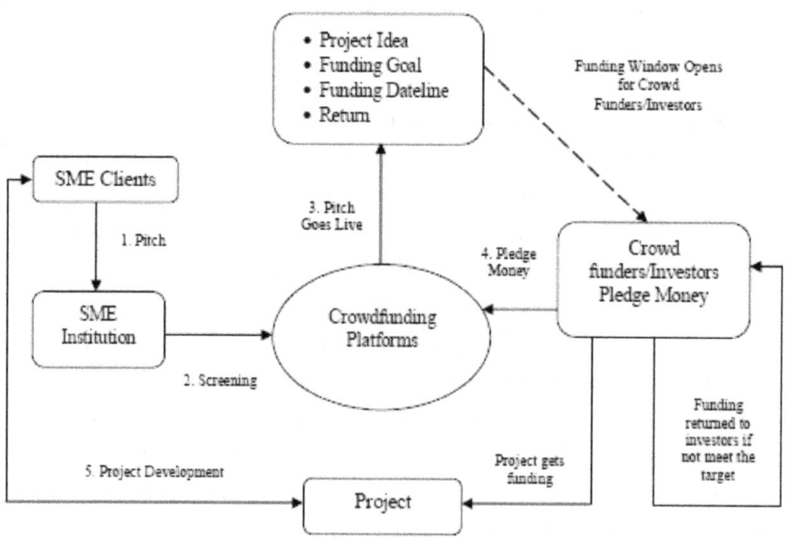

The following are the modus operandi of Integrated Islamic Crowdfunding Small Medium Enterprise Model (ICSME):

1. SME clients plan to initiate businesses. This group is less capable financially, but they have entrepreneurial skills (after undergoing training/program). They need to raise the funding from crowd funders or investors to implement the projects. They pitch their idea through microfinance institutions (Arrow 1).
2. SME Institution's uploads and submits the potential of particular projects' proposals to the platform which is known as Web-Based Platform and Social Networks. SME Institution can establish and manage its own Web-Based Platform and Social Network or outsourcing from external parties. The projects have to be funded within a predefined time frame. In this model, this research proposed to use *Murabahah*-based crowdfunding, *Sadaqah*-based crowdfunding, and *Hibah*-based crowdfunding. The platform provides an intermediate service to act as a link between an entrepreneur and potential crowd-funders (Arrow 2 and 3).
3. Crowd funders or investors choose projects that they want to support and a joint venture in. Crowd funders or investors browse the web to search requests and finally choose the projects they are willing to provide the fund or capital. (Arrow 4).
4. Crowd funders or investors transfer/send funds through payment gateways. SME institutions can have their own payment gateways through collaboration with existing financial institutions or crowdfunding platforms. Once the target amount of funds from crowd funders is reached, the system will update the status of projects and keep track of received funds until it is ready to be distributed. If the fund is not reached to its target, the fund will be returned to the crowd funders or investors (Arrow 4).
5. If the fund is successfully raised, the system distributes the fund to microfinance institutions and notifies them to get ready managing and supervising the projects they proposed earlier (Arrow 5).
6. SME institutions manage and supervise their identified projects. SME Institution must track the progress regularly and updates the progress into the system until the particular projects completed and started to commence by the clients. This will ensure transparency between them and the crowd funders. The system communicates with SME institutions as for control and audit purposes through a simple communication media such as short message services (SMS) or WassUp etc. (Arrow 5)
7. Later, within the specified time framework of project, SME clients via SME institutions need to provide a return (for P2P-based crowdfunding) and non-monetary return (for reward-based crowdfunding) to the crowd funders or investors.

## SIGNIFICANCE OF THE STUDY

From the Integrated Islamic Crowdfunding, Small Medium Enterprise Model (ICSME) developed, it can be seen that the Islamic crowdfunding and SMEs can complement each other. Islamic crowdfunding can be used to boost the economy and provide financial support for SMEs. Thus, from a broader perspective, this model could bring a significant impact on SMEs as well as society and economy as a whole. The impacts as follows:

### Impact on the SMEs

As this model incorporates the use of Islamic crowdfunding for SMEs, it brings benefits to SMEs. For instance, this integration of Crowdfunding with the SMEs will be useful in achieving a higher profile for the business involved and enhance the image of the SMEs. In addition, the focus of crowdfunding on business and project financing eliminates risky speculation. Furthermore, this model can increase the success of SMEs by helping their business development. Integrated Islamic Crowdfunding Small Medium Enterprise Model (ICSME) can also assist in the growth of SMEs from micro to small, to medium and large scales enterprises.

### Impact on Society and Economy

The model is also anticipated to bring benefits to the society and economy. As this model emphasizes on financing, it creates an environment of innovation and diversification of economic activity. It also helps to stimulate private ownership among SMEs. Integrated Islamic Crowdfunding Small Medium Enterprise Model (ICSME) enables SMEs to reach to affordable financial services. This model provides seed capital to develop the SME sector and give them access to finance. In addition, as this model incorporates crowdfunding, it can play an intermediary role in assisting corporate sector and investors in doing their corporate social responsibility by funding SMEs. On the other hand, this model creates employment opportunities and helps poor clients to generate income and thus alleviate poverty. Meanwhile, since Islamic crowdfunding could be considered as s one of the redistribution schemes, it helps to increase wealth, consumption and investment that later can boost the economy. Furthermore, as this study proposed the use of crowdfunding as the main resource, it helps to achieve efficiency of allocation of resources in the economy.

## Impact on Academic and Theoretical

For academic and theoretical, the proposed model adds to the existing literature in the areas of enterprises and Islamic crowdfunding. This study provides new literature on the avenue for effective utilization of Islamic crowdfunding for socio-economic development, particularly in Malaysia. This model is expected to positively change the perceptions of stakeholders about the dynamics and potentials of this social financer.

# FUTURE RESEARCH

Several limitations in this study are: firstly, since this study is just a conceptual paper, we did not incorporate the management, operational and regulatory outcomes which later can be a possible area of research in the future. Secondly, the model validation needed via carrying out the empirical investigation to measure investor behavioral intention in investing in the proposed model. Lastly, industrial expert's feedbacks needed for further enhancement of the model via carrying out an interview session with them to obtain comprehensive feedback on the proposed model.

# CONCLUSION

The study intends to propose a viable model or framework in overcoming the issue of financial accessibility that haunting the SMEs in Malaysia. As mentioned in the literature, the issue of financial problems found to be one of the root causes of the underdevelopment of SME in Malaysia. Therefore, to solve this issue, the current study proposes a solution using the Integrated Islamic Crowdfunding Small Medium Enterprise Model (ICSME). To differentiate with existing literature, we incorporate the element of crowdfunding and Islamic finance, subsequently, make the model looks more solid and original. We claim, that this model can support providing enough access to SMEs to develop their projects or business.

# REFERENCES

Agrawal, A., Catalini, C., & Goldfarb, A. (2013). Some Simple Economics of Crowdfunding. *National Bureau of Economic Research (NBER) Working Paper No. w19133.*

Agrawal, A., Catalini, C., & Goldfarb, A. (2015). Crowdfunding: Geography, Social Networks, and the Timing of Investment Decisions. *Journal of Economics & Management Strategy*, *24*(2), 253–274. doi:10.1111/jems.12093

Allison, T. H., Davis, B. C., Short, J. C., & Webb, J. W. (2015). Crowdfunding is a Prosocial Microlending Environment: Examining the Role of Intrinsic Versus Extrinsic Cues. *Entrepreneurship Theory and Practice*, *39*(1), 53–73. doi:10.1111/etap.12108

Asutay, M. (2007). Conceptualization of the Second Best Solution in Overcoming the Social Failure of Islamic Finance: Examining the Overpowering of Homoislamicus by Homoeconomicus. *IIUM Journal in Economics and Management*, *15*(2), 167–195.

Bank Negara Malaysia. (2016). Retrieved from http://www.bnm.gov.my/. Accessed on 10 April 2019.

Belleflamme, P., Lambert, T., & Schwienbacher, A. (2010). *Crowdfunding: An Industrial Organization Perspective*. Workshop on Digital Business Models: Understanding Strategies, Held in Paris in June 2010.

Belleflamme, P., Lambert, T., & Schwienbacher, A. (2013a). Crowdfunding: Tapping the right crowd. *Journal of Business Venturing*, *29*(5), 585–609. doi:10.1016/j.jbusvent.2013.07.003

Brüntje, D., & Gajda, O. (2016). *Crowdfunding in Europe, State of the Art in Theory and Practice*. Switzerland: Springer International Publishing.

Colombo, M. G., Franzoni, C., & Rossi-Lamastra, C. (2015). Internal Social Capital and the Attraction of Early Contributions in Crowdfunding Projects. *Entrepreneurship Theory and Practice*, *39*(1), 75–100. doi:10.1111/etap.12118

Dusuki, A. W., & Abdullah, N. I. (2007). Why do Malaysian customers patronize Islamic banks? *International Journal of Bank Marketing*, *25*(3), 142–160. doi:10.1108/02652320710739850

Erol, C., Kaynak, E., & El-Bdour, R. (1990). Conventional and Islamic banks: Patronage behavior of Jordanian customers. *International Journal of Bank Marketing*, *8*(4), 25–35. doi:10.1108/02652329010004231

Fazlan, S., & Mohammad, A. (2007). *The Efficiency of Islamic Banks: Empirical Evidence from the MENA and Asian Countries Islamic Banking Sectors*. Paper presented at the Fifth International Islamic Finance Conference, September 3-4, Kuala Lumpur. Academic Press.

Freedman, S., & Jin, G. (2014). *The Signaling Value of Online Social Networks: Lessons from Peer-to-Peer Lending*. National Bureau of Economic Research (NBER) Working Paper No. 19820, 48 -70.

Gleasure, R., & Feller, J. (2016). Emerging technologies and the democratization of financial services: A metal triangulation of crowdfunding research. *Information and Organization*, *26*(4), 101–115. doi:10.1016/j.infoandorg.2016.09.001

Gorbatai, A. D., & Nelson, L. (2015). Gender and the Language of Crowdfunding. *Academy of Management Proceedings*, *1*, 2015.

Herzenstein, M., Sonenshein, S., & Dholakia, U. M. (2011). Tell Me a Good Story and I May Lend You Money: The Role of Narratives in Peer-to-Peer Lending Decisions. *JMR, Journal of Marketing Research*, *48*(2), 138–149. doi:10.1509/jmkr.48.SPL.S138

Hulme, M., & Wright, C. (2006). *Internet-based social lending: Past, present and future*. Social Futures Observatory 2006.

International Organization of Securities Commissions (IOSCO). (2004). *Islamic Capital Market Fact-Finding Report*, July 2004, p. 10 available at www.iasplus.com/resource/ioscoislamiccapitalmarkets.pdf (Accessed on 22 Feb 2018).

Kuppuswamy, V., & Bayus, B. L. (2018). Crowdfunding Creative Ideas: The Dynamics of Project Backers. In *H. L. Cumming D., The Economics of Crowdfunding* (pp. 151–182). Cham, Switzerland: Palgrave Macmillan. doi:10.1007/978-3-319-66119-3_8

Lu, C.-T., Xie, S., Kong, X., & Yu, P. S. (2014). Inferring the Impacts of Social Media on Crowdfunding. *WSDM '14. Proceedings of the 7th ACM international conference on Web search and data mining*, 573-582. 10.1145/2556195.2556251

Marom, D., Robb, A., & Sade, O. (2016). *Gender Dynamics in Crowdfunding (Kickstarter): Evidence on Entrepreneurs, Investors, Deals and Taste Based Discrimination*. Social Science Research Network.

Marzban, S., Asutay, M., & Boseli, A. (2014). *Shariah--compliant Crowdfunding: An Efficient Framework for Entrepreneurship development in Islamic Countries*. Paper presented at the Harvard Islamic Finance Forum, Boston, USA. Academic Press.

Ministry of Economic Affairs Malaysia. (2018). *Mid-term Review of the Eleventh Malaysia Plan: 2016 – 2020*. Kuala Lumpur: Percetakan Nasional Malaysia Berhad.

Mollick, E. R. (2013). The dynamics of crowdfunding: Determinants of success and failure. *Social Science Research Network. The Electricity Journal*, *29*(1), 1–20.

Mollick, E. R. (2014). The Dynamics of Crowdfunding: An Exploratory Study. *Journal of Business Venturing*, *29*(2), 1–16. doi:10.1016/j.jbusvent.2013.06.005

Moritz, A., & Block, J. (2016). Crowdfunding: A literature review and research directions. In D. Brüntje, & O. Gajda (Eds.), *Crowdfunding in Europe, State of the Art in Theory and Practice* (pp. 25–53). Switzerland: Springer International Publishing. doi:10.1007/978-3-319-18017-5_3

National SME Development Council. (2012a). *SME Annual Report 2011–2012*. Available at http://www.smecorp.gov.my/index.php/en/resources/2015-12-21-11-07-06/sme-annual-report (Accessed on 10 April 2019). (2012b). *SME Masterplan 2012 – 2020: Catalysing Growth and Income*. Available at http://www.smecorp.gov.my/index.php/en/resources/2015-12-21-11-07-06/sme-masterplan (Accessed on 10 April 2019). (2013). *SME Annual Report 2012 – 2013*. Available at http://www.smecorp.gov.my/index.php/en/resources/2015-12-21-11-07-06/sme-annual-report (Accessed on 10 April 2019). (2014). *SME Annual Report 2013 – 2014*. Available at http://www.smecorp.gov.my/index.php/en/resources/2015-12-21-11-07-06/sme-annual-report (Accessed on 10 April 2019). (2016). *SME Annual Report 2015 – 2016*. Available at http://www.smecorp.gov.my/index.php/en/resources/2015-12-21-11-07-06/sme-annual-report (Accessed on 10 April 2019). (2018). *SME Annual Report 2017 – 2018*. Available at http://www.smecorp.gov.my/index.php/en/resources/2015-12-21-11-07-06/sme-annual-report (Accessed on 10 April 2019)

Robb, A., & Robinson, D. (2014). The capital structure decisions of new firms. *Review of Financial Studies*, *27*(1), 153–179. doi:10.1093/rfs/hhs072

Smith, S., Windmeijer, F., & Wright, E. (2014). Peer Effects in Charitable Giving: Evidence from the (Running) Field. *Economic Journal (London)*, *125*(35), 1053–1071.

Thaker, M. A. M., & Thaker, H. M. T. (2018). SMEs Financing and the Potential of Crowdfunding. Working paper.

Zhang, J., & Liu, P. (2012). Rational Herding in Microloan Markets. *Management Science*, *58*(3), 892–912. doi:10.1287/mnsc.1110.1459

## ADDITIONAL READING

Pitchay, A.P., Thaker, M.A.M.T., Azhar, Z., Mydin, A. A., & Thaker, H.M. T. (2019). Factors persuade individuals' behavioral intention to opt for Islamic bank services. *Journal of Islamic Marketing*. Forthcoming article.

Thaker, M. A. M. T., & Allah Pitchay, A. (2018). Developing waqf land through the crowdfunding-waqf model (CWM): The case of Malaysia. *Journal of Islamic Accounting and Business Research, 9*(3), 448–456. doi:10.1108/JIABR-05-2016-0062

Thaker, M. A. M. T., Pitchay, A. P., Thaker, H. M. T., & Amin, M. F. B. (2019). Factors influencing consumers' adoption of Islamic mobile banking services in Malaysia: An approach of partial least squares (PLS). *Journal of Islamic Marketing, 10*(4), 1037–1056. doi:10.1108/JIMA-04-2018-0065

Thaker, M. A. M. T., Thaker, H. M. T., & Pitchay, A. P. (2018). Modeling crowdfunders' behavioral intention to adopt the crowdfunding-waqf model (CWM) in Malaysia: The theory of the technology acceptance model. *International Journal of Islamic and Middle Eastern Finance and Management, 11*(2), 231–249. doi:10.1108/IMEFM-06-2017-0157

## KEY TERMS AND DEFINITIONS

**Crowdfunding:** The practice of funding a project or venture by raising money from a large number of people who each contribute a relatively small amount, typically via the Internet.

**Hibah:** A gift of an asset(s) made voluntarily by a donor during his/her lifetime to the beneficiary without any consideration.

**Integrated:** Two or more things combined in order to become more effective.

**Islamic Finance:** Corporations in the Muslim world, including banks and other lending institutions, raise capital in accordance with Sharia, or Islamic law. It also refers to the types of investments that are permissible under this form of law.

**Murabahah:** Referred to as cost-plus financing, it is an Islamic financing structure in which the seller provides the cost and profit margin of an asset.

**Profit and Loss Sharing:** Method of finance used by Islamic financial or Shariah-compliant institutions to comply with the religious prohibition on interest on loans that most Muslims subscribe to.

**Sadaqah:** The concept of voluntary giving in Islam, *fi sabillilah* (for the cause of Allah).

**Small Medium Enterprise:** Non-subsidiary, independent firms that employ fewer than a given number of employees. This number varies across countries. Small firms are generally those with fewer than 50 employees, while micro-enterprises have at most 10, or in some cases 5, workers.

# Compilation of References


Aaker, D. A., & Adler, D. A. (2001). *Developing business strategies*. Sons New York, NY: John Wiley.

Abduh, M., Omar, M., & Duasa, J. (2011). The Impact of Crisis and Macroeconomic Variables towards Islamic Banking Deposits. *American Journal of Applied Sciences*, *8*(12), 1413–1418. doi:10.3844/ajassp.2011.1378.1383

Abdul Rahim, F. (2016). Fintech Pitch for Islamic Bank: Three New Areas of Services. Paper submitted to meet course requirements IB5013 Islamic Banking Practices, Masters In Islamic Finance Practice (MIFP) INCEIF, September 2016 Semester.

Abdullah, N., & Hanafi, H. (2007). *A comparative approach of money lending activities practiced by the financial institution and "Ah Long" in Malaysia. Law Conference 2007*, April 18th-20th, Sintok, Kedah, 257-267.

Abdullah, O. (2016). Impact of Fintech to Islamic finance. Retrieved from https://www.islamicfinance.com/2016/04/impact-Fintech-islamic-finance/

Achrol, R. S., & Kotler, P. (1999). Marketing in the network economy. *Journal of Marketing*, *63*(Special Issue), 146–163. doi:10.1177/00222429990634s114

Adelakun, O. J. (2011). The Nexus of Private Savings and Economic Growth in Emerging Economy: A Case of Nigeria. *Journal of Economics and Sustainable Development*, 2(6), 31–45.

Ager, S. N. S., Abdullah, M., Shahwahid, F. M., Wahab, N. A., & Saidpudin, W. (2015). An analysis of the definition of halal: shari'ah vs statutes. In World Academic and Research Congress. 2015 (World-AR 2015) Ar-Rahim Hall, YARSI University, Jakarta, Indonesia, Dec. 9-10, 2015.

Aghion, P., & Bolton, P. (1997). A theory of trickle-down growth and development. *The Review of Economic Studies*, *64*(2), 151–172. doi:10.2307/2971707

Agostino, D. (2013). Using social media to engage citizens: A study of Italian municipalities. *Public Relations Review*, *39*(3), 232–234. doi:10.1016/j.pubrev.2013.02.009

Agrawal, A., Catalini, C., & Goldfarb, A. (2013). Some Simple Economics of Crowdfunding. *National Bureau of Economic Research (NBER) Working Paper No. w19133*.

Agrawal, A., Catalini, C., & Goldfarb, A. (2015). Crowdfunding: Geography, Social Networks, and the Timing of Investment Decisions. *Journal of Economics & Management Strategy*, *24*(2), 253–274. doi:10.1111/jems.12093

Ahmed, H. (2002). Financing microenterprises: An analytical study of Islamic microfinance institutions. *Islamic Economic Studies, 9*(2), March.

Ahmed, S., & Hassan, M. (2003). Survey and case investigations on application of quality management tools and techniques in SMIs. *International Journal of Quality & Reliability Management*, *20*(7), 795–826. doi:10.1108/02656710310491221

AITI. (2018). AITI. Retrieved June 12, 2019, from https://www.aiti.gov.bn/SitePages/Surveys.aspx

Akaike, H. (1971). Autogressive Model Fitting for Control. *Annals of the Institute of Statistical Mathematics*, *23*(1), 163–180. doi:10.1007/BF02479221

Akram, N., & Akram, M. I. (2015). Savings Behaviour in Muslim and Non Muslim Country in Context to the Interest Rate. *Pakistan Journal of Applied Economics*, *25*(2), 161–177.

Al Quran[1].

Albers, A., Gladysz, B., Pinner, T., Butenko, V., & Stürmlinger, T. (2016). Procedure for defining the system of objectives in the initial phase of an industry 4.0 project focusing on intelligent quality control systems. *Procedia Cirp*, *52*, 262–267. doi:10.1016/j.procir.2016.07.067

Aldrich, D. F. (1999). *Mastering the Digital Marketplace: Practical Strategies for Competitiveness in the New Economy*. John Wiley & Sons.

Ale Ebrahim, N., Ahmed, S., & Taha, Z. (2003). Virtual R&D teams in small and medium enterprises: A literature review.

Alexakis, C., Dasilas, A., & Grose, C. (2013). Asymmetric Dynamic Relations between Stock Prices and Mutual Fund Units in Japan. An Application of Hidden Cointegration Technique. *International Review of Financial Analysis*, *28*, 1–8. doi:10.1016/j.irfa.2013.02.001

Alexander, M. (2012). *Decision-Making using the Analytic Hierarchy Process (AHP) and SAS / IML* (pp. 1–12). Baltimore, MD: Social Security Administration.

Al-Jafari, M. K., Salameh, H., & Al-Asil, K. (2013). An Empirical Investigation of the Price Relationship between Open-end Mutual Funds and Amman Stock Exchange Index. *Advances in Management & Applied Economics*, *3*(5), 1–20.

Allen, D. E., & Macdonald, G. (1995). The Long-run Gains from International Equity Diversification: Australian Evidence from Cointegration Tests. *Applied Financial Economics*, *5*(1), 33–42. doi:10.1080/758527669

Allison, T. H., Davis, B. C., Short, J. C., & Webb, J. W. (2015). Crowdfunding is a Prosocial Microlending Environment: Examining the Role of Intrinsic Versus Extrinsic Cues. *Entrepreneurship Theory and Practice*, *39*(1), 53–73. doi:10.1111/etap.12108

Alsayed, K. (2017). Fintech: The new barrier to entry in Islamic finance, *Islamic Finance News*, August 23, 2017.

Amit, R., & Zott, C. (2001). Value creation in E-business. *Strategic Management Journal*, *22*(6–7), 493–520. doi:10.1002mj.187

Andam, Z. R. (2003). E-Commerce and e-Business. *E-ASEAN Task Force UNDP-APDIP*, 47.

Anderson, J. C., Hernande, S., Jessup, E. L., & North, E. (2018). Perceived Safe and Adequate Truck Parking: A Random Parameters Binary Logit Analysis of Truck Driver Opinions in the Pacific Northwest. *International Journal of Transportation Science and Technology*, *7*(1), 89–102. doi:10.1016/j.ijtst.2018.01.001

Ang, L. (2011). Community relationship management and social media. *Journal of Database Marketing and Customer Strategy Management*, *18*(1), 31–38. doi:10.1057/dbm.2011.3

Anonim. (2013). Undang-Undang no 20, tahun 2008 tentang Usaha Mikro Kecil dan Menengah. Kementerian Koperasi dan Usaha Mikro, Kecil dan Menengah.

Anonim. (2015). Indikator Industri Kecil dan Menengah Indonesia. Badan Pusat Statistik, Jakarta.

Antony, J., Jiju Antony, F., Kumar, M., & Rae Cho, B. (2007). Six sigma in service organisations: Benefits, challenges and difficulties, common myths, empirical observations and success factors. *International Journal of Quality & Reliability Management*, *24*(3), 294–311. doi:10.1108/02656710710730889

APJIII. (2017). *Indonesia Internet Usage for Business Sector 2017*. Retrieved from https://apjii.or.id/downfile/file/SurveiPenggunaanInternetSektorBisnis2017versienglish.pdf

Arif, A. M. M. (2009). The licensing system under the Malaysian moneylenders act 2003. *International Journal of Economics and Management*, *3*(1), 1–21.

Arnaboldi, M., Busco, C., & Cuganesan, S. (2017). Accounting, accountability, social media, and big data: Revolution or hype? *Accounting, Auditing, & Accountability Journal*, *30*(4), 762–776. doi:10.1108/AAAJ-03-2017-2880

*Asean Today*. (2018). Better late than never? Brunei and its role in the Fintech revolution. Retrieved from https://www.aseantoday.com/2018/06/better-late-than-never-brunei-and-its-role-in-the-Fintech-revolution/

Asian Development Bank (ADB). (2001). *ADB Annual Report 2001*. ISSN 306-8370 (print). Retrieved from https://www.adb.org/documents/adb-annual-report-2001. Accessed on 29 September 2014.

Askari, H., Iqbal, Z., & Mirakhor, A. (2009). New issues in Islamic finance and economics, progress and challenges. Singapore: John Wiley & Sons (Asia).

Asutay, M. (2007). Conceptualization of the second best solution in overcoming the social failure of Islamic banking and finance: Examining the overpowering of Homoislamicus by Homoeconomicus. *IIUM Journal of Economics and Management*, *15*(2), 167–196.

Asutay, M. (2007). Conceptualization of the Second Best Solution in Overcoming the Social Failure of Islamic Finance: Examining the Overpowering of Homoislamicus by Homoeconomicus. *IIUM Journal in Economics and Management*, *15*(2), 167–195.

Attanasio, O. P., & Weber, G. (2010). Consumption and Saving: Models of Intertemporal Allocation and Their Implications for Public Policy, *Journal of Economic Literature*. *American Economic Association*, *48*(3), 693–751.

Attewell, P. (1992). Technology diffusion and organizational learning: The case of business computing. *Organization Science*, *3*(1), 1–19. doi:10.1287/orsc.3.1.1

Autoriti Monetari Brunei Darussalam. (n.d.). *Autoriti Monetari Brunei Darussalam.* Retrieved from http://www.ambd.gov.bn/

Awirya, A. A., Rahmayani, K., & Prirayani, J. (2012). The opportunity of profit-sharing scheme implementation on moneylender in expanding Islamic banking service, evidence from traditional market in Surabaya, Indonesia. In Jurnal BPPK, 4, 1-17. Jakarta: Badan Pendidikan dan Pelatihan Keuangan (BPPK) Kementerian Keuangan Republik Indonesia (Kemenkeu RI).

Bailey, J. P., & Bakos, Y. (1997). An Exploratory Study of the Emerging Role of Electronic Intermediaries. *International Journal of Electronic Commerce*, *1*(3), 7–20. doi:10.1080/10864415.1997.11518287

Bailey, W., & Lim, J. (1992). Evaluating the Diversification Benefits of the New Country Funds. *Journal of Portfolio Management*, *18*(3), 74–80. doi:10.3905/jpm.1992.409405

Bakos, Y. (1991). A Strategic Analysis of Electronic Marketplaces. *Management Information Systems Quarterly*, *15*(3), 295. doi:10.2307/249641

Bakos, Y. (1998). The emerging role of electronic marketplaces on the Internet. *Communications of the ACM*, *41*(8), 35–42. doi:10.1145/280324.280330

Bamford, D. R., & Greatbanks, R. W. (2005). The use of quality management tools and techniques: A study of application in everyday situations. *International Journal of Quality & Reliability Management*, *22*(4), 376–392. doi:10.1108/02656710510591219

Banerje, E. A., & Newman, A. (1993). Occupational choice and process of development. *Journal of Political Economy*, 101, 274-298.

Bank Negara Malaysia. (2016). Retrieved from http://www.bnm.gov.my/. Accessed on 10 April 2019.

Bappenas. (2015). *Masterplan Arsitektur Keuangan Syariah Indonesia*. Jakarta: Bappenas Press.

Barnes, N. G., Lescault, A., & Wright, S. (2013). *2013 Fortune 500 are bullish on social media.* Retrieved May 2, 2019 from www.umassd.edu/cmr/socialmediaresearch/2013fortune500/

Barro, R. J. (1974). Are Government Bonds Net Wealth? *Journal of Political Economy, 82*(6), 1095–1117. doi:10.1086/260266

Barslund, M., & Tarp, F. (2008). Formal and informal rural credit in four provinces of Vietnam. *The Journal of Development Studies, 44,* 4, 485-503. DOI: 798 doi:10.1080/00220380801980

Basu, R. (2004). *Implementing quality: A practical guide to tools and techniques.* London, UK: Thomson Learning.

Basu, R., & Wright, J. N. (2012). *Quality beyond six sigma.* Routledge. doi:10.4324/9780080515502

Baughn, C. C., Chua, B. L., & Neupert, K. E. (2006). The normative context for women's participation in entrepreneurship: A multicountry study. *Entrepreneurship Theory and Practice, 30*(5), 687–708. doi:10.1111/j.1540-6520.2006.00142.x

Baumol, W. J. (1990). Entrepreneurship: Productive, unproductive, and destructive. *Journal of Political Economy, 98*(5), 893–921. doi:10.1086/261712

Baur, C., & Wee, D. (2015). Manufacturing's next act. *McKinsey Quarterly, Jun.*

Bayazit, O. (2003). Total quality management (TQM) practices in Turkish manufacturing organizations. *The TQM Magazine, 15*(5), 345–350. doi:10.1108/09544780310502435

Beckert, J. (2009). The social order of markets. *Theory and Society, 38*(3), 245–269. doi:10.100711186-008-9082-0

Belleflamme, P., Lambert, T., & Schwienbacher, A. (2010). *Crowdfunding: An Industrial Organization Perspective.* Workshop on Digital Business Models: Understanding Strategies, Held in Paris in June 2010.

Belleflamme, P., Lambert, T., & Schwienbacher, A. (2013a). Crowdfunding: Tapping the right crowd. *Journal of Business Venturing, 29*(5), 585–609. doi:10.1016/j.jbusvent.2013.07.003

BenMark, G. (2014). *Why the COO should lead social-media customer service.* Retrieved July 16, 2019 from http://www.mckinsey.com/business-functions/marketing-and-sales/our-insights/why-the-coo-should-lead-social-media-customer-service

Ben-Zion, U., Choi, J. J., & Hauser, S. (1996). The Price Linkages between Country Funds and National Stock Markets: Evidence from Cointegration and Causality Tests of Germany, Japan and UK Funds. *Journal of Business Finance & Accounting, 23*(7), 1005–1017. doi:10.1111/j.1468-5957.1996.tb01037.x

Bidault, M., & Cummings, T. (1994). *Advanced Manufacturing Technology and Work Design.* Chichester: Wiley.

Bio Malaysia & ASEAN Bioeconomy Conference. (2015). *Halal economy : Opportunity and Challenges*. Retrieved from http://biomalaysia.bioeconomycorporation.my/speakerssliders/day1/session2perlis/BioMalaysia 2015-v4(17.08.2015).pdf

BizBrunei. (2019). Brunei's Instagram penetration highest in the world. Bizbrunei (Online) Retrieved from https://www.bizbrunei.com/2019/04/bruneis-instagram-penetration-highest-in-the-world/

Blackshaw, P. (2006). *The consumer-generated surveillance culture*. Retrieved June 28, 2019 from http://www.clickz.com/showPage.html?page=3576076

Bolton, B., & Thompson, J. (2004). *Entrepreneurs: Talent, temperament, techniques* (2nd ed.). Oxford, UK: Elsevier Butterworth-Henemann.

Borneo Bulletin. (2016, Nov. 11).

Bozeman, B. (2000). Technology transfer and public policy: A review of research and theory. *Research Policy*, *29*(4/5), 627–655. doi:10.1016/S0048-7333(99)00093-1

BPS. (2018). *Berita Resmi Statistik No. 07/01/Th. XXII, 15 Januari: Profil kemiskinan di Indonesia September 2018*. Jakarta: Badan Pusat Statistik (BPS).

BPS. (2019). *Berita resmi statistik no. 57/07/Th. XXII, 15 Juli: Tingkat ketimpangan pengeluaran penduduk Indonesia maret 2019*. Jakarta: Badan Pusat Statistik (BPS).

Brady, J. E., & Allen, T. T. (2006). Six Sigma literature: A review and agenda for future research. *Quality and Reliability Engineering International*, *22*(3), 335–367. doi:10.1002/qre.769

Braun, V., & Clarke, V. (2006). Using thematic analysis in psychology. *Qualitative Research in Psychology*, *3*(2), 77–101. doi:10.1191/1478088706qp063oa

Brewer, C. (2014). *Designing better maps. A guide for GIS users*. Esri Press.

Brouthers, L. E., Nakos, G., Hadjimarcou, J., & Brouthers, K. D. (2009). Key factors for successful export performance for small firms. *Journal of International Marketing, 17*(3), 21-38.

BruDirect. (2019). Development of 4th Industrial Revolution. BruDirect (Online). Retrieved from http://brudirect.com/news.php?id=65263

Bruhn, M., Schoenmueller, V., & Schäfer, D. (2012). Are social media replacing traditional media in terms of brand equity creation? *Management Research Review*, *35*(9), 770–790. doi:10.1108/01409171211255948

Bruijl, G. (2018). *The Relevance of Porter's Five Forces in Today's Innovative and Changing Business Environment*. SSRN Electronic Journal; doi:10.2139srn.3192207

Brunei Government. (2015). *Brunei Darussalam Key Indicators 2014*. Brunei Darussalam: Department of Statistics, Department of Economic Planning and Development, Prime Minister's Office.

Brüntje, D., & Gajda, O. (2016). *Crowdfunding in Europe, State of the Art in Theory and Practice*. Switzerland: Springer International Publishing.

Bruton, G. D., Ahlstrom, D., & Li, H.-L. (2010). Institutional theory and entrepreneurship: Where are we now and where to we need to move in the future. *Entrepreneurship Theory and Practice*, *34*(3), 421–440. doi:10.1111/j.1540-6520.2010.00390.x

Bryant, C. (1989). Entrepreneurs in the rural environment. *Journal of Rural Studies*, *5*(4), 337–348. doi:10.1016/0743-0167(89)90060-0

Burns, T., & Stalker, G. M. (1961). *The Management of Innovation* (3rd ed.). London, UK: Tavistock Publications.

Burrough, P. A., McDonnell, R., & McDonnell, R. A. (2000). Principles of Geographical Information System, New York: Oxford University Press.

Burrough, P. A., McDonnell, R., McDonnell, R. A., & Lloyd, C. D. (2015). *Principles of Geographical Information Systems*. OUP Oxford.

Burton, J. (1998). How, When, And Why To Buy Stocks. *Medical Economics*, *75*(13), 86–94.

Cafferky, M. (2005). *The Porter Five-forces Industry Analysis Framework For Religious Nonprofits: A conceptual analysis*.

Candramila, W., Sumarsono, S. H., Suryobroto, B., & Moeis, M. R. (2015). Face Shape Variation Among Sundanese People form Western Java, Indonesia. *Hayati Journal of Biosciences*, *22*(1), 34–40. doi:10.4308/hjb.22.1.34

Cardon, M. S., Wincent, J., Singh, J., & Drnovsek, M. (2009). The nature and experience of entrepreneurial passion. *Academy of Management Review*, *34*(3), 511–532. doi:10.5465/amr.2009.40633190

Castells, M. (2011). *The Rise of the Network Society* (3rd ed.). Oxford, UK: John Wiley & Sons.

Catto-Smith, C. (n.d.). *The weekly link Halal logistics a fast-growing market*. Retrieved from http://www.halalrc.org/images/Research Material/Literature/Halal logistics a fast-growing market.pdf

Centenaro, A., & Laimer, C. G. (2017). Cooperative Relationship and Competitiveness in Supermarket Sector. *Review of Business Management.*, *19*(63), 65–81. doi:10.7819/rbgn.v0i0.3070

Chaleunsinh, C., Akihiko, O., Koichi, F., & Fumiharu, M. (2015). An analysis on borrowing behavior of rural households in Vientiane municipality: Case study of four villages. *Southeast Asian Studies, 3,* Supplementary Issue, March, 113–133.

Chambers, R. (1996). *Relaxed and Participatory Appraisal. Notes of Practical Approaches and Methods:* Brighton: Institute of Development Studies.

Chambers, R. (1997). *Responsible Well-being*: A Personal Agenda for Development. *World Development*, *25*(11), 1743–1754. doi:10.1016/S0305-750X(97)10001-8

Chambers, R. (1994). The Origins and Practice of Participatory Rural Appraisal. *World Development, 22*(7), pp. 953-969, 1994 Copyright 0 1994 Elsevier Science Ltd. 0305750X(94) E0029.

Chandadarot, K., & Liv, D. (2011). *Impact of micro finance services in Cambodia*. Phnom Penh: Cambodia Microfinance Association.

Chandararot, K. (2002). The development of micro finance in Cambodia. *Cambodia Development Review, 6*(3), 1–4.

Chapra, M. U., & Khan, T. (2008). *Regulasi dan pengawasan bank syariah*. Jakarta: Bumi Aksara.

Charantimath, P. M. (2011). *Total quality management* (2nd ed.). Boston, MA: Pearson Education.

Chatta, J. A. (2017). Fintech and Islamic finance: A regulatory perspective. *Global Halal Investing Journal*, December, 2017. Retrieved from https://journal.wahedinvest.com/Fintech-and-islamic-finance-a-regulatory-perspective/

Chen, A. H.-L., Cheng, K., & Lee, Z.-H. (2011). The behavior of Taiwanese investors in asset allocation. *Asia-Pacific Journal of Business Administration, 3*(1), 62–74. doi:10.1108/17574321111116405

Chen, C.-J., Huang, J.-W., & Hsiao, Y.-C. (2010). Knowledge management and innovativeness: The role of organizational climate and structure. *International Journal of Manpower, 31*(8), 848–870. doi:10.1108/01437721011088548

Chen, X. P., Yao, X., & Kotha, S. (2009). Entrepreneur passion and preparedness in business plan presentations: A persuasion analysis of venture capitalists' funding decisions. *Academy of Management Journal, 52*(1), 199–214. doi:10.5465/amj.2009.36462018

Chircu, A. N., & Kauffman, R. J. (2013). *E-Commerce and V-Business*. Routledge.

Choi, H. J. (2009). Technology transfer issues and a new technology transfer model. *The Journal of Technology Studies, 35*(1), 49–57. doi:10.21061/jots.v35i1.a.7

Chonlaworn, P., & Pongpirodom, P. (2015). *Can Nano Finance unleash The Grassroots from Loan Shark Problems?* EIC Analysis. April. 1. Retrieved from https://www.scbeic.com/ en/detail/product/1255

Chow, G. C. (1993). Capital Formation and Economic Growth in China. *The Quarterly Journal of Economics, 108*(3), 809–842. doi:10.2307/2118409

Chu, P. K. K. (2010). The Price Linkages between the Equity Fund Price Levels and the Stock Markets: Evidences from Cointegration Approach and Causality Analysis of Hong Kong Mandatory Provident Fund (MPFs). *International Review of Financial Analysis, 19*(4), 281–288. doi:10.1016/j.irfa.2010.08.001

Chu, P. K. K. (2011). Relationship between Macroeconomic Variables and Net Asset Values (NAV) of Equity Funds: Cointegration Evidence and Vector Error Correction Model of the Hong Kong Mandatory Provident Funds (MPFs). *Journal of International Financial Markets, Institutions and Money*, *21*(5), 792–810. doi:10.1016/j.intfin.2011.06.003

CIKL. (2011). *Roadmapping capacity building needs in consumer protection in ASEAN, country report: Brunei Darussalam (final).* Revised 3 June. Project under the Special Services Agreement between the ASEAN Secretariat and Consumers International Kuala Lumpur (CIKL) Office.

Clegg, B., Rees, C., & Titchen, M. (2010). A study into the effectiveness of quality management training: A focus on tools and critical success factors. *The TQM Journal*, *22*(2), 188–208. doi:10.1108/17542731011024291

CO. US Chamber of Commerce. (2019). Retrieved October 3, 2019 from https://www.uschamber.com/co/run/business-financing/business-financing-challenges

Cohen, W., & Levinthal, D. (1989). Innovation and Learning: The two Faces of R & D. *Economic Journal (London)*, *99*(397), 569–596. doi:10.2307/2233763

Coleman, B. E. (2006). Microfinance in Northeast Thailand: Who benefits and how much? *World Development, 34*(9), 1612–1638. DOI: dev.2006.01.006 doi:10.1016/j.world

Colombo, M. G., Franzoni, C., & Rossi-Lamastra, C. (2015). Internal Social Capital and the Attraction of Early Contributions in Crowdfunding Projects. *Entrepreneurship Theory and Practice*, *39*(1), 75–100. doi:10.1111/etap.12118

Constantiou, I. D., & Kallinikos, J. (2015). New games, new rules: Big data and the changing context of strategy. *Journal of Information Technology*, *30*(1), 44–57. doi:10.1057/jit.2014.17

Cooper, J. R. (1998). A Multidimensional Approach the Adoption of Innovation. *Management Decision*, *36*(8), 493–501. doi:10.1108/00251749810232565

Cornwall, A. (2000). *Making Differences? Gender and Participatory Development.* IDS Discussion Paper 378. Institute Development Studies.

Coy, P. (2017). When Does a Lender Become a Loan Shark? In *Bloomberg Businessweek, April* 15. Retrieved from https://www.bloomberg.com/news/articles/2017-04-05/when-does-a-lender-become-a-loan-shark

Crescentrating, M. (2018). *Mastercard-Crescentrating GMTI 2018 Global Muslim Travel Index 2018.* Retrieved from https://www.halalmedia.jp/wp-content/uploads/2018/04/GMITI-Report-2018.pdf

CrescentRating. (2018). Global Muslim Travel Index 2018. (April). Retrieved from https://www.crescentrating.com/download/thankyou.html?file=X7UrOM8Y_GMITI-Report-2018-web-version%281%29.pdf

Crouch, R. L. (1972). Macroeconomics. New York: Harcourt Brace Javanovich.

Cuihua, C., Sheng, L., Pengfei, L., & Lu, W. 2016. Active Shop Scheduling of Production Process Based on RFID Technology. In *MATEC Web of Conferences* (Vol. 42, p. 04004). EDP Sciences. 10.1051/matecconf/20164204004

Daft, R. L. (1978). A Dual Core Model of Orgaizational innovation. *Academy of Management Journal*, *20*, 193–211.

Daft, R. L., & Armstrong, A. (2012). *Organization Theory and Design* (2nd ed.). Toronto, Canada: Nelson Education.

Dahlstrom, R. F., Dwyer, R., & Chandrashekaran, M. (1995). Environment, Structure and Performance in Interfirm Exchange. *Journal of Business-To-Business Marketing*, *2*(2), 37–58. doi:10.1300/J033v02n02_04

Dale, B. (2003). *Managing quality* (4th ed.). Oxford, UK: Blackwell Publishers.

Daley, S., & Sautet, F. (2005). *Microfinance in action: The Philippine experience.* Mercatus Policy Series, Mercatus Center's Global Prosperity Initiative, George Mason University. February.

Damanpour, F., & Damanpour, J. A. (2001). E-business e-commerce evolution: Perspective and strategy. *Managerial Finance*, *27*(7), 16–33. doi:10.1108/03074350110767268

De Aghion, B. A., & Morduch, J. (2005). *The economics of microfinance.* Cambridge, MA: The MIT Press.

Deb, B. J., Sengupta, K., & Ray, B. D. (Eds.). (2008). *Globalization and north east India.* New Delhi, India: Ashok Kumar Mittal.

Dekay, S. H. (2012). How large companies react to negative Facebook comments. *Corporate Communications*, *17*(3), 289–299. doi:10.1108/13563281211253539

Deloitte. (2013). *Who says banks can't be social? Become a social bank, inside and out.* Ontario, Canada, Deloitte LLP.

DeMers, J. (2017). *Why Instagram Is The Top Social Platform For Engagement (And How To Use It).* Retrieved August 20, 2019 from https://www.forbes.com/sites/jaysondemers/2017/03/28/why-instagram-is-the-top-social-platform-for-engagement-and-how-to-use-it/

Department of Agriculture and Agri-food. (2009). *Mid-term Plan 2008-2011.* Retrieved from http://www.agriculture.gov.bn/DOA2009/pdf%20Publication/Pelan%20Strategik%202008-2013.pdf

Deshpande, R. S., & Arora, S. (Eds.). (2010). *Agrarian crisis and farmer suicides: Land reforms in India* (Vol. 12). New Delhi, India: Sage.

Ding, Q., Akoorie, M., & Pavlovich, K. (2009). Understanding the specificity and complexity of inter-firm knowledge flows in alliance networks. *Interdisciplinary Journal of Contemporary Research in Business*, *1*(7), 8–33.

Drew, E., & Healy, C. (2006). Quality management approaches in Irish organizations. *The TQM Magazine*, *18*(4), 358–371. doi:10.1108/09544780610671039

Duflos, E., Luchtenburg, P., Ren, L., & Chen, L. Y. (2013). *Microfinance in Myanmar, sector assessment*. IFC Advisory Services in East Asia and the Pacific. January.

Duncan, S. (2016). *Brands, Handle Negative Criticism on Social Media Like a Champ*. Retrieved August 11, 2019 from https://www.salesforce.com/blog/2016/03/brands-handle-negative-criticism-social-media-champ.html

Dusuki, A. W. (2008). Banking for the poor: The role of Islamic banking in microfinance initiatives. *Humanomics*, *24*(1), 49–66. doi:10.1108/08288660810851469

Dusuki, A. W., & Abdullah, N. I. (2007). Why do Malaysian customers patronize Islamic banks? *International Journal of Bank Marketing*, *25*(3), 142–160. doi:10.1108/02652320710739850

Dusuki, A. W., & Abozaid, A. (2007). A critical appraisal on the challenges of realizing Maqasid al-Shariah in Islamic banking and finance. *IIUM Journal of Economics and Management*, *15*(2), 143–166.

Duvall, A. (2004). *The impact of interest rate ceilings on microfinance. Donor Brief No. 18, May. CGAP Donor Information Resource Centre*. DIRECT.

Easy access savings accounts. (n.d.). Retrieved from http://www.bibd.com.bn/

Economy of the Organisation of Islamic Cooperation. (n.d.). *Arabian Business*. Retrieved from http://www.arabianbusiness.com/muslim-tourism-sector-said-be-worth-over-138bn--growing-656633.html

Edelman, B., Jaffe, S., & Kominers, S. D. (2011). *To Groupon or Not to Groupon: The Profitability of Deep Discounts*. 24.

Edwards, J. (2013). *Twitter's "dark pool": IPO doesn't mention 6541 million users who abandoned Twitter*. Retrieved May 26, 2019 from www.businessinsider.com/twitter-total-registered-users-v-monthlyactive-users-2013-11

Eisenmann, T., Parker, G., & Van Alstyne, M. (2006). Strategies for two-sided markets. *Harvard Business Review*, *84*, 92-101, 149.

Emery, M., Wall, M., & Macke, D. (2004). From theory to action: Energizing entrepreneurship (E2), strategies to aid distressed communities grow their own. *Journal of the Community Development Society*, *35*(1), 82–96. doi:10.1080/15575330409490123

Eng, T.-Y. (2004). The Role of E-Marketplaces in Supply Chain Management. *Industrial Marketing Management*, *33*(2), 97–105. doi:10.1016/S0019-8501(03)00032-4

Eridilek, A. (1986). Issues in international technology transfer. *Economic Impact*, *4*(56).

Erol, C., Kaynak, E., & El-Bdour, R. (1990). Conventional and Islamic banks: Patronage behavior of Jordanian customers. *International Journal of Bank Marketing*, *8*(4), 25–35. doi:10.1108/02652329010004231

Etter, M., Ravasi, D., & Colleoni, E. (2017). *Social Media and the Formation of Organizational Reputation. Academy of Management Review*. In-Press.

Evans, D. S., Hagiu, A., & Schmalensee, R. (2006). *Invisible Engines: How Software Platforms Drive Innovation and Transform Industries*. doi:10.7551/mitpress/3959.001.0001

Evans, D. S., Schmalensee, R., Noel, M. D., Chang, H. H., & Garcia-Swartz, D. D. (2011). *Platform Economics: Essays on Multi-Sided Businesses* (SSRN Scholarly Paper No. ID 1974020). Retrieved from Social Science Research Network website: https://papers.ssrn.com/abstract=1974020

EY. (2016). *Banking in emerging markets GCC Fintech play* 2017.

Faizal, P. R. M., Ridhwan, A. A. M., & Kalsom, A. W. (2013). The Entrepreneurs Characteristics from al-Quran and al-Hadis. *International Journal of Trade. Economics and Finance*, *4*(4), 191–196.

Fazlan, S., & Mohammad, A. (2007). *The Efficiency of Islamic Banks: Empirical Evidence from the MENA and Asian Countries Islamic Banking Sectors*. Paper presented at the Fifth International Islamic Finance Conference, September 3-4, Kuala Lumpur. Academic Press.

Febianto, I., & Ashany, A. M. (2012). The impact of qardhul hasan financing using zakah funds on economic empowerment (Case study of Dompet Dhuafa, West Java, Indonesia). *Asian Business Review*, *1*(1), 15–20. doi:10.18034/abr.v1i1.139

Finmark Trust & UNCDF. (2013). *Survey highlights, finscope Myanmar 2013. A survey by Finmark Trust and The United Nations Capital Development Fund*. UNCDF.

Fintech And Islamic Finance. (2017). Retrieved from https://islmFintech.com/Fintech-and-islamic-finance/

Fleishman Hillard Majlis. (2011). The Market Opportunity of the Muslim World. Bio Malaysia & ASEAN Bioeconomy Conference. (2015). *Halal economy : Opportunity and Challenges*. Retrieved from http://biomalaysia.bioeconomycorporation.my/speakerssliders/day1/session2perlis/BioMalaysia 2015-v4(17.08.2015).pdf

Flora, C. B., & Flora, J. L. (2004). *Rural communities: Legacy and change* (2nd ed.). Boulder, CO: Westview Press.

Foerch, T., Ki, O., Thein, S., & Waldschmidt, S. (2016). Myanmar's financial sector a challenging environment for banks, 3rd Edition, October. Yangon: The Deutsche Gesellschaft für Internationale Zusammenarbeit (GIZ).

Fotopoulos, C. B., & Psomas, E. L. (2009). The impact of "soft" and "hard" TQM elements on quality management results. *International Journal of Quality & Reliability Management*, *26*(2), 150–163. doi:10.1108/02656710910928798

Fotopoulos, C., & Psomas, E. (2009). The use of quality management tools and techniques in ISO 9001: 2000 certified companies: The Greek case. *International Journal of Productivity and Performance Management*, *58*(6), 564–580. doi:10.1108/17410400910977091

Fountas, G., Sarwar, M. T., Anastasopoulos, P. C., & Blatt, A. (2018). Analysis of Stationary and Dynamic Factors Affecting Highway Accident Occurrence: A Dynamic Correlated Grouped Random Parameters Binary Logit Approach. *Accident; Analysis, and Prevention*, *113*, 330–340

Franz, J. C. (1990). The Sultanate of Brunei: Oil Wealth and problems of Development. (M. Schmitz, & A. Sharp, Trans.) In Universitat Nuremberg, Nuremberg.

Freedman, S., & Jin, G. (2014). *The Signaling Value of Online Social Networks: Lessons from Peer-to-Peer Lending*. National Bureau of Economic Research (NBER) Working Paper No. 19820, 48 -70.

Ganesan, S., & Kesley, J. (2006). Technology transfer: International collaboration in Sri Lanka. *Construction Management and Economics*, *24*(7), 743–753. doi:10.1080/01446190600704703

Gardner, J. (2015). *Regulating moneylending in Singapore: Looking at Alla sides*. Research Policy Report CBFL-Rep-JG1, July. Centre for Banking and Finance Law (CBFL), Faculty of Law, National University of Singapore.

Gartner, W. B. (1985). A conceptual framework for describing the phenomenon of new venture creation. *Academy of Management Review*, *10*(4), 696–706. doi:10.5465/amr.1985.4279094

Georgakopoulos, D., & Jayaraman, P. P. (2016). Internet of things: From internet scale sensing to smart services. *Computing*, *98*(10), 1041–1058. doi:10.100700607-016-0510-0

Germidis, D. (1977). *Transfer of Technology by Multinational Corporationns*. Paris, France: Development Centre of the Organisation for Economic Co-operation and Development.

Giaglis, G. M., Klein, S., & O'Keefe, R. M. (2000). *The Role of Intermediaries in Electronic Marketplaces: Assessing Alternative Hypotheses for the Future*.

Gibson, D. V., & Smilor, R. W. (1992). *Technology Transfer in Consortia and Strategic Alliances*. Maryland: Rowman and Littlerfield Publisher.

GIFR. (2017). *Global Islamic Finance Report*. Retrieved July 10, 2019 from http://www.gifr.net/gifr_2017.htm

Glasgow loan shark 'charged 719,000% interest'. (2011, April 6). Retrieved from https://www.bbc.com/news/uk-scotland-glasgow-west-12991640

Gleasure, R., & Feller, J. (2016). Emerging technologies and the democratization of financial services: A metal triangulation of crowdfunding research. *Information and Organization*, *26*(4), 101–115. doi:10.1016/j.infoandorg.2016.09.001

Global WebIndex. (2017). *GWI Social*. Retrieved August 18, 2019 from https://cdn2.hubspot.net/hubfs/304927/Downloads/GWI%20Social%20Summary%20Q3%202017.pdf

Gold, A. H., Malhotra, A., & Segars, A. H. (2001). Knowledge management: An organizational capabilities perspective. *Journal of Management Information Systems*, *18*(1), 185–214. doi:10.1080/07421222.2001.11045669

Google Consumer Barometer. (2018). *Trended Data*. Retrieved September 10, 2019 from https://www.consumerbarometer.com/en/trending/?countryCode=ID&category=TRN-NOFILTER-ALL

Gopalakrishnan, S., Kessler, E. H., & Bierly, R. S. (1999). Innovation Speed: A Conceptual Model of Context, Antecedents and Outcomes. *Academy of Management Review*, *21*(4), 1143–1191.

Gopi, M., & Ramayah, T. (2007). Applicability of theory of planned behavior in predicting intention to trade online: Some evidence from a developing country. *International Journal of Emerging Markets*, 2(4), 348–360. doi:10.1108/17468800710824509

Gorbatai, A. D., & Nelson, L. (2015). Gender and the Language of Crowdfunding. *Academy of Management Proceedings*, *1*, 2015.

Granger, C. W. (1969). Investigating Causal Relations by Econometric Models and Cross Spectral Methods. *Econometrica*, *37*(3), 424–438. doi:10.2307/1912791

Greene, W. H. (2002). *Econometric Analysis*. New York: Prentice Hall.

Greenspan, A. (2002). FRB: Testimony, Greenspan—Monetary policy report to the Congress, U.S. Senate—July 16, 2002. Retrieved May 20, 2019, from https://www.federalreserve.gov/boarddocs/hh/2002/july/testimony.htm

Grigoli, F., Herman, A., & Hebbel, K. S. (2014). World Saving. *IMF Working Paper*, *204*(14), 1–55. doi:10.5089/9781498393454.001

Groome, J. (1978). *Farming in Brunei: current systems and prospects for beef production*. (Master's thesis). Durham University (Online). Retrieved from http://etheses.dur.ac.uk/9736/1/9736_6529.PDF?UkUDh:CyT

Guidelines, N. O. FTU/G-1/2017/1, Fintech Regulatory Sandbox Guidelines. AMBD, Brunei Darussalam. Retrieved from https://www.ambd.gov.bn/SiteAssets/fintech-office/FTSG%20v1_final.pdf

Hage, J. (1980). *Theories of Organizations*. New York: John Wiley & Sons.

Hagemeyer, C., Gershenson, J. K., & Johnson, D. M. (2006). Classification and application of problem-solving quality tools: A manufacturing case study. *The TQM Magazine*, *18*(5), 455–483. doi:10.1108/09544780610685458

Hagiu, A. (2014). Strategic Decisions for Multisided Platforms. *MIT Sloan Management Review*, *55*, 92–93.

Haller, M. H., & Alviti, J. V. (1977). Loansharking in American cities: Historical analysis of a marginal enterprise. *The American Journal of Legal History*, *21*(2), 125–156. doi:10.2307/845211

Hall, R. E. (1978). Stochastic Implications of the Life Cycle-Permanent Income Hypothesis: Theory and Evidence. *Journal of Political Economy*, *86*(6), 971–987. doi:10.1086/260724

Hamdan, A. R., Fathi, M. S., & Mohamed, Z. (2018). Evolution of Malaysia's technology transfer model facilitated by national policies. *IACSIT International Journal of Engineering and Technology*, *7*(2), 196–202. doi:10.14419/ijet.v7i2.29.13317

Hanna, R., Rohm, A., & Crittenden, V. L. (2011). We're all connected: The power of the social media ecosystem. *Business Horizons*, *54*(3), 265–273. doi:10.1016/j.bushor.2011.01.007

Harris, L., & Rae, A. (2009). Social networks: The future of marketing for small business. *The Journal of Business Strategy*, *30*(5), 24–31. doi:10.1108/02756660910987581

Harris, M. L., & Gibson, S. G. (2008). Examining the entrepreneurial attitudes of US business students. *Education + Training*, *50*(7), 568–581. doi:10.1108/00400910810909036

Hartrisari, H., Imanto, H., & Suyamto, D. (2013). Decision Support Planning for Food Security (case study at Jawa barat province). SEAMEO BIOTROP. Bogor.

Hartrisari. (2007). Sistem Dinamik. Konsep Sistem dan Pemodelan untuk Industri dan Lingkungan. SEAMEO BIOTROP. Bogor.

Hassan, A. (2005). *Evaluating the performance of managed funds: The cases of equity, ethical funds and Islamic index.* Durham Theses, Durham University, 1–293. Retrieved November 8, 2018 from http://etheses.dur.ac.uk/2731/

Hassan, P. H., & Binti, D. N. H. (2010). *Everyday finances and consumption in Brunei Darussalam.* (Doctoral Thesis), University of Southampton.

Hasting, J. S., & Ashto, L. T. (2008). Financial Literacy, Information, and Demand Elasticity: Survey and Experimental Evidence from Mexico, *Working Paper* 14538.

Hasting, J., & Tejeda-Ashton, L. (2008). Financial Literacy, Information and Demand Elasticity: Survey and Experimental Evidence from Mexico, *NBER Working Paper, 14538.*

Hastings, J. S., & Mitchell, O. S. (2011). How Financial Literacy and Impatience Shape Retirement Wealth and Investment Behaviors, *National Bureau of Economic Research Working Paper Series, 16740*, 1-26

Hayton, J. C., George, G., & Zahra, S. A. (2002). National culture and entrepreneurship: A review of behavioural research. *Entrepreneurship Theory and Practice*, *26*(4), 33–52. doi:10.1177/104225870202600403

Heeks, R. (1998). Small Enterprise Development and the 'Dutch Disease' in a Small Economy: The Case of Brunei, *IDPM Discussion Paper Series Paper*, No. 56, Development Policy and Management, University of Manchester.

Henning, K., Wolfgang, W., & Johannes, H. (2013). Recommendations for Implementing the Strategic Initiative INDUSTRIE 4.0: Securing the Future of German Manufacturing Industry. *Final Report of the Industrie, 4.*

Herbel, D., Croweley, E., & Lee, M. (2010). *Good practices in building innovative rural institutions to increase food security*. FAO Issue.

Hermann, M., Pentek, T., & Otto, B. (2016, January). Design principles for industrie 4.0 scenarios. In *2016 49th Hawaii International Conference on System Sciences (HICSS)*, (pp. 3928-3937). IEEE.

Herzenstein, M., Sonenshein, S., & Dholakia, U. M. (2011). Tell Me a Good Story and I May Lend You Money: The Role of Narratives in Peer-to-Peer Lending Decisions. *JMR, Journal of Marketing Research*, *48*(2), 138–149. doi:10.1509/jmkr.48.SPL.S138

Hj Abu Bakar, R. (2016). Youth must see agriculture as a business opportunity. The BT Archive (Online). Retrieved from https://btarchive.org/news/national/2016/04/24/youth-must-see-agriculture-business-opportunity

Hj Abu Bakar, R. (2019). Flexing digital economy muscle key to enabling growth in other sectors. The Scoop (Online). Retrieved from https://thescoop.co/2019/01/31/flexing-digital-economy-muscle-key-to-enable-growth-in-other-sectors/

Hockenson, L., & Molla, R. (2013). *Facebook grows daily active users by 25 percent, mobile users by 45 percent*. Retrieved May 29, 2019 from http://gigaom.com/2013/10/30/facebook-grows-dailyactive-users-by-25-percent-mobile-users-by-45-percent/

Hofstede, G. (2001). *Culture's Consequences: Comparing Values, Behaviours, Institutions, and Organizations across Nations*. Thousand Oaks, CA: Sage.

Honig, M. (1996). Retirement Expectations: Differences by Race, Ethnicity, and Gender. *The Gerontologist*, *36*(3), 373–382. doi:10.1093/geront/36.3.373 PMID:8682335

Hossain, F., & Knight, T. (2008). *Financing the poor: Can microcredit make a difference? Empirical observations from Bangladesh*. Brooks World Poverty Institute (BWPI) Working Paper 38. University of Manchester, Manchester.

Hossain, M. D. (2002). *Al-Qard al-Hasan: A Practical Approach*. Retrieved from sarjoon.weebly.com/uploads/3/4/7/9/3479157/al-qarz.doc

Hossain, F. (2002). Small loans, big claims. *Foreign Policy*, (132), 79–82. doi:10.2307/3183463

Hulme, M., & Wright, C. (2006). *Internet-based social lending: Past, present and future*. Social Futures Observatory 2006.

Hyrynsalmi, S., Mäkilä, T., Järvi, A., Suominen, A., Seppänen, M., & Knuutila, T. (2012). App Store, Marketplace, Play! An Analysis of Multi-Homing in Mobile Software Ecosystems. *IWSECO@ICSOB*.

Idris, A. (2018). Incorporate agriculture in school curriculum, says minister at PMO. Borneo Bulletin (Online). Retrieved from https://borneobulletin.com.bn/incorporate-agriculture-in-school-curriculum-says-minister-at-pmo/

Imarat Consultants. (n.d.). *An Overview of the Global Halal Market South East Asia Driving the Halal. Media*. Retrieved from http://www.halalrc.org/images/Research Material/Presentations/ overview of global halal market.pdf

International Fund for Agricultural Development (IFAD). (2009). *Gender in Agriculture Source book*.

International Organization of Securities Commissions (IOSCO). (2004). *Islamic Capital Market Fact-Finding Report*, July 2004, p. 10 available at www.iasplus.com/resource/ ioscoislamiccapitalmarkets.pdf (Accessed on 22 Feb 2018).

Iqbal, Z., & Mirakhor, A. (2011). An introduction to Islamic finance: Theory and practice, 2nd Edition. Singapore: John Wiley & Sons (Asia). doi:10.1002/9781118390474

Iqbal, Z., & Mirakhor, A. (2008). *Pengantar keuangan Islam: Teori dan Praktik*. Jakarta: Kencana.

Ira Sugita. (2017). *Halal in Singapore*. Singapore. Retrieved from https://gain.fas.usda.gov/Recent GAIN Publications/Halal in Singapore _Singapore_Singapore_3-28-2017.pdf

Irfan, M., Arif, G. M., Ali, S. M., & Nazli, H. (1999). *The structure of informal credit market in Pakistan*. Pakistan Institute of Development Economics (PIDE) Research Report No. 168. Islamabad: PIDE.

Ishikawa, K. (2012). Introduction to Quality Control. *Productivity Press*.

Islam, N. (2018, March 15). *Making Digital Marketplaces Fairer [Keynote Paper presented in the "World Consumers Right Day 2018" on 15 March 2018 at Osmani Sriti Auditorium Organized by Ministry of Commerce, People's Republic of Bangladesh]*.

Islamic Fintech can take Brunei to new heights. (2016, Nov. 11). Retrieved from http://www. business.gov.bn/Lists/News/DispItem.aspx?ID=683

Islam, M. Z., Jasimuddin, S. M., & Hasan, I. (2015). Organizational culture, structure, technology infrastructure and knowledge sharing: Empirical evidence from MNCs based in Malaysia. *Vine*, *45*(1), 67–88. doi:10.1108/VINE-05-2014-0037

Islam, M. Z., Jasimuddin, S. M., & Hasan, I. (2017). The role of technology and socialization in linking organizational context and knowledge conversion: The case of Malaysian service organizations. *International Journal of Information Management*, *37*(5), 497–503. doi:10.1016/j. ijinfomgt.2017.06.001

Ismail, A. G., Shamim, S., & Possumah, B. T. (2011). Bringing work back in Islamic perspectives. *Prosiding PERKEM*, *5*(2), 247–262.

ISRA. (2010). ISRA conpendium: For Islamic finance terms, Arabic-English. Kuala Lumpur: International Shari'ah Research Academy for Islamic Finance (ISRA).

ISRA. (2015). *Sistem keuangan Islam: Prinsip dan operasi*. Jakarta: Rajawali Pers.

Jagadeesh, D. (2015). The Impact of Savings in Economic Growth: An Empirical Study Based on Botswana. *International Journal of Research in Business Studies and Management, 2*, 10–21.

JAKIM. (2015). Manual Procedure for Malaysia Halal Certification (Third Revision) 2014. [Third Revision]. *Manual Procedure for Malaysia Halal Certification, 2014*, 67. doi:10.1017/CBO9781107415324.004

Jamaludin, N., Smith, M., & Gerrans, P. (2012). Mutual fund selection criteria: Evidence from Malaysia. *Asian Review of Accounting, 20*(2), 140–151. doi:10.1108/13217341211242187

Johan, E. (2018). New Challenges in ASEAN Regional Market: International Trade Framework on Halal Standard. *Jurnal Dinamika Hukum, 18*(1), 93. doi:10.20884/1.jdh.2018.18.1.809

Johansen, S. (1991). Estimation and Hypothesis Testing of Cointegration Vectors in Gaussian Vector Autoregressive Models. *Econometrica, 59*(6), 1551–1580. doi:10.2307/2938278

Joyce, S. (2011). *2011 UMass study of Fortune 500 companies and social media: 23% blog, 62% use Twitter, 58% Facebook*. Retrieved May 8, 2019 from www.q4blog.com/2011/10/27/2011-umassstudy-of-fortune-500-companies-and-social-media-23-blog-62-use-twitter-58-facebook/

Kagan, J. (2019, October 6). Loan Shark Definition. Retrieved from https://www.investopedia.com/terms/l/loansharking.asp

Kaino, T. (2006). Rural credit markets in Myanmar: A study of formal and non-formal lenders. *Asian Journal of Agriculture and Development, 3*(1,2), 1-15.

Kallas, Z. (2010). Butchers' Preferences for Rabbit Meat; AHP Pairwise Comparisons Versus a Likert Scale Valuation. Retrieved from https://www.semanticscholar.org/

Kaplan, A. M., & Haenlein, M. (2010). Users of the world, unite! The challenges and opportunities of *Social Media. Business Horizons, 53*(1), 59–68. doi:10.1016/j.bushor.2009.09.003

Karaivanov, A., & Kessler, A. (2013). *A friend in need is a friend indeed: Theory and evidence on the (dis)advantages of informal loans*. Simon Fraser University, Department of Economics Working Papers. Retrieved from http://www.sfu.ca/econ-research/RePEc/sfu/ sfudps/dp13-03.pdf

Karaivanov, A., & Kessler, S. (2017). *(Dis)Advantages of Informal Loans – Theory and Evidence*. May. Retrieved from http://www.sfu.ca/~akaraiva/KKpaper_current.pdf

Karim, M. R. A. (2010). *Analysing The Characteristics And Performance Of Islamic Funds: A Critical Review Of The Malaysian Case*. Durham Theses, Durham University, 1–366. Retrieved November 8, 2018 from http://etheses.dur.ac.uk/521/

Karim, N., Tarazi, M., & Reille, X. (2008). Islamic microfinance: An emerging market niche. *CGAP Focus Note*, No. 49.

Kazumi, T., & Kawai, N. (2017). Institutional support and women's entrepreneurial self-efficacy. *Asia Pacific Journal of Innovation and Entrepreneurship, 11*(3), 345–365. doi:10.1108/APJIE-12-2017-041

Khalid, A. M., Haji Masr, M., Muhammad, N., & Pang, W. L. (2018). *Halal Meat and Meat Products Processing*. Brunei Darussalam: ERIA; Retrieved from http://www.eria.org/uploads/media/RURB_2018_Chapter_4_Halal_meat_Brunei.pdf

Khan, A. A. (2008). *Islamic microfinance: Theory, policy and practice*. Birmingham: Islamic Relief Worldwide.

Khandelwal, P. (2010). Money lender drives man to commit suicide. In *Hindustan Times*, August 12. Retrieved from http://www.hindustantimes.com/delhi/money-lender-drives-man-to-commit-suicide/story-KSixMHviIbkhvUTcoiqZ1H.html

Khan, M. A. (1989). *Economic teachings of prophet Muhammad*. Islamabad: International Institute of Islamic Economics and Institute of Policy Studies.

King, D., Chung, H. M., Lee, J. K., & Turban, E. (1999). Electronic commerce: A managerial perspective. Prentice Hall PTR.

Kirchner, S., & Schüßler, E. (2019). *The Organization of Digital Marketplaces: Unmasking the Role of Internet Platforms in the Sharing Economy*.

Kirs, P., & Bagchi, K. (2012). The impact of trust and changes in trust: A national comparison of individual adoptions of information and communication technologies and related phenomenon. *International Journal of Information Management*, *32*(5), 431–441. doi:10.1016/j.ijinfomgt.2012.02.003

Koh, T. K., & Fichman, M. (2010). *Multi-Homing Users' Preferences for Two-Sided Exchange Networks* (SSRN Scholarly Paper No. ID 1635615). Retrieved from Social Science Research Network website: https://papers.ssrn.com/abstract=1635615

Kondo, M. (2003). The "bombay 5-6": Last resource informal financiers for Philippine micro-enterprises. *Kyoto Review of Southeast Asia*, Issue 4, October.

Korsching, P. F., & Allen, J. C. (2004). Local entrepreneurship: A development model based on community interaction field theory. *Journal of the Community Development Society*, *35*(1), 25–43. doi:10.1080/15575330409490120

Kotler, P. R. (1997). *Marketing Management: Analysis, Planning, Implementation and Control*. Englewood Cliffs, NJ: Prentice Hall.

Kotler, P., Kartajaya, H., & Setiawan, I. (2010). *From Products to Customers to the Human Spirit: Marketing 3.0*. Hoboken, NJ: John Wiley & Sons. doi:10.1002/9781118257883

Kotter, J. P. (1979). *The General Managers*. New York: Free Press.

Kube, G., & Rinn, T. (2014). Industry 4.0-The next revolution in the industrial sector.

Kumar, V., Rajan, B., Gupta, S., & Pozza, I. D. (2017). Customer engagement in service. *Journal of the Academy of Marketing Science*.

Kuppuswamy, V., & Bayus, B. L. (2018). Crowdfunding Creative Ideas: The Dynamics of Project Backers. In *H. L. Cumming D., The Economics of Crowdfunding* (pp. 151–182). Cham, Switzerland: Palgrave Macmillan. doi:10.1007/978-3-319-66119-3_8

Kwok, K. Y., & Tummala, V. M. R. (1998). A quality control and improvement system based on total control methodology (TCM). *International Journal of Quality & Reliability Management*, *15*(1), 13–48. doi:10.1108/02656719810197288

Laderchi, R. C. (2001). *Participatory methods in the analysis of poverty: a critical review.* QEH Working Paper Series No. 62, Oxford. Retrieved from http://www2.qeh.ox.ac.uk/Re- PEc/qeh/qehwps/qehwps62.pdf

Laforet, S. (2008). Size, strategic, and market orientation affects on innovation. *Journal of Business Research*, *61*(7), 753–764. doi:10.1016/j.jbusres.2007.08.002

Lagrosen, Y., & Lagrosen, S. (2005). The effects of quality management–a survey of Swedish quality professionals. *International Journal of Operations & Production Management*, *25*(10), 940–952. doi:10.1108/01443570510619464

Lakic, V. (n.d.). Colombia Loan Shark Network Booming in Mexico. Retrieved from https://www.occrp.org/en/daily/6910-colombia-loan-shark-network-booming-in-mexico

Lam, S. S. (1996). Applications of quality improvement tools in Hong Kong: An empirical analysis. *Total Quality Management*, *7*(6), 675–680. doi:10.1080/09544129610559

Lasi, H., Fettke, P., Kemper, H. G., Feld, T., & Hoffmann, M. (2014). Industry 4.0. *Business & Information Systems Engineering*, *6*(4), 239–242. doi:10.100712599-014-0334-4

Lee, G. L., Burcher, P. G., & Waddell, D. (2008). The challenges for quality managers in Britain and Australia. *The TQM Journal, 20*(1), pp. 45-58.

Lee, J., Kao, H. A., & Yang, S. (2014). Service innovation and smart analytics for industry 4.0 and big data environment. *Procedia Cirp*, *16*, 3–8. doi:10.1016/j.procir.2014.02.001

Leonard-Barton, D., & Sinha, D. (1993). Developer-User Interaction and User Satisfaction in Internal Technology Transfer. *Academy of Management Journal*, *36*(5), 1125–1139.

Leong, K., Li, H., & Xu, H. (2018). *Exploiting the unbanked: Evidence from Singapore's unlicensed moneylending market.* Discussion Paper Series IZA DP No. 11786. IZA Institute of Labor Economics. August.

Liao, C., Chuang, S. H., & To, P. L. (2011). How knowledge management mediates the relationship between environment and organizational structure. *Journal of Business Research*, *64*(7), 728–736. doi:10.1016/j.jbusres.2010.08.001

Lim, D., Morse, E., Mitchell, R., & Seawright, K. (2010). Institutional environment and entrepreneurial cognitions: A comparative business system perspective. *Entrepreneurship Theory and Practice*, *34*(3), 491–516. doi:10.1111/j.1540-6520.2010.00384.x

Lim, S., Othman, R., Zain, M., Yusob, A., & Pengiran, S. R. (2012). Implicit leadership theories of Bruneians. *Journal of Asia-Pacific Business, 13*(4), 302–319. doi:10.1080/10599231.2012.718674

Lin, B. W., & Berg, D. (2001). Effects of cultural difference on technology transfer projects: An empirical study of Taiwanese manufacturing companies. *International Journal of Project Management, 19*(5), 287–293. doi:10.1016/S0263-7863(99)00081-2

LIPKA. M. (2017). Muslims and Islam: Key findings in the U.S. and around the world. Retrieved November 5, 2018, from http://www.pewresearch.org/fact-tank/2017/08/09/muslims-and-islam-key-findings-in-the-u-s-and-around-the-world/

Llanto, G. M., & Fukui, R. (2003). *Rural finance and microfinance development in transition countries in Southeast and East Asia.* PIDS Discussion Paper Series, No. 2003-12, Philippine Institute for Development Studies (PIDS), Makati City.

LOAN SHARK. meaning in the Cambridge English Dictionary. (n.d.). Retrieved from https://dictionary.cambridge.org/dictionary/english/loan-shark

Loan sharks trap poor people. (n.d.). Retrieved from http://vietnamnews.vn/society/482580/loan-sharks-traps-poor-people.html#259EbmV0HFO01xAX.99

Lok-Dessallien, R. (1998). Review of Poverty Concepts and Indicators. SEPED Series on Poverty Reduction. New York, Social Development and Poverty Elimination Division, UNDP.

Lom, M., Pribyl, O., & Svitek, M. (2016, May). Industry 4.0 as a part of smart cities. In *Smart Cities Symposium Prague (SCSP),* 2016 (pp. 1-6). IEEE. 10.1109/SCSP.2016.7501015

Loverigde, S. (1996). On the continuing popularity of industrial recruitment. *Economic Development Quarterly, 10*(2), 151–158. doi:10.1177/089124249601000202

Low, S.-W., & Ghazali, N. A. (2007). The Price Linkages between Malaysian Unit Trust Funds and the Stock Market: Short run and Long run Interrelationships. *Managerial Finance, 33*(2), 89–101. doi:10.1108/03074350710715827

Lu, C.-T., Xie, S., Kong, X., & Yu, P. S. (2014). Inferring the Impacts of Social Media on Crowdfunding. *WSDM '14. Proceedings of the 7th ACM international conference on Web search and data mining*, 573-582. 10.1145/2556195.2556251

Lukač, D. (2015, November). The fourth ICT-based industrial revolution" Industry 4.0"—HMI and the case of CAE/CAD innovation with EPLAN P8. In Telecommunications Forum Telfor (TELFOR), 2015 23rd (pp. 835-838). IEEE.

Lumpkin, G. T., & Gregory, G. D. (2004). E-Business Strategies and Internet Business Models. *Organizational Dynamics, 33*(2), 161–173. doi:10.1016/j.orgdyn.2004.01.004

Lusardi, A., & Mitchell, O. S. (2007). Baby Boomer Retirement Security: The Roles of Planning, Financial Literacy, and Housing Wealth. *Journal of Monetary Economics, 54*(1), 205–224. doi:10.1016/j.jmoneco.2006.12.001

Lu, Y. (2017). Industry 4.0: A survey on technologies, applications and open research issues. *Journal of Industrial Information Integration*, *6*, 1–10. doi:10.1016/j.jii.2017.04.005

Lynskey, M. J. (1999). The transfer of Resources and Competencies for developing Technological Capabilities-The case of Fusitsu-ICL. *Technology Analysis and Strategic Management*, *11*(3), 317–335. doi:10.1080/095373299107384

Madia, S. A. (2011). Best practices for using social media as a recruitment strategy. *Strategic HR Review*, *10*(6), 19–24. doi:10.1108/14754391111172788

Mahadevan, B. (2000). Business models for Internet-based e-commerce: An anatomy. *California Management Review*, *42*(4), 55–69. doi:10.2307/41166053

Mahanti, J. (2008). *Women Helping Women Through Nano Finance Institution.* Retrieved from http://www.ashanet.org/detroit/Projects/BISWA/Nano_Finance_Report_ Jan2008.pdf

Mahfouz, S. S. (2012). *Investment Characteristics Of Islamic Investment Portfolios: Evidence From Saudi Mutual Funds And Global Indices.* Durham Theses, Durham University, 1–277. Retrieved November 8, 2018 from http://etheses.dur.ac.uk/4440/

Maierbrugger, A. (2014) Brunei limits agricultural land use to 1% to protect tropical forests. Retrieved from http://investvine.com/brunei-limits-agricultural-land-use-to-1-to-protect-tropical-forests/

Malaysia World's Islamic Finance Marketplace. (2016). Islamic Finance Technology & Innovation. Kuala Lumpur: Bank Negara Malaysia, April 29, 2016.

Malaysian, I. C. M. (2013). New Shariah Advisory Council Resolutions. *Bulletin on the Islamic Capital Market*, *8*(2), 3–6.

Mallick, D. (2009). Microfinance and moneylender interest rate: Evidence from Bangladesh. Munich Personal RePEc Archive (MPRA). May. Retrieved from http://mpra.ub.uni-muenchen.de/17800/

Mallick, D. (2012). Microfinance and moneylender interest rate: Evidence from Bangladesh. *World Development*, *40*(6), 1181–1189. doi:10.1016/j.worlddev.2011.12.011

Marom, D., Robb, A., & Sade, O. (2016). *Gender Dynamics in Crowdfunding (Kickstarter): Evidence on Entrepreneurs, Investors, Deals and Taste Based Discrimination.* Social Science Research Network.

Marzban, S., Asutay, M., & Boseli, A. (2014). *Shariah--compliant Crowdfunding: An Efficient Framework for Entrepreneurship development in Islamic Countries*. Paper presented at the Harvard Islamic Finance Forum, Boston, USA. Academic Press.

Matallin, J. C., & Nieto, L. (2002). Mutual Funds as an Alternative to Direct Stock Investment: A Cointegration Approach. *Applied Financial Economics*, *12*(10), 743–750. doi:10.1080/09603100110038693

Mayer, R. (2012). Loan sharks, interest-rate caps, and deregulation. *Washington and Lee Law Review, 69*(2), Article 10, Spring 3-1, 807-845.

Mayer, R. (2010). *Quick cash: The story of the loan shark.* Illinois: Northern Illinois University Press.

McAfee, A., Brynjolfsson, E., Davenport, T. H., Patil, D. J., & Barton, D. (2012). Big data: The management revolution. *Harvard Business Review, 90*(10), 60–68. PMID:23074865

McCaw, M. (2018). Islamic Finance Embraces Fintech. Retrieved from http://www.bobsguide.com/guide/news/2018/Apr/5/islamic-finance-embraces-fintech/

McKinsey Asia, P. F. S. Survey (2017). *Asia's digital banking race: Giving customers what they want.* Retrieved September 22, 2019 from https://www.mckinsey.com/~/media/McKinsey/Industries/Financial%20Services/Our%20Insights/Reaching%20Asias%20digital%20banking%20customers/Asias-digital-banking-race-WEB-FINAL.ashx

Mensah, H. K., Azinga, S. A., & Sodji, J. A. M. (2015). Challenges faced by small and medium-size enterprises in accessing credit facilities from financial institutions: An empirical assessment incorporating the perceptions of both borrowers and financiers. Retrieved October 1, 2019 from https://www.researchgate.net/publication/286238910

Meyer, R. L. (2002). *Track record of financial institutions in assisting the poor in Asia.* Asian Development Bank (ADB) Institute Research Paper 49, December. Tokyo: ADB.

Mi, M., & Zolotov, I. (2016). February. Comparison between multiclass classifiers and deep learning with focus on industry 4.0. In 2016 Cybernetics & Informatics (K&I) (pp. 1-5).

Miguel, P. A. C., Satolo, E., Andrietta, J. M., & Calarge, F. A. (2012). Benchmarking the use of tools and techniques in the Six Sigma programme based on a survey conducted in a developing country. *Benchmarking: An International Journal, 19*(6), 690–708. doi:10.1108/14635771211284279

Ministry of Economic Affairs Malaysia. (2018). *Mid-term Review of the Eleventh Malaysia Plan: 2016 – 2020.* Kuala Lumpur: Percetakan Nasional Malaysia Berhad.

Mishkin, F. S. (2010). The Economic of Money, Banking, and Financial Markets. New York: The Addison-Wesley.

MiTi. (2012). *Development of the halal industry.* Retrieved from http://www.miti.gov.my/miti/resources/fileupload/Chap 21.pdf

Mitic, M., & Kapoulas, A. (2012). Understanding the role of social media in bank marketing. *Marketing Intelligence & Planning, 30*(7), 668–686. doi:10.1108/02634501211273797

Mitra, A. (2012). *Fundamentals of quality control and improvement.* Hoboken, NJ: John Wiley & Sons.

Mitra, S. K. (2009). Exploitative microfinance interest rates. *Asian Social Science, 5*(5). doi:10.5539/ass.v5n5p87

Mohamad, M. (1970). *The Malay dilemma*. Singapore: Asia Pacific Press.

Mohammad Yousef, A. (2014). Integration of social media in business. *International Journal of Business and Social Science*, *5*(8), 202–209.

Mohd Zain, M., Asyraf, A. R., & Mohd Rafi, Y. (2014). Spirituality in Islamic Entrepreneurship: Motivation and Achievements of Successful Entrepreneurs in Kelantan. *Journal ofTechno Social*, *6*(2), 27–36.

Mollick, E. R. (2013). The dynamics of crowdfunding: Determinants of success and failure. *Social Science Research Network. The Electricity Journal*, *29*(1), 1–20.

Mollick, E. R. (2014). The Dynamics of Crowdfunding: An Exploratory Study. *Journal of Business Venturing*, *29*(2), 1–16. doi:10.1016/j.jbusvent.2013.06.005

Moritz, A., & Block, J. (2016). Crowdfunding: A literature review and research directions. In D. Brüntje, & O. Gajda (Eds.), *Crowdfunding in Europe, State of the Art in Theory and Practice* (pp. 25–53). Switzerland: Springer International Publishing. doi:10.1007/978-3-319-18017-5_3

Mosconi, F. (2015). *The new European industrial policy: Global competitiveness and the manufacturing renaissance*. Routledge. doi:10.4324/9781315761756

MUIS. (2018). *MUIS Annual Report 2017*. Retrieved from https://www.muis.gov.sg/-/media/Files/Corporate-Site/Annual-Reports/MUIS_AR_Full_2017.pdf

Murakami, S. (2013). Social capital in Vietnam, Cambodia and Laos. *The Senshu Social Capital Review* No. 4, 65-110.

Murphy, A., & Taylor, M. (2004). SMEs and e-business. *Journal of Small Business and Enterprise Development*, *11*(3), 280–289. doi:10.1108/14626000410551546

Musari, K. (2016a). *Nanofinance, redefine the microfinance for the very micro society.* A poster was presented at the 13th Indonesian Regional Science Association International Institute (IRSA) and was hosted by Department of Economics, Faculty of Economics and Business, Brawijaya University, at Atria Hotel, Malang. July 25-26.

Musari, K. (2016c). *Redefining the Islamic nanofinance and its institutional strengthening: Lesson learned from Asian countries.* A paper was presented at 11th International Conference on Islamic Economics and Finance (ICIEF) "Rethinking Islamic Economics and Finance: Paving The Way Forward for Inclusive and Sustainable Development" with Organizer and Host Institution Kulliyyah of Economics and Management Sciences International Islamic University Malaysia (IIUM) and Co-Organizers Islamic Research and Training Institute (IRTI), Islamic Development Bank (IDB) and International Association of Islamic Economics (IAIE), Kuala Lumpur. October 11-13.

Musari, K. (2016d). Yuk, Perangi Riba, & Rentenir! In Jawa Pos Radar Jember Daily Newspaper, Perspektif. July 18. pp. 1, 11.

Musari, K. (2017). *Nanofinance, addressing the Islamic microfinance gap through global Islamic humanitarian institution*. E-Proceedings of Conference on Philanthropy for Humanitarian Aid 2017 "Philantrophy for Humanitarian Aid as Mechanism to Alleviate Poverty and Maintain Human Dignity" held by International Research Centre of Islamic Economics and Finance (IRCIEF) International Islamic University College Selangor (KUIS) in collaboration with Islamic Research and Training Institute (IRTI) International Islamic Development Bank (IDB) and Sultan Sharif Ali Islamic University (UNISSA) at UNISSA, Brunei Darussalam, May 23-24, 170-183.

Musari, K. (2018). Menyambut BUMDes Center dan Bank Wakaf Mikro. In Jawa Pos Radar Jember Daily Newspaper, Perspektif. September 14, pp. 21 and 31.

Musari, K., & Simanjuntak, R. (2015). *Reconstruction the bank for poor family through Islamic linkage program (Case study in Indonesia)*. A paper was presented at 4th International Conference on "Inclusive Islamic Financial Sector Development" held by Islamic Research and Training Institute Islamic Development Bank (IRTI-IDB) and International Islamic University (IIU) Islamabad at Faisal Mosque, IIU Islamabad, Pakistan. November 17-18.

Musari, K. (2016b). Economic sustainability for Islamic nanofinance through sukuk-waqf linkage program (Case study in Indonesia). [IJISEF]. *International Journal of Islamic Economics and Finance Studies*, *2*(3), 83–94.

Musari, K. (2019). Promoting qard al-hasan in nanofinance to counter the moneylender in Southeast Asia. *Studia Islamica*, *26*(1), 1–16. doi:10.15408di.v26i1.5990

Musari, K., & Simanjuntak, R. (2016). Nanofinance, redefinition of microfinance for the very micro society through philanthropy linkage program (Case study in Indonesia, Cambodia, Thailand, India). [AARJSH]. *Asian Academic Research Journal of Social Science and Humanities*, *3*(4), 455–463.

Muslim Population in the World. (n.d.). Retrieved October 31, 2018, from http://www.muslimpopulation.com/

Mustapa Mohamed. (2018). World Halal Week 2016 Speech. Retrieved from http://www.miti.gov.my/index.php/pages/view/3195

Nadaraja, K. (2016). Malay reaction to the 1930s economic depression in Malaya. *Jebat: Malaysian Journal of History, Politics, & Strategy*, *43*(1), 46–64.

Najeeb, S. F., & Lahsasna, A. (2016). Qard hasan: Its shari'ah rules and applications in Islamic finance. In H. Khalid, M. N. Barom, & N. S. Shirazi. (2016). Essential Perspectives in Islamic Economics and Finance. Kuala Lumpur: Kulliyyah of Economics and Management Sciences, International Islamic University Malaysia (IIUM).

Narayan-Parker, D., Chambers, R., Shah, M. K., & Petesch, P. (2000). *Voices of the Poor: 32 Crying Out for Change*. New York, N.Y.: Published for the World Bank, Oxford University Press. doi:10.1596/0-1952-1602-4

National SME Development Council. (2012a). *SME Annual Report 2011 – 2012*. Available at http://www.smecorp.gov.my/index.php/en/resources/2015-12-21-11-07-06/sme-annual-report (Accessed on 10 April 2019). (2012b). *SME Masterplan 2012 – 2020: Catalysing Growth and Income*. Available at http://www.smecorp.gov.my/index.php/en/resources/2015-12-21-11-07-06/sme-masterplan (Accessed on 10 April 2019). (2013). *SME Annual Report 2012 – 2013*. Available at http://www.smecorp.gov.my/index.php/en/resources/2015-12-21-11-07-06/sme-annual-report (Accessed on 10 April 2019). (2014). *SME Annual Report 2013 – 2014*. Available at http://www.smecorp.gov.my/index.php/en/resources/2015-12-21-11-07-06/sme-annual-report (Accessed on 10 April 2019). (2016). *SME Annual Report 2015 – 2016*. Available at http://www.smecorp.gov.my/index.php/en/resources/2015-12-21-11-07-06/sme-annual-report (Accessed on 10 April 2019). (2018). *SME Annual Report 2017 – 2018*. Available at http://www.smecorp.gov.my/index.php/en/resources/2015-12-21-11-07-06/sme-annual-report (Accessed on 10 April 2019)

Nguyen, N. T. D., & Aoyama, A. (2015). The impact of cultural differences on technology transfer Management practice moderation. *Journal of Manufacturing Technology Management*, *26*(7), 926–954. doi:10.1108/JMTM-09-2013-0130

Nohong, M., Sanusi, A., & Nurqamar, I. F. (2018, May). Suriadi Harun Strategic Model in Increasing the SMEs Competitive Advantage in South Sulawesi. *International Journal of Administrative Science & Organization*, *25*(2), 57–65.

Nor Ai'han Mujar, N. H. (2015). The economics of halal industry. *Journal of Experimental Psychology. General*, *136*(1), 23–42.

Nord, W. R., & Tucker, S. (1987). *Implementing Routine and Radical innovation*. Lexington, KY: Lexington Books.

Norton, A., Bird, B., Brock, K., Kakande, M., & Turk, C. (2001). A rough guide to PPAs Participatory Poverty Assessment: An introduction to theory and practice, Department for International Development's Social Development Department, Overseas Development Institute.

Novak, S. (2005). *The small manufacturer's toolkit: A guide to selecting the techniques and systems to help you win*. Boca Raton, FL: CRC Press.

Obaidullah, M. (2008). Introduction to Islamic microfinance. India: The Islamic Business and Finance Network (IBF Net) and Islamic Relief Worldwide.

Obaidullah, M., & Khan, T. (2008). Islamic microfinance development, challenges and initiatives. *Policy Dialogue Paper No. 2*, Islamic Research and Training Institute, Islamic Development Bank. Retrieved July 6, 2011 from http://www.imad.in/mf-obaidullah1.pdf

Obaidullah, M., & Khan, T. (2008). Islamic microfinance development: Challenges and initiatives. Policy Dialogue Paper No. 2. Jeddah: Islamic Research and Training Institute (IRTI) Islamic Development Bank (IDB).

O'Connor, T, (2017, April 18). Retrieved February 9, 2018, from IntheBlack: https://www,intheblack,com/articles/2017/04/18/religion-and-ethnicity-drive-savings-habits

Oh, Y., bin Pg Hamir, A. M. H., & Mohd Shah, M. A. S. bin. (2018). The viability of halal food industry for Brunei economic diversification: SWOT analysis. *People: International Journal of Social Sciences, 3*(3), 1220–1233. doi:10.20319/pijss.2018.33.12201233

OJK. (2018). *Bank wakaf mikro, program pemberdayaan masyarakat melalui pendirian bank wakaf mikro - LKM Syariah.* A public socialization material by Financial Services Authority (OJK) in Forum Merdeka Barat 9, March 27.

Olayan, H. B. (1999). Technology Transfer in Developing Nations. *Research Technology Management, 42*(3), 43–48. doi:10.1080/08956308.1999.11671283

Omar, M. (2017). "Fintech & entrepreneurship" at the Islamic Fintech Dialogue 2017, Fintech & Entrepreneurship, Kuala Lumpur, Oct. 11, 2017.

Omar, M. A., Abduh, M., & Sukmana, R. (2013). *Fundamentals of Islamic Money and Capital Markets*. Singapore: John Wiley & Sons.

Oses, N., Legarretaetxebarria, A., Quartulli, M., García, I., & Serrano, M. (2016). Uncertainty reduction in measuring and verification of energy savings by statistical learning in manufacturing environments. [IJIDeM]. *International Journal on Interactive Design and Manufacturing, 10*(3), 291–299. doi:10.100712008-016-0302-y

Oukil, M. S. (2013). Entrepreneurship and entrepreneurs in an Islamic context. *Journal of Islamic and Human Advanced Research, 3*(3), 111–131.

Ovesen, J., & Trankell, I. (2014). Symbiosis of microcredit and private moneylending in Cambodia. *The Asia Pacific Journal of Anthropology, 15*(2), 178–196. doi:10.1080/14442213.2014.894116

Oxford Business Group. (2014). *The Report: Brunei Darussalam 2013.* London, UK: Oxford Business Group.

Pacific, A. (2010). Global Halal Industry : An Overview. *Global Islamic Finance Report 2013*, 140–159. Retrieved from http://www.gifr.net/gifr2013/ch_13.PDF

Packman, C. (2014). *Payday lending: Global growth of the high-cost credit market.* New York: Palgrave Macmillan. doi:10.1057/9781137361103

Paelke, V. (2014, September). Augmented reality in the smart factory: Supporting workers in an industry 4.0. environment. In *Proceedings of the 2014 IEEE emerging technology and factory automation (ETFA)* (pp. 1-4). IEEE. 10.1109/ETFA.2014.7005252

Pagani, M. (2013). Digital Business Strategy and Value Creation: Framing the Dynamic Cycle of Control Points. *Management Information Systems Quarterly, 37*(2), 617–632. doi:10.25300/MISQ/2013/37.2.13

Pan, J., Vorvoreanu, M., & Zhou, Z. (2014). Social media adoption in disaster restoration industry. *Construction Innovation, 14*(3), 346–369. doi:10.1108/CI-03-2013-0014

Parpart, E. (2014). BOT Considers 'Nano-Financing' for Grass-Roots People. *Nation (New York, N.Y.)*, *25*(October). Retrieved from http://www.nationmultimedia.com/business/BOT-considers-nano-financing-for-grass-roots-peopl-30246202.html

Parusheva, S. (2017). Social Media Banking Models: A case study of a practical implementation in banking sector. Икономически изследвания, *3*, 125-141.

Parveen, F., Jaafar, N. I., & Ainin, S. (2016). Social media's impact on organizational performance and entrepreneurial orientation in organizations. *Management Decision*, *54*(9), 2208–2234. doi:10.1108/MD-08-2015-0336

Penyusun, T. (2015) Indeks Pembangunan Desa 2014: Tantangan pemenuhan standar pelayanan minimum desa. Kenenteian PPN/Bappenas dan Badan Pusat Statistik, Jakarta.

Peprah, C. (2016). *Challenges SMEs face in acquiring loans from banks: A comparative study between Finland and Ghana*. (Unpublished doctoral dissertation). Centria University of Applied Sciences.

Perera, N., & Sutrisna, M. (2010). The Use of Analytic Hierarchy Process (AHP) in the Analysis of Delay Claims in Construction Projects in the UAE. *The Built & Human Environment Review*, *3*(1), 29–47.

Personal, M., Archive, R., Puah, C., Voon, S., & Entebang, H. (2009). Halal Industry : key challenges dan Opportunities, (10679).

Pierce, J. L., & Delbecq, A. L. (1977). Organization Structure, Individual Attitudes, and Innovation. *Academy of Management Review*, *2*(1), 27–37. doi:10.5465/amr.1977.4409154

Pojanavatee, S. (2013). The Price Linkage between Stock Market and Equity Mutual Funds of Thailand. *The Macrotheme Review*, *2*(5), 128–137.

Polsaram, P., Kulsiri, P., Techasermsukkul, L., Dar Htwe, T., & Kwanchainond, K. (2011). Small and medium enterprises development policies of 4 ASEAN countries: Brunei Darussalam, Cambodia, Lao PDR, and Myanmar. *Japan Overseas Development Corporation (JODC)*. Retrieved from http://www.asean.org/storage/images/documents/SME%20Policies%20in%204%20ASEAN%20Countries%20-%20Brunei%20Darussalam.pdf

Popovici, G. (2012). *Understanding the Factors Affecting Savings of Dutch Households*, Groningen: University of Groningen and "Alexandru Ioan Cuza" University of Iasi.

Porter, M. (1998). *Competitive Advantage*. USA: Waterstone. doi:10.1007/978-1-349-14865-3

Porter, M. E. (1980). *Competitive Strategy: Techniques for Analyzing Industries and Competitors*. New York: Free Press.

Porter, M. E. (2008). The Five Competitive Forces That Shape Strategy. *Harvard Business Review*, 19. PMID:18271320

Prahasta, E. (2002). Sistem Informasi Geografis. Konsep dasar Informasi Geografis. I nformatika. Bandung.

Preece, D. A. (1989). *Managing the Adoption of New Technology*. London, UK: Routledge.

Raible, M. (2013). *Industrial Organization theory and its contribution to decision-making in purchasing*.

Rajak, W. (2018). Brunei is world's 4th highest in social media penetration—The Bruneian. Retrieved June 10, 2019, from https://www.thebruneian.news/brunei-is-worlds-4th-highest-in-social-media-penetration

Rask, M., & Kragh, H. (2004). Motives for e-marketplace Participation: Differences and Similarities between Buyers and Suppliers. *Electronic Markets*, *14*(4), 270–283. doi:10.1080/10196780412331311720

Ratnam, K. J. (1985). *Technology and society*. Pulau Pinang: Universiti Sains Malaysia.

Ray, S. K., & Singh, S. (2010). Blog content based recommendation framework using wordnet and multiple ontologies. *Proceedings of the International Conference on Computer Information Systems And Industrial Management Applications*, 432-437. Cracow, Poland, 10.1109/CISIM.2010.5643502

Revuelto-Taboada, L., Canet-Giner, T., & Balbastre-Benavent, F. (2011). Quality tools and techniques, EFQM experience and strategy formation. Is there any relationship?: The particular case of Spanish service firms. *Innovar (Universidad Nacional de Colombia)*, *21*(42), 25–40.

Rice, M. P., O'Connor, G. C., Peters, L. S., & Morone, J. G. (1998). Managing Discontinuous Innovations. *Research Technology Management*, *41*(3), 52–58. doi:10.1080/08956308.1998.11671210

Robb, A., & Robinson, D. (2014). The capital structure decisions of new firms. *Review of Financial Studies*, *27*(1), 153–179. doi:10.1093/rfs/hhs072

Robbins, S. P. (1996). *Organizational Behavior: Concepts Controversies Applications* (7th ed.). Englewood Cliffs, NJ: Prentice Hall International.

Robinson, M. S. (2001). The microfinance revolution: Sustainable finance for the poor. Washington: International Bank for Reconstruction and Development (IBRD)-World Bank. doi:10.1596/0-8213-4524-9

Roblek, V., Meško, M., & Krapež, A. (2016). A complex view of industry 4.0. *SAGE Open*, *6*(2). doi:10.1177/2158244016653987

Rochet, J.-C., & Tirole, J. (2006). Two-sided markets: A progress report. *The Rand Journal of Economics*, *37*(3), 645–667. doi:10.1111/j.1756-2171.2006.tb00036.x

Rowland-Jones, R., Thomas, P. T., & Page-Thomas, K. (2008). Quality management tools & techniques: Profiling SME use & customer expectations. *The International Journal for Quality and Standards, 1*(1). Retrieved from http://www.bsieducation.org/Education/downloads/ijqs/paper6.pdf

Rubmann, M., Lorenz, M., Gerbert, P., Waldner, M., Justus, J., Engel, P., & Harnisch, M. (2015). *Industry 4.0*. Boston, MA: Boston Consulting Group.

Rusliyadi, M., Jamil, M. A., & Kumalasari, R. T. (2019). *Analysis of household food security policy: Case of food security village programme*, Indonesia. *Asian Journal of Agriculture and Rural Development*, *9*(1), 19–32.

Rusliyadi, M., Jamil, M. A., Maseleno, A., Kumalasari, R. T., & Othman, M. (2019). Agricultural extension policy, agricultural growth and poverty reduction in Indonesia. *IACSIT International Journal of Engineering and Technology*, *7*(4), 5539–5550. doi:10.14419/ijet.v7i4.13337

Rusliyadi, M., & Libin, W. (2018). *Agriculture development programs for poverty reduction evidences from Indonesia and China* - comparative study case. *Asian Journal of Agriculture and Rural Development*, *8*(2), 104–118.

Rusnah, M., Edil, A. S., & Mohd Rizal, M. (2008). Corporate social responsibility: An Islamic perspective. *Journal of Accounting Perspectives*, *1*, 43–56.

Ryan, D., & Jones, C. (2016). *Understanding digital marketing: Marketing strategies for engaging the digital generation*. Kogan Page Publishers.

Saad, N. (2012). Microfinance and prospect for Islamic microfinance products: The case of Amanah Ikhtiar Malaysia. *Advances in Asian Social Science*, 1(1).

Saeed, A. (2004). Islamic banking and finance: In search of a pragmatic model. In V. Hooker, & A. Saikal (Eds.), *Islamic perspectives on the new millenium*. Singapore: ISEAS. doi:10.1355/9789812305367-009

Sage, A. P. (1991). *Decision Support Systems Engineering*. New York: John Wiley.

Sakai, K. (2008). Headwinds lashing Japan's moneylenders. In *Finance, Japan Spotlight,* November/December. pp. 50-51. Retrieved from https://www.jef.or.jp/journal/jef_contents_pdfloader.asp?c=3547andt=

Sanders, A., Elangeswaran, C., & Wulfsberg, J. (2016). Industry 4.0 implies lean manufacturing: Research activities in industry 4.0 function as enablers for lean manufacturing. *Journal of Industrial Engineering and Management*, *9*(3), 811–833. doi:10.3926/jiem.1940

Sandman, J. (n.d.). The New Loan Sharks: Payday Lenders Have More Tricks Up Their Sleeves - AARP ... Retrieved from https://www.aarp.org/money/scams-fraud/info-12-2012/the-new-loan-sharks.html

Santiago, A., & Roxas, F. (2015). Reviving farming interest in the Philippines through agricultural entrepreneurship education. *Journal of Agriculture, Food Systems, and Community Development*, *5*(4), 15–27.

Scheuermann, C., Verclas, S., & Bruegge, B. (2015, August). Agile factory-an example of an industry 4.0 manufacturing process. In *2015 IEEE 3rd International Conference on Cyber-Physical Systems, Networks, and Applications* (pp. 43-47). IEEE.

Schmidt, R., Möhring, M., Härting, R. C., Reichstein, C., Neumaier, P., & Jozinović, P. (2015, June). Industry 4.0-potentials for creating smart products: empirical research results. In *International Conference on Business Information Systems* (pp. 16-27). Cham, Switzerland: Springer. 10.1007/978-3-319-19027-3_2

Schmidt, J. B., & Calantone, R. J. (1998). Are Really New Product Development Projects Harder to Shut Down? *Journal of Product Innovation Management*, *15*(2), 111–123. doi:10.1111/1540-5885.1520111

Schrader, H. (1994). Money Lenders and Merchant Bankers in India and Indonesia. In F. J. A. Bouman, & O. Hospes (Eds.), Financial landscapes reconstructed: The fine art of mapping development. Colorado and Oxford: Westview Press. pp. 341-356.

Sciulli, L. M. (1998). How Organization Structure Influences Success in Various Types of Innovation? *Journal of Retail Banking Services*, *20*, 13–18.

Scott, A. C. (2014). *Ethnic Differences in Reliance On Family Versus Personal Savings in the Face of a Financial Shock,* Unpublished Master's Thesis of University of Colorado.

Seater, J. J. (1993). Ricardian Equivalence, Journal of Economic Literature, 31, 142-190

Secretariat, A. S. E. A. N. (2018). *ASEAN key figures 2018, December*. Jakarta: ASEAN Secretariat.

Securities Commission. (2007). *Best Practices in Islamic Stockbroking Services undertaken by Participating Organisations*. Kuala Lumpur: Securities Commission.

Securities Commission. (2011). *List of Shariah-compliant Securities by the Shariah Advisory Council of the Securities Commission Malaysia*. Kuala Lumpur: Securities Commission.

Securities Commission. (2017). *Annual Report 2017*. Kuala Lumpur: Securities Commission.

Segrado, C. (2005). Case study: Islamic microfinance and socially responsible investment. *MEDA Project*, University of Torino MED. Retrieved July 2, 2012 from http://www.gdrc.org/icm/islamic- microfinance.pdf

Seibel, H. D. (2005). Islamic microfinance in Indonesia. Division Economic Development and Employment Sector Project Financial Systems Development. Retrieved July 6, 2011 from http://www.gtz.de/de/dokumente/en- islamic-mf-indonesia.pdf.pdf

Seibel, H. D., & Kunkel, C. R. (1999). *Microfinance in Laos: A case for women's banking?* Working Paper, No. 1999,3, Universität zu Köln, Arbeitsstelle für Entwicklungsländerforschung (AEF), Köln.

Seibel, H. D., Llanto, G., & Quiñones, B. (2000). *How values create value: Social capital in microfinance - the case of the Philippines.* Working Paper, No. 2000,2, Universität zu Köln, Arbeitsstelle für Entwicklungsländerforschung (AEF), Köln. May.

Sen, A. (1981). *Poverty and famines: An essay on entitlement and deprivation.* Oxford, UK: Clarendon Press.

Shafiq, S. I., Sanin, C., Toro, C., & Szczerbicki, E. (2015). Virtual engineering object (VEO): Toward experience-based design and manufacturing for industry 4.0. *Cybernetics and Systems, 46*(1-2), 35–50. doi:10.1080/01969722.2015.1007734

Shah, S. A. (2018, November 26). Bursa includes UOB Kay Hian Securities in Islamic stockbroking list. *The Malaysian Reserve*. Retrieved from https://themalaysianreserve.com/

Shahbandeh, M. (2019). Global halal market - Statistics & Facts. Retrieved March 17, 2019, from https://www.statista.com/topics/4428/global-halal-market/

Shahin, A., Arabzad, S. M., & Ghorbani, M. (2010). Proposing an integrated framework of seven basic and new quality management tools and techniques: A roadmap. *Research Journal of Internatıonal Studıes,* (17), 183-195.

Shankar, R., & Khan, S. (2012), The Next Generation Social Banking Ecosystem: A Road Map for Banks, Happiest Minds Technologies. 1-13. Retrieved August 01, 2019 from http://www.happiestminds.com/whitepapers/The-Next-Generation-Social-Banking-Ecosystem--A-Road-Map-for-Banks.pdf

Shapiro, T. M. (2004). The Hidden Cost of Being African American: How Wealth Perpetuates Inequality. *Regional Science and Urban Economics, 30,* 238.

Sharma, R. A. (1989). *Organizational Theory and Behavior. New Delhi* , India: McGraw-Hill.

Shiri, N., Mohammadi, D., & Hosseini, S. M. (2012). Entrepreneurial intention of agricultural students: Effects of role model, social support, social norms and perceived desirability. *Archives of Applied Science Research, 4*(2), 892–897.

Shukle, R. (2015). How to Handle Customer Complaints via Social Media. Retrieved June 03, 2019 from https://www.socialmediaexaminer.com/how-to-handle-customer-complaints-via-social-media/

Siddiqui, M. S., Parker, M. C., Koczian, G., Adeyemi-Ejeye, F., Quinlan, T., Walker, S. D., ... Habel, K. (2016, June). CHARISMA: Converged heterogeneous advanced 5G cloud-RAN architecture for intelligent and secure media access. In *2016 European Conference on Networks and Communications (EuCNC)* (pp. 240-244). IEEE.

Sitepu, J. (2005). *Manajemen Strategik.* Jakarta: Gramedia Group.

Smart Shield International Sdn Bhd. (2016). *Study on Halal Industry Investment in Brunei Darussalam*. Retrieved from http://www.eria.org/old/events/Brunei_Halal_EN.pdf

Smith, L. R., & Sanderson, J. (2015). I'm Going to Instagram It! An Analysis of Athlete Self-Presentation on Instagram. *Journal of Broadcasting & Electronic Media*, *59*(2), 342–358. doi:10.1080/08838151.2015.1029125

Smith, S., Windmeijer, F., & Wright, E. (2014). Peer Effects in Charitable Giving: Evidence from the (Running) Field. *Economic Journal (London)*, *125*(35), 1053–1071.

Sousa, S. D., Aspinwall, E., Sampaio, P. A., & Rodrigues, A. G. (2005). Performance measures and quality tools in Portuguese small and medium enterprises: Survey results. *Total Quality Management & Business Excellence*, *16*(2), 277–307. doi:10.1080/14783360500054434

Spagnoletti, P., Resca, A., & Lee, G. (2015). A Design Theory for Digital Platforms Supporting Online Communities: A Multiple Case Study. *Journal of Information Technology*, *30*(4), 364–380. doi:10.1057/jit.2014.37

Statista Internet. (2018). *Mobile Internet & Apps*. Retrieved August 28, 2019 from https://www.statista.com/markets/424/topic/538/mobile-internet-apps/

Stern, S., & Ibarra, P. (2011). Digital government: Creating the social media game plan. *Government Finance Review*, *27*(5), 8–14.

Stock, T., & Seliger, G. (2016). Opportunities of sustainable manufacturing in industry 4.0. *Procedia Cirp*, *40*, 536–541. doi:10.1016/j.procir.2016.01.129

Sulianti, K. T. D., Fathorazz, M., & Ayu Wulandari, G. (2018). Mapping the Competitive Advantage of SMEs in East Java, Indonesia. *Jurnal Dinamika Manajemen*, *9*, 1.

Suppiah, U. (2014). *History of moneylending during British era: A case study of chettiars as the major money lenders*. A conference paper in 23th International Conference of Historians of Asia 2014 (IAHA2014) held by Universiti Utara Malaysia and Malaysian Historical Society, August 23-27, in Alor Setar, Kedah, Malaysia, 850-867.

Suppiah, U., & Raja, S. S. (2013). Sejarah asal-usul dan kegiatan ekonomi chettiar di Tanah Melayu. *Jebat: Malaysian Journal of History, Politics, and Strategy*, *40*(1), 63–90.

Tajvidi, R., & Karami, A. (2017). (in press). The effect of social media on firm performance. *Computers in Human Behavior*. doi:10.1016/j.chb.2017.09.026

Tan, B., Pan, S., Lu, X., & Huang, L. (2015). The Role of IS Capabilities in the Development of Multi-Sided Platforms: The Digital Ecosystem Strategy of Alibaba.com. *Journal of the Association for Information Systems*, *16*(4), 248–280. doi:10.17705/1jais.00393

Tarí, J. J., & Sabater, V. (2004). Quality tools and techniques: Are they necessary for quality management? *International Journal of Production Economics*, *92*(3), 267–280. doi:10.1016/j.ijpe.2003.10.018

Taylor, M. J. (1992). Post-16 options: Young people's awareness, attitudes, intentions and influences on their choice. *Research Papers in Education*, *7*(3), 301–335. doi:10.1080/0267152920070305

Teece, D. J. (1977). Technology Transfer by Multinational Firms: The Resource Cost of Transferring Technological Know-How. *Economic Journal (London)*, *87*(346), 242–261. doi:10.2307/2232084

Tenner, A. R., & DeToro, I. J. (1992). *Total Quality Management*. New York: Addison-Wesley.

Teo, S., & Cheong, S. (1994). Difficulties faced by SMEs in obtaining financing from financial institutions. *Journal of Enterprising Culture*, *2*(4), 955–968. doi:10.1142/S0218495894000355

Thaker, M. A. M., & Thaker, H. M. T. (2018). SMEs Financing and the Potential of Crowdfunding. Working paper.

Thames, L., & Schaefer, D. (2016). Software-defined cloud manufacturing for industry 4.0. *Procedia CIRP*, *52*, 12–17. doi:10.1016/j.procir.2016.07.041

Thamsen, P. U., & Wulff, S. (2016). Industry 4.0 and current Trends in the Pump industry-A Look back on the ACHEMA 2015. *Chemieingenieurtechnik (Weinheim)*, *88*(1-2), 15–19. doi:10.1002/cite.201690002

The Scoop. (2018, July 15). Millennials driving e-commerce, says new report from AITI. Retrieved June 11, 2019, from The Scoop website: https://thescoop.co/2018/07/15/millennials-driving-ecommerce-report-aiti/

Thomas, M. (2011). *Social media in finance: Users want tangible benefits, not friendship, Deutsche Bank Research, E-Banking Snapshot 37*, pp. 1-4. Retrieved July 16, 2019 from http://www.dbresearch.com/PROD/DBR_INTERNET_EN-PROD/PROD0000000000273185.pdf

Thomson Reuters and DinarStandard. (2017). Outpacing The Mainstream. *State of the Global Islamic Economy Report*, *2017*(18). doi:10.100700348-013-1600-9

Thomson Reuters and DinarStandard. (2018). *State of Global Islamic Economy Report 2018/19. Dubai International Financial Centre*. Retrieved from https://haladinar.io/hdn/doc/report2018.pdf

Thomson Reuters and EFICA Fintech Roundtable. (2017). *Fintech: A Source of Positive Change*, in collaboration with White Paper Media. UAE.

Timans, W., Ahaus, K., & Van Solingen, R. (2009). A Delphi study on Six Sigma tools and techniques. *International Journal of Six Sigma and Competitive Advantage*, *5*(3), 205–221. doi:10.1504/IJSSCA.2009.028093

Ting, S.-C. (2014). *The Relationship between Customers' Switching Cost and Repurchase Intention: The Moderating Role of Satisfaction*. doi:10.4236/jssm.2014.74028

Tiwary, D. (2017). In 80% farmer-suicides due to debt, loans from banks, not moneylenders. In *Indian Express,* January 7. Retrieved from http://indianexpress.com /article/india/in-80-farmer-suicides-due-to-debt-loans-from-banks-not-moneylenders-4462930/

Tlaiss, H. A. (2015). How Islamic business ethics impact women entrepreneurs: Insights from four Arab middle eastern countries. *Journal of Islamic Business Ethics*, *129*(4), 859–877. doi:10.100710551-014-2138-3

Tsang, E. W. K. (1997). Choice of International Technology Transfer Mode: A Resource-based View. *Management International Review*, *37*, 151–165.

Turban, E., King, D., Lee, J. K., & Viehland, D. W. (2004). *Electronic commerce 2004: A managerial perspective* (International edition). Retrieved from https://trove.nla.gov.au/version/42646354

Turban, E., Sharda, R., & Delen, D. (2014). Business intelligence and analytics: Systems for decision support. Pearson Higher Ed.

Turnell, S. (2005). A Survey of Microfinance Institutions in Burma. *Burma Economic Watch*, *1*, 26–50.

Tushman, M. J., & Anderson, P. (1986). Technological Discontinuities and Organizational Environments. *Administrative Science Quarterly*, *31*(3), 439–465. doi:10.2307/2392832

Udo, G. J., & Ehie, I. C. (1996). Advanced Manufacturing Technologies: Determinants of Implementation Success. *International Journal of Operations & Production Management*, *16*(12), 6–26. doi:10.1108/01443579610151733

Utterback, J. M. (1994). *Mastering the Dynamics of Innovation*. Boston, MA: Harvard Business School Press.

Vallerand, R. J., & Houlfort, N. (2003). Passion at work: toward a new conceptualization. In S. W. Gilliland, D. D. Steiner, & D. P. Skarlicki (Eds.), *in Emerging Perspectives on Values in Organizations*. Greenwich, CT: Information Age Publishing.

Van de Ven, A. H. (1993). The development of an infrastructure for entrepreneurship. *Journal of Business Venturing*, *8*(3), 211–230. doi:10.1016/0883-9026(93)90028-4

Varghese, A., & Tandur, D. (2014, November). Wireless requirements and challenges in Industry 4.0. In *2014 International Conference on Contemporary Computing and Informatics (IC3I)*, (pp. 634-638). IEEE.

Vathana, R. T. M. S., Dalis, P., Bopharath, S., & Dorina, P. (2016). *Credit access, multiple sources of borrowings and household wellbeing: The case of eleven villages in Cambodia.* Final Report for Partnership for Economic Policy (PEP) with funding from the Department for International Development (DFID) of the United Kingdom (or UK Aid), and the Government of Canada through the International Development Research Center (IDRC). May.

Vendramin, S. (2016). *Why Banks Need Instagram*. Retrieved May 12, 2019 from https://medium.com/@stefanovendramin/why-banks-need-instagram-3b66747093b7

Vibriyanti, D. (2014). The Effect of Socio-Demographic Variables on Household Saving: The Analysis of the 2007 IFLs Data. Developing Country Studies, 4(1), 73–84.

Vieneris, Y. P. (1977). Macroeconomics Model and Policy. New York: Wiley & Sons.

Vijaykumar, S., Saravanakumar, S. G., & Balamurugan, M. (2015). Unique sense: Smart computing prototype. *Procedia Computer Science*, *50*, 223–228. doi:10.1016/j.procs.2015.04.056

Vogel-Heuser, B., & Hess, D. (2016). Guest editorial Industry 4.0–prerequisites and visions. *IEEE Transactions on Automation Science and Engineering*, *13*(2), 411–413. doi:10.1109/TASE.2016.2523639

Vuong, Q. H. (2014). *Vietnam's political economy: A discussion on the 1986-2016 period.* Centre Emile Bernheim (CEB) Working Paper No. 14/010, May. Solvay Brussels School of Economics and Management, Université Libre de Bruxelles. Brussels, Belgium.

Walker, H. F., Elshennawy, A., Gupta, B., & McShane-Vaughn, M. (2012). *The certified quality inspector handbook.* Milwaukee, WI: ASQ Quality Press.

Wallach, E. J. (1983). Individuals and organizations: The cultural match. *Training and Development Journal*, *37*(2), 28–36.

Wan Omar, M., & Mohd Ali, M. N. (2010). Brand Loyalty and Relationship Marketing in Islamic Banking System. *Canadian Social Science*, *6*(1), 25–32.

Wang, Z. Z., Nie, D. X., Chen, X., & Huang, G. Q. (2016). IoT-based real-time production logistics synchronization system under smart cloud manufacturing. *International Journal of Advanced Manufacturing Technology*, *84*(1-4), 147–164. doi:10.100700170-015-7220-1

Wan, J., Wang, S., Li, D., & Zhang, C. (2016). Implementing smart factory of industrie 4.0: An outlook. *International Journal of Distributed Sensor Networks*, *12*(1). doi:10.1155/2016/3159805

Wannasupchue, W., Othman, M., Abidin, U. F. U. Z., Ishak, F. A. C., & Mohamad, S. F. (2019). Current Trends and Opportunities for Halal Restaurants in Thailand: A Conceptual Framework. *International Journal of Academic Research in Business and Social Sciences*, *9*(1), 235–247. doi:10.6007/IJARBSS/v9-i1/5392

Wasli, W. (2018). Jobseekers, youths encouraged to start vertical farming. The Scoop (Online). Retrieved from https://thescoop.co/2018/09/15/jobseekers-youths-encouraged-to-start-vertical-farming/

Watson, K., Hogarth-Scott, S., & Wilson, N. (1998). Small business start-ups: Success factors and support implications. *International Journal of Entrepreneurial Behaviour & Research*, *4*(3), 217–238. doi:10.1108/13552559810235510

We are Social. (2017). *Digital in 2017*. Retrieved September, 26 2019 from https://www.juancmejia.com/wp-content/uploads/2017/03/Digital-2017-WeAreSocial-y-HootSuite.pdf

Webster, A. (1993). Comparative advantages and long run Dutch disease effects: The international trade of Trinidad and Tobago. *Development Policy Review*, *11*(2), 153–155. doi:10.1111/j.1467-7679.1993.tb00034.x

Weinberg, B. D., & Pehlivan, E. (2011). Social spending: Managing the social media mix. *Business Horizons*, *54*(3), 275–282. doi:10.1016/j.bushor.2011.01.008

Werner, T., & Weckenmann, A. (2012). Sustainable quality assurance by assuring competence of employees. *Measurement*, *45*(6), 1534–1539. doi:10.1016/j.measurement.2012.02.025

West, J., & Mace, M. (2010). Browsing as the killer app: Explaining the rapid success of Apple's iPhone. *Telecommunications Policy*, *34*(5–6), 270–286. doi:10.1016/j.telpol.2009.12.002

White, L. (2018, September 4). Police hunt loan sharks riding Britain's rising tide of debt. Retrieved from https://www.reuters.com/article/us-britain-lending-loansharks/police-hunt-loan-sharks-riding-britains-rising-tide-of-debt-idUSKCN1LK1LX

Wildman, M., & Torres, R. M. (2001). Factors identified when selecting a major in agriculture. *Journal of Agricultural Education*, *42*(2), 46–55. doi:10.5032/jae.2001.02046

Wilkinson, K. P. (1991). *The rural community in America*. New York: Greenwood Press.

Williams, R. (2016). Understanding and Interpreting Generalized Ordered Logit Models. *The Journal of Mathematical Sociology*, *40*(1), 7–20.

Williamson, O. E. (1985). *The Economic Institutions of Capitalism: Firms, Markets, Relational Contracting*. New York: Free Press.

Winsteadt, R. O. (1947). *The Malays: A cultural history*. Singapore: Kelly & Walsh.

Wolfe, K., Hsu, C. H. C., & Kang, S. K. (2004). Buyer Characteristics Among Users of Various Travel Intermediaries. *Journal of Travel & Tourism Marketing*, *17*(2–3), 51–62. doi:10.1300/J073v17n02_05

Wollasa, L. K. (2011). *Investment Efficiency, Savings and Economic Growth in Sub Saharan Africa*. Retrieved July 18, 2017, from http://www,politicalarticles, net/blog/ 2011/09/05/ investment-efficiency-savings-and-economic-growth-in-sub-saharan-africa/

World Bank Global Financial Inclusion. (2015). *Global Financial Inclusion (Global Findex) Database*. Retrieved August 10, 2019 from https://datacatalog.worldbank.org/dataset/global-financial-inclusion-global-findex-database

World Bank. *(2012) The World Bank Data Bank*. Retrieved from http://databank.worldbank.org/data/views/reports/tableview.aspx

World Bank. (2017). *World Bank Open Data*, Retrieved March 10, 2017, from http://data,worldbank,org/

WTO. (2018). *World trade statistical review 2018*. Retrieved from www.wto.org/statistics

Xuxin. (2019). Brunei among countries with highest social media penetration, Xinhua. Feb. 1, 2019. Available at http://www.xinhuanet.com/english/2019-02/01/c_137792631.htm (Accessed: 27 June 2019).

Yakub, K. (2012) *An Ethnographic Study of Wasan Rice Farm in Brunei Darussalam.* (Master's Thesis). Ritsumeikan Asia Pacific University. Retrieved from http://r-cube.ritsumei.ac.jp/bitstream/10367/3915/1/51110003.pdf

Yang, P. Q. (2000). *Ethnic Studies: Issues and Approaches.* New York: State University of New York Press.

Yang, Z., & Fang, X. (2005). Online service quality dimensions and their relationships with satisfaction: A content analysis of customer reviews of securities brokerage services. *International Journal of Service Industry Management, 15*(3), 302–326. doi:10.1108/09564230410540953

Yin, R. (1994). Case study research: Design and methods (2nd ed.). Beverly Hills, CA.

Zain, M., Yusob, A., Othman, R., Lim, S., & Idris, P., & Siti Rozaidah, D. (2015). Attributes of effective leadership from the perspectives of implicit leadership theory (ILT): A study in Brunei. *International Journal of Science Commerce and Humanities, 3*, 58–64.

Zain, M., Yusob, A., Othman, R., Lim, S., & Idris, P. (2014). Brunei implicit leadership theories: Impacts of expectation gap. *Review of Strategic and International Studies, 6*, 12–21.

Zakaria, Z. (2008). Tapping into the world halal market: Some discussions on Malaysian laws and standards. *Shariah Journal, 16*(3), 603–616.

Zapata, N. R. (2006). Credit decision and rationing rules: A study of informal lenders in the Philippines. *Philippine Management Review, 13*, 117–126.

Zauro, N. A., Saad, R. A. J., & Sawandi, N. (2016). The moderating effects of financial inclusion on qardhul hassan financing acceptance in Nigeria: A proposed framework. *International Journal of Economics and Financial Issues, 6*(S7), 143–148.

Zhang, J., & Liu, P. (2012). Rational Herding in Microloan Markets. *Management Science, 58*(3), 892–912. doi:10.1287/mnsc.1110.1459

Zhu, K., Kraemer, K. L., & Xu, S. (2006). The Process of Innovation Assimilation by Firms in Different Countries: A Technology Diffusion Perspective on E-Business. *Management Science, 52*(10), 1557–1576. doi:10.1287/mnsc.1050.0487

Zolkepli, I. A., & Kamarulzaman, Y. (2015). Social media adoption: The role of media needs and innovation characteristics. *Computers in Human Behavior, 43*, 189–209. doi:10.1016/j.chb.2014.10.050

Zoller, A. S. (1999). Are you Satisfied with your Technology Alliance? *Research Technology Management, 64*(3), 10–12. doi:10.1080/08956308.1999.11671266

# About the Contributors

**Patricia Ordonez de Pablos** is a professor in the Department of Business Administration in the Faculty of Business and Economics at The University of Oviedo (Spain). She completed her education in The London School of Economics (UK). Her teaching and research interests focus on the areas of strategic management, knowledge management, organizational learning, human resource management, intellectual capital, information technologies, with special interest in Asia (Bhutan, China, Laos, Myanmar). She is Editor-in-Chief of the International Journal of Learning and Intellectual Capital (IJLIC) and International Journal of Asian Business and Information Management (IJABIM), respectively. She has edited books for IGI-Global, Routledge and Springer.

**Mohammad Nabil Almunawar** is currently a senior assistant professor at the School of Business and Economics, Universiti of Brunei Darussalam (UBDSBE), Brunei Darussalam. He received his bachelor's degree in 1983 from Bogor Agricultural University, Indonesia, master's degree (MSc) from the Department of Computer Science, University of Western Ontario, London, Canada in 1991 and Ph.D. from the University of New South Wales in 1998. Dr. Almunawar has published more than 100 papers in refereed journals, books, book chapters, and international conference proceedings. He has more than 30 years of teaching experience in the area of information systems. His overall research interests include applications of IT in management, e-business/commerce, digital marketplace/platform, digital business ecosystem, health informatics, information security, and cloud computing. Currently, he focuses his research on digital platform and digital business ecosystem.

**Muhamad Abduh** was born in Jakarta, May 1981. He completed his Bachelor of Science (Statistics) from Bogor Agricultural University (IPB) in September 2004 and his first master degree, Magister Hukum Islam (Fiqh Al-Mu'amalat), from Ibn Khaldun University in September 2006. He completed his second master degree, Master of Economics from the International Islamic University Malaysia (IIUM) in June 2009. Under the supervision of Prof. Dato' Dr. Mohd Azmi Omar, former

IRTI-IDB Director, Abduh completed his PhD in Business Administration with specialization in Islamic Banking and Finance in December 2011. Abduh has written more than 60 journal articles, book chapters and text-books in the area of Islamic finance. Currently, Abduh is a Senior Assistant Professor and Programme Leader for Accounting and Finance at UBD School of Business and Economics (UBD-SBE).

* * *

**Alif Abdullah** received his BSc in Computer Science from the University of Chester from the United Kingdom in 2017. In 2019 he was accepted into the Universiti Brunei Darussalam (UBD) as Master of Management (MM) by research student under UBD School of Business and Economics and currently doing research on adoption of digital marketplace in Brunei Darussalam.

**Moha Asri Abdullah**, Professor (Ph.D.) at KENMS, IIUM; Deputy dean of INHART, IIUM; Director of IEC Sdn. Bhd., and National Panel of Evaluation Committee for Research Grants, MOHE. He is a former Director of Innovation and Commercialisation Office at the university, a former Deputy Dean at the Research Management Centre (IIUM) and Head of the Department of Economics. He was a Visiting Research Scholars of Economic Research Centre, Japan and University of Auckland, AUT and Massey University, New Zealand. More than 60 papers in renowned journals and presented a number of papers in the international conferences/forums. He has conducted more than 35 research projects from different funding agencies, local and international alike. He also has been a consultant to a number of agencies and involved in a wide range of consultancy works. He has been an editor and author of more than 15 books. He expertise in Small Business/SMEs, Entrepreneurship and Venture Capital, Economic Development, and Halal Industry. His research interest areas include Halal entrepreneurship and capital venture, Small Business/SMEs, and Halal Micro-credit.

**Shochrul Rohmatul Ajija** was born in Mojokerto, May 25, 1986. She holds a Bachelor of Economics degree in education from the Development Economics Study Program, FEB, Airlangga University in 2004-2008, and a Master of Economics (M.Ec) degree in Kulliyah of Economics and Management Science, International Islamic University Malaysia in 2009-2011. She is a lecturer at the Airlangga University S1 Development Economics Study Program, Founder and Chair of the Islamic Cooperative, Baitul Maal wat Tamwil (BMT) Mandiri Ukhuwah Persada (MUDA), and Deputy Director of Perwira Cendekia Institute.

**Muhammad Anshari** is researcher and academic staff at School of Business & Economics. His professional experience started when he was IT Business Analyst at Astra International. Research Fellowship from The Government Republic of China (Taiwan) at National Taiwan University (Jan-Dec, 2014). Research Fellowship from King Saud University - the Kingdom of Saudi Arabia 2009. Details of research interests are as below. He received his BMIS (Hons) from International Islamic University Malaysia, his Master of IT (E-Business) from James Cook University Australia, and his PhD programme from Universiti Brunei Darussalam. His research interests include E-Health & Mobile Health, FinTech, Big data in business, ICT & Area, Studies (ASEAN/Borneo) ICT in Education,Smartphone adoption, millenial & digital business.

**Faizal Asfan** is a master holder in Islamic Banking, IIiBF, IIUM, Malaysia. Research in Islamic Equity Broking. An ex-Investment banker in Islamic Equity Broking, a senior lecturer in Finance.

**Md. Siddique E Azam**, pursuing his Ph.D. at International Institute for Halal Research and Training (INHART), IIUM after completing his MBA in January 2018 from IIUM as well. Previously he also studied M.Sc. in Agriculture Education at Sher-e-Bangla Agricultural University, Dhaka, Bangladesh. He obtained his bachelor's degree in agriculture science from Hajee Mohammad Danesh Science and Technology University, Bangladesh. Alongside serving in banking industry in Bangladesh, he has contributed a few publications in different journals. He foresees the Muslim entrepreneurs receiving action civics education which will provide them knowledge and skills to develop the economy as practicing Muslim.

**Muhammad Khairul Hidayatullah Haji Basir** is an assistant lecturer at the Faculty of Islamic Economics and Finance, Universiti Islam Sultan Sharif Ali (UNISSA). He has a Bachelor of Arts (Honours) in Economics from Universiti Brunei Darussalam and a Master in Development Studies from the University of Melbourne, Australia. He went to the University of Oxford, UK for global mobility programme. He teaches courses in Principles Macroeconomics, Business Creativity and Innovation, and Corporate Entrepreneurship. Khairul's research interests revolve around socio-economic development. He has received the best paper award and has presented papers at conferences in Australia, Brunei, Malaysia, Philippines and Thailand. His journal article publications include Youth Unemployment and the Rentier Economy, Economic Issues in Brunei, and Case Study of Zakat Institution in Brunei. He was also invited to be a panel forum for BigBWN Project to talk about Entrepreneurial and Youth Employability Journey. He is an author of Managing Oil Wealth: Lessons for Brunei to Learn from Norway.

**Boon Cheong Chew** obtained his first degree-Bachelor of Engineering (Civil) from Faculty of Civil Engineering University of Technology Malaysia (UTM) as well as his master degree-Master of Technology Management from Faculty of Management. He spent four-year time working in one of the Malaysian Best Managed Companies, YTL Corporation Bhd under one of the divisions-YTL Cement Bhd. In 2007, he obtained the scholarship (funded by the Minister of Higher Education) and went for further study in the University of Edinburgh Scotland. He obtained his PHD on 26 June 2012.

**Mohammed Haneef**, PhD, is currently Professor at the Department of Economics, International Islamic University Malaysia (IIUM). PhD from the School of Development Studies, University of East Anglia, UK. Held Fellowships at the Centre for Muslim-Christian Understanding, Georgetown University and the Oxford Centre for Islamic Studies. Published books and articles and conducted research in various areas of Economics, Development Studies and Islamic economics including Co-editor of Islamic Economics: Principles and Applications (ISRA, 2018). Current research interests in philosophical issues in economics, socio-economic impact of awqaf and social economics/finance. Jointly heading Islamic microfinance project called 'I-Taajir'. Actively involved in numerous public and private executive training programs, specializing in Islamic economics and contemporary development issues. Executive Committee Member, International Association for Islamic Economics (IAIE), 2012 to date and International Council of Islamic Finance Educators (ICIFE), 2014 -2019. Investment Committee member for Affin Islamic Funds 2001-2014 and Permodalan MARA Berhad, 2016 to date. Director, Centre for Islamic Economics, 2013-2018 and currently, Director of Academic Development, IIIT East and Southeast Asia.

**Abdurrahman Haqqi** graduated with bachelor degree from Kuwait University, Kuwait then MCL and Ph. D in Law from International Islamic University Malaysia. Joined International Islamic University Malaysia as lecturer then joined Universiti Brunei Darussalam before currently as Senior Assistant Professor at Faculty of Shariah and Law, Universiti Islam Sultan Sharif Ali (UNISSA), Brunei Darussalam. Published 18 books, 40 articles in journals and more than 700 articles in magazines and newspapers.

**Ahmad Hudaifah** is a lecturer at Universitas Internasional Semen Indonesia who specializes research interest in Islamic microfinance, cooperative and Islamic philanthropy economics. His area of academic work has intensified into the community practice and industry service through direct engagement on the project and consultation. He is also actively involved in disseminating and scaling up such research and teaching topics via conference, regular meeting and communal forum.

**Saifuddin Isa** is a researcher in Faculty of Technology Management and Technopreneurship, Universiti Teknikal Malaysia Melaka. His current research is looking at the advances tools and techniques in quality management particularly for Industrial Revolution 4.0. Additionally, his also has background in industry, as he frequently visited some company in High Technology Industries.

**Norma Md Saad** is a Professor at the Department of Economics, Faculty of Economics and Management Sciences, International Islamic University Malaysia. Her areas of specialization are Islamic Economics and Islamic Finance as well as International Trade. Her teaching and research have been focused on waqf, Islamic microfinance and also the intra-trade patterns of major economic blocs and their impact on regional integration. She is actively doing research on the area of Islamic Economics and Finance, implementing equity-based models of Islamic microfinance and investigating the efficiency of corporate entities in managing Waqf institutions in Malaysia and other selected countries. Prof. Norma has published a few books (which also includes chapter in a book) in the area of Waqf, Islamic Finance, International Trade, Macroeconomics, and Business Mathematics. She has also published some of her works in the internationally recognized refereed journals.

**Mustafa Mohammad** is presently an Associate Professor and Head of the Department of Economics, KENMS, International Islamic University Malaysia [IIUM] where he has been teaching for the past 20 years. He teaches both theoretical and applied courses at postgraduate and undergraduate levels. Dr. Mustafa earned the Best Teacher Award at the Kulliyyah Level in 2003, and thereafter won several quality academic awards in 2008, 2009, 2012, 2013 and 2014. He has published more than 70 refereed journal articles and presented more than 80 papers, mostly at international conferences. He is also actively involved in funded and commissioned research projects. His present research areas of interest are Waqf, Zakat, Islamic Microfinance and Maqasid al-Shari'ah. He has supervised more than 50 dissertations at PhD and Master Levels. He is also a journal editorial member and reviewer panel to 11 academic entities. Dr. Mustafa has long experience in translations, Arabic and English. He undertook projects for MIFC, BNM, IBFIM, AIBIM, IFSB, ISRA and other international organizations. He is involved in consultancy and several training workshops and lectures on Islamic economic, banking, finance, Zakat and Waqf. He conducted training in Singapore, Sri Lanka, Bangladesh, Philippines, Indonesia, Uganda, South Africa and Malaysia involving Board of Directors, investors, academicians, Shari'ah scholars and practioners. He is a co-founder and advisor to the IIUM-CIMB Islamic i-Taajir Entrepreneurial microfinance project at the International Islamic University Malaysia. Dr. Mustafa graduated with Bachelor and Master of Economics from IIUM, and PhD in Finance from Universiti Sains Malaysia.

**Rizal Abd Hamid Mohd Syaiful** graduated with his first Bachelor Degree of Human Resources Management from University Utara Malaysia (UUM) as well as his Master Degree of Business Administration from UUM. Subsequently, he obtained his Doctor of Philosophy in Quality and Technology Manufacturing from Strathclyde University, School of Engineering, Design Manufacture Engineering Management, United Kingdom. He worked as a Business Development Executive at Era Riang and Human Resource Officer at ONKYO Electric (Malaysia) Private Limited.

**Hassanudin Mohd Thas Thaker** is a lecturer in the Department of Economics and Finance, Sunway University, Malaysia. He holds a PhD in Business Administration (Finance) from International Islamic University (IIUM). His research interest includes international trade, balance of payment, econometrics, corporate finance, Islamic banking and finance, financial economics and housing/properties market. He has published in International Journal of Housing Markets and Analysis, Jurnal Pengurusan, Journal of Financial Reporting and Accounting, Qualitative Research in Financial Markets, International Journal of Islamic and Middle Eastern Finance and Management, Journal of Islamic Marketing, and International Journal of Business and Systems Research. He has been awarded with Emerald Literati Award for Research Excellence in 2017.

**Mohamed Asmy Mohd Thas Thaker** obtained his B.Economics (Hons), Master of Economics and PhD Economics from International Islamic University Malaysia (IIUM). Upon completion of his PhD, he joined IIUM in October 2014 as Assistant Professor at Department of Economics. He is majoring in economic development, SMEs, Islamic economics, Waqf, Zakat and Islamic banking & finance. Currently, he is research fellow of Centre of Islamic Economics, IIUM and life member of Malaysian Economic Association. He has published numbers of publications in cited refereed journals, and chapters in books and presented papers at national and international conferences. Some of his papers have won Distinguished and Best Paper awards. Recently, his thesis also won Bronze award at international exhibition. His work is made possible by his receipt of support in the form of grants from various agencies and organizations nationally and internationally.

**Khairunnisa Musari** is a Ph.D. in Islamic Economics. She is a lecturer at the Department of Islamic Economics, Postgraduate Program and Faculty of Islamic Economics Business (FEBI), State Institute for Islamic Studies (IAIN) of Jember. She is a Deputy Coordinator of Central Indonesia for Central Board (DPP) of the Indonesian Association of Islamic Economist (IAEI), Secretary II for Provincial Board of East Java (DPW) of IAEI, a Secretary of Indonesian Economist Association (ISEI) of Jember and Member of Expert Board of Islamic Economic Society (MES) of Lumajang. She has a great attention for sukuk, waqf, esham, fiscal & monetary policies, microfinance, and nanofinance. She is listed as the Top 300 Most Influential Women in Islamic Business & Finance 2019 by Cambridge-IFA. This time, she intensely sounds about nanofinance with qardhul hassan for the poor to counter the loan shark and financing the poor.

**Choong Pai Wei** is a lecturer at Department of Economics and Finance, Sunway University Business School. She is currently completing her PhD in Economics at Universiti Kebangsaan Malaysia. Her areas of interest are mainly in international production sharing, trade and industry. She has publication in Jurnal Ekonomi Malaysia (December 2018 issue) and International Journal of Economics and Management (the forthcoming issue). She has more than twenty-year teaching experiences in private higher learning institutions.

**Siti Fatimahwati Pehin Dato Musa** has been a lecturer in Economics at Universiti Brunei Darussalam School of Business and Economics (UBDSBE) since 2008. She has a PhD in Agricultural Economics and Rural Development from Newcastle University, United Kingdom, 2016, MSc in International Economics from Bradford University, United Kingdom, 2007 and Bachelors of Education (Major in Economics) from Universiti Brunei Darussalam, 2006. Her research interest revolves around development economics, agricultural economics specifically issues on food security and youth in agriculture. She has presented her papers in a number of conferences overseas: Qatar, United Kingdom, Phuket and South Korea. She has also published a chapter on CSR on Brunei in Green Behavior and Corporate Social Responsibility in Asia (Emerald Group Publishing) and Scopus-indexed journal articles on issues of youth unemployment in Brunei.

**Pg Siti Rozaidah Pg Hj Idris** has been a lecturer in leadership at Universiti Brunei Darussalam School of Business and Economics (UBDSBE) since 2008. She has a PhD in Management Learning and Leadership from the Lancaster University Management School (LUMS) United Kingdom, 2016, MA in Human Resource Development & Consulting from LUMS, 2007 and a Bachelor's Degree in Accounting and Financial Management from University of Sheffield, 2006. Her current research interests are public sector leadership and cultural studies on leadership. Other areas of interest are in human resource development policies and employability. She has also published several chapters on CSR initiatives in Brunei in a book entitled Green Behavior and Corporate Social Responsibility in Asia (Emerald Group Publishing) and Scopus-indexed journal articles on unemployment issues in Brunei. She has also represented Brunei at the APEC HRD Working Group Meetings under the

Capacity Building Network from 2009 to 2014. She has also been invited as a guest speaker and trainer for several leadership development programmes. She welcomes research collaboration in the areas of leadership, human resource development and cross-cultural management.

**Ahmad Rafiki** is currently as a lecturer in Faculty Economics and Business at Universitas Medan Area, Indonesia. Previously he was an Assistant Professor in Department of Business Administration of University College of Bahrain. He obtained his BBA with a major of Marketing from MARA University of Technology (UiTM), Masters in Management from International Islamic University of Malaysia (IIUM), and PhD in Economics and Muamalat Administration from Islamic Science University of Malaysia (USIM). He is holding Certified Islamic Marketer (CIMA) from the International Islamic Marketing Association (IIMA). He had published a number of articles in refereed journals, and became the editorial advisory board and reviewer in reputable international journals.

**Safayet Rahman** is an assistant professor at Southeast University, Bangladesh. He has completed his BBA and MBA from the University of Dhaka. His research interests include Management, Knowledge Management, International Business.

**Wasiaturrahma Wasiaturrahma** is an active lecturer in the Department of Economics, Faculty of Economics and Business, Airlangga University. She completed her doctoral education in the Airlangga University. She is very active in financial and monetary research and community service.

# Index

## P



## Q



## R



## S



## T



## V



## W

www.ingramcontent.com/pod-product-compliance
Lightning Source LLC
LaVergne TN
LVHW080606300926
849162LV00005B/1055